IMPORTAN

HERE IS YOUR REGISTRATION CODE TO
YOUR PREMIUM McGRAW-HILL ONLINE RESOURCES.

MW00597658

For key premium online resources you need THIS CODE to gain access. Once the code is entered, you will be able to use the Web resources for the length of your course.

If your course is using **WebCT** or **Blackboard**, you'll be able to use this code to access the McGraw-Hill content within your instructor's online course.

Access is provided if you have purchased a new book. If the registration code is missing from this book, the registration screen on our Website, and within your WebCT or Blackboard course, will tell you how to obtain your new code.

Registering for McGraw-Hill Online Resources

TO gain access to your McGraw-Hill web resources simply follow the steps below:

1. USE YOUR WEB BROWSER TO GO TO: **www.mhhe.com/connelly**
2. CLICK ON **FIRST TIME USER**.
3. ENTER THE REGISTRATION CODE* PRINTED ON THE TEAR-OFF BOOKMARK ON THE RIGHT.
4. AFTER YOU HAVE ENTERED YOUR REGISTRATION CODE, CLICK **REGISTER**.
5. FOLLOW THE INSTRUCTIONS TO SET-UP YOUR PERSONAL UserID AND PASSWORD.
6. WRITE YOUR UserID AND PASSWORD DOWN FOR FUTURE REFERENCE. KEEP IT IN A SAFE PLACE.

TO GAIN ACCESS to the McGraw-Hill content in your instructor's **WebCT** or **Blackboard** course simply log in to the course with the UserID and Password provided by your instructor. Enter the registration code exactly as it appears in the box to the right when prompted by the system. You will only need to use the code the first time you click on McGraw-Hill content.

Thank you, and welcome to your McGraw-Hill online Resources!

REGISTRATION CODE

DGEA-WKZY-5Q4W-9JKN-D33L

*YOUR REGISTRATION CODE CAN BE USED ONLY ONCE TO ESTABLISH ACCESS. IT IS NOT TRANSFERABLE.

0-07-305441-0 T/A CONNELLY, DIGITAL RADIO PRODUCTION

Digital Radio Production

Donald W. Connelly
Western Carolina University

Boston   Burr Ridge, IL   Dubuque, IA   Madison, WI   New York   San Francisco   St. Louis
Bangkok   Bogotá   Caracas   Kuala Lumpur   Lisbon   London   Madrid   Mexico City
Milan   Montreal   New Delhi   Santiago   Seoul   Singapore   Sydney   Taipei   Toronto

Higher Education

DIGITAL RADIO PRODUCTION
Published by McGraw-Hill, an imprint of The McGraw-Hill Companies, Inc., 1221 Avenue of the Americas, New York, NY 10020. Copyright ©2005. All rights reserved. No part of this publication may be reproduced or distributed in any form or by any means, or stored in a database or retrieval system, without the prior written consent of The McGraw-Hill Companies, Inc., including, but not limited to, in any network or other electronic storage or transmission, or broadcast for distance learning.

This book is printed on acid-free paper.

1 2 3 4 5 6 7 8 9 0 DOC/DOC 0 9 8 7 6 5 4

ISBN   0-07-282253-8

Editor in Chief: Emily Barrosse
Publisher: Phil Butcher
Sponsoring Editor: Phil Butcher
Signing Representative: Lisa Berry
Marketing Manager: Leslie Oberhuber
Developmental Editor: Laura Lynch
Production Editor: Chanda Feldman
Editorial Assistant: Françoise Villeneuve
Manuscript Editor: Marie Deer

Design Manager: Preston Thomas
Text Designer: Maureen McCutcheon
Cover Designer: Preston Thomas
Art Editor: Katherine McNab
Illustrators: Katherine McNab and Ayelet Arbel
Photo Research: Nora Agbayani
Supplements Producer: Louis Swaim
Production Supervisor: Randy Hurst
Media Producer: Christie Ling

Composition: 10/14 Palatino by TBH Typecast, Inc.
Printing: PMS 301, 45# New Era Matte, R. R. Donnelley & Sons/Crawfordsville, IN

Cover: © 2002 Getty Images, Inc.

Library of Congress Cataloging-in-Publication Data

Connelly, Donald W.
      Digital radio production / Donald W. Connelly.—1st ed.
          p. cm.
      Includes bibliographical references and index.
      ISBN 0-07-282253-8 (softcover)
      1. Digital audio broadcasting.   2. Radio—Production and direction.   I. Title.
TK6562.D54C66 2004
621.3845—dc22

2004055208

The Internet addresses listed in the text were accurate at the time of publication. The inclusion of a website does not indicate an endorsement by the authors or McGraw-Hill, and McGraw-Hill does not guarantee the accuracy of the information presented at these sites.

www.mhhe.com

To my family: Debie, Amanda and Mike, and Sarah Grace

Brief Contents

Contents

8 Producing Commercials, Promos, and News   215

9 Communicating with the Listener: Announcing   241

Preface

Scope and Focus

One unique aspect of the history of the radio industry is its creative adaptability, demonstrated through radio's success in overcoming every new medium threatening to replace it. *Digital Radio Production* offers a fresh, insider's approach to a constantly evolving industry. Now, more than ever, the old axiom is true: "You are either moving forward or you are moving backward." Remaining stationary is not an option in the radio industry.

Written for an industry in motion, *Digital Radio Production* is designed to equip today's students with a well-rounded and comprehensive grounding in radio production. Although the production person's job is to produce commercial and programming elements, radio broadcasting today demands a broad knowledge of sales, promotions, programming, and other key areas of the station from every employee. That is why *Digital Radio Production* takes a holistic approach to radio production and the production person. Although radio is all about communicating and delivering a message to listeners, the business environment and technology cannot be ignored. In many respects, the traditional technical skills of a radio production person have transitioned into audio data and system management skills. For a producer, an excellent knowledge of computers and software is the norm rather than the exception. Regardless of the technology, however, the core element of radio production remains the same, communicating with the listener.

Digital Radio Production holds the humanity of radio communication at center stage, and in its technical approach to making that communication possible, this book is first and foremost digital. The twenty-first century is not about vinyl records or reel-to-reel tape recorders. The approach focuses on new technologies and trends, with chapters that introduce students to concepts vital to a successful radio career. Some of the special features of this text include:

- an explanation of the role of the production person in today's broadcast industry
- easy-to-understand, cutting-edge presentations about digital audio recording, storage, manipulation, audio processing, and special effects
- current state-of-the-industry basics in commercial writing and production techniques, recognizing the role the sales department plays in production
- benchmark chapters about station promotion and imaging and taking the station on location
- a discussion about the Internet and digital audio transmission methods for everything from transferring a commercial to another station to high-definition radio production techniques
- a no-nonsense approach to how programming and production go hand-in-hand in today's industry

- a valuable insider's approach to getting a first job in radio . . . and it's not what you think!

Although each chapter covers a different group of core skills and background information, all are interrelated. Each chapter features suggested activities to involve the student outside of class, industry web sites for more information, and a chapter-by-chapter Pro Speak glossary of industry terms.

In addition, three special features make *Digital Radio Production* truly different, placing it in a league of its own in terms of making technology accessible to students:

1. Nearly 100 audio examples, covering virtually every aspect of production from microphone technique to commercial production samples, are included on the demonstration CD and are described in the text.

2. Another CD features an outstanding selection of production music with over 200 music loops and a custom studio-tracking session, with suggested activities written for this text.

3. A fully functional trial edition of Adobe Audition multitrack recording software is included with this text for students to use, experiment with, and learn the latest in digital technology.

Structure

The first chapter of this book, "The Production Person," sets the stage for the rest of the text by explaining the business and programming aspects of radio, identifying the key players and departments, and describing the integral role of the production person in each area of the station.

Radio is a technology- and hardware-based industry, and chapters 2 through 5 focus on the science and hardware of digital radio production. Students are introduced to "Basic Sci-

ence: Analog and Digital Audio" in chapter 2, including analog sound and how humans hear as the foundation for analog-to-digital conversion and the practical uses of digital audio. Chapter 3, "Microphones and Their Role in Radio Production," is an in-depth examination of microphones, mounts, cables, windscreens, and preamplifiers in addition to special-purpose and wireless microphones. "Control, Mixing, and Monitoring," chapter 4, focuses on control boards, mixing, and monitoring across the on-air, production, and portable console platforms. There is also an in-depth discussion of the importance of metering in digital production. "Basic Concepts in Digital Recording" introduces students to recording, mixing, and mastering using digital audio workstations and a variety of digital media in chapter 5. It also features instruction in the basic set-up and operation of Adobe Audition and Pro Tools digital recording software.

The foundation of knowledge developed in the first five chapters is a basis to advance into the artistic and creative side of production in chapters 6 through 10. "Audio Processing," chapter 6, is an introduction to the creative use of dynamic, dimensional, and frequency processing including voice, effects, and broadcast audio processors. In this chapter, care is taken to emphasize not only what can be created using audio processing but also the perceptual effect it can have on listeners.

"The Art of Sixty-Second Story Telling," chapter 7, introduces commercial production as a part of the sales process and approaches commercial creation from the point of view of moving a project from a sales order to an on-air product. This chapter is not about writing so much as it is about how to create well-crafted solutions to a client's marketing problems. "Producing Commercials, Promos, and News," chapter 8, begins with the talent selection process and advances through production pre-planning, production, and delivery to the client. This chapter includes in-depth discussions on the use of music and sound effects. The chapter also includes a section on the special challenges of news production. Chapter 9, "Communicating with the Listener: Announcing," begins with the philosophy of how to communicate one-on-one with listeners and advances to show planning, delivery, voice tracking, news, and sports delivery. The chapter also includes sections on working with producers and production directors as well as a section on developing your voice.

"Promotion and Station Imaging," chapter 10, is unique to *Digital Radio Production* and introduces the concepts of branding and positioning to station promotion and imaging. There is an in-depth examination of effective production for liners, sweepers, station IDs, jingles, and imaging placement. The section on contest promotion moves from the initial tease to post-prize-award promotion.

Chapter 11, on location work, begins by explaining the unique relationship between the sales, promotion, and production departments that result in successful live broadcasts. Entitled "Fieldwork: Taking the Station on Location," this chapter includes detailed sections on digital remote broadcast transmission methods and producing commercial, sports, and news remotes.

"Interfacing with the Net," chapter 12, is a straightforward chapter that addresses audio production for the Internet and explores the unique programming and business relationship radio enjoys with the Internet. Although covering webcasting, the focus of chapter 12 is on audio production and radio's more creative uses of the Internet.

Chapter 13, "From Here to There: Radio and Audio Transmission in a Digital World," introduces the student to the many digital transmission methods radio has available for everything from transferring commercials from one station to another, to using ISDN lines for voice tracking and live remotes. Unique to the chapter are sections on high-definition radio and radio production for high-definition radio.

"Programming, Production, and Measuring Success," chapter 14, explores the relationship between radio production and radio programming. Included are sections on the radio production person's role in programming, music and format selection, and format delivery methods ranging from live to automated voice tracking. The chapter also discusses Arbitron audience ratings and how they are used to measure a radio station's success.

The last chapter, "Getting Your First Job in Radio," is unique in a production text from the standpoint that it provides students with the key information they need to secure their first position in radio broadcasting, with advice from someone who spent over twenty years in radio management. Chapter 15 has the information the career services office does not provide to broadcasting students. This tightly focused chapter's topics range from arranging an internship to completing an audition CD, including a special section on electronic resumes and auditions and creative approaches to delivering an application.

CDs and Supplements Package

Digital Radio Production is accompanied by several powerful learning tools. The demonstration CD included with the text features nearly 100 audio concepts and demonstrations discussed throughout the text. Students have the advantage of being able to experience what they are reading about 24/7. The demonstration CD includes a number of unedited recordings created for this text, such as a shuttle launch at the Kennedy Space Center, a real Baldwin steam locomotive captured in the Great Smoky Mountains, and a recording made deep in a national forest demonstrating some of the most basic principles of sound. The audition CD examples included on the demonstration disc from chapter 15 are actual student and professional auditions.

The music CD that accompanies *Digital Radio Production* features twenty cuts of production music written especially for this text. What is so unique about these is that each selection has been written as a production exercise. Students are treated to a raw multitrack recording session in which they can edit, mix, and master over 100 new musical selections. Additionally, there are over 200 music loops for students to compose their own production music with on the music CD. Beginners to masters will find something on the music CD that excites their creativity.

Also included with the text is a fully operational trial version of Adobe Audition. Adobe Audition is one of the de facto standards of radio production adopted by some of the largest broadcast companies. Students get to work with this incredibly powerful digital audio software as a learning tool on their personal computers and to create projects outside of class, experimenting with up to 128 tracks.

Digital Radio Production, with its demonstration CD, music CD, and Adobe Audition, is a complete production package featuring the information and tools a student needs to become a successful production person. Additionally, there is a full complement of instructor and student ancillaries supporting this text, including a complete and online learning center, packed with additional resources, exercises, and self-study quizzes, at http://www .mhhe.com/connelly. Also available are the Instructor's Resource CD, and test banks.

Acknowledgments

In writing this first edition of *Digital Radio Production* as a brand new text, I'm grateful to have had the opportunity to start fresh, based on where the industry is now and where it is going.

When my wife and I both fell in love with the mountains of Western North Carolina and made the tough decision to change careers, there were so many terrific people who helped in our transition from the industry to academics. My sincere thanks are due Dr. Kathleen Wright at Western Carolina University. As the head of the communication department, she took a chance and gave me the opportunity to excel at the profession of teaching. I would also like to thank my faculty mentor, Dr. "Newt" Smith of Western's English department. When I told Newt I had been approached to write this text he looked me square in the eye and in his best North Carolina drawl said, "If you don't do this, I will kick your ____." People who know him will tell you he wasn't kidding.

Digital Radio Production is unique with its industry-leading digital audio software, audio demos, and music CD. Thanks are due to Hart Shafer of Adobe Audition for sharing my vision and love of production so that students can have the opportunity to work with one of the most powerful digital audio programs there is.

I have worked with a lot of great people in my broadcasting career and I would sincerely like to thank everyone who assisted me with this project. I would particularly like to thank Rick Green, general manager; Jim Underwood, general sales manager; Jim Poling, director of operations; and Frank Lovre, chief engineer of Clear Channel Communications' Florida's Radio Networks, where I was affiliate relations director. Also, a big thanks to Dave Green, director of production services, and Mike Sprysenski, director of engineering, at Clear Channel Communications, Orlando.

I owe a special note of thanks to one of the best voices and imaging talents in the country, Jeff Laurence and his Autumn Hill Studios. Jeff's voice is heard on over 120 radio stations and, additionally, he is the voice of many national television commercials. Jeff provided valuable insight, help, and guidance in developing the chapter on promotion and station imaging.

Dr. Bruce H. Frazier is the Carol Grotnes Belk Distinguished Professor in Commercial and Electronic Music at Western Carolina University. Bruce is a good friend and an incredibly talented professional. The Academy of Television Arts and Science has twice recognized him for his contributions to dramatic underscore and sound mixing for television programs. He has also been nominated for several Emmys for his role as music editor on the TV series *Quantum Leap* and a Golden Reel nomination for his work on *JAG*. I am still amazed at how Bruce took my basic concept for music to accompany the text and created over twenty "musical exercises" for students to work with. My sincerest thanks go to Bruce for his contribution to this text.

Before taking on this project, the longest written work I had ever prepared was my master's thesis, many years ago. I learned so much working with Dr. John Slater, associate professor of communication at Western Carolina University. John is an accomplished writer and editor and deserves my deepest gratitude and a special recognition for serving as my non-industry reader/editor. John is an incredibly patient man and taught me that wordcrafting really is hard work. I will for-

ever be grateful to him as a colleague and friend.

I would also like to extend my thanks to Lynn Distler, president, Comrex Corporation, and to Robert Eaton of Electro-Voice, who took the time to be interviewed for the text.

I also extend my gratitude to all of those who patiently reviewed this first edition. I truly appreciated their insight and the contributions that they made to the text. My thanks to:

Stephen Adams, Cameron University

Steve Buss, California State University, Sacramento

Vincent M. Ditingo, New York Institute of Technology

Dana Vance Elderkin, North Carolina State University

Karen Holp, The University of Oklahoma

Heather Hundley, California State University, San Bernardino

José M. Maunez-Cuadra, University of Central Florida

Patrick J. Piotrowski, The University of Texas at El Paso

David D. Sabaini, Indiana State University

and Stanley Sollars, Ball State University.

I want to extend my sincere thanks to Phil Butcher and the incredible team at McGraw-Hill including David Sutton and Chanda Feldman, production editors; Marcella Tullio and Françoise Villeneuve, editorial assistants; Leslie Oberhuber, marketing manager; Christie Ling, media producer, for her experienced guidance and help in bringing my vision for *Digital Radio Production* to life. I would like to extend my very special thanks to Laura Lynch, who was my editor on the project and was always there with wisdom and advice when something came up.

Finally, I must express my deepest gratitude to my wife Debie for her incredible support during this project. I have worked a lot of odd hours in the radio business, but this project topped them all. For the last two years, most of my evenings and my spare time have been spent in front of a computer, writing the text and preparing the audio cuts. Debie's support and encouragement were invaluable. Now, with the publication of *Digital Radio Production*, she'll probably wonder who the stranger is finally joining her for dinner and an evening at home.

About the Author

N ow Director of Electronic Media at Western Carolina University, Don Connelly began his broadcast career as an undergraduate with a morning radio show, winning production awards from the Missouri Broadcasters Association while still in school. Upon graduation, he began teaching and simultaneously managing a public radio station. The station attracted national attention for its large audience and its consistent ability to generate more community funding per capita than any other public station in the country.

Don later ventured to leave behind a tenured teaching position and enter commercial broadcasting full-time. This led to eighteen years of commercial experience, managing and developing radio stations in Florida. Prior to his return to academia and joining the faculty at Western Carolina, Connelly was with Clear Channel Communications in Orlando, Florida, as Affiliate Relations Director for Florida's Radio Networks.

Throughout his extensive career, Don had always maintained a keen interest in production, and he has earned numerous production awards, including two "best of competition" awards at the Broadcast Education Association Media Festival.

Photo by John Ashcraft and Mark Haskett, Western Carolina University

CHAPTER 1

The Production Person

Introduction

This book is about radio production. We'll begin with a discussion of the production person and the industry in which he or she works.

Due largely to consolidation during the last few years, the radio industry has dramatically changed how it operates. Even small-market broadcasters are modeling themselves after larger companies and buying up stations to form small groups. By locating two or more stations in a market within a single facility, operational and staffing costs can be significantly reduced. Broadcasters are requiring staff to be multi-skilled, and just about anyone in the station may be called upon to participate in production.

Parts of this chapter may sound like a radio management text to you; however, it is vitally important to your success that you understand how a radio station operates and the role a production person plays in it.

One reason people are drawn to production is that the job is challenging in its broad scope. Production people are involved in just about every aspect of a radio station's operation and on-air sound. Through creative commercials, promotional announcements, and services offered to the on-air announcers, promotion, news, and sports departments, a production person is an integral part of the station.

Another, less obvious, reason people are drawn to production is the mastery of technology. Everyone desires to be the master of something, and the technology offers a certain mystery and excitement with which to be creative (see Fig. **1.1**). There is always the opportunity to create something seemingly from nothing.

Before you enter the radio industry, though, it is imperative that you understand what a radio station is, how it operates, and the role production people play in each station's success.

As a senior vice-president of Infinity Broadcasting, whose nearly two hundred radio stations generate an income of over a billion dollars per year, David Pearlman has summed up his view of what it takes for a career in broadcasting:

> To best prepare for a career in the new world of radio, one must refine a total knowledge of the business. For example, although a successful PD [program director] must understand the musical nuances of the format, he or she is now asked to manage the P & L [profit and loss] of their department and initiate revenue-generating opportunities. . . . It is imperative to develop effective communications skills and an understanding of marketing and sales, even if your ultimate goal is an on-air shift.

The Radio Station as a Business: The Profit Perspective

Every radio station has a specific purpose for being on the air. However, before that purpose can be accomplished or even understood, you must understand with absolute clarity what a radio station is first and foremost. A radio station is a business. It has one primary purpose: to make a profit for its owner. Even noncommercial public radio stations have bills to pay and must balance their ledger sheets each month.

And yet, although radio stations are a business, they are unique. Radio stations operate at the pleasure of the people of the United States of America. Radio stations are given an eight-year license, or franchise, by the Federal Communications Commission (FCC) to use a frequency or dial position. The FCC has rules and regulations with which the owner and employees of a radio station must comply. A radio station owner never owns or takes pos-

Figure 1.1

A digital audio workstation offers the opportunity to create commercials, promotional announcements, and creative features for the on-air staff. Production people often assist the promotion, news, and sports departments as well.

session of the radio frequency; it remains the property of the people of the United States. The FCC has the power to issue large forfeitures (fines) and even revoke the license of a radio station for a violation of its rules and regulations.

The FCC has established that the primary responsibility of a radio station is to serve the public's interest, convenience, and necessity in the community in which the station operates; this is often referred to as a station's social responsibility. If the station owner serves the community during the license period, the station license is renewed for another eight-year period.

Like any business, a radio station has operational expenses, such as retirement of debt or paying off the mortgage, radio **spectrum use fees,** building and tower rental, music copyright fees, payroll, and so on. If a radio station cannot meet its expenses it will be sold, leased to someone else to operate, or transferred to the entity holding the largest debt against the radio station. In a worst-case scenario, the station will "go dark," meaning to go off the air, existing in some form of bankruptcy until someone purchases the remaining assets of the radio station.

If a radio station does not produce a profit, it is very difficult for it to meet its legal and service obligations to the community. That is why, as a business, a radio station must make a profit. For a radio station to grow and expand services, it must produce financial gains.

Although many think of radio as an art form, the cold, hard reality is that radio stations are not referred to as the radio arts. Radio stations are referred to as the radio industry. The purpose of any industry is to produce profit for its owners and contribute to the economic well-being of the community in which it operates.

Radio Broadcasting Revenues

The radio broadcasting industry is a big business. Annual revenues from advertising sales are approximately twenty billion dollars a year. A radio station represents a substantial investment, often costing millions of dollars to purchase. At the beginning of this chapter, it was made very clear that the purpose of a radio station is to make a profit for the station owner so that the station can meet its legal and social obligations to the community. There is a saying in management that "you are only as good as your last quarter's balance sheet." For the most part, this is true.

Station managers have two clear obligations to their ownership: to make a return on the investment (profit) and to show continuing growth or new business. As a part of this business environment, managers who oversee several stations in a single market or region employ strict cost-accounting measures to ensure that the return on investment and projected annual growth are met. Even successful small-market managers have learned that these procedures can lead to reduced operating costs and increased profits.

As a part of this cost-accounting process, a manager examines every line item of the station budget and asks a simple question: Does this line item produce profit or significantly contribute to the profitability of the radio station? If the answer is yes, then the item is left in place. If the answer, on the other hand, is no, then some serious questions have to be answered. Sometimes a line item involves a person or a position. Can the line item be eliminated as a cost? If it cannot be eliminated entirely, can the line item be transferred to another department capable of accomplishing the same task more efficiently, thus lowering station costs and increasing profits? It is very difficult for a manager to justify keeping a line item that does not produce profit or significantly contribute to the profitability of the radio station.

That brings us to the production person. The production person is a line item on someone's spread sheet. How does he or she demonstrate profitability? How do you keep your line item in the budget? After all, the production person is not like the account executive who sells the ads and brings in cash to the radio station. You are also not like the disc jockey who is on the air getting high audience ratings, and thus increasing the value of the station's **commercial inventory.** So how do you show profitability? One of the keys to your success in radio is an understanding that the production director and the production people work for the sales department. In fact, everyone in the radio station works for the sales department. With this basic understanding of radio as a business and the necessity to make a profit, you can enter the industry a step ahead of others who are only focused on the art form.

The Role of the Radio Production Person

The production person is in effect the Renaissance person of the radio station. Production people must master a number of different skills and be several things to several different departments. As you prepare for a career in radio it is very important that you understand the vital role the production person plays in the industry.

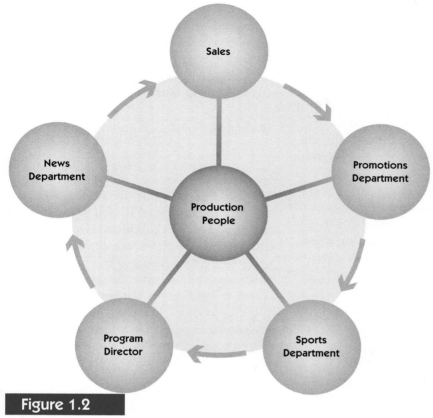

Figure 1.2

The production department is the hub around which the radio station revolves; its spokes reach to every department and provide critical support services and creative products.

The production department is the hub around which the radio station revolves; its spokes reach to every department and provide critical support services and creative product such as commercials, promotional announcements, and assistance in producing news, sports, and public affairs programming (see Fig. **1.2**). The power that turns the wheel is the sales department. Most of the projects in a radio station involve an account executive and a production person in some respect. The air staff depends on the support of production people, the account executives in the sales department depend on production people, and the promotions department depends on production people. In general, production people support the station's format with creative services.

Although production people do not get the listeners' attention like the on-air staff, and they don't get the glory of bringing in a huge new sales contract, what they do get—if they have done their job properly and supported the radio team—is respect as talented craftspeople whose skills are vital in making the radio station profitable.

What Makes a Good Production Person?

Great production people know the power of radio as a medium. More importantly, they are enthusiastic about the station they are working for and confident in their abilities to assist the station in achieving market dominance. This level of job satisfaction comes with education, mastery of skills, confidence in your abilities, and a genuine desire to see both you and everyone around you succeed.

Good production people have many qualities, including computer literacy, creativity, basic writing skills, a knowledge of music, and an ability to express themselves artistically through the medium.

Computer Literacy

A large part of a production person's job involves the use of computers and software in the recording, storage, and manipulation of audio. A production person is required to be computer literate and technically skilled with the hardware and software of the industry. The production person must always be a learner and be open to new technologies and techniques that help deliver a more creative and effective product in a more cost-efficient manner.

Thanks to digital production techniques, there is always going to be a new piece of software, hardware, or a new production style to help you be more creative and efficient. Every day brings you a new and different challenge. For example, until recently, radio stations and ad agencies were still sending commercials to one another on reels of magnetic tape or CDs. This practice became outdated when the Internet and **MP3** audio arrived with their immediate savings in time and cost. Advertising agencies could extend deadlines and deliver a commercial to hundreds of radio stations for pennies, versus hundreds or thousands of dollars for overnight shipping of reels of tape. It's positive changes like this that make your job easier and improve the quality of the product that the production person can look forward to.

Creativity

Did you ever color outside the lines? Do you take time to play "what if" and just have some fun every day? The production person has the seemingly impossible task of taking words, using hardware and software, and creating a thirty- or sixty-second "theater-of-the-mind event" so exciting that listeners are stimulated to go somewhere they have never been or to buy something they never knew they needed.

As a production person you are asked, on a daily basis, to take an idea from a brainstorming session the salesperson had with the client and turn that idea into a cinematically suggestive radio commercial that gets the listeners' immediate attention and projects an image of products or services onto their mind's eye. Your task is to create something that transforms a listener into a customer walking into a sponsor's business; it's what retailers refer to as "in-store traffic."

Production people must work outside the box. They must challenge themselves from time to time to come up with a concept or approach that is something other than a bland meat-and-potatoes concept for a commercial or promotion.

Writing Skills

Although many stations employ copy writers, many others do not; in that case, you're it. A good production person must be able to write a commercial or station promotional announcement when necessary. These writing skills need to be matched with knowledge gained from working alongside salespeople, so that the production person can assemble a powerful commercial to increase store traffic and deliver the results the client expects. You need to have a good understanding of what makes a commercial "work" for the client and which elements are necessary for a great commercial and which are not.

There are also going to be those times when the client has given the salesperson a piece of commercial copy, considered by the client to be a great work of art, and you are assigned the task of editing four-and-a-half pages of handwritten copy into an effective sixty-second commercial.

From a basic writing standpoint, how do you structure the price and product placement within the ad? How many times does the client's name need to be mentioned? Where does the address go, does the client's phone number need to be in the ad, does the client's web address need to be in the ad, what makes an effective commercial? By working with the salesperson, you can develop the knowledge of what kinds of ads produce results for the client and what kinds of ads do not. This even includes becoming familiar with the kinds of people the client is trying to attract to its business, including such things as lifestyle, consumer habits, and product preferences.

Musicology

Music is powerful. Combined with just the right words it can be even more powerful. It can motivate people to make buying decisions, to take part in community activities,

and to continue listening to your radio station. A production person works with an exclusive library of music (see Fig. **1.3**). This library consists of specially written, copyright-cleared production music, just like the production music included with this text. What makes it so special is that the musical selections are thirty or sixty seconds long. The music has been written specifically for use as a part of a commercial, even to the point that some music is industry-specific. In other words, it has the qualities or thematic style associated with a particular type of business.

A production person needs to be familiar with his or her production music library and have an excellent knowledge of the radio station's musical format, even if it is not his or her favorite style of music. Production music has to complement and enhance not only a client's commercial but also the station's musical format, as well. Music can give a commercial terrific impact when matched to the right copy. Likewise, it can create a serious distraction when a mismatch occurs (see demo CD, cuts 1 and 2). Selecting the right production music for a commercial or station promotional announcement (promo) is a skill that comes with experience, but it also requires taste and an ear for selecting music that complements the advertiser's business and the station's format.

Artistic Expression

A painter selects brushes, paints, and canvas. A production person selects microphones, computers, software, and music and voice talent, blending them to create commercials and program elements to support the station format, create interest, and motivate listeners. A lot of production people become truly talented and gifted artists—the person who has the ability to mix just the right amount of each

Figure 1.3

Production music is specially written, copyright-cleared music intended for use in commercials. Each station purchases or leases a library of production music that complements its musical format. *T. Garret Adams, photographer, courtesy of TM Century, Inc.*

of the preceding elements to trigger the "wow" factor in a listener.

The Radio Station as an Organization

The production person is but one member of a team that is charged with making the radio station a success. The sooner you understand how you fit within the radio station's organization, the quicker you are going to understand your responsibilities with regard to the radio station's success. By understanding your position and how you relate to the rest of the radio station, you can avoid many time-wasting and costly misadventures.

The Business Side

Most successful radio stations, even some small-market stations, typically have an organizational chart clearly outlining the radio station's structure (see Fig. **1.4**). To complement the organizational chart, there should be written job descriptions for each of the positions on the organizational chart. As a new employee, you should ask for a copy of each so you know where you fit in and what your specific duties are.

General Manager

At the top of the organizational chart is the general manager, or GM, as they are often called. The GM is responsible for *everything*.

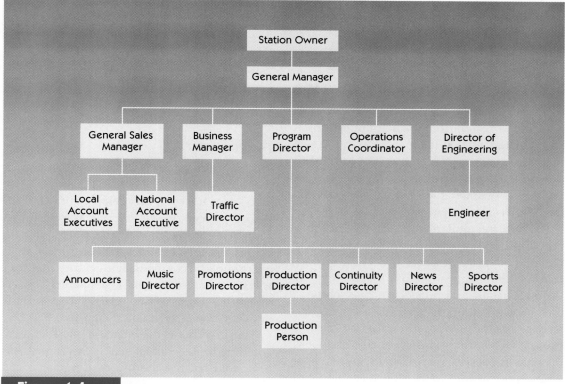

Figure 1.4

An organizational chart for a radio station is a graphic representation of the station staff and who it reports to. Depending on the market size, some of the jobs represented here may be combined and assigned to one person. For example, the general sales manager may also be the national account executive.

Along with a staff, the GM develops a business plan to guide the station to a position of sales and audience dominance in the marketplace. Using the resources of the station department heads, the GM oversees and coordinates all planning, including growth and income projection, programming, marketing, and execution of the station's business plan.

The GM is the parent figure within the station who guides and settles the disputes that sometimes arise between departments. In addition, the GM is a headhunter, with the responsibility to search for the new staff necessary to

meet the station's needs as it grows. The GM is the person who makes the ultimate decision to hire or terminate employees.

You may also find yourself working in an environment where there are multiple radio stations under one roof. Typically, there is one group or market manager over all the stations. In some cases, the stations in a particular geographic area may be located close together, and the GM for all of the stations is known as a regional manager. The exact wording of the title and responsibilities varies from company to company, but the end result is the same:

The GM, or market manager, is at the top of the organizational chart.

General Sales Manager

Working very closely with the GM is the general sales manager, or GSM. The general sales manager is responsible for helping to project and generate station income through the sale of radio commercials, or inventory. In addition to a return, or profit, the general sales manager's business plan reflects growth or an increase in sales revenues.

Advertising dollars come from three primary areas: local advertising sales, regional/national advertising sales, and NTR, or nontraditional revenue. Nontraditional revenue includes events and projects such as job fairs, boat shows, station magazines, or other radio station sidelines that produce revenue for the station. Depending on market size, the GSM may have a local and a national sales manager who report to him or her. Further, the GSM may employ the services of a national firm to represent the station to national clients, often referred to as a **national rep.**

Business Manager

A business manager does just what the name implies. This is the person held fiscally responsible for the operation of the radio station, controlling every aspect of the money that flows in and out. The business manager advises the general manager and general sales manager on financial matters and keeps them abreast of the station's billing and collections. Business managers also track the station's financial performance to determine profitability and whether the station is meeting sales and growth projections. The business manager is responsible for establishing the station's commercial billing and collection practices. It is the business manager who determines who gets credit and who gets taken off the air because they did not pay their advertising bill. You may also find the business manager being referred to as the controller.

Traffic Director

Working alongside the business manager is the traffic director, or TD. The TD is the person who keeps track of every salable minute of advertising inventory the station has to offer. Account executives consult the traffic director before signing a contract with an advertiser to make sure the commercial inventory that they want to sell to the client is available. The TD schedules every commercial, station promo, or event that is to run on the air (see Fig. **1.5**).

The TD advises the business manager as to what percentage of available inventory has been sold so that the business manager can alert the GM and GSM. This information is used to determine advertising rates. If the station is consistently sold out and demand for commercials is high, rates go up. If the station has a large amount of available inventory, rates are adjusted so that the inventory can be sold.

Account Executive

At the street level is the account executive, or AE, also sometimes called a marketing consultant, sales representative, or salesperson. The station AEs target and call on local businesses to sell them advertising. This level of sales is typically referred to as direct or retail sales. The AEs may also call on local advertising agencies hired by businesses to handle their advertising. Typically, AEs not only sell commercials but also market station promo-

Program Log

Program Time		Max Units	Program	Break Type	Length	Advertiser Spot Title	ISCI	Cart
Start	Break Len							
9:10:00	0:01:00	2	JBB 9 AM HR GEM	Commercial	01:00	CINGULAR WIRELESS CINGULAR/COOL DAD/60	WFSR-1962	7330
9:20:00	0:00:01	1	JBB 9 AM HR GEM	Adjacency				
9:30:00	0:03:00	4	JBB 9 AM HR GEM	Commercial	01:00	CHARTER CHARTER/INTERRUPT/6	CCIN0036	7416
					01:00	NATIONWIDE NATIONWIDE/FAMILY	NWI010960	7356
					01:00	SOUTHEAST TOYOTA SE TOYOTA/MAR CARS	TJRA0820	7529
9:40:00	0:04:00	5	JBB 9 AM HR GEM	Commercial	01:00	RAMCELL RAMCELL/39 99 DEAL/60	RCNC9768	7381
					01:00	TOUGHMAN TOUGHMAN/WEEK	API3282.MP3	7494
					00:30	HARDEES HARDEES/CINAMMON	HD308750	7294
					00:30	HARDEES HARDEES/6 DOLLAR	HD308676	7296
					00:30	DR HENRY WONG WONG/YARD SALE/30		7573
					00:30	MOUNTAIN AREA HOSPICE/HORSE		7534
9:50:00	0:02:00	3	JBB 9 AM HR GEM	Commercial	01:00	JIM COOK CHEVROLET JIM COOK/JBB+TAG/60		7031
					01:00	INGLES INGLES/MOVIE MONT	ING1011+TAG ING1002	7302
9:52:00	0:01:00	1	JBB 9 AM HR GEM	Premiere Gem	01:00	PREMIERE NETWORK GM/On Star System	R-0340-ON-6	9535

Sign On:_____   Time: _____   Sign Off: _____   Time: _____

Figure 1.5

The traffic director creates the station's daily program log that lists every commercial, station promotional announcement, or event that is to run on the air.

tions and nontraditional revenue-generating events, as well.

The general manager, general sales manager, business manager, traffic director, and account executives comprise the "business side of the house."

The Programming Side

Program Director

The "programming side of the house" is headed up by the program director, or PD. The PD is responsible for everything that ends up on the air. PDs direct and shape the station's overall sound and make all of the decisions regarding programming, with the final approval resting with the general manager. Program directors do not generally make decisions based on hunches or gut feelings. There is a great deal of audience research, skill, and judgment involved on the part of the PD in making programming decisions. That said, you must also understand that sometimes, in smaller markets, programming *is* based on hunches. In fact, sometimes it is based on what the owner's mother likes.

PDs have three responsibilities with respect to programming. First, they must maintain the listener base the station currently has. Second, they must attract new listeners. Third, they must show consistent audience growth and achieve audience ratings goals. To accomplish these three objectives, PDs use a number of research tools to track the station's progress. These include both **quantitative** (ratings numbers) and **qualitative** (lifestyle) research. Such research includes audience ratings services, focus groups, surveys, and **call-out research** conducted by the station to judge listeners' feelings about the station's music.

The PD uses research to help develop an overall programming strategy for the station. This includes music selection, music flow and rotation of songs, air personalities and presentation style, the number of commercials that can run **(commercial inventory load)** on an hour-by-hour basis, the style of **imaging** used to promote the station, when and if there is news, traffic reports and weather, and the overall sound and attitude of the station, among other things. These are just a few of the elements that make up the station's programming.

Another aspect of the program director's job is the oversight of music copyright concerns. This includes being familiar with the specific copyright agreements that a station has and monitoring the station's music use. Regular reports are required by **ASCAP, BMI,** and **SESAC,** which are the major organizations that represent artists' interests with regard to copyright.

Great program directors are talent coaches. They are involved in each personality's show, reviewing and helping the on-air staff to develop and increase the quality of the product (see Fig. **1.6**). They teach their disc jockeys, and for that matter anyone working on-air, to communicate with the station's listeners while routinely doing an on-air show (air shift) themselves. Program directors are deeply involved with promotion and marketing of the station's sound. Program directors are also required to control a budget with regard to talent and promotion expenses, and they help initiate new revenue-generating promotional opportunities.

Like many of the jobs in a radio station, the PD's position is constantly evolving and changing with the industry. In a market where there are several stations under one roof, there may be one PD who works with individual program coordinators for each station. In this situation, the PD is elevated to looking at the big picture, and the program coordinators handle the day-to-day details that consume a lot of a regular PD's time.

Music Director

In addition to the PD, many stations have a music director. A music director works closely with the program director to research and select the music that ends up on the air. The music director develops the lists of music (playlists) for the various times of the day (dayparts) and creates the music rotation order so that the music always appears fresh and forward-moving on the radio station. Usually, the music director consults with the program director on the overall sound of the

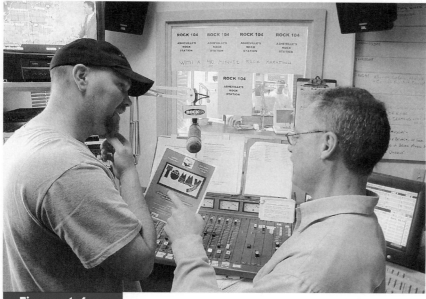

Figure 1.6

Program directors are involved in each personality's show, reviewing and helping the on-air staff to develop and increase the quality of the product. They teach disc jockeys, and for that matter anyone working on-air, to communicate effectively with the station's listeners.

station's music product and for final music approval, including songs that are being added or dropped from the station's playlist.

Promotions Director

Closely aligned with the program director and the general sales manager is the promotions director. A promotions director works with the program director, the general sales manager, and the account executive to create sales-driven, format-centered promotions for the radio station. These are revenue-generating events that the radio station hosts or co-hosts with a sponsor (see Fig. 1.7). The promotions director is responsible for both the internal and external marketing of the radio station to listeners.

Internal marketing involves using all of the resources of the radio station to promote the station to existing listeners. This includes on-air contests and giveaways, promotions of special station events such as movie premieres, and just about anything else sales and programming can think of to be competitive in the market. **External marketing,** on the other hand, is when the radio station goes outside its listener base and seeks new listeners through other media such as billboards, newspapers, and television promotion.

Public Service/ Community Affairs Director

Many times station promotions involve a community group or organization as a public

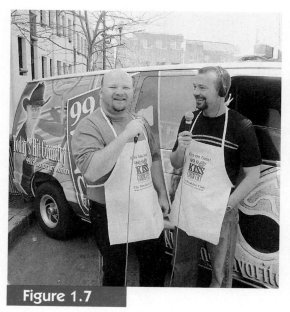

Remote broadcasts are an important part of a station's public visibility. The promotions director coordinates sales-driven, format-centered promotions for the radio station. This promotion was tied to a chili cook off and a KISS the cook event.

service function of the radio station. The public service or community affairs director of the radio station is the person who is responsible for interfacing with the community. When a community leader or group comes to the station and asks assistance in promoting an event such as a live broadcast from a pet adoption day at the Humane Society, the community affairs director serves as a liaison between the community group and the station. It is not unusual for the duties of the community affairs director to be combined with another position.

Production Director

The production director is another individual responsible in part for the sound of the radio station. Production directors work closely with the program director so that all of the creative product that the production department turns out fits the station's format, style, and personality. The production director directs the production staff in producing commercials, station promotional announcements, and station imaging. The production director also maintains a close relationship with the general sales manager and account executives so that they are aware of the production department's talents and creative abilities. Occasionally, if the client's idea is a little too creative and one that may not fit the station format or style, the production director may be placed in the awkward position of sending the GSM or an AE to the program director to clear a client's commercial idea.

The production director also works closely with the radio station's promotion department. The promotion department comes up with and directs all of the creative ways to involve the station with the listeners and the community. There is an old saying in radio: "If it's worth doing, it's worth promoting." Each event the promotion department dreams up has to have support from the production department to sell it to the listener in a creative fashion. The more creative, the better.

The production director, like many others in radio management, has a staff to lead. It is the production director's job to put his or her production people to use in the most cost-effective manner possible. The production director must know each staff member's creative strengths and weaknesses. Production directors also serve as coaches for staff members, guiding and helping them to produce the best creative product possible. By developing the staff, production directors are able to schedule production more effectively and give those clients that require the most attention to the most creative and productive people.

The production director is often asked to assign production people collaborate with the news department on the production of public affairs programs. Such a partnership reflects the most efficient use of the news person's time. Although most news people are quite competent at news production, it makes more sense for them to serve as talent on long-form public affairs shows and to allow the production person to perform the routine editing and final on-air preparation of the show. Radio stations are required by the FCC to produce some kind of public affairs programming on a regular basis to serve their community.

The production director has to be able to work with deadlines and ensure that every commercial is produced on time and is ready to go on the air as scheduled. An ad not ready to air on time is an expensive error—the station is left with an ad that did not run, for which it lost money, and an unsold time slot, for which it also lost money. It is very important that you understand that each minute of inventory has a very real cash value. Finally, the production director is also required to work with budgets for new equipment, software upgrades and support packages, production music, and production payrolls, among other things.

Production Person

Although you are called a production person and you work in the production department, you play a vital role in the sales department. In addition to the other station staff a production person works with, a good production person seeks to develop a synergy with each of the AEs, so that he or she more clearly understands the styles and types of commercials the AEs want for their clients (see Fig. **1.8**). By working with the AEs to develop effective commercials that produce results for the clients, the production person is putting finan-

cial success of the radio station first and foremost. When you cooperate in this way, you will be noticed by the AE and the GSM because you are helping them reach the station's projected budgets. There is nothing more exciting than having an AE return to the radio station and tell everyone that the thirty-five-thousand-dollar contract he or she just landed with a new car dealership was because the dealer loved the commercial *you* created for it. This is how the production person contributes to the station's profitability. Production people get pay raises and bonuses based on their contribution to the success of the sales department and the station.

Production people also play a vital role on the air through entertainment and news production. Production people help produce the comedy bits, the ongoing elements, imaging, promotional announcements, and a lot of the things critical to being on the air that gives the station its unique sound and personality. The on-air morning team may give a production person a concept or idea for a show feature that makes the radio station leap out of the radio at the listener with vivid sound imagery. Although their job is not as flashy as that of the morning teams, and no one ever asks for an autographed picture of a production person, their creativity and skill are what helps the morning team and the other on-air staff sound great and get higher ratings. Great ratings translate into higher advertising rates, which mean that your radio station makes budget.

Continuity Director

A production person works closely with the station's continuity director. The continuity director is the person who is responsible for writing all the commercials that turn listeners into customers for your station's clients. Continuity directors are an interface between the

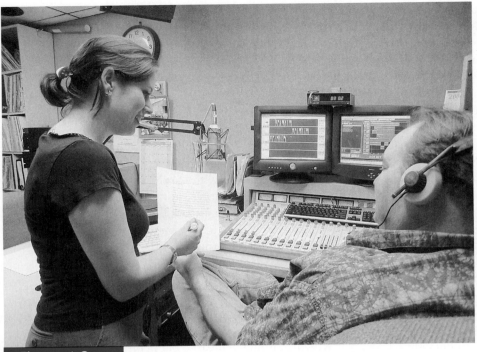

Figure 1.8

Production people work with the station's account executives to develop effective commercials that produce results for the clients. Production people play a vital role in the advertising sales process.

sales department and the production department. Not only do they prepare the copy, they work with the AE to get the copy approved by the client before it goes to production. This allows a production person to focus his or her time and energy on the creative presentation of the ad, as opposed to having to create the script from scratch.

The continuity director knows the station's commercial policies and is familiar with federal, state, and local laws that advertising must comply with. The continuity director also works with the program director to determine what kinds of ads are suitable for what dayparts. Would your radio station accept an ad for a "gentlemen's club" (expensive strip bar) during the daytime, or does your station only allow such ads to run between 11 p.m. and 3 a.m., if at all?

In larger markets the continuity director may have a small staff of copy writers. In smaller markets, though, don't be surprised to find that there is no continuity director and that all of the duties of the continuity director fall to the production person.

News Director

Another important individual in the radio station is the news director. The news director reports either to the general manager or to the program director, depending on the station.

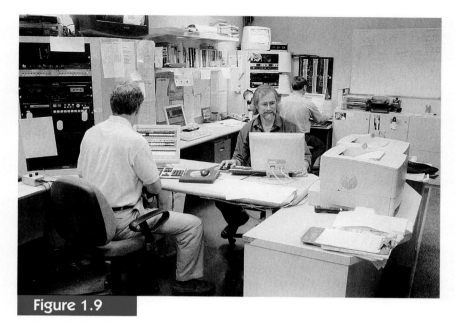

Figure 1.9

Because of industry consolidation, program directors typically work with smaller news and sports staffs. This newsroom handles the news and sports for six radio stations in one market.

Generally, the news director meets on a regular basis with the program director to make sure that the style of news that is being presented fits the format (see Fig. **1.9**). A rock station might want news written for 18-to-34-year-olds with a bit of an edge or attitude in the presentation. Even the length of a newscast is determined somewhat by the format and the age group or **demographic** (demos) the station is trying to attract. People from younger demographic groups tend to want short-and-to-the-point newscasts; people from older demographic groups tend to want more in-depth stories and a longer-format newscast. Of course, this description is based on a radio station having a commitment to news. Many radio stations have a "news" department in name only. This generally consists of one member of the morning team being desig-

nated the "news director" and preparing short-format (two minutes or less) newscasts using material prepared by a service for the morning show.

Sports Director

In addition to a news director, a station may have a sports director. The sports director is responsible for the sports programming that is on the station. This might include daily sportscasts, any long-form sports coverage such as college football, and doing play-by-play for local sporting events (see Fig. **1.10**). As with the news director, not every radio station employs a sports director, and in many cases the station uses the services of one of the top-rated television sports anchors from the area for their sportscasts. This is both a cost-saving

In addition to daily sportscasts, a sportscaster might be actively involved in play-by-play coverage of local sports.

measure and a promotional opportunity to be associated with a popular television station.

Engineer

Engineers are the people who keep your studios in excellent shape and keep your radio station on the air. Most engineers have excellent technical skills and understand that their job is to make sure everything is working all of the time. A good relationship with your station engineer is vital to a production person. Regular communications with the engineer can help you maintain audio quality and get good technical advice and assistance when needed.

This is not an easy job, and you may rarely see the engineers, as they often work late at night, during "down time," or when your production studios are not in use. Most stations have specific policies about the repair of

equipment, and generally your role as a production person is confined to reporting any problem accurately. Do not try to play junior engineer and make repairs yourself. This is especially important in a union shop, in which the engineers and station staff are members of trade unions.

The Radio Team in Action

From a practical standpoint, not every radio station has all of the staff described in the preceding section. Many times several jobs are combined into one position in smaller markets. For example, the general manager may also be the general sales manager, and the business manager may also be the traffic director. But, for the moment, assume you are in a larger market and let's walk a commercial order through fictional WBSP-FM so you can have some idea of how things come together. The process of getting a commercial on the air is truly a team effort, with a lot of communication going on among the various staff members at each stage of the ad's creation. At all times during the process an eye is kept on the deadlines for copy writing, ad production, client approval, and the first day the commercial is to be aired.

From a Budget to a Commercial

Earlier in the year, fictional radio station WBSP's general manager created an annual budget for the radio station based on a specific return on investment that the owner seeks. With the help of the general sales manager, the GM establishes the sales budgets for each quarter of the year. Because it is the GSM's job to carry out this budget and reach the projected station incomes in each quarter, the GSM assigns the account executives businesses to call on and to consult with about using radio to increase their retail sales. After meeting with a new business, the AE develops a plan to meet the client's needs and desires. The plan ensures that the client uses radio effectively and includes a schedule of ads to run on WBSP-FM.

An AE often checks with the business department before proposing a schedule to a client to see if the client can afford to be on the station and that he or she has acceptable credit. Some clients by their very nature are required to pay cash in advance. Bars, concerts, restaurants, and political candidates most often are required to pay cash in advance. Nor is it unusual for a new start-up business to be required to pay in advance until it establishes a credit history with the radio station.

The AE then meets with the client again, and because the AE has done an excellent job of researching and meeting all of the client's needs, the client agrees to use WBSP-FM in his or her media mix of advertising. Let's assume this is the case. The AE returns to WBSP-FM and submits the advertising plan and sales order to the GSM for his or her review and approval. With the GSM's approval, the sales order travels to the business department where a credit check is run on the business, a credit limit is established, and the client is cleared to go on the air.

From the business department, the sales order moves to the traffic department. Here the available commercial time (inventory) is scheduled according to the sales order. Most good AEs check with the traffic department before they propose a schedule to a client; that way they know the inventory they are proposing (pitching) to the client is available. Once the order clears traffic, it heads to the continuity director, where the ad is written. The AE has already had a meeting with the client to determine what will be advertised and how the ad should be produced. In some cases, though, the client simply asks the AE to produce a great-sounding ad. The continuity director works through the AE to get client approval of the written script. At this point, the script is given a unique client name and number to identify the ad, and a production order is created and sent to production.

When the script and production order arrive, the production director assigns the job to a production person, and the job is given a specific deadline for production. At this point, the production person who has been assigned the job meets briefly with the AE to discuss any special requirements or desires the client might have. After the ad is produced, the production person contacts the AE and assists him or her with the technical aspects of getting client approval. Such assistance might include making a CD for the AE to play to the client in person or assisting the AE in calling the client and playing the ad on the phone to get the client's approval. The production person always works with or through the AE; he or she never contacts a client directly unless specifically told to do so by the AE. Once the ad is approved, the production person places the ad in whatever digital audio storage device the radio station uses for commercial playback on the air. The production order is completed and filed, and traffic is notified that the ad is ready to air.

Traffic generates the daily logs that tell the on-air staff what ads get played when. After the ad plays at the predetermined times, the on-air announcer verifies this by signing the program log. In some cases this will be an actual signature on a piece of paper, in others it will be an electronic signature in the form of a computerized confirmation report of what actually ran on the radio station. From the completed and verified logs the business department generates the billing and sends out the bills to the clients.

Although the process of moving a commercial project through a radio station sounds complicated, much of the "paper trail" is handled by computer and occurs simultaneously in the various departments.

The basic organizational structure or radio stations is quite similar from one station to the next, with the business side and the programming side working together to ensure the station's financial success.

Suggested Activities

1. Arrange a tour of a local radio station and explain your interest in radio production and how a radio station operates.
2. While there, observe the number of studios and how the station and each studio is laid out.

3. Ask questions about how the radio station is structured and who performs the different jobs in the radio station.

Web Sites for More Information

For more information about:

- *how radio stations operate as a business,* visit the Radio Advertising Bureau at www.rab.com
- *issues facing the broadcast industry,* visit the National Association of Broadcasters at www.nab.org
- *how the FCC regulates broadcasting,* visit the FCC at www.fcc.gov

Pro Speak

You should be able to use these terms in your everyday conversations with other professionals.

ASCAP—American Society of Composers, Authors, and Publishers. A membership-based performing rights organization that protects the copyrights of members' works by licensing and distributing royalties for the performances of their copyrighted works.

BMI—Broadcast Music, Incorporated. A membership-based performing rights organization that protects the copyrights of members' works by licensing and distributing royalties for the performances of their copyrighted works.

call-out research—Research conducted by a radio station or a research firm to ask listeners questions about how they perceive the station's music format; often used to keep a station's music format on track from week to week.

commercial inventory—The number of commercials that a radio station has to offer for sale. Commercial inventory can be broken down into weekly, daily, and hourly inventory.

commercial inventory load—How many commercials are actually scheduled to run in a given time period such as an hour, half hour, or quarter hour.

demographic—Statistical data about particular groups of people. Radio uses standardized age groupings consisting of persons 12 and older, 18–34, 25–54, and 35–64. These age groups are also broken down into statistical data for males and females.

external marketing—Any medium or marketing tool outside the radio station such as billboards, newspaper ads, and television commercials used to promote the radio station.

imaging—Radio station imaging consists of the short live and recorded elements that are used between segments of a station's programming that tie everything together, creating a station's signature sound. As an example, "Kansas City's home for good-time rock-and-roll oldies, Super Cool 107.9."

internal marketing—Any marketing tool or promotion tool used on a radio station to attract more listeners such as contests, T-shirts, bumper stickers, etc.

MP3—Motion Picture Experts Group Layer 3 audio compression compresses, or shrinks, CD-quality audio files by a factor of twelve or more, maintaining the original perceived CD-quality sound so that audio files can be transferred via the World Wide Web.

national rep—A national representative is a person or a company that represents a radio station to large national advertising agencies handling regional or national products.

quantitative research—Research centered on numerical or statistical data; most commonly audience ratings research to determine the number of listeners a radio station has.

qualitative research—Research centered on a person or group's lifestyle choices. For example, the radio station targets 18-to-34-year-old single males living in Jackson County who rent an apartment, make monthly car payments on a 2002, or newer, vehicle, eat out three times a week, drink domestic beer, and go to the movies twice a month.

SESAC—Society of European Stage Authors and Composers. A membership-based performing rights organization that protects the copyrights of members' works by licensing and distributing royalties for their performance.

spectrum use fees—Fees charged by the FCC to broadcasters for the use of the public airwaves.

CHAPTER 2

Basic Science: Analog and Digital Audio

It's an Analog World

A production person works with sound every day of his or her life. Before you can efficiently use the equipment in the radio station to perform your job, you need to understand what is moving through the equipment and how it reacts with the environment around you.

It is difficult to use a microphone properly without an understanding of sound and basic acoustics. Likewise, it is very difficult to master the hardware and software with which you record, store, and manipulate digital audio without some understanding of the raw material (sound) you are working with. Although you are living in a digital age, digital sound is not sound's natural state. To understand digital sound you must first understand nature-based analog sound, including how your own ears work.

The Beginnings of Sound

Deep in the forests of the Great Smoky Mountains of western North Carolina, far from any four-lane highway or city, there is a 13,000-acre tract of four-hundred-year-old old-growth trees that reach over a hundred feet into the air. One of the unique aspects of this part of the forest is that some of the oldest trees occasionally lose limbs, or in some cases collapse due to age or weather, which brings up an age-old question. If a tree falls in the forest and there is no one there to hear the event, does it make a sound?

On a windy day a tree is about to give way and send tons of lumber crashing to the forest floor. As the winds blow, the tree is pushed forward, forcing the molecules of air surrounding it from their original resting places and shoving them into other air molecules. Energy is transferred from one air molecule to another, creating a chain reaction, or wave, moving away from the tree.

The chain reaction of one molecule being pushed into another creates an area of high pressure between the molecules, known as compression. The high-pressure compression pushes up a crest in the wave (see Fig. **2.1**). However, the molecules really don't move very far from their original position or average resting space. The wave is very similar to what happens in a sports stadium when the crowd does "the wave." Someone gives a signal, and rows of people begin standing up and sitting down, creating crests in the wave of people. And while the wave moves all the way around the stadium, participants stay in or very close to their seats, or their average resting place.

As the winds let up and the tree returns to its original position, it no longer is pushing the molecules out of the way in that particular direction. In fact, as the tree returns to its original position it pulls apart the molecules that it forced close together. As the molecules are pulled apart, low-pressure trenches are created between the high-pressure crests in the wave in a process referred to as rarefaction.

The sequence of a single compression crest, or high-pressure point, and a rarefaction trench, or low-pressure point, is one complete cycle and is represented by the sine wave (see Fig. **2.2**). The cycles repeat themselves over and over, traveling away from the object that started the original vibrations until the wave runs out of energy. The continuous wave is called a sound wave.

Identifying Sounds

The primary way in which sound waves are differentiated from one another is by using electronic equipment to count the number of cycles in the sound wave in one second of time, or the cycles per second. The number of

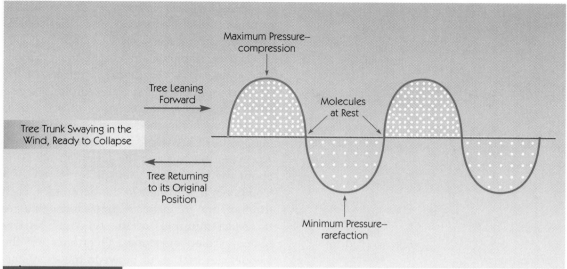

Maximum Pressure–
compression

Tree Leaning
Forward

Tree Trunk Swaying in the
Wind, Ready to Collapse

Molecules
at Rest

Tree Returning
to its Original
Position

Minimum Pressure–
rarefaction

Figure 2.1

As the vibrations leave the tree trunk, one air molecule is pushed into another, creating an area of high pressure between the molecules known as compression. When the tree returns to its original position it pulls apart the molecules of air that it forced close together. As the molecules are pulled apart, low-pressure trenches are created between the high-pressure crests in the wave in a process referred to as rarefaction.

cycles per second is designated as the **frequency** of the sound wave. Interestingly, humans perceive the frequency of a sound as pitch. As a general rule, the fewer the cycles per second, the lower in pitch the sound appears. The generic term "bass" describes a broad range of low-pitched frequencies. The higher the number of cycles per second, the higher in pitch the sound appears. The generic term "treble" describes a broad range of these high-pitched frequencies. Every sound source has a unique frequency that can be identified.

Heinrich Hertz was a nineteenth-century researcher who did pioneering work with radio waves and theorized about cycles per second. In his honor, the term hertz is used in place of the term "cycles per second" and is

abbreviated as Hz. If a sound has 180 cycles per second it becomes 180 hertz, or 180 Hz.

A human being with excellent hearing can hear a range of sound waves from near 20 Hz, at the low end of the scale, to near 20,000 Hz, at the upper end of the scale. The range of sound each person hears varies depending on the person's physical condition. The complete range of audible frequencies is referred to as the sound frequency spectrum (see demo CD, cut 3).

There are many sounds that are beyond the range of human hearing; even though we cannot hear them, however, such sounds are often perceived by feeling them. Sounds below 20 Hz are called **infrasonic** and are sometimes referred to as sub-bass. Sounds above 20,000 Hz are called **ultrasonic.** Not all people are able to sense the presence of these sounds.

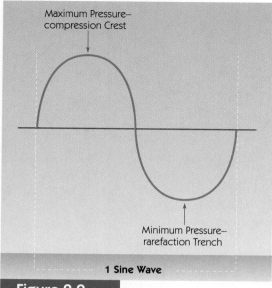

Maximum Pressure–
compression Crest

Minimum Pressure–
rarefaction Trench

1 Sine Wave

Figure 2.2

A sine wave is one complete cycle of a compression crest and a rarefaction trench. The cycles repeat themselves over and over, traveling away from the object that started the original vibrations until the wave runs out of energy. The continuous wave is called a sound wave.

To this point, all of the frequencies discussed have been a single pure tone or frequency, as represented by the sine wave. A pure tone is referred to as a fundamental frequency or first **harmonic.** Harmonics are sounds that are created by multiplying the original fundamental frequency. Not all sounds in life are pure tones; most are made up of a combination of tones. Consider the case of the doomed tree in the forest; the tree trunk makes a low rumbling sound as it bends back and forth at its base, sending vibrations into the ground around it. The wind whistles through the leaves, the leaves are hitting one another thrashing about in the wind, and there is the occasional creaking sound as the tree trunk becomes weak. There is the snap of

twigs, a few birds singing; in all, a multitude of fundamental frequencies and other sounds are coming from the tree.

Each fundamental frequency has harmonics, or tones, that are exact multiples of the original frequency. As an example, starting with a fundamental frequency of 400 Hz as the first harmonic, the second harmonic is 800 Hz; the third harmonic is 1,200 Hz, and so on. Applying this to a real-life situation, 400 Hz is about the top end of the primary range of a trombone. In addition to the harmonics, each fundamental frequency also has tones that are *not* exact multiples of the fundamental frequency, called **overtones.** Overtones are the frequencies that occur between the exact harmonic frequencies. In the case of the trombone, the harmonics and overtones extend from the primary frequency of about 400 Hz to nearly 10,000 Hz.

Most sounds that you perceive are a combination of the fundamental frequency, the harmonics, and the overtones. Timbre, or the tone quality, is the term used to describe this unique combination of tones that distinguishes one sound from another. Musical instruments, when played properly, create many tonal combinations that are quite pleasing to the ear. Typically, engineers talk about bass, midrange, and treble. These broad definitions can be further defined and divided.

Sub bass   The sub bass is typically 16 Hz to 50 Hz. These are the sounds that pipe organs do such an incredible job of reproducing, down to 32 Hz, with some large pipe organs capable of 16 Hz. These are the sounds that you don't really hear as much as you feel them. Such frequencies are associated with the power and fullness of a sound. However, if these sounds occur continuously or too often, or are too loud, the sound becomes muffled. The very un-technical term used to describe this condition of the sound is "down in the mud" or "muddy."

Low bass   The low-bass region of 50 Hz to 80 Hz is where some of the distinctive qualities of musical instruments begin to appear. In this range are instruments like the bottom end of a kick drum, tuba, and the lower notes of a bass, among others. This range is well into the hearing range of most people.

One of the interesting qualities of the sub-bass and low-bass regions of sound is that humans have a very difficult time sensing the direction these sounds originate from. Sounds at these frequencies lose their directionality to us. This is why a stereo, or surround-sound speaker system, only has one sub-bass speaker or **subwoofer.** It can be placed just about anywhere in the room, since you are not capable of sensing which direction the sub-bass sounds are coming from.

Upper bass   The upper-bass frequencies include the sounds from 80 Hz to 315 Hz. This is an area that includes some of the lower ranges of the human voice and frequencies that provide warmth and body to sound. The sounds in this frequency range are very satisfying to the human ear and include instruments such as the piano, drums, and stringed instruments like the bass and cello. Some horns are also in this range.

Lower midrange   In the lower midrange are the frequencies between 315 Hz and 2,500 Hz. The human voice extends into this range, and it is these frequencies that provide us with our basic sense of speech intelligibility. Many of the sounds in this frequency range are harmonics and overtones of lower frequencies. Sounds in this range add a rich quality and intensity to music.

Midrange   The midrange frequencies include the band between 2,500 Hz and 5,000 Hz. Of all the frequency bands, this is the one that humans are most sensitive to, for several

reasons. Many of the frequencies from 2,500 Hz through 3,500 Hz contribute to speech intelligibility, particularly sounds like *m, b,* and *v.* Starting at 3,500 Hz, and extending into the bottom end of the lower treble (to about 6,500 Hz), are frequencies that add definition, realism, and clarity. In fact, it is the sounds in this area that give us a sense of realism and help us to pinpoint direction. People perceive sounds in this range as being nearby, which is a quality called presence.

Another interesting acoustic quality of this range is what happens around 5,000 Hz, or about dead center of the presence range. If you boost the sound level at 5,000 Hz, the listener perceives that there has been a significant boost over the entire midrange, making vocals sound tight and very nearby.

Lower treble   The lower-treble range includes the frequencies from 5,000 Hz to 12,500 Hz. This includes vocal sibilance, or the sizzle produced as some people use words containing the letters *s, c, x,* and *z.* Amazingly, female sibilance can range as high as 11,000 Hz to 12,000 Hz. Natural sibilance is fine and adds an intimate quality or presence to vocals. However, this is the frequency range in which a person who has a sibilance problem will stand out.

Upper treble   The upper-treble frequencies include those from 12,500 Hz to 20,000 Hz. Earlier it was stated that a person with excellent hearing could hear sounds as high as 20,000 Hz. The reality, however, is that most people cannot hear much past 16,000 Hz. In the upper-treble range are found those sounds that provide a sense of airiness, sizzle, crispness, and brilliance. One of the downsides to this frequency range is that any electronic noise or hiss appears here if present in the signal.

So far, the number of cycles per second has been discussed in terms of hertz. As the number of hertz increases, metric terms are used to simplify the terminology. For example, instead of using the term 1,000 Hz, the metric term kilo, which means 1,000, is substituted. Thus, 1,000 Hz becomes 1 kilohertz, or 1 kHz. After kilo, the next metric step is mega, meaning one million (one million Hz becomes 1 mHz). An electrical signal with a frequency of 100 kHz or more is classed as a radio frequency. As an example, rather than saying a radio station's frequency is 90,500,000 Hz on the FM dial, we say the station is at 90.5 mHz.

When you listen to the radio you are not listening to the radio frequency, such as 90.5 mHz. Humans cannot perceive radio frequencies. You are listening to the audible sounds between 20 Hz and 20,000 Hz that were piggybacked onto the radio frequency to deliver them to your radio. In other words, the radio frequency serves as a carrier to send the audio to your radio.

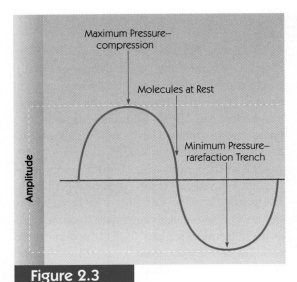

Figure 2.3

The size of a sound wave is measured from the bottom of the trench to the top of the crest and is called amplitude. Subjectively, the amplitude represents the loudness or softness of a sound wave. The amplitude of a sound wave is measured in decibels.

Loudness

Sound is created from vibration and from the compression and rarefaction of molecules that follow. Specific sounds are identified using frequency, harmonics, and overtones. Because you are going to be dealing with sound on a daily basis, it is important for you to be able to determine how loud a sound is, how loudness is measured, and the effect loudness has on people.

A vibration sets off a cycle of compression and rarefaction of air molecules, creating a sound wave. The stronger the vibration and the more molecules that are forced into the cycles, the greater the height of the crest and depth of the trench of the sound wave. In other words, the taller the sound wave is in physical size, the louder the sound. The size of the sound wave is measured from the bottom of the trench to the top of the crest and is called **amplitude.** Subjectively, the amplitude

represents the loudness or softness of a sound wave (see Fig. **2.3**).

The amplitude of a sound wave is measured in **decibels.** The decibel is a unit of measurement developed by Alexander Graham Bell and represents one tenth of a "bel." A decibel is a mathematical calculation based on ratios of two quantities. The quantities can be acoustic sound pressure or electrical energy, such as voltage. Unless you are going into engineering, it is not necessary for you to know the formulas, as they involve advanced engineering and mathematics beyond the scope of this book.

A sound wave passing through the air causes variations in the air pressure rising above or dropping below the **barometric air pressure.** The variations in air pressure accurately track up and down with the compression and rarefaction of the sound wave. The variation in air pressure is called the sound-pressure level (SPL). Sound, or acoustic energy, is measured in decibels of sound-pressure level, or dB-SPL, on a sound-pressure meter. A sound-pressure meter includes a microphone and a calibrated electronic filter so that the microphone and meter react to sound just like your ears do.

Scientifically, microphones are transducers, or devices that change one form of energy into another form of energy. In this case, a microphone converts acoustic energy, or sound pressure, into electrical energy. Microphones, by their very nature, measure the compression and rarefaction of a sound wave and convert it into electrical energy. When a microphone converts acoustic energy to electrical energy, the sound wave is converted into an audio signal. Audio is a Latin word and means "I hear"; it usually refers to a signal or electrical waveform. Audio depends on wires, fiber optics, or radio frequencies to carry it from place to place.

When a microphone converts a sound wave to an audio signal, the audio signal is an identical electrical copy of the sound wave. That is, it is analogous to the sine wave or acoustic waveform that it represents. In analog audio, the voltage of the audio signal varies in amplitude the same way that the sound pressure varies in amplitude before it enters the microphone.

Humans can hear sounds from 0 dB-SPL, the threshold of hearing, to sounds that exceed 120 dB-SPL (the threshold of pain; see Fig. **2.4**). The difference between the softest sound and the loudest sound created by something is called its **dynamic range.**

You must use caution when it comes to your hearing. At a sound-pressure level of 120 dB-SPL, humans begin to experience pain. At extremely high sound-pressure lev-

els, excruciating pain and serious physical damage to your hearing occur. Likewise, extended exposure to high sound-pressure levels causes temporary loss of hearing that can last several hours and in some cases become permanent.

The National Institute for Occupational Safety and Health (NIOSH) has established safe levels of noise exposure for workers in industry. The maximum continuous safe sound-pressure exposure limit for an eight-hour workday is 85 dB-SPL. However, even at 85 dB-SPL and less, many employers require workers to wear hearing protection. Safe-exposure limits get shorter as the sound pressure increases. A worker exposed to 94 dB-SPL has a safe-exposure time limit of one hour. At 106 dB-SPL, the safe-exposure time limit is three minutes and forty-five seconds!

To give you some meaningful comparisons, normal conversational speech is at about 60 dB-SPL, a ringing telephone has about 80 dB-SPL, and a hair dryer 90 dB-SPL. At the upper end of the spectrum, an ambulance siren creates 120 dB-SPL, and a jet engine at takeoff is about 140 dB-SPL.

If you have ever attended a rock concert, where sound pressures can reach 100 to 110+ dB-SPL, you now know why everyone was yelling at each other when they went home. They were suffering temporary hearing loss. At extreme sound-pressure levels, your eardrums can be blown in or imploded. One of the side effects of military service is that many service personnel suffer permanent hearing loss due to exploding artillery shells and other ordnance.

Recording studios typically have a sound-pressure meter sitting on the main console to observe music-playback levels (see Fig. **2.5**). Long recording or mixing sessions can take their toll on the engineer's ears, causing a temporary loss of hearing and causing the engineer

	Sound Pressure Levels
195dB	Space Shuttle at Lift-off, Measured 800 Meters from Launch Tower
140dB	Jet Engine at Take-off
120dB	Ambulance Siren
	Threshold of PAIN
110dB	Rock Concert
90dB	Hair Dryer
80dB	Average Phone Ringing
70dB	Vacuum Cleaner
60dB	Normal Conversation
30dB	Whisper
20dB	Rustling Leaves
10dB	Normal Breathing
0dB	Threshold of Hearing

Dynamic Range

Figure 2.4

Sound pressure is measured in decibels of sound-pressure level (dB-SPL). Humans can hear sounds from 0 dB-SPL, the threshold of hearing, to sounds that exceed 120 dB-SPL, the threshold of pain. The difference between the softest sound and the loudest sound created by something is called its dynamic range.

to make poor judgments when it comes to the recording mix. Likewise, many radio stations have preset maximum-volume controls for headphones and monitor speakers so that you cannot exceed safe limits of exposure.

Frequency and Loudness

Frequency and loudness are not related, and they are independent of one another. Your ears, though, react differently to sounds depending on their frequency. If the frequency of a sound is varied, the perception of its loudness also varies, even though the frequency remains at a constant sound level (see demo CD, cut 4). Likewise, if the amplitude or loudness of a frequency is varied, our perception of pitch is affected, even though the pitch remains at a constant frequency (see demo CD, cut 5).

Figure 2.5

Sound-pressure meters are a valuable studio tool. Many radio stations have preset maximum-volume controls for headphones and monitor speakers so that you cannot exceed safe limits of exposure. Long production sessions can take their toll on a producer's ears, causing a temporary loss of hearing and causing poor judgments when it comes to the final mix.

This phenomenon occurs because your ears are not equally sensitive to all of the audible frequencies. We do not hear the sub-bass and bass frequencies as well as we hear the mid-range frequencies. In fact, your ears are likely very insensitive to low frequencies at low levels. You also do not hear the lower-treble and upper-treble frequencies as well as you hear the midrange frequencies. Your ears are most sensitive to the middle frequencies. Remem-ber the engineer's trick of boosting the frequencies at 5,000 Hz? That is about the frequency that your ears are most sensitive to. The name of this phenomenon, in which you hear different frequencies at different levels, is the equal-loudness principle. (Which really is backward; it should be called the unequal-loudness principle.)

The equal-loudness principle is the reason why sound-pressure meters have calibrated electronic filters to measure sounds accurately the way humans hear them.

Velocity

From the moment the tree began to wobble back and forth in the forest at the start of this chapter, the emphasis has been on movement: the molecules of air displaced by the tree and moving away from it. If there is movement, then the speed, or velocity, of the movement can be measured. Unlike the relationship we just saw in the equal-loudness principle, the speed of a sound wave has little or no impact on the perceived frequency or loudness of the sound wave. In fact, the speed of sound is fairly constant. At sea level, when the temperature is 70 degrees Fahrenheit, sound travels through air at 1,130 feet per second. Sound does change velocity in cooler or hotter air temperatures, moving faster as the temperature rises and more slowly as the temperature drops. Each Fahrenheit degree of temperature variation produces a change of 1.1 feet per second up or down.

The speed of sound also varies with the medium it is passing through. Sound passing through water travels at around 4,900 feet per second, in wood about 11,700 feet per second, and in steel, sound is transmitted at a screaming 19,000 feet per second.

A practical use of this knowledge is estimating the distance to an event or sound source. For example, if you cover a space shuttle launch at the Kennedy Space Center, the press area is several miles from the launch pad for safety reasons. Reporters see the engines ignite and the shuttle clear the tower and head downrange before the first sound ever reaches the press site. In fact, it takes about fifteen seconds for the sound to travel the distance from the launch pad to the press site. From the time you see any event until you hear its sound, count the seconds, and then multiply by 1,130 feet per second, to determine the distance. In the case of the Space Center and the press area, this comes to about 16,350 feet, or right at three and one-tenth miles (see demo CD, cut 6). (The same thing works for figuring out how far away lightning is. See the flash, count the seconds until you hear the roar of the thunder, and then multiply by about 1,130 feet per second to determine your distance from the lightning.)

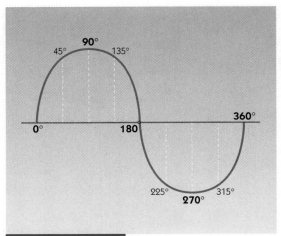

Figure 2.6

One cycle is divided into 360 degrees. The sound wave begins with zero amplitude, zero degrees, and after one complete cycle of compression and rarefaction ends at zero amplitude, 360 degrees. The crest of maximum positive amplitude occurs at 90 degrees. The point at which the sine wave passes through zero again is 180 degrees, and as the sound wave continues to lose sound pressure it bottoms out at maximum rarefaction, or 270 degrees.

Phase

Acoustical phase is the term used to describe the difference in time between two or more sound waves as they travel from one place to another. In a concert hall, the sounds of an orchestra may all leave the stage at the same time, but because of physical obstacles, reflections, and other acoustic conditions, the same sound may arrive at the listener's ears at various times, altering the original sound. Phase is essentially a difference in time between two sine waves. The difference can range from a few microseconds (micro = millionths) to an extreme of several seconds, depending on the acoustical conditions present. To measure this difference in time, sound waves are divided into segments for comparison to other sound waves.

The length of a sine wave is measured in degrees. One cycle is divided into 360 degrees (see Fig. **2.6**). The wave begins at zero amplitude, zero degrees, and after one complete cycle of compression and rarefaction ends at zero amplitude, 360 degrees. In addition to the starting and stopping points, other major points in a sound wave can be identified. The crest of maximum positive amplitude occurs at 90 degrees into the sine wave, or about one-fourth of the way through the 360-degree cycle. As the pressure decreases, the sound wave passes back through zero on its way to

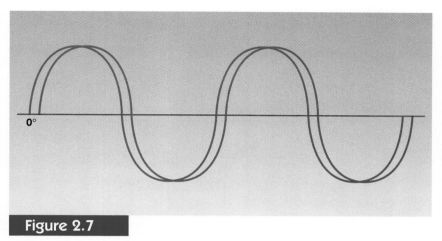

0°

Figure 2.7

Waves that are in phase reinforce one another, and the amplitude or loudness of the sound is increased. For example, if two trumpeters are side by side and start playing the same note at the identical time, then the sound is in phase and is amplified or made louder. In a perfect world, when two identical sound waves, of the same frequency and perfectly in phase, are combined, they double in amplitude or loudness.

the lowest negative pressure in the sound wave. The point at which the sine wave passes through zero is 180 degrees, or half of the way through the cycle. The sound wave continues to lose sound pressure until it bottoms out in the area of maximum rarefaction or negative pressure, the trench. This point is at 270 degrees, or three-quarters of the way through the sound wave, just before the sound wave begins its upward movement before coming to the end of one cycle, or 360 degrees. Phase is a difference in time between two sine waves, measured in degrees.

Phase causes some interesting acoustical conditions to occur. When two sound waves start together and their degree interval remains the same, the waves are said to be in phase. Waves that are in phase reinforce one another, and the amplitude or loudness of the sound is increased (see Fig **2.7**). For example, if two trumpeters are side by side and start

playing the same note at the identical time, then the sound is in phase and is amplified or made louder. In a perfect world, when two identical sound waves, of the same frequency and perfectly in phase, are combined, they double in amplitude or loudness.

When two sound waves start at different times and their degree interval is not the same, however, the waves are said to be out of phase. Waves that are out of phase weaken each other and decrease the amplitude or loudness. Using a variation on our previous example, if the two trumpeters are playing the same note but start at slightly different times, the sound is out of phase and is weaker. Again, in a perfect world, two identical sound waves of the same frequency that are exactly 180 degrees out of phase cancel each other out (see Fig. **2.8**).

These two conditions explain why a theater or concert hall has "sweet spots," where the

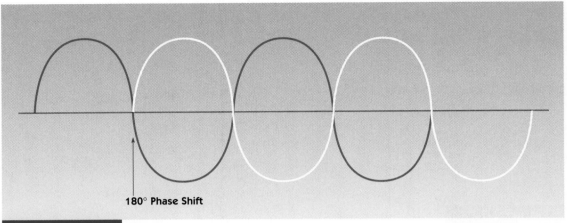

180° Phase Shift

Figure 2.8

When two sound waves start at different times and their degree interval is not the same, the waves are said to be out of phase. Waves that are out of phase weaken each other and decrease the amplitude or loudness. In a perfect world, two identical sound waves of the same frequency that are exactly 180 degrees out of phase cancel each other out.

sound is in phase and is just perfect, and "dead spots," where the sound is out of phase, and certain sounds cancel each other out and are lost. Unfortunately for performers and listeners alike, there is no such thing as the perfect concert hall.

In reality, sound waves get started at different times, even in a great orchestra. If the sounds are together in compression and rarefaction and just slightly out of phase, it is called **constructive interference.** Constructive interference tends to increase the amplitude, reinforcing the sound waves. However, if the sounds have gotten off to such a poor start that the compression and rarefaction are occurring at different times, it is called **destructive interference** (see demo CD, cut 7). Destructive interference tends to decrease the amplitude and weaken the sound waves.

A practical application of phase relationships might be encountered when placing a pair of stereo microphones to record a musical group. Place the microphones in the sweet spot of the room and you get a great recording; place them in a field of destructive interference and some of the audio frequencies may be weak and cancel themselves out. Even when the sound is in phase, it is possible to improperly place two microphones and cause phase problems as the same sound enters one microphone before the other. Microphone placement is discussed in detail in chapter 3.

Your Ears: How They Work and How to Take Care of Them

To this point in the chapter the focus has been on sound: its frequencies, harmonics, overtones, velocity, and phase. Sound waves passing through the air eventually impact a human ear (if someone is present). The sound wave, consisting of compression and rarefac-

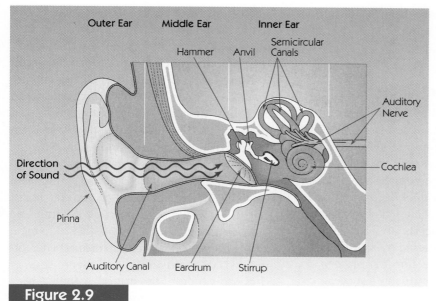

Figure 2.9

The outer, middle, and inner ear convert sound waves into electrical impulses that our brain interprets and identifies as sound.

tion, enters through the outer ear and travels through the external ear canal until reaching the eardrum (see Fig. **2.9**).

The compression and rarefaction of the sound wave push and pull the eardrum back and forth. Attached to the back of the eardrum are three bones: the hammer, anvil, and stirrup. These three interconnected bones act as a mechanical lever, amplifying the sound pressure and transferring it to the cochlea. The cochlea is a small snail-shaped organ that contains a microscopic amount of fluid, in which about 30,000 hair cells are located. Each hair cell is attached to the auditory nerve; they generate the electrical signals sent to the brain that you perceive as sound. When the electrical signals from each of your two ears reach the brain stem, the two sets are combined and the signal eventually ends up in the auditory cortex of the brain. Once in the auditory cor-

tex, the electrical signals are interpreted by the brain and, finally, perceived by you as sound.

Constant exposure to high-pressure sound levels damages the microscopic hair cells in the cochlea, in severe cases breaking the hairs off. As the hair cells are damaged or lost, your hearing is affected proportionately.

In addition to this method of sound arriving at the brain, there is another way you perceive sound. Sound can also be transmitted to the brain through the central nervous system. Exposure to high-sound pressure levels, such as those produced by a gun shot, can cause unexplained excitability, tension, fatigue, headaches, and nausea. When your body has to absorb powerful sound-pressure levels, it reacts negatively. Your heart rate jumps first, signaling alarm. Your blood pressure increases, muscles begin to contract, and as a result of the instinctive fear you are experiencing, adrenaline is released. In addition, your pupils typically dilate, your mouth becomes dry, and your stomach becomes upset.

You Only Get One Set of Ears

As you progress in this text you are going to be given tips on how to listen to or monitor sound. Don't think for one moment that the speakers or headphones you are using on a daily basis can't damage your hearing. When you combine them with all of the other sounds that you are exposed to on a daily basis, including live music concerts and car stereos, your hearing can be impaired over time.

In many ways, production people can be the victims of their own industry's success. By using the latest advances in studio equipment, production people work with gear that produces incredibly clean, distortion-free sound at higher sound-pressure levels. According to the House Ear Institute, although the audio is clean and sounds great, the downside is that production people are listening at a level of 10 to 15 dB-SPL higher than in the past. Hearing screenings conducted at major industry trade shows, involving professionals from the audio and music industries who volunteered to have their hearing tested, have shown that up to twenty-six percent of those tested had some form of hearing loss.

You can preserve your hearing by listening to your work in the studio at a maximum sound-pressure level of 85 dB-SPL, or lower. This applies both to the speakers in the studio and to the headphones you may be using as you record voice tracks. Smart producers in recording studios monitor sound levels with a sound-pressure meter near the mixing position. You can purchase an inexpensive sound-pressure meter at any electronics store (such as Radio Shack).

If you are in a band, attend concerts frequently, or like to watch or participate in a motor sport, use inexpensive (less than a dollar) foam ear plugs that can reduce the ambient sound level up to 30 dB-SPL. You still get to hear the concert or see the race, just not at earsplitting levels. Other often-overlooked sources of loud noise are gas-powered lawn mowers, string trimmers, and lawn blowers. Again, inexpensive foam ear plugs can prevent hearing loss. Although loud sounds can be a thrill, keep in mind that the end result could be impaired or permanent hearing loss or constant ringing in the ears, just to name a couple of common hearing disorders. The bottom line is that you only get one set of ears.

Ironically, one of the critical listening tests to judge if a commercial or program is mixed properly is to turn the monitors *down* to a low level and see if everything is still clear and intelligible. There is nothing wrong with mixing your projects at lower levels; this is how many pros prefer to mix, particularly in long sessions.

To Answer the Age-Old Question

With your new knowledge of analog sound, go back to the first part of the chapter and ask yourself the original question again. If a tree falls in the forest and there is no one there to hear the event, does it make a sound? Well . . . does it?

It's a Digital World

The first analog sound recording and playback device was Thomas Edison's phonograph. It operated with a hand-cranked spring-driven motor that, when wound tightly, provided several minutes of cylinder playing time. (Edison's original design used a cylinder to record and play back sound; it was Emile Berliner who developed the flat record that could be easily mass-produced.) Whereas analog audio served us well throughout its long history, it was plagued with many problems inherent in the mechanical, magnetic, and vinyl media used for recording and playback. Additionally, analog recordings have a limited dynamic range and when copies are made, each generation degrades slightly from the last.

Digital audio eliminates almost all of the problems associated with recording and storing analog audio; in addition, digital audio provides an incredible dynamic range of up to 144 dB. The most obvious advantage of digital recording is that once sound or audio is converted to a digital format, it can be stored, manipulated, and played back on a variety of devices. Digital audio can be transported and sent anywhere that computer data can be transmitted, even attached to an e-mail message. A further advantage of digital audio, although some in the music industry would consider it a distinct disadvantage, is that each copy is identical to the original, with no loss of quality or degradation of the audio.

The Foundation of Digital Audio

The origins of digital audio technology can be traced to the development of the binary number system, or base-two number system (1 and 0), in the late 1700s. In 1840, Samuel Morse invented the telegraph and a binary system of communications based on dots and dashes, called the Morse code. More recently, Harry Nyquist, working at the Bell Labs in 1929, determined that it was possible to convert an analog audio signal into a digital form.

Nyquist had one problem, though; he was eighteen years ahead of his time. It was not until Bell Labs developed the transistor, in 1947, that the Nyquist theorem could be tested!

The first electronic digital computer, using the binary numbers 1 and 0, was developed during World War II to calculate artillery range charts. ENIAC (Electronic Numerical Integrator and Computer) weighed in at a monstrous thirty tons and guzzled about 200 kilowatts of electricity. It was about twenty-five years later that digital audio recorders were demonstrated, in the early 1970s, and in 1982 Sony released the first compact disc (CD) player.

Whereas analog audio depends on an analogous relationship between the original sound wave and its electrical counterpart, digital audio does not. Digital sound does not occur in nature, it is created from nature. Digital audio uses numerical representations to record and play back an analog audio signal's amplitude and frequency.

Digital audio can be stored in one of three ways; *magnetically,* on a computer hard drive, a flash memory card, or digital audio tape; *optically,* on a CD, **SACD,** or one of the many digital versatile disc (DVD) formats; or in a *magneto-optical* format, which is a combination of the magnetic and optical formats. A good example of a magneto-optical format is a minidisc, or **MD.** With enough inventiveness, just about any medium that can store computer data can store digital audio, provided there is enough storage space.

Analog-to-Digital Conversion

Analog audio goes through two basic stages, ADC and DAC, to become digital audio. ADC is the analog-to-digital conversion that takes

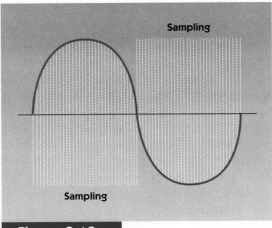

Figure 2.10

The first step of turning an analog signal into a digital audio signal is sampling. At a number of points in the analog audio signal's sine wave, the A/D converter samples, or reads, the voltage of the analog audio signal. Each of these samples, or voltage readings, is assigned a binary number to represent that specific point in the sine wave. The higher the sample rate, the more accurately the original frequency response can be recorded and played back.

place before the audio can be recorded, stored, or manipulated digitally by a computer. DAC is the digital-to-analog conversion so that the audio can be played back on speakers or headphones. From a terminology standpoint, ADC is often expressed as A/D and, likewise, DAC is expressed as D/A. A small microprocessor (computer chip) makes the A/D and D/A conversion within the digital audio equipment.

The actual A/D conversion is a fairly simple process. The first step of turning an analog audio signal into a digital audio signal is sampling (see Fig. **2.10**). At a number of points in the analog audio signal's sine wave, the A/D converter samples, or reads, the voltage of the analog audio signal. Each one of these sam-

ples, or voltage readings, is assigned a binary number to represent that specific point in the sine wave. The process of assigning a binary number to each of the samples or voltage readings is called **quantization.**

The number of samples that need to be taken is based on the Nyquist theorem. Nyquist said that the highest reproducible audio frequency in a digital system is one half the sampling rate; the audio frequency is often called the Nyquist frequency.

Humans can hear up to 20,000 Hz. Based on the Nyquist theorem, twice the number of samples of the highest frequency we want to be able to record and play back must be taken. In this case, $2 \times 20,000$ Hz, or at least 40,000 samples need to be taken per second. At this sampling rate, however, some frequencies, harmonics, and overtones that are just above 20,000 Hz might be lost. To ensure good quality audio, the industry set the upper audio frequency to 22,050 Hz, resulting in a sampling rate of 44,100 Hz or 44.1 kHz ($2 \times 22,050 = 44,100$). This is the standard sampling rate used to store audio data on a CD. The sample rate determines the frequency response of the signal that is recorded and played back. The higher the sample rate, the more accurately the original frequency response can be recorded and played back.

To prevent any unwanted ultrasonic frequencies from getting into the A/D converter and causing undesirable side effects during the A/D conversion (a process called aliasing), an anti-aliasing filter is placed on the input of an A/D converter. An anti-aliasing filter blocks all frequencies above a predetermined point. With a sampling frequency of 44,100 Hz it might be set to block all frequencies above 22,050 Hz.

4-Bit Audio System = 16 Quantizing Levels

1111
1110
1101
1100
1011
1010
1001
1000
0111
0110
0101
0100
0011
0010
0001
0000

Sampling

Sampling

4-Bit System

Figure 2.11

The number of samples and the number of bits in each sample word determines how accurately the original sine wave is reproduced. The four-bit system above only produces 16 binary words, or levels of quantization, and cannot accurately reproduce the sine wave. A 16-bit system provides 65,536 binary words that can be assigned to each sample. A 24-bit system provides 16,777,216 binary words. The higher the bit rate, the more accurately the sine wave can be reproduced.

Each time a voltage sample is taken, a binary number consisting of 1s and 0s is created and assigned to the sample to represent the voltage reading. The binary digits are called "bits," (short for "binary digits"). Each binary number created and assigned to a sample is called a digital word, sample word, or just plain old "word."

Obviously, with only the digits 1 and 0 to work with, not many different digital words can be formed to represent and record the thousands of different voltage readings that are taken each second during sampling (see Fig. **2.11**). In a two-bit system (using 1 and 0) there are only four digital words, or voltage steps, that can be formed: 1-1, 1-0, 0-1, and 0-0. The solution to the problem is to increase the length of the digital word with more bits, or more 1s and 0s. Using 8 bits results in 256 different words, or voltage steps, which can be assigned to represent each one of the samples. Although this works, the audio does not sound very good; this quality is similar to that of an inexpensive digital telephone-answering machine. At 16 bits, however, there are 65,536 different binary words that can be assigned to represent a sample; suddenly, a magic number of sorts is reached.

The number of bits in each sample word determines the dynamic range of the audio signal. Dynamic range is the difference between the softest and the loudest sound, or in this case the signal-to-noise ratio. The ratio is a comparison of the audio signal's power to the electrical noise, or hiss, which may be inherently present in a circuit. The higher the signal-to-noise ratio, the cleaner the audio sounds. A 16-bit digital audio signal has a dynamic range of 96 decibels.

Compact discs use a sample rate of 44.1 kHz, as mentioned earlier. For each of the 44,100 samples taken during one second of time, a 16-bit binary word is created to represent the voltage reading, or step, of the sample. The result is excellent quality sound that is the standard by which most people, particularly consumers, judge digital audio. Although this sample rate and bit rate create excellent quality audio, they still do not produce a perfect recreation of the original analog sine wave. However, in 1982, when the CD was released, it was certainly state-of-the-art. To create a perfect copy of an analog sine wave, more samples and binary words are needed.

Digital-audio workstations feature sample rates as high as 192 kHz, meaning that each second of audio is sliced into 192,000 individual samples. Bit rates are as high as 24 bits, creating 16,777,216 different binary words, or voltage steps, that can be used to represent the voltage reading of any one of the individual samples. The dynamic range of 24-bit audio is an incredible 144 decibels, easily capable of reproducing the softest sound to the loudest crescendo of an orchestra.

During playback, the digital-to-analog conversion is the reverse of the process previously described. The D/A converter reads each sample's binary word and recreates the assigned voltage step. When all of the samples are combined, the analog audio sine wave is recreated and can be sent to headphones or monitor speakers so that our analog ears can hear the sounds.

Practical Uses of Digital Audio

One of the unique qualities of digital audio is that it is nothing more than computer data, binary words consisting of 1s and 0s. With the digital audio tools on the market, the only real limits to your creative abilities are the limitations *you* place on yourself. Your creative opportunities extend not only to the end product you deliver to the listener, but to the hardware and software you select to record, store, and manipulate digital audio.

There was a time when broadcast quality standards and equipment were designed like battleships, intended to last for ten or fifteen years. Thanks to digital audio, hardware and software are continually improving and evolving. There is always going to be something new and exciting to be creative with.

At one time, digital audio recording involved a machine the size of a kitchen stove. Today, add a professional-quality soundcard and inexpensive software to your home computer, and you can create a digital audio workstation that is capable of outperforming machines that cost tens of thousands of dollars just a few years ago. Laptop computers can be outfitted with 192 kHz, 24-bit digital multitrack software and turned into studio-quality recorders. Portable CD recorders provide excellent quality for location recording on a medium that is virtually universal. News people are using portable recorders with no mov-

Figure 2.12

Portable CD recorders provide excellent quality for location recording on a medium that is virtually universal. Some news people prefer portable recorders with no moving parts, just flash-memory cards that are inserted and removed to record on. A single card is capable of holding over three days of recorded material.

ing parts, just flash-memory cards that are inserted and removed, to record on. A single card is capable of holding over three days of recorded material (see Fig. **2.12**).

Radio stations use mainframe computer servers to record, store, and play back digital audio. By linking a number of broadcast facilities over a wide-area computer network, several stations can create and share the same audio files.

The storage of digital audio, or how you store your projects and files, is again wide open for creativity. There is mainframe server storage for a station or group of stations, storage in individual digital-audio workstations, and storage in portable "hot-swappable" hard

drives. "Hot-swappable" means that the hard drive is literally designed to be "plug-and-play" in ports on digital equipment. Devices using these drives do not have to be shut down or rebooted each time a hard drive is inserted or removed. Each staff member can carry his or her own hard drive to various digital audio workstations.

In addition to these more permanent solutions, there is the ability to store audio on mini-discs, CDs, and DVDs, all of which have rewritable versions. Another storage option available to a radio station is rental of computer server space from a third party.

The manipulation of digital audio includes such possibilities as editing out all of the mistakes you made when you voiced your last commercial, of course, but it offers much more than that as well. Manipulation involves altering the audio in any way. For example, digital audio processors allow radio stations to have incredible tools at their disposal for doing everything from eliminating background noise to creating rich-sounding reverb. Outboard equipment that would have cost thousands of dollars and have occupied racks of equipment space just a few years ago is now available as "plug-ins," or software, that can easily be added to your digital audio workstation.

One of the great features of digital audio manipulation is time compression and expansion. If you create a commercial that ends up being 63 seconds, you can digitally squeeze it to 60 seconds. Run the commercial through a time-compression program and suddenly your 63-second commercial is 60 seconds long, with no changes in pitch or timbre. However, there may be slight changes in spacing between words. Another plug-in allows you to alter voices through pitch shifting—taking the voice up or down as you desire. Again, about the only limit to the manipulation of digital audio is your imagination.

Specific production techniques and the hardware and software for recording, editing, mixing, and mastering of creative audio products are discussed in detail later in this text. Overall, digital audio offers the broadcaster the best cost-to-benefit ratio of any audio system that can be employed in the operation of a radio station. Even if you toss out all of the unlimited creative benefits of digital audio, it is still the most cost-effective way that exists to record, store, and manipulate audio.

Suggested Activities

1. If your university has a speech and hearing clinic, visit the clinic and request a standard hearing test. Most universities offer such services free to students. The test can provide knowledge of your hearing strengths and make you aware of any weaknesses.
2. Save the results of your test to use as a reference point for future hearing tests later in life.

Web Sites for More Information

For more information about:

- *protecting your hearing,* visit the House Ear Institute at www.hei.org
- *Harry Nyquist and his accomplishments,* visit the Institute of Electrical and Electronics Engineers at www.ieee.org/organizations/history_center/legacies/nyquist.html

Pro Speak

You should be able to use these terms in your everyday conversations with other professionals.

acoustical phase—A difference in time between two or more sine waves, measured in degrees.

amplitude—Amplitude represents the strength, or loudness, of a sound or audio signal without regard for its frequency. The height of the sine wave can be measured either in decibels, for sound, or voltage, for audio signals.

barometric air pressure—A measure of the weight of the atmosphere, or air, pressing down on earth. It averages approximately 29.92 inches of mercury at mean sea level, which is the equivalent of 14.7 pounds per square inch. Barometric pressure varies with altitude, getting lighter as the altitude increases.

constructive interference—When two sine waves are just slightly out of phase with one another but are still together in their cycles of compression and rarefaction. Constructive interference tends to increase the amplitude, reinforcing the sound waves.

decibels—A unit of measurement developed by Alexander Graham Bell to measure the loss of signal over one mile of telephone line. Because the bel is such a large unit, most measurements are made in tenths (deci) of a bel, thus the decibel. A decibel can be expressed as a volume of acoustic sound-pressure level or, for audio signals, as a voltage reading.

destructive interference—When two sine waves are out of phase with one another and their cycles of compression and rarefaction are occurring at different times. Destructive interference tends to decrease the amplitude and weaken the sound waves.

dynamic range—The difference between the softest and loudest part of a sound, measured in decibels (dB). A dynamic range of 95 dB, for example, indicates that the loudest sound is 95 dB louder than the softest sound.

frequency—The number of complete cycles that occur in one second of time; expressed as cycles per second, or hertz.

harmonic—A harmonic is a sound created by multiplying the fundamental frequency or first harmonic. The second harmonic is two times the fundamental; the third harmonic is three times the fundamental, etc.

Hertz, Heinrich—Hertz (1857–1894) proved that electricity could be transmitted in electromagnetic waves, which travel at the speed of light. In 1933 his name was adopted as the international metric term used for radio and electrical frequencies: hertz (Hz), as in kilohertz (kHz) and megahertz (mHz).

infrasonic—Sounds or audio signals that fall below the average person's hearing range, typically 20 Hz and lower.

MD—Minidisc is a registered trademark of Sony and refers to a disc enclosed in a small cartridge. The 2½-inch-diameter disc records and plays back near-CD-quality audio using a combination magnetic/optical system.

overtone—A sound or audio signal that occurs in between the harmonics or multiples of a fundamental frequency.

quantization—The process of assigning a binary number to each of the samples or voltage readings taken during the analog-to-digital audio conversion.

SACD—A joint product of Sony and Philips that uses a two-layer, CD-sized disc to reproduce both 5.1 surround sound and standard stereo using Direct Stream Digital encoding, which is a one-bit system with a sampling rate of 2,822,400 samples per second.

subwoofer—A speaker designed to handle those sounds from 16 Hz to about 100 Hz.

ultrasonic—Sounds or audio signals occurring above the average person's hearing range, typically above 20,000 Hz.

CHAPTER 3

Microphones and Their Role in Radio Production

Microphones are one of the key tools you use to create sound pictures for listeners. In this chapter you are going to learn about the different microphone types and how to put them to use creatively. One of the interesting things for you to discover about microphones is that regardless of price, just about every microphone is better than another microphone at recording some particular thing. Just because one microphone is more expensive than another does not make it the best microphone. In fact there is no such thing as a "best" microphone. It does not exist.

Microphones as Transducers

As much as it sounds like something from Star Trek, a microphone is a transducer, a device that transforms one form of energy into another. A microphone converts sound waves, or acoustic energy, into electrical energy. The electrical energy created is an analogous waveform (an exact replica) of the original sound wave. Of course, the quality of the microphone does have an effect on the process. A higher quality microphone generates a more accurate replica of the original sound wave.

Prior to a sound entering the microphone, it is referred to as **sound,** or acoustic energy. Once the microphone converts sound to electrical energy, it becomes **audio.** Microphones are electro-mechanical devices and are divided into two distinct types, dynamic and electrostatic. The classification is based on how the **mic** (pronounced "Mike") converts sound to audio.

Dynamic Microphones

There are two different types, differentiated by their physical structure, within the dynamic microphone category: moving-coil microphones and ribbon microphones. One of the quirks of the industry is that a moving-coil microphone is called a **dynamic microphone** and a **ribbon microphone** is called a "ribbon," even though they both are technically dynamic microphones. From this point on in the text, moving-coil microphones are referred to as dynamic microphones.

Dynamic Microphones

A dynamic microphone works using magnetic inductance, a principal of physics you probably learned in ninth-grade science. Place a coil of wire within a magnetic field and move it back and forth through the magnetic field. The result is that electricity (alternating current) is generated or induced in the coil of wire. The Western Electric Company made the first moving-coil microphones in the early 1930s.

A dynamic microphone has a very thin plastic circular diaphragm at the face of the microphone (see Fig. **3.1**). Attached in the center, on the back of the diaphragm, is a tiny coil of very fine wire surrounded by a permanent magnet mounted within the microphone's body. As the sound wave hits the diaphragm and coil of wire, they move back and forth, just like your eardrum. The movement of the coil of wire back and forth through the magnetic field generates a very-low-voltage electrical signal, an analogous waveform, which travels down the wires leading away from the microphone (again, see Fig. **3.1**).

Generally, dynamic microphones accurately reproduce a wide frequency range and

Figure 3.1

The elements of a dynamic microphone. As the sound wave hits the diaphragm it moves back and forth, just like your eardrum. The movement of the coil of wire back and forth through the magnetic field generates a very-low-voltage electrical signal, an analogous waveform, which travels down the wires leading away from the microphone.

have a transparent sound, meaning they do not color or change the original sound.

Dynamic Microphone Characteristics

Radio announcers like directional dynamic microphones because of the deep, rich qualities they can add to a good announcer's voice. This is due to the **proximity effect** or the "I can sound like James Earl Jones" effect (see Fig. **3.2;** see demo CD, cut 8). The closer you move to the face of the microphone, the lower your voice appears to go, taking on a richer, bassy quality. Announcers experiment to find the distance from the mic that makes their voice sound best; this is called "working the mic." Likewise, the proximity effect occurs when a directional dynamic microphone

is placed closer to a sound source like a drum or other instrument rich in bass. Nondirectional dynamic microphones do not exhibit the proximity effect. Directional characteristics of microphones are discussed later in the chapter.

Dynamic Microphone Applications

Generally, dynamic microphones are very rugged and can withstand a number of different adverse environments. They operate over a wide temperature range and are not generally affected by inclement weather conditions. Dynamic microphones are used extensively in radio. Because of their design, they are also excellent for use in high-sound-pressure-level environments, like on stage at a rock concert.

Figure 3.2

The closer you move to the face of a directional dynamic microphone, the lower your voice appears to go, taking on a richer, bassy quality. Announcers experiment to find the distance from the mic that makes their voice sound best; this is called "working the mic." This announcer is about one inch from the microphone windscreen.

Dynamic microphones generate very little internal electrical **noise** or hiss. Electrical noise is an undesirable audio quality in any audio device.

Dynamic microphones are available in a variety of models, quality levels, and price ranges. Some are designed for very specific purposes, such as for studio use, for news reporters, or for use at live remotes with public-address systems. Retail prices for professional dynamic microphones range from a low of about $125 to a high of nearly $1,000, with excellent microphones available in the $300-to-$500 range.

Later in this chapter you will learn how properly to place and use dynamic microphones.

Ribbon Microphones

The ribbon microphone, although quite different from a dynamic in its design, works using magnetic inductance. Harry Olson, working for the RCA research laboratories, developed the ribbon microphone in 1931. To this day, radio stations use photos and drawings of classic ribbon microphones as logos and trademarks.

Internally, a very thin corrugated metal ribbon is suspended vertically between two poles of a large permanent magnet. At the top and bottom of the metal ribbon are the signal leads, or wires, coming off the ribbon and going to the microphone cable (see Fig. **3.3**).

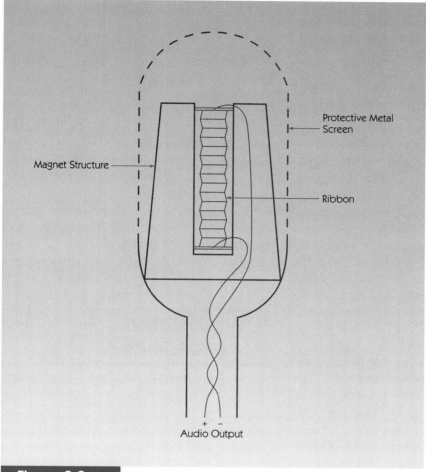

Magnet Structure

Protective Metal Screen

Ribbon

+ –
Audio Output

Figure 3.3

The elements of a ribbon microphone. As the sound wave hits the ribbon, it moves back and forth, just like your eardrum. The movement of the ribbon back and forth through the magnetic field generates a very-low-voltage electrical signal, an analogous waveform, which travels down the wires leading away from the microphone.

As the sound wave hits the metal ribbon, it is moved back and forth, just like the diaphragm in the dynamic microphone. This movement causes the metal ribbon to cut back and forth through the magnetic field, and a very-low-voltage signal is generated in the ribbon and travels down the microphone cable.

Generally, ribbon microphones are known for their accurate reproduction over a wider frequency range than dynamic mics and for having a very natural, "warm," sound. Modern ribbon microphones have a very good extended-high-frequency response that engineers refer to as "open" or very natural sounding (see demo CD, cut 9).

Ribbon Microphone Characteristics

There are a couple of characteristics of the ribbon microphone you need to know about, or you'll kill one before you ever get a chance to use it! The ribbon in older vintage ribbon microphones is very fragile due to the fact that it is only 1.8 **microns** (1.8 millionths of a meter) thick. You should never blow into any microphone to test it; in the case of a ribbon microphone you could easily stretch or snap the ribbon in two. Likewise, never take a ribbon microphone outside unless it is in a case; a breeze can stretch or snap the ribbon. Ribbon microphones are usually encased in a protective cover when not in use.

Ribbon microphones have acoustic qualities that producers and voice talent like. Ribbons tend to have a very smooth, warm, natural sound at the lower frequencies, with an open high-frequency response. Ribbons make great voice microphones and are also used for a number of musical instruments in recording studios. The **transient response** (ability to handle those fast-attack, slow-to-trail-off sounds like consonants in speech) of a ribbon microphone is generally better than that of the dynamic microphone.

Announcers like directional ribbon microphones because they exhibit the proximity effect just like directional dynamic microphones, while featuring the smoother, warmer, and richer acoustic quality of ribbons. A unique feature of a ribbon is that the proximity effect starts as much as three to five feet from the microphone (see demo CD, cut 10).

Ribbon Microphone Applications

Ribbon microphones are found primarily in recording and production studios and are rarely used as on-air radio microphones, due to their cost and fragility. Ribbons are used by many top producers. The classic RCA series 44 and 77 ribbon microphones that were made from the mid-1930s through the 1950s are prized for the unique warm, rich, natural sound they produce on vocals. Additionally, many of these older microphones have historic value (see Fig. **3.4**).

Depending on the history of the microphone and its condition, a vintage ribbon microphone can easily top the $2,500 mark. Currently manufactured ribbon microphones range in price from $650 to $3,500.

Electrostatic Microphones

The electrostatic mic was invented shortly after Lee DeForest invented the vacuum tube amplifier in 1906. The theory behind the design is based on an early electrical component called a condenser. The name of the condenser was later changed to "capacitor" to reflect more clearly its function within an electrical circuit.

Although the microphone operates on electrostatic principles and is technically a capacitor, the industry has stuck with the original name of "condenser." From this point on in the text this microphone type is referred to as a **condenser microphone.**

Condenser Microphones

How a Condenser Microphone Works

At the front of the microphone there is a very thin circular diaphragm (see Fig. **3.5**). This di-

The classic RCA series 77 DX ribbon microphones were made starting in the mid-1930s and are prized for the unique warm, rich, natural sound they produce on vocals. Additionally, many of these microphones have historic value based on the radio station or studio in which they were used. This particular microphone is over 50 years old.

aphragm is made of a flexible plastic material coated with a very thin layer of gold for conductivity. One impressive feature of the diaphragm is that it is only a couple of microns thick.

Right behind the diaphragm, and parallel to it, is a rigid back plate. The diaphragm and the back plate are separated by an air space of just a few hundredths of an inch. The assembly created by the back plate, the air space, and the diaphragm is a capacitor (also known as a condenser). For a capacitor to work it must have a polarizing voltage.

Positive (+) voltage is applied to the back plate, and the diaphragm serves as the negative (–) side of the circuit. The voltage passing through the back plate and diaphragm sets up an electrostatic field of energy in the air space between the two. As long as the microphone remains in an absolutely silent room the electrostatic field and the voltage passing through the capacitor remain constant.

When a sound wave hits the diaphragm, it moves back and forth in relation to the back plate. As the movement occurs, the stable electrostatic field is upset, or changed, causing the voltage passing through the mic to vary and creating an analogous waveform (an exact replica) of the original sound wave. The output of a condenser microphone is very weak. For the microphone to be functional, a **preamplifier** is placed very near the microphone element to amplify the signal to a usable level. Depending on the microphone model, the preamplifier may be located inside the microphone or be a separate unit located near the microphone.

Power for the preamplifier can be provided with a separate power supply, a battery power supply located within the microphone itself, or with **phantom power** provided by a control board or portable mixer. Phantom power is a system of sending the necessary voltage for the condenser microphone down the microphone cable. Phantom power in professional equipment is 48 volts, direct current. Phantom power supplies of between 18 and 24 volts are common in **"prosumer"** equipment.

Electret-Condenser Microphones

An **electret-condenser microphone** differs from a condenser microphone in that the diaphragm or the backplate, depending on the

Figure 3.5

A condenser microphone has a very thin diaphragm with a parallel, rigid, back plate. The diaphragm and the back plate are separated by an air space of just a few hundredths of an inch. The assembly created by the back plate, the air space, and the diaphragm is a capacitor or, as it is more commonly known, a condenser.

particular design, holds a permanent electrical charge. Because there is a permanent electrical charge present, there is no need for the separate polarizing power supply. The only power an electret-condenser microphone requires is a small battery to operate the preamplifier, which is usually included inside the microphone.

Generally speaking, electret-condenser microphones can be made much smaller, with a good example being the very tiny lavalier or body microphones used in television and film production.

Condenser Microphone Characteristics

Condensers are generally very sensitive, high-performance, microphones that deliver incredibly accurate sound reproduction and are used for the most critical applications. A unique characteristic of the condenser microphone is its sensitivity. In fact, some condensers are sensitive enough to pick up instantaneous variations in barometric pressure (atmospheric pressure) within a room.

Because condensers are so sensitive, they offer excellent high frequency and transient response (fast-attack, slow-to-trail-off sounds). A condenser microphone typically has a slight peak in the high frequencies that gives the microphone a very bright, crisp sound that helps to create a very open, natural quality.

Whereas you see on-air talent working close to the face of a dynamic microphone to get a **"bass boost,"** that is usually not the case with a condenser. Talent typically backs off a condenser microphone as much as one to two feet to achieve a very natural open presence in their voice, rather than the proximity effect common to dynamic and ribbon microphones (see demo CD, cut 11).

Although the microphone's sensitivity is an advantage in a production studio, it presents some really unusual problems for on-air use. For example, a high-quality condenser is capable of picking up the sound of air rushing out of an air conditioning vent, the sounds of control board switches, and any other stray noise in an on-air studio. A condenser microphone mounted directly on a microphone stand easily picks up stray building vibrations, such as the thud of a person walking across a studio floor or the rumble of traffic that is passing by the studio, and so forth. To solve vibration problems, condenser microphones are suspended in shock mounts isolating them from any type of vibration. Microphone shock mounts are discussed later in this chapter.

Condenser Microphone Applications

Condenser microphones are used in the studio or in the field, provided the particular model is matched to the application. Generally, condensers are fairly rugged and can withstand a lot of adverse environments. Condenser microphones often see duty on news crews and on entertainment television and film sets.

Condenser microphones come in a variety of models, quality levels, and price ranges. There is also a class of specialty electret-condenser microphones called lavaliers or **lavs.** Sometimes they are referred to as body microphones. Many of these microphones are so tiny there appears to be nothing on the end of the slim 3-millimeter-diameter microphone

Figure 3.6

A lavalier microphone, or lav, is a specialty class of electret-condenser microphones. Sometimes lavs are referred to as body microphones, as they can easily be hidden on clothing due to their small size.

cable (see Fig. **3.6**). Lavs are discussed in detail later in the chapter.

Retail prices for condenser microphones extend from just under $200 for an inexpensive electret-condenser microphone to $5,000 for a high-end studio condenser microphone (see Fig. **3.7**). There are a number of superior condenser microphones available in the $400-to-$600 range.

Digital Condenser Microphones

Several condenser microphone models are equipped with preamplifiers that include A/D (analog-to-digital) converters. The output of these microphones consists of binary numbers rather than analog waveforms. **Digital condenser microphones** offer the advantage of being able to be plugged directly into the digital inputs of a control board, or digital recorder, for higher audio quality.

From left to right, the Sennheiser shotgun microphone, Neumann U-87, and AKG 414 all represent outstanding condenser microphones. The Sennheiser is often used in television and motion picture production; the Neumann U-87 and AKG 414 are typically studio microphones. Prices range from about $1,000 to over $3,000.

Microphone Pickup or Directional Patterns

Learning to use microphones includes not only selecting the right type of microphone for the job but also placing it in the right position to capture the best sound. Pros talk about being "on-mic" or in the "sweet spot." They are referring to having the microphone positioned so that the direction it is most sensitive to is aimed in exactly the right spot to capture the best sound.

Each microphone, regardless of whether it is a dynamic, ribbon, or condenser, has a specific pickup **pattern** or direction from which it picks up sound and is most sensitive. Usually,

this is straight into the front of the microphone. Another term for the pickup pattern is the polar response of the microphone. The inherent pattern of a microphone type can be changed or modified by designing a special case in which to house the element.

Usually, such microphones have slots or openings in the microphone body behind the head of the microphone. The openings create an acoustical environment within the microphone that reinforces some frequencies or sounds coming into the front of the microphone and cancels out others coming from the rear of the microphone. By changing the design of the microphone body, the pickup pattern can be altered to change the direction in which the microphone is sensitive.

FRONT

REAR

Figure 3.8

The omnidirectional, or nondirectional, microphone pattern is just what the name implies. A microphone with this type of pattern is sensitive to sound from all directions, regardless of where the microphone is pointed. The polar pattern illustration shows the 360-degree sensitivity.   *Image provided courtesy of Shure Incorporated.*

The Five Basic Microphone Directional Patterns

Omnidirectional

The **omnidirectional,** or nondirectional, microphone pattern is just what the name implies. A microphone with this type of pattern is sensitive to sound from all directions, regardless of where the microphone is pointed (see Fig. **3.8**). The polar pattern illustration shows the 360-degree sensitivity. An omnidirectional microphone has no "dead spot" and picks up everything. Because the microphone is sensitive in all directions, you have no control over what the microphone picks up other than to turn it on or off.

Omnidirectional microphones are often issued to radio news crews as handheld interview microphones because, even in confusing

situations, such as covering breaking news, if the microphone is turned on something will be recorded to go on-air (see demo CD, cut 12).

Bidirectional

A **bidirectional** microphone pattern provides the user a great deal of control over what sounds the microphone picks up, since it is most sensitive to the front and rear. The pickup pattern looks like a figure eight and is ideal for interviewing people with one person on the front side and the other person on the back side of the microphone (see Fig. **3.9**). In a recording studio or at a live remote, careful placement between two people provides great pickup on each person and blocks other unwanted sounds from the sides (see demo CD, cut 13). The polar pattern illustration for the

Figure 3.9

A bidirectional microphone provides the user a great deal of control over what sounds the microphone picks up. The polar pattern above shows the microphone is most sensitive to the front (0°) and to the rear (180°). A bidirectional microphone is least sensitive to the sides at 90° and 270°. A bidirectional microphone is ideal for conducting interviews. *Image provided courtesy of Shure Incorporated.*

bidirectional microphone shows that it is most sensitive at 0 and 180 degrees (front and back). At 90 and 270 degrees (left and right) the microphone is least sensitive.

Cardioid

A **cardioid** microphone pattern is shaped like a heart and provides a greater level of control over unwanted sounds, such as room reverberation or noise (see Fig. **3.10**). Cardioid pattern microphones are often referred to as **unidirectional** microphones, meaning that they pick up sound from one particular direction. Other than the omnidirectional and bi-

directional patterns, in fact, all other microphone patterns are referred to as unidirectional or single-direction microphones.

The ratio of direct sound to room reverberation that the microphone picks up is called the direct-to-reverberant sound ratio. Because the cardioid microphone pattern has a higher direct-to-reverberant sound ratio, cardioid-pattern microphones can be placed about one-and-a-half times further away from a sound source than an omnidirectional pattern microphone and still maintain the sweet spot.

The polar pattern for a cardioid microphone shows it is most sensitive at 0 degrees, or straight into the face of the microphone. This is termed as being "on axis." The cardioid pattern is least sensitive at 180 degrees, or "off axis" (see demo CD, cut 14). From the head of the microphone forward is where it is most sensitive to sound, and from the head to the rear of the microphone it is least sensitive.

A cardioid pattern is truly directional and is one of the most popular patterns for this reason. For example, if an announcer uses a cardioid-pattern microphone in a radio studio, the face of the microphone is aimed at the announcer and the dead spot might be aimed at the door to the studio. People coming and going during the show cannot be heard because they are on the dead side of the microphone. Or the dead spot could be aimed at equipment or other staff in the studio, such as a telephone call screener, or producer, whose sounds you don't want going on-air.

In a talk-radio studio, the use of supercardioid-pattern microphones allows a producer to isolate and control the level of each guest individually. By arranging the guests around a table and carefully placing the microphones, each guest is on-mic, but at the same time each guest is in the other microphones' dead spots (see Fig. **3.11**).

Figure 3.10

A cardioid microphone pattern is shaped like a heart and provides a greater level of control over unwanted sounds, such as room reverberation or noise. Cardioid pattern microphones are often referred to as unidirectional microphones, meaning that they pick up sound from one particular direction. *Image provided courtesy of Shure Incorporated.*

Overall, a cardioid pattern gives you a great deal of control over what sounds are picked up and what sounds are not picked up, depending on microphone placement.

Super-Cardioid

A **super-cardioid** microphone pattern is a refinement of the cardioid pattern. The super-cardioid pattern shows that it is most sensitive at 0 degrees, or on axis, and least sensitive at 180 degrees, or off axis (see Fig. **3.12**). However, notice that the sides of the super-cardioid pattern are narrower than those of the cardioid pattern, giving the user more directional control. Because of the improved direct-to-rever-

berant sound ratio, super-cardioid microphones can be placed nearly twice as far from a sound source as the omnidirectional microphone and still maintain the sweet spot. The cardioid and super-cardioid pattern are the two most popular used in radio.

Hyper-Cardioid

A **hyper-cardioid** microphone pattern is a further refinement of the cardioid pattern. The design goal is to be able to move the microphone further from the sound source without increasing the apparent room reverberation. A hyper-cardioid microphone can pick up sound at slightly more than twice the distance from a

Super-cardioid microphones are used around the desk in this talk-radio
studio to allow individual level control of the guests. Each guest is on-mic,
but at the same time each guest is in the other microphones' dead spots. The
computer monitors display caller information to the show hosts.

sound source as can the omni-directional pattern microphone, while still maintaining the
same direct-to-reverberant sound ratio (see
Fig. **3.13;** see demo CD, cut 15).

A hyper-cardioid pattern is a very narrow
and highly directional pattern typically found
in **"shotgun"** type microphones used by radio
and television news crews, in television studios, and for location film shoots.

The name shotgun comes from the early
hyper-cardioid designs that required a large
microphone structure to accomplish the task.
At the time, the microphones employed long
tubes on the front of the mic to attain the desired pattern and some did look like a shotgun. Today hyper-cardioid microphones are
usually less than eighteen inches in length and
about an inch in diameter. Shotgun micro-

phones and their radio applications are discussed in detail later in this chapter.

Multi Pattern Microphones

Some microphone models have one or more
elements, or pickups, within the microphone.
These are known as multidirectional or poly-
directional microphones, meaning that their
patterns can be switched or altered. Generally,
multidirectional microphones are either ribbons or condensers. Such microphones are
more expensive but offer the user up to four or
five different pickup patterns from which to
choose, making the microphone more versatile for production (see Fig. **3.14**).

Another popular multidirectional microphone type is based on separate components

Figure 3.12

A super-cardioid microphone pattern is a refinement of the cardioid pattern. The super-cardioid pattern shows that it is most sensitive at 0 degrees, or on axis, and least sensitive at 180 degrees, or off axis. However, notice that the sides of the super-cardioid pattern are narrower than those of the cardioid pattern, giving the user more directional control. *Image provided courtesy of Shure Incorporated.*

or capsules. The microphone element, or capsule, is designed to detach easily from the microphone body. By purchasing different capsules, one microphone body can have any one of a number of different microphone patterns, depending on which capsule is attached to the microphone body at the time. Modular types of microphones are often called microphone systems or system mics and offer a variety of options when budgets are limited (see Fig. **3.15**).

Stereo Microphones

Several companies manufacture stereo microphones that have two elements within the mi-crophone. Stereo microphones offer an easy way for a production person to capture a stereo music image without setting up two microphones and running two cables (see Fig. **3.16**). Such microphones can provide a unique sound picture for a remote or sports broadcast when used for the background or ambient sound. As tempting as it might seem, stereo radio stations do not use stereo microphones for announcers. The reason is that any movement of the announcer's head left or right causes the announcer's voice to shift left or right in the stereo speakers. Due to the acoustics in a car, this would cause the announcer's voice to appear to fade in and out around the driver.

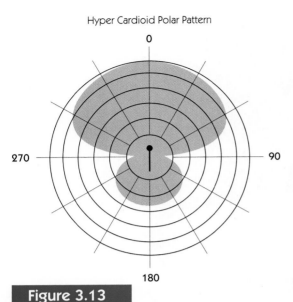

Hyper Cardioid Polar Pattern

0

270

90

180

Figure 3.13

The polar pattern for a hyper-cardioid microphone pattern shows that it is most sensitive to the front of the microphone at 0°. Notice how the pattern is similar to a bi-directional microphone in that it has extreme rejection to the sides at 90° and 270°. The combined side and rear rejection of sound allow the hyper-cardioid microphone to pick up sound clearly at slightly more than twice the distance from a source than an omnidirectional microphone and still maintain the same direct-to-reverberant sound ratio. *Image provided courtesy of Shure Incorporated.*

Figure 3.14

This AKG 414 condenser microphone can be switched among four different pickup patterns. Depending on the application, the microphone can be a cardioid, super-cardioid, omnidirectional, or bidirectional microphone, as represented by the symbols below the small switch.

Factors to Consider in Selecting a Microphone

Although selecting the proper microphone type and directional pattern is important, there are three other qualities that you might consider when selecting a microphone: frequency response, sensitivity, and overload/maximum sound-pressure level.

Frequency Response

Just like your ears, a microphone has a range of frequencies that it can "hear," called the frequency response. Ideally, a microphone should pick up all frequencies at the same level or within a narrow decibel range. For professional microphones, the range is plus or minus three decibels (dB). This means that no sound picked up by the microphone is three decibels louder or three decibels softer than

Figure 3.15

Modular types of microphones are often called microphone systems or system mics and offer a variety of options. By selecting different capsules, the user can have any one of a number of different microphone patterns on one microphone body. Shown from left to right are a bidirectional capsule, mic body, omnidirectional capsule, and cardioid capsule. Below is an assembled microphone body and capsule.

any other sound the microphone is capable of picking up. A microphone's frequency range is called the **frequency-response curve.**

A microphone's frequency response curve is graphically charted to document the microphone's performance. Most charts begin at 20 Hz and track to 20 kHz along a horizontal line, with the various frequencies listed in between (see Fig. **3.17**). A vertical scale lists the decibels (dB) of amplitude or loudness. In theory, the frequency-response curve of a perfect microphone is a flat line from 20 Hz to 20 kHz, indicating that the microphone does not favor one frequency over another or has little sound coloration.

The Polar Frequency Response

Another aspect of the frequency-response curve of a microphone is how the microphone perceives sounds that are not coming directly into the face of the microphone. This is called the microphone's **polar frequency response.** In theory, when a sound enters the front of a microphone on axis, or at 0 degrees, the microphone is the most sensitive and treats all sounds equally, reproducing the best sound quality. This is sometimes referred to as the **centerline** of the microphone. As you may have noticed, when you turn your head from side to side, the way you hear a particular

Figure 3.16

This Rode microphone has two capsules arranged as a coincident stereo pair to pick up sound. Stereo microphones offer an easy way for a production person to capture a stereo music image without setting up two microphones and running two cables. Such microphones can provide a unique sound picture for a remote or sports broadcast when used for the background or ambient sound.

sound changes. The same thing is true for a microphone.

As a directional microphone is turned away from a sound source, off centerline, the sensitivity and the frequency response of the microphone degrades and changes (see demo CD,

cut 16). This is called **off-axis coloration** of the sound, and it gets progressively worse as the angle to the sound source increases. High frequencies are lost first, making the microphone sound muddy the further it is moved **off axis** or is turned away from the sound source.

Sensitivity

Like people's ears, some microphones are more sensitive to sound than others. The **sensitivity** of a microphone is connected to its output. Generally, a sensitive microphone has a higher output voltage and does not have to be placed as close to the sound source to do its job. Likewise, a sensitive microphone does not have to be amplified as much when its signal gets to the control board or mixer. Condenser microphones are generally the most sensitive microphones with the highest output levels.

Overload and Maximum Sound-Pressure Level

Microphones distort and in some cases just plain stop functioning under extremely high instantaneous sound-pressure levels, which is very similar to what your ears do. Such a failure is called **overload.**

Typically, dynamic and condenser microphones reproduce the highest sound-pressure levels without distorting the sound. Under some circumstances, the element in a ribbon microphone can be stretched or blown out if placed too close to a sound source like an electric bass guitar amplifier.

As with your ears, the sound pressure a microphone can handle before distorting and failing is expressed in dB-SPL (decibels of

Figure 3.17

A microphone's frequency response is graphically charted to document the microphone's performance. Most charts begin at 20 Hz and track to 20 kHz along a horizontal line with the various frequencies listed in between. A vertical scale lists the decibels (dB) of amplitude or loudness. *Image provided courtesy of Shure Incorporated.*

sound-pressure level) and is listed as a part of a microphone's specifications, as its **maximum sound-pressure level.** For example, dynamic microphones are capable of handling sound pressures in excess of 125 dB-SPL; condenser microphones can handle up to 150 dB-SPL. Again, humans start to experience pain and hearing loss at 120 dB-SPL.

If you remember, the dynamic microphone is basically a small generator with a coil of wire moving back and forth in a magnetic field. So it stands to reason that the louder the sound, the more the diaphragm moves back and forth, generating a higher microphone output voltage. At some point the microphone may generate a high enough voltage to overload the input of whatever it is plugged into. For example, if a microphone that generates one volt of signal output is plugged into a control board that can only handle three quarters of a volt as the maximum input, that extra quarter of a volt from the microphone causes the control board input

to be overloaded. The overload results in the sound being distorted. Often this is misdiagnosed as a bad microphone.

The maximum output of a microphone can be determined by looking at the particular model's specification sheet. Likewise, the maximum input voltage that your recorder or control board can handle can also be determined by looking at its specification sheet.

Gain Staging

Gain staging is the term applied to matching the maximum microphone output voltage to the maximum input voltage of the device the microphone is plugged into. The maximum voltage ratings can be determined by reading the equipment specifications.

To prevent overloading of a recorder or control board, a number of microphones have built-in switchable "pads." A pad is the term

Figure 3.18

This AKG 414 condenser microphone has a built-in pad on the left that can be switched to lower the audio output by either 10 or 20 decibels. The switch on the right is a frequency roll-off switch used to adjust the amount of low-frequency bass the microphone picks up.

used for a preset, or fixed, volume control. For example, a 10-dB pad lowers the audio output of a microphone 10 dB below whatever is coming into the microphone. The user can select between two or more pads to reduce the output of the microphone (see Fig. **3.18**). In addition to microphones, many recorders, consoles, and other devices also have built-in switchable pads to lower the input or output level so as not to overload the electronic circuits.

By matching the output of the microphone to the input of the control board or recorder (gain staging), you are assured of a clean

audio signal with no distortion. As simple as this sounds, failing to gain-stage the microphone and equipment is one of the most common mistakes made using microphones.

Microphone Mounts

There are a number of ways to mount a microphone properly, ranging from a factory mount designed for a particular microphone model to the ultimate microphone stand—you.

People

Often, people become microphone stands. As silly as it sounds, people are quite well designed for the purpose. Radio and TV news people hold microphones for field interviews. Many times, to get just the right sound, a person is required to hold a microphone to get into tight spaces or close enough to the sound source. Since humans are pretty flexible they can easily position a microphone just about anywhere. However, a person should grasp the microphone firmly and not change hand positions, or the movement creates a thumping noise through the body of the microphone. Likewise, clothing needs to be kept clear of the microphone, as any movement may cause a rustling sound that the microphone can pick up.

Floor Stands

Microphone floor stands come in a variety of styles and materials. Stands usually consist of one of two types, a permanent base or a folding-leg base, both with a vertically telescoping pole to mount the microphone on.

A permanent base stand has a round or triangular base that is made of cast iron and is fairly heavy, at 20 to 30 pounds, and some-

Figure 3.19

A folding-leg stand has three legs that fold neatly to allow the stand to be easily transported for location and concert sound work. A useful addition to any floor stand is a "baby boom," or an arm about three feet long with a sliding counterbalance weight that mounts to the top of the mic stand.

times more. A folding-leg stand has three legs that fold neatly to allow the stand to be easily transported for location and concert sound work. The telescoping pole usually extends from three feet to a little over five feet (see Fig. **3.19**).

A useful addition to a floor stand is a "baby boom," or an arm about three feet long with a sliding counterbalance weight that mounts to the top of the mic stand. It gives the stand ad-

ditional reach either horizontally or vertically. The mic is mounted on one end of the boom and the counterbalance weight is adjusted to balance the boom at whatever angle it is placed. Quality floor stands range in price from $60 to $150. "Baby" booms are about $40 extra.

Floor Booms

A floor boom is a large stand with an extended arm to hold a microphone over the sound source. Typically, they are on casters or wheels so they can be easily moved, as most have a very heavy iron base. A "small" floor boom extends vertically over six feet, and the boom arm extends out five to six feet (see Fig. **3.20**). Occasionally, you may find one of these in a radio station. A small floor boom costs about $300.

Desk Stands

Desk stands are usually miniature versions of a company's floor stands. Some have short, telescoping mounts for the microphone, and some do not (see Fig. **3.21**). Typically, radio desk stands are a little larger and heavier, whereas desk stands intended for television are small and less obtrusive. A disadvantage of a desk stand is that any vibration in the table is transmitted directly through the stand to the microphone, producing a thumping sound. This often occurs when someone is nervously tapping his or her fingers on the table or tapping a foot against a table leg.

Desk-Mounted Microphone Arms

For radio, it's best to mount a microphone so that it is adjustable for height and reach, since

Figure 3.20

Solid-base floor stands come in a variety of styles and materials from the half stand with short boom (center) to large rolling floor booms. Finishes vary from bright chrome to nonreflective black.

no two people who work at a radio control board are the same size and shape. A desk-mounted mic arm is a cantilever arm mounted on a swivel. The arm is spring-loaded to counterbalance the weight of the microphone and to allow the arm to be positioned at any height (see Fig. **3.22**).

The microphone is also mounted on a swivel, so it can be turned in any direction. The arm allows the microphone to be positioned anywhere within a range and "hang" there for

the announcer to use. Often, desk arms are mounted on a twelve-inch riser to raise the arm above any equipment on the desk.

Clips, Clamps, and Goosenecks

Necessity is the mother of invention when it comes to mounting a microphone in an unusual circumstance. There are a number of very creative products on the market to help solve the problem (see Fig. **3.23**). There are

Figure 3.21

A desk stand can easily position a microphone when an announcer is sitting in a fixed position. A disadvantage of a desk stand is that any vibration in the table is transmitted directly through the stand to the microphone, producing a thumping sound. This often occurs when someone is nervously tapping his or her fingers on the table or tapping a foot against a table leg.

Figure 3.23

When a situation calls for something out of the ordinary, many technicians open a bag of clips, clamps, and an occasional gooseneck (center). There are no hard and fast rules here, except that the microphone must be mounted securely so it can pick up the sound. There are eight mic mounts in this picture that can be arranged in a number of combinations.

Figure 3.22

A desk-mounted mic arm is spring-loaded to counterbalance the weight of the microphone and to allow the arm to be positioned anywhere within a range and "hang" there for the announcer to use. This arm is mounted on a twelve-inch tall base to place the arm above the control board.

generic microphone clips that look like large clothespin-type devices, which are basically spring-loaded clamps. Just about any size microphone can be placed in them.

There are microphone quick-release adapters, swivel adapters, and microphone thread adapters to match microphones to microphone stands. There are also a number of different screw-type "C clamps" designed to clamp down on something (table, desk, the pole of a mic stand, etc.) and hold a microphone.

Figure 3.24

A shock mount is a mic mount situated within a larger supporting mount. The inner mount holds the microphone at its base and is suspended on what looks like tiny bungee cords. The suspension system isolates and absorbs building vibrations so they can't reach the mic and be picked up.

One of the more unusual microphone mounts is a **gooseneck.** A gooseneck is a flexible piece of metal conduit about sixteen inches long that can be twisted, turned, and bent in just about any direction you can imagine (see Fig. **3.23**). Whatever you do, though, don't bend, or flex, a gooseneck with the microphone turned on because a gooseneck makes a creaking noise that is picked up by the mic.

Of course, there's always **gaffer's tape.** Tape the microphone to something, keeping in mind not to cover any vents on the microphone body. Although gaffer's tape looks like duct tape, the two are different products with different properties and adhesives. Gaffer's tape is designed to have strong holding abilities and to be removed without leaving a sticky residue. Duct tape is intended to seal

permanently and leaves a sticky residue all over everything.

Shock Mounts

All microphone mounts have one common fault, regardless of whether they are made of steel, plastic, or carbon fiber. The mount transfers mechanical noise and vibration from the stand into the microphone body, producing unwanted rumble and thumping sounds.

A **shock mount** is a mic mount situated within a larger supporting mount (see Fig. **3.24**). The inner mount holds the microphone and is suspended on what look like expensive rubber bands or tiny bungee cords. The rubber suspension system isolates and absorbs the vibrations so they can't reach the mic.

Why You Need a Shock Mount

A microphone mounted on a floor stand is essentially connected to the floor. Any mechanical vibration in the floor travels up the microphone stand into the body of the microphone. Such sounds include vibrations from air conditioning and heating systems, a person walking across the floor, and general building noise originating anywhere within a building (see demo CD, cut 17). Vehicle traffic passing by a building can introduce ground vibrations into the building foundation. The foundation passes the rumble into the floor, into the microphone stand, and finally to the microphone.

Desk stands and microphone arms are also notorious for passing any vibration on the desk into the microphone. This includes someone tapping fingers on the desk, bumping the desk with a chair, or slapping the desk to emphasize points when speaking.

Generally, the more sensitive a mic is, the greater the need to shock-mount it. A large number of microphones come with a factory shock mount. When purchased separately, shock mounts cost from $50 to $200.

Microphone Placement

Using a microphone is part science and part art. Part science from the standpoint that there are some basic rules to use as guides; part art from the standpoint of capturing the exact sound *you* want from an event, musical instrument, or voice talent. Once you learn the basic rules, you can start practicing your art.

It would be nice to have a chart that told you where to place the microphone on radio talent and each different instrument or sound source you might encounter, but no such chart exists. The art of sound recording is just too subjective and open to creativity. Although there are certainly guidelines to follow, much of microphone placement is based in science with a lot of additional experimentation. The experimentation is challenging and fun as you try different microphone placements to capture the sound you are seeking.

Microphone Myths and the Science behind Microphone Placement

There are at least three myths with regard to how microphones operate and, thus, their proper placement. First, microphones do not reach out to capture sound, nor is there such a thing as a working distance or "microphone reach" measured in inches and feet. The fact is that sound waves have to travel to the microphone and impact the diaphragm in order to start the process of converting acoustic energy to electrical energy.

How effective a microphone is at picking up sound at a particular distance from the sound source depends on a number of factors, including the initial sound-pressure level of the source you want to record and the background, or ambient, noise level present. For example, if you hike into the boonies in one of the national parks with a digital recorder and a microphone, you might be amazed to hear sounds that are hundreds of feet away, or even the sound of a stream cascading down a mountainside a quarter-mile away (see demo CD, cut 18). Does this mean the microphone has a quarter-mile reach? Absolutely not. What it means is that there is almost no background noise present to interfere with the sound, allowing it to reach your location.

A second microphone myth is that directional microphones somehow pull in or enhance sound waves coming from the front of the microphone. The fact is that directional microphones do not enhance or pull in sound from any particular direction, just as microphones do not reach out for sound. Directional microphones are designed to *reject* sound from specific directions. In the case of a cardioid microphone, sound is slightly rejected from the sides and entirely rejected from the rear of the microphone. This gives the impression that the sound to the front of the microphone is enhanced, when in reality, the front is simply the only active side of the microphone left to pick up sound.

A third myth surrounding microphones is that hyper-cardioid shotgun microphones somehow focus and zoom in on sounds, pulling them in and making them appear closer. Here again, hyper-cardioid microphones do not focus and do not zoom in, and they certainly don't pull in sound. What hyper-cardioid microphones are capable of doing is *rejecting* sound from the sides and rear of the microphone so that the active side of the microphone has a very narrow pickup pattern. It is the extreme rejection of the sound from the sides and rear that gives the impression that the microphone is focused and pulling in sound.

During a nature recording session for this text, a hyper-cardioid shotgun mic was used to capture the sounds of whitewater rafters as they passed through a rough section of a popular river. The goal was to record their hoots and hollers as they went crashing through the water. Their speaking voices were clearly recorded from over 75 feet away as they talked to one another before hitting the rapids, with a state highway only 30 feet behind the mic (see demo CD, cut 19). Listen carefully to the cut. Can you hear any traffic? The shotgun mic did what it was designed to do: it rejected the vehicle sounds, which are not in the recording.

Regardless of the directional qualities of a microphone, unwanted sounds can still enter a directional microphone by being reflected off walls and objects.

Basic Microphone Placement Guidelines

Using a simple three-step process, you can properly place a microphone on just about any sound source. First, identify the source of the sound. What is creating the sound? For an announcer, it is his or her mouth. At a news event, what is the source of the sound you are to capture? Is it the fire engine racing to the scene of the fire, or the crackling of the fire itself? What did your producer ask for? In the case of a musical instrument, something has to vibrate to cause a sound to be generated. For example, on a violin, piano, or guitar, it is the strings. Regardless of the situation, identify the source of the sound.

Second, once you have identified the sound source, focus your attention on the sound's amplifier. Something is amplifying the sound so that you can hear it. In the case of radio talent, the people's mouths are the amplifiers. On a piano, it is the sounding board that the strings are mounted to; on a tuba, it is the huge bell-shaped opening at the end of all the plumbing; on an acoustic guitar, it is the guitar body. Outdoors, the sound reverberating off buildings or objects often serves to amplify sound. Regardless of the situation, identify what is amplifying the sound.

Third, with the sound source and the amplifier in mind, determine the direction that the amplifier is aimed and the direction the sound waves are traveling. Place the microphone in the sound's direct path, facing the amplifier.

The question now is, how far away from the sound source do you place the microphone? And the answer is: within the critical distance.

Critical Distance

You perceive sound as a combination of the direct sound from a source and the reverberant sounds from the space surrounding the source. Earlier we discussed the direct-to-reverberant sound ratio, which is the ratio of direct sound to the reverberant sound that you hear. At a certain distance from each sound source the direct sound and the reverberant sound are equal, and the ratio between the two is 1. Everything between the sound source and this point is part of the **critical distance.**

The critical distance depends on the sound source. A source that is louder and is more directional in nature has a longer critical distance. Likewise, a softer sound that is non-directional has a much shorter critical distance. For example, if you are standing in front of a blaring trombone, its direct sound path is several feet long before you can begin to hear the reverberant sound from the room you are in. At the opposite end of the spectrum, if you are trying to record someone whispering, you leave the direct sound path and begin to hear the reverberant sound from the room fairly quickly.

Microphone Placement within the Critical Distance

Ideally, a microphone should be placed within the critical distance from the sound source to obtain the most accurate and intelligible recording. However, there are times when, for effect, a production person intentionally places a microphone outside the critical distance to capture more room reverberation or reverberant sound.

There are questions that come into play in microphone placement that cross the line between science and art. Science says that, to get the perfect recording, you place the microphone one way. But art says that to get the effect you are seeking, you might place it another. For example, try placing a microphone very near the source and another a few feet away, recording each on a separate track. When you listen to the playback, mix the ratio of the direct mic track to the ambient mic track and see the incredible range of sounds that you can create (see demo CD, cut 20). The best sound is usually achieved by experimentation.

Great recording engineers and production people are not known for their ability to place a mic in just the right place according to a book or chart. They are known for their creativity in capturing sound, sometimes by some very unconventional methods. You should feel free to experiment to achieve the sound *you* or your client wants.

Stereo Microphone Placement Guidelines

The goal in recording or broadcasting an event in stereo is to recreate a broad, life-like, sound field between two speakers during playback. A stereo recording requires at least two microphones, one for left channel, one for right channel. How these microphones are placed determines the stereo image you capture. There are four possible ways to capture a stereo sound field.

The Spaced Pair or A-B Stereo Configuration

This is the simplest and most straightforward way to create a stereo image. Two identical omnidirectional microphones are placed on stands in front of the band or event to be

1 ft.

3 ft.

3–to–1 Rule

Figure 3.25

The three-to-one rule for stereo mic placement states that when using a spaced pair of microphones they should be placed three feet apart for every one foot they are from the sound source. Although not the preferred method for stereo recording, using the three-to-one rule helps ensure that phase cancellations are kept to a minimum.

phase. As covered in chapter 2, when a sound arrives at a pair of mics out of phase it can be canceled out and disappear from the stereo image. Essentially, there is going to be both constructive and destructive interference of the sounds. To prevent this, observe the three-to-one rule.

The three-to-one rule states that when using a spaced pair of microphones, they should be placed three feet apart for every one foot they are from the sound source. Using the three-to-one rule helps ensure that phase cancellations are kept to a minimum (again, see Fig. **3.25**).

By listening to the stereo microphone placement in mono (left and right combined into a single channel), you can tell when you are getting phase cancellation and acoustic losses in the recording. The sound takes on a fuzzy, nondirectional quality, and things that should appear in the center of the stereo image seemingly disappear or become quite faint.

The X-Y Stereo Configuration

X and Y in the **X-Y stereo configuration** represent your left and right ears, respectively. There are two methods of obtaining an X-Y recording, with a **coincident pair** of microphones or a **near-coincident pair** of microphones. The object of this type of mic placement is to eliminate or reduce the possible phase cancellation that can occur with the spaced-pair mic technique.

A coincident microphone pair includes two cardioid (or other directional-type) microphones placed in a horizontal position facing the group or instrument, with one microphone stacked directly above the other. With the two microphone *heads* (the part of each microphone that contains the sound pickup) remaining one above the other and acting as a

recorded. However, if you desire less room ambiance, two cardioid microphones can be used instead. The two microphones are spaced apart, facing the band, with each microphone angled slightly outward to the left and right edges of the sound source to form the **spaced pair** (see Fig. **3.25**).

There is one potential problem to be aware of with a spaced pair. Because the microphones are spaced apart, some sound will arrive at one microphone before it arrives at the other, and vice versa. Due to the different arrival times, the sound may or may not be in

A coincident microphone pair includes two cardioid (or other directional-type) microphones placed in a horizontal position facing the group or instrument. The degree of angle at which you aim the microphones determines the size of the stereo image that is recorded. Because the microphone heads are so close together, a coincident microphone pair introduces very little phase shift and produces an accurate stereo picture.

rotation point, the top microphone head should be aimed toward the left side of the sound source. The lower microphone head is aimed toward the right side of the sound source (see Fig. **3.26**). The degree of angle at which you aim the microphones determines the size of the stereo image that is recorded. Because the microphone heads are so close together, a coincident microphone pair introduces very little phase shift and produces an accurate stereo picture.

A near-coincident microphone pair includes two cardioid (or other directional-type) microphones placed in a horizontal position facing the group or instrument, with one mi-crophone stacked directly above the other. With the two microphone *bodies* (the part of each microphone that is below the micro-phone head) remaining one above the other, the top microphone should be aimed toward the left side of the sound source, using the midpoint of the mic body as the rotation point. Using the same procedure, the lower microphone is aimed toward the right side of the sound source (see Fig. **3.27**).

The two microphone heads should gener-ally be four to seven inches apart. This posi-tioning of the microphones allows for just a little bit of phase shift and adds an open sound with some width and depth to the

A near-coincident microphone pair includes two cardioid (or other directional-type) microphones placed in a horizontal position facing the group or instrument. The two microphone heads should generally be four to seven inches apart. This positioning of the microphones allows for just a little bit of phase shift and adds an open sound with some width and depth to the stereo image. The angle of the microphones can be varied to adjust the stereo image.

stereo image. The angle of the microphones can be varied to adjust the stereo image.

Stereo Microphones

Stereo microphones usually have two elements arranged within the microphone head in a coincident X-Y pair. This is a convenient way to record stereo using only one microphone body, one microphone mount, and one microphone cable. The other advantage, or disadvantage depending on your viewpoint, is that the aiming of the X-Y pair is fixed, giving you consistency of the stereo image, espe-

cially on live remote broadcasts. Stereo microphones work well as crowd mics for sports broadcasts, adding a realistic ambiance.

Middle/Side Microphones

Another way to capture a stereo image using just one microphone is with a **middle/side microphone** (M/S). A middle/side microphone has two directional elements within a single microphone. The first of these is a cardioid element facing straight forward to pick up the direct sound and is the middle element, or M, in middle/side. The second is located behind

Front-facing Cardioid Pattern

Bidirectional, Side-facing Pattern

Figure 3.28

A middle/side microphone has two directional elements within the microphone. The middle element is a cardioid pattern facing straight forward to pick up the direct sound. The side element is located behind the cardioid element and is a bidirectional microphone pattern aimed out each side of the microphone.

the cardioid element and is a bidirectional microphone element with the bidirectional pattern aimed out each side of the microphone (see Fig. **3.28**).

By combining the sound from the cardioid element and the left half of the bidirectional pattern the left channel is formed, likewise for the right. Most mid/side microphones have adjustable patterns to vary the size of the stereo image.

Stereo microphones are offered in a wide variety of directional patterns. Prices range from $100 to $5,000 for a high-end condenser stereo mic.

Windscreens and Pop Filters

A **windscreen** or **pop filter** protects a microphone's diaphragm from blasts of wind or plosive speech sounds. A plosive speech sound is created when you obstruct the flow of air through your mouth and nose prior to making the sound and suddenly release the air when you make the sound or say the letter. The plosive sounds include the letters *b, d, g, k, t,* and the most famous plosive of all, the letter *p.* Many people deliver a significant blast of air along with the letter *p.* It is called "popping your Ps" (see demo CD, cut 21). The blast of air is so strong that the letter is lost, and all that is heard from the mic is what sounds like a loud thump, or small explosion. This occurs because the diaphragm bottomed out or was forced all the way to the limits of its ability to travel by the blast of air.

Good announcers learn to "pull their Ps," or slightly restrict the plosive, so that this condition does not occur. But you are not always going to be working with experienced talent. Other sounds that can cause problems are the sibilant sounds, like *s* and *ch.*

Pop Filters

A pop filter is a small, acoustic-foam windscreen built into the head of the microphone in an effort to eliminate those nasty thumping sounds from plosives and sibilant sounds (see demo CD, cut 22). In theory, the acoustic foam allows the sound through, and the blasts of air from the plosives get lost in the foam and

Figure 3.29

A pop filter helps prevent the nasty thumping sounds from plosives and sibilant speech. This particular condenser microphone has an easily removable pop filter that allows, depending on the application, the microphone to be used with or without the filter.

never make it to the diaphragm (see Fig. **3.29**). However, not everyone speaks the same and, in many cases, the built-in pop filter just can't handle a serious "p popper."

If the microphone's built-in pop filter is not stopping your popper, turn the microphone 90 degrees to the left or right and have the popper talk across the face of the microphone so that the plosive blast of air goes past the microphone instead of directly into it (see Fig. **3.30;** see demo CD, cut 23). However, some people can still pop a mic, even under these circumstances.

A more aggressive approach for a pop filter is to use a **"popper stopper"** or external pop filter. These mount on the mic stand and are placed a few inches off the face of the microphone. They appear to be a fine mesh cloth, similar to women's stockings, stretched over a small circular frame (see Fig. **3.31**). "Popper stoppers" are acoustically transparent, and the mesh stops or protects the microphone from the blasts of air created by the plosive sounds. If one is not enough, try a second placed behind the first.

Popper stoppers are also sometimes called **spit screens** as they offer the additional benefit of stopping spit from reaching the face of the microphone and building up a film on the microphone face. As gross as it sounds, it is something to think about if you are using something like a $2,000 voice-over microphone.

Internal pop filters and popper stoppers are intended for indoor use and cannot provide adequate protection from the wind outdoors.

Windscreens

A microphone can be protected outdoors from the wind with a foam windscreen. Made from special acoustic foam to fit the microphone, windscreens come in various shapes and sizes. A foam windscreen slides over the head of the microphone and is held in place by friction or a small piece of Velcro (see Fig. **3.32**). The sound passes through the foam with only a very slight effect on the high frequencies. The wind gets lost in the foam, loses its power, and never makes it to the diaphragm (see demo CD, cut 24).

Foam windscreens are also popular inside radio stations because they allow announcers

Figure 3.30

If a microphone's built-in pop filter is not stopping an announcer from "popping," turn the microphone 90 degrees to the left or right and have the announcer talk across the face of the microphone so that the plosive blasts of air go past the microphone instead of directly into it.

to work microphones very closely for the proximity effect and not pop their Ps or sizzle their Ss.

Microphone Cables

There are two types of microphone cables, distinguished by their physical structure and electrical properties.

Balanced Cables

Professional microphone cables are **balanced** lines, meaning that they have a wire for positive (+), a wire for negative (–), and a braided, or foil, shield that encases the positive and negative wires (see Fig. **3.33**).

A balanced microphone line is always preferred, as it is the least susceptible to electrical noise and hum or to radio-signal interference. Electrical interference occurs in a number of ways, such as laying a mic cable close to an AC power line. If you are close to a radio station, a mic cable can serve as a very good antenna and help a portable audio mixer or recorder to act as a radio. In some location situations, two-way radios can cause interference.

The shield in a balanced mic cable protects the audio traveling on the wires by being connected to earth ground through the equipment the line is plugged into. The shield picks

Figure 3.31

"Popper stoppers" are acoustically transparent, and the mesh stops or protects the microphone from the blasts of air created by the plosive sounds. Popper stoppers are also sometimes called "spit screens," as they offer the additional benefit of stopping spit from reaching the face of the microphone.

Figure 3.32

Foam windscreens are popular in radio stations because they allow announcers to work microphones very closely for the proximity effect and not pop their Ps or sizzle their Ss. A foam windscreen slides over the head of the microphone and is held in place by friction or a small piece of Velcro, as highlighted above.

up the interference and carries it harmlessly to ground. Balanced mic cables can be run up to a thousand feet without serious audio degradation.

Unbalanced Cables

An **unbalanced** mic **cable** has only one conductor, positive (+), with the shield as the negative (–) (again, see Fig. **3.33**). This presents two problems. First, unbalanced cables are highly susceptible to electrical noise and radio-signal interference, since the shield is also the negative (–) of the audio signal. Second, such cables need to be kept as short as possible due to the electrical noise and radio-signal interference they are capable of picking up. With very few exceptions, such as adapting a professional microphone to a "prosumer" type minidisc recorder, unbalanced mic cables should be avoided if possible.

Balanced Male and Female XLR

Shield Hot 2

Cold 3 1

Shield 1

Cold Hot 3 2

1 — Shield
3 — Negative
2 — Positive

Balanced Tip, Ring Sleeve

Ring Sleeve Sleeve Ring Tip

Tip

Ring
Tip
Sleeve

Unbalanced Tip, Ring

Sleeve Sleeve Tip

Tip

Tip
Sleeve

Figure 3.33

From left to right, a balanced male and female XLR connector, a balanced male TRS tip, ring, sleeve connector, and an unbalanced male T/S (tip and sleeve) connector.

Microphone Connectors

XLR "Cannon" Connectors

Professional microphone cables use three-pin **XLR connectors.** The connector is also called a "Cannon connector." The connector is named after James Cannon of the Cannon Electric Company, who developed the first three-pin connector in the late 1920s.

The XLR connector is a cylindrical metal housing with three protected connector pins or sockets. The male connector has protruding pins; the female connector has pin sockets. Typically, outputs are male and inputs are female (see Fig. **3.33**).

The pins and sockets are numbered 1, 2, and 3. Pin number one is the shield, or earth ground, and is slightly longer than the other two pins. This is so that the first thing that connects is the ground, to eliminate any electrical pop when the other two pins are mated together. Pin number two is the positive (+), and pin three is the negative (−). An XLR connector is a balanced connector, just like the mic cable that it is attached to.

A professional microphone has a male connector built into its base. Microphone cables have a male and a female connector; the female end plugs into the microphone. The male connector plugs into the console or recorder.

Quarter-Inch Connectors

The TRS Connector

TRS connectors are sometimes used in radio, but more typically they are in the concert industry on musical instruments, mics, and portable mixers or consoles. The TRS connector is often called a quarter-inch phone plug since it is one-quarter-inch in diameter and looks just like the plugs used by operators in the days when they literally connected each telephone call by patching in a cable with a plug on the end of it. TRS male connectors are called plugs, and the female connectors are called jacks.

TRS stands for tip, ring, and sleeve. Looking at the connector, the "tip" of the connector is the positive (+). A small black insulator ring separates the tip from the next part of the connector, called the "ring"; the ring is the negative (−). Another small black insulator separates the ring from the final part of the connector, called the sleeve; the sleeve is the shield or earth ground (again, see Fig. **3.33**).

A TRS connector is a balanced connector, just like the XLR connector. Professional microphone cables are often made with a female XLR connector on one end and a male TRS connector on the other. This type of connector is used to plug a professional microphone into a portable mixer or console.

Occasionally TRS connectors are used as "stereo" connectors. For example, stereo headphones use a TRS with the tip being positive left channel, the ring being positive right channel, and the sleeve being a common negative. In such instances the TRS is used as an unbalanced connector.

The T/S Connector

A **T/S connector** (tip/sleeve) is an unbalanced quarter-inch phone plug. The tip is positive (+) and the sleeve is the shield or negative (−) (see Fig. **3.33**). Unbalanced T/S connectors are generally found on public address amplifiers, speaker cables, and consumer-type microphones. Occasionally you'll encounter a microphone cable with a female XLR connector on one end and a T/S plug on the other to plug a better quality microphone into consumer gear.

Mini-TRS and T/S Connectors

The mini-plug was developed in the consumer electronics industry and found its way into the professional world though "prosumer" type equipment, like minidisc recorders, used in many radio news operations. The mini-plug is sometimes referred to as an eighth-inch mini-plug or a 3.5-millimeter mini-plug.

The plug is constructed like the standard one-quarter-inch phone plug, just a lot smaller. It comes in TRS and T/S configurations. It is not unusual to find a female XLR connector on one end of a microphone cable and a TRS mini-plug on the other end so that a professional microphone can be plugged into a minidisc recorder or other portable gear.

Microphone Cable Care

A microphone cable is not just a plain old piece of wire. It is a special cable designed to offer low impedance (resistance to electrical flow) so that it can more easily pass low-level microphone signals. It is also designed to be flexible under a variety of conditions.

Figure 3.34

Microphone cable should be rolled up using the natural looping of the cable as a guide. Once looped, it should be tied with a Velcro cable tie-wrap, as this cable is, or with a reusable plastic cable wrap. It is also acceptable to use a small piece of gaffer's tape.

Microphone cable should be rolled up using the natural looping of the cable as a guide. Once looped, it should be tied with a Velcro cable tie-wrap, a reusable plastic cable wrap, or a piece of gaffer's tape (see Fig. **3.34**). Each of these makes it very easy to hang the cable up or stack it. Another acceptable way to roll and store cable is with a microphone cable reel.

NEVER wrap a mic cable around your bent arm from hand to elbow or in a figure-eight hand to elbow. This twists and kinks the wire within the cable, which causes the cable to fail. In addition to causing the wire to fail at some point, the kinks and twists formed by this method of wrapping a cable make it unable to lie flat or hang straight from a microphone stand.

Microphone Preamplifiers

Boosting Microphone Signals

A microphone preamplifier, in its most basic form, is a voltage multiplier. It takes the low-voltage signal from the microphone and amplifies it to a line-level signal. Without getting too involved in electronics theory, professional audio is usually either at mic level or line level.

Figure 3.35

Rack-mounted outboard microphone preamplifiers have adjustable input-level controls to match the output level of the microphone (gain-staging). Mic preamps also have output-level controls to match the input level of a control board or digital recorder. Many preamplifiers feature analog-to-digital converters with digital outputs designed to feed directly into a digital console or recorder.

Mic level is a very low-level signal measured in millivolts (millivolt = thousandths of a volt). Line level is typically 1 volt but can be as high as nearly 2 volts.

A preamplifier's design is critical, since a microphone's signal is very weak. Preamplifiers boost whatever signal is present. If the audio contains noise and distortion from the microphone or a bad microphone cable, the noise and distortion are amplified along with the original signal. Ideally, microphone cable runs should be kept as short as practicable to help prevent this.

Broadcast and production control boards and portable mixers have internal microphone preamplifiers. Such preamplifiers are designed to work with a wide range of microphones and have a limited number of adjustments, if any, to boost and shape the sound.

In a quest for sonic perfection, a producer or voice talent typically turns to a stand-alone preamplifier known as an "outboard" preamp, often referred to as a voice processor. Outboard gear is rack-mounted, separate from the main console (see Fig. **3.35**). Preamplifiers also exist in virtual form within digital audio workstations. A virtual preamplifier is software-based and emulates the same controls, functions, and effects as the hardware version of the preamplifier.

Professional preamplifiers have adjustable input-level controls to match the output level of the microphone (**gain-staging**). Mic preamps also have output-level controls to match the input level of a control board or digital recorder. Many preamplifiers feature analog-to-digital converters with digital outputs designed to feed directly into a digital console or recorder.

Depending on the design, a preamplifier or voice processor may have additional audio processors, including compressors, limiters, equalizers, de-essers (to eliminate sibilant "s" sounds), and other user-selectable settings to tailor or shape the sound (again, see Fig. **3.35**). You will learn about setting up a mic preamplifier or voice processor in chapter 6. Outboard microphone preamplifiers cost from $200 to nearly $4,000.

Selecting a Microphone Preamplifier

Golden-eared engineers and producers have written quite a bit about the perfect preamplifier. Selecting the "best" outboard microphone preamplifier is like selecting which flavor of **Krispy Kreme donut** is best. You have to try them all before you know which one *you* like! Engineers and voice talent try different microphone and preamplifier combinations until they find the one that's just right for their specific purpose or application. In a typical radio station, a microphone preamplifier is selected for the staff by the station engineer and the production director. However, if you are putting together your own voice-over studio, you may get the opportunity to select what you think sounds the best for your voice.

A professional voice-over artist experiments to find the exact microphone and preamplifier combination that makes his or her voice sound the best. Just as with microphones, there is no "best" microphone preamplifier; it does not exist. By now you should have realized that sound is very subjective on a person-to-person basis. Regardless of published equipment specifications, more than anything else you must learn to let your ears be the final judge of what sounds good and what does not.

Special-Purpose Microphones

Lavalier or Body Microphones

Lavs, as they are called, are often referred to as body mics, since they are so small and can easily be hidden from view on television or in film use.

Lavs serve a very useful purpose in radio. Often news people do interviews with subjects who have no idea in the world how to use a microphone. These people turn their heads and move about, drifting in and out of the microphone pickup pattern. This kind of movement makes it very difficult to understand what they are saying. A lav comes in handy in a talk-radio studio, or on location, since it is clipped to the subject. People can move all they want to and they are always on-mic.

Lavs are generally electret-condenser microphones, although there are a few moving-coil lavs on the market. The electret-condenser lav requires only a small battery power source or phantom power for the microphone's preamplifier. A "large" lav mic is about the size of an eraser on a pencil. Tiny body mics are sometimes only slightly larger in diameter than the three-millimeter (less than one-eighth of an inch) cable they are mounted on (see Fig. **3.6** earlier in the chapter).

Lavs are designed for placement below the chin, in the area of the chest. Because the talent does not speak directly into the microphone, most lav mics have an omnidirectional pickup pattern. The microphone is designed to be below and behind the sound source (the mouth and chin), so designers boost the high-frequency response or roll off the low-frequency response to make the microphone sound more natural. The high-frequency boost

Figure 3.36

With headset microphones, these two sportscasters are always "on mic" as they follow the action on the court and are free to use their hands to produce the broadcast. Notice the backup headset laying on top of the remote audio console for guests or in case one of their headsets fails.

explains why a lav sounds so funny when someone picks it up and speaks directly into it (see demo CD, cut 25).

Although the lav is a tiny microphone, its price is not. Top-quality lav mics intended for use in the radio, television, and film industry cost $300 to $400.

Shotgun Microphones

Shotgun microphones work by using a tube placed in front of the element with a series of openings along each side of the tube. As sound enters the microphone directly from the front, it also enters the side openings in succession one after the next, in phase, adding upon itself until it reaches the element at the rear of the mic. Sound from the rear of the microphone enters the openings in the reverse order, out of phase, canceling itself out and making the microphone highly directional.

Shotguns are designed primarily for use in radio and television news and the film industry. Shotguns have the ability to pick up sound at more than twice the distance of an omni-directional microphone and retain the same direct-to-reverberant sound ratio (see demo CD, cut 26). Radio news reporters use short shotguns for press conferences and "on-the-run" interviews to get a good clean pickup on the subject and eliminate unwanted sound or background noise. Shotgun microphones range in price from $300 to $2,000.

Headset Microphones

Headset microphones are designed to allow the talent to work with a microphone hands-free, as the microphone is attached to a pair of headphones (see Fig. **3.36**). Broadcasters use headset microphones primarily for news/ sports coverage and radio talk shows where the announcer needs to have his or her hands free to keep statistics or take notes. The added benefit of a headset microphone is that no matter where the talent looks, or what the talent does, he or she is always on-mic.

Headset microphones can be either moving-coil or electret condenser and are usually classed as "noise-canceling microphones." They are intended to be used close to the lips and to block out unwanted background noise.

Wireless Microphones

Wireless microphones provide talent the freedom to move about at a remote broadcast without being attached to a microphone cable. They also allow a production person to place a microphone at a distant location, such as on the backboard in a basketball game to capture the swish of the ball going through the hoop. Although not often thought of for radio, wireless microphones can be used to solve a lot of remote broadcast sound pickup problems. A professional wireless microphone has three separate components, a microphone, a transmitter, and a receiver. Occasionally, the microphone and transmitter are combined into a handheld microphone.

Transmitters

Professional wireless transmitters are low-power radio transmitters into which a microphone is plugged. The transmitters share frequencies in the VHF (Very High Frequency channels, 2–13) and UHF (Ultra High Frequency channels, 14–69) television bands. Most professional wireless transmitters are frequency-agile and can be tuned to any one of a number of channels. For example, in the UHF band (preferred by professionals), there are 256 frequencies.

Types of Transmitters

Professional wireless transmitters come in three varieties: self-contained, body-packs, and plug-ons.

A self-contained microphone/transmitter appears to be a regular handheld microphone, only slightly larger in size due to the transmitter that is contained in the microphone body.

Body-packs are smaller than a pack of cigarettes, and in some cases not much bigger than a cigarette lighter (see Fig. **3.37**). Body-packs operate on batteries, have a small **"rubber ducky"** flexible antenna, and are typically clipped to the back of a person's clothing with a belt clip or taped to an object. Most body-pack transmitters have been designed for use with a lavalier, or body mic.

Plug-ons are small transmitters that plug into the base of the microphone and are used for handheld microphones (again, see Fig. **3.37**). They are very popular because they can turn any microphone into a wireless by just plugging the transmitter into the microphone.

Radio stations use self-contained microphone/transmitters and plug-on transmitters effectively during live remote broadcasts to free up talent so they can move around without worrying about someone tripping over a mic cable. In many situations a radio station's remote truck is parked on the street as a portable billboard, and the talent is positioned inside the sponsoring business with a wireless mic.

A plug-on transmitter can also be attached to the microphone level output of a portable microphone mixer at a sporting event, such as a football game, to transmit the announcers'

Figure 3.37

Left to right, wireless transmitters known as body-packs operate on batteries, have a small "rubber ducky" antenna, and are designed for use with a lavalier, or body mic. Usually the transmitter is smaller than a pack of cigarettes. Self-contained microphone/transmitters are popular for live remote broadcasts to free up talent so they can move around without worrying about someone tripping over a mic cable. Plug-ons are small transmitters that plug into the base of the microphone and are used to turn any handheld microphone into a wireless.

voices from the press box to the remote truck in the parking lot, where a more powerful transmitter sends the signal back to the radio station.

However, these wireless transmitters are not usually referred to as plug-ons; they are often called by their unflattering industry nickname, **"butt-plugs,"** since they plug into the butt of the microphone.

Wireless transmitters have an effective line-of-sight range from 100 to 1,000 feet, depending on conditions. Professional wireless microphone transmitters are not inexpensive, with many models costing $1,000 per transmitter.

Wireless Receivers

A wireless receiver is a specially designed radio receiver that is tuned to match the wireless transmitter frequency in use. There are two basic types of receivers, single and diversity. A single receiver is one radio tuner and one antenna. Under most circumstances these work just fine, but occasionally they can experience noise, signal dropouts, and other interference, depending on the location and physical surroundings.

A **diversity receiver** has two tuners and two antennas combined to receive the signal (see Fig. **3.38**). The two receivers are connected internally by a small microprocessor that automatically selects the better signal from the two identical receivers, or, if necessary, combines the signals from the two receivers to get the best usable signal. Although diversity receivers are more expensive (near $2,000), they provide better reliability and are most often chosen by professionals who cannot afford to have poor audio quality or signal dropout.

Making the Final Selection

Selecting a microphone by type and pattern for a project is not necessarily an easy task for a beginner. What complicates things is that microphone selection and placement are not

Figure 3.38

A diversity wireless microphone receiver has two built-in tuners and two antennas to receive the signal. The two receivers are connected internally by a small microprocessor that automatically selects the better signal from the two identical receivers, or, if necessary, combines the signals from the two receivers to get the best usable signal.

Microphone selection is, many times, a very personal decision on the part of the technician. A microphone is often chosen for the unique acoustic qualities it imparts in a particular recording situation. Sometimes the unconventional yields a very pleasing result, and many times the most expensive microphone does not yield the "best" sound. For someone starting in the industry, the best thing you can do is to observe and ask questions, just like the three-year-old who constantly asks "Why?" Also, read industry trade publications, especially interviews with top engineers and producers. If you are observant, trends and patterns of how professionals select and use microphones will become evident to you.

Suggested Activities

1. Collect a dynamic and condenser microphone, and a ribbon if one is available, and place them close together in one of the studios available at your school. Have someone stand in one spot and speak into the microphones. Simultaneously record each microphone on a separate track. Play back the recordings and see if you can find three distinct qualities that make each microphone different from the others.
2. Using the same setup as above, experiment with the proximity effect, making recordings with the talent three feet from the microphones, two feet from the microphones, one foot from the microphones, six inches from the microphones, and finally two inches off the face of the microphones. How was the proximity effect for each microphone?
3. Place a directional microphone in the studio and have the talent speak directly into

exact sciences but rather subjective judgments of technicians, engineers, and producers. In many cases, such decisions are based on accepted practice within an industry. As an example, one microphone thought to be a great voice microphone in radio is rarely used in recording studios for vocals. Likewise, there are even more different microphone preferences between television and film.

the face of the microphone on its center-line, or 0-degree axis. Slowly rotate the microphone away from the talent, calling out the approximate position of the microphone as you go. When does the pickup pattern begin to take effect? In your judgment, how was the frequency response of the microphone affected?

4. If available, experiment with a lav mic, recording the talent with the microphone placed in a number of locations on the body as suggested in this chapter. Where is the best place to use your lav microphone?

5. Take a shotgun microphone and an omni-directional microphone outside and record some birds or other sounds, with both microphones in the same location. Then compare the recordings. Can you name at least three different sound qualities produced by each?

Web Sites for More Information

For more information about:

- *condenser microphones,* visit AKG at www.akg-acoustics.com

- *digital condenser microphones,* visit Neumann USA at www.neumannusa.com

- *dynamic or moving-coil microphones,* visit Electro-Voice at www.electrovoice.com

- *dynamic or moving-coil microphones,* visit Shure, Inc. at www.shure.com

- *general knowledge about microphones,* patterns, and applications, visit the Shure

Technical Support Knowledge Base at www.shure.com

- *powered ribbon microphones,* visit Royer Labs at www.royerlabs.com

- *ribbon and digital microphones,* visit Beyerdynamic at www.beyerdynamic.com

- *shotgun microphones,* visit Sennheiser USA at www.sennheiserusa.com

- *wireless microphones,* visit Lectrosonics at www.lectrosonics.com

Pro Speak

You should be able to use these terms in your everyday conversations with other professionals.

audio—Latin, "to hear"; sound that has been converted into electrical energy.

balanced microphone cable—A microphone cable or line in which there is a positive wire, a negative wire, and a shield or earth ground surrounding the positive and negative wires.

bass boost—Another term for proximity effect.

bidirectional—A microphone pattern that has maximum sensitivity at 0 and 180 degrees and maximum rejection at 90 and 270 degrees.

butt-plug—A wireless transmitter designed for plugging into the base of a microphone.

cardioid—A heart-shaped microphone pattern with maximum sensitivity at 0 degrees and maximum rejection at 180 degrees.

centerline—An imaginary line extending straight out from the face of a microphone, or 0-degree axis.

coincident pair—Stereo microphone placement in which the two microphones are placed one above the other in a horizontal position facing the sound source. With the heads serving as the rotation point, one is aimed at the right side of the sound source, the other at the left side.

condenser microphone—A microphone that uses an electrostatic field to convert sound into audio and requires a polarizing voltage and a preamplifier.

critical distance—Everything between the sound source and the point at which the ratio of direct-to-reverberant sound is equal, or 1; abbreviated Dc.

digital condenser microphone—A condenser microphone with a built-in preamplifier that includes an analog-to-digital converter and digital output only.

diversity receiver—A wireless microphone receiver using two tuners and two antennas to eliminate noise and dropouts.

dynamic microphone—A moving-coil microphone.

electret-condenser microphone—A condenser microphone that, although it does not require a polarizing voltage, does require a battery to run the preamplifier.

frequency-response curve—Graphically shows how a microphone responds to various frequencies, called flat if the microphone treats all frequencies equally.

gaffer's tape—Available in colors, gaffer's tape has the strength of duct tape without the sticky mess afterward.

gain staging—Matching a microphone's maximum output voltage to the preamplifier's maximum input voltage to prevent overload.

gooseneck—A piece of flexible metal conduit used to support a microphone.

hyper-cardioid—An elongated heart-shaped cardioid pattern used primarily in shotgun microphones to allow the microphones to be moved farther from the sound source without increasing the apparent room reverberation.

Krispy Kreme donut—A Southern delicacy, wonderfully light donuts slathered in mouth-watering sugar frosting, often used to entice the crew to show up in the morning; a sugar-delivery device.

lav—The abbreviation for the word lavalier, which comes from the French word lavaliere or "pendant," a microphone worn on the body. Pronounced like "lava" from a volcano, just dropping the last a.

maximum sound-pressure level—The maximum dB-SPL that a microphone can reproduce before going into distortion and then failure.

mic—Pronounced "Mike"; industry abbreviation for microphone ("mics" is used for more than one mic).

micron—An outdated term still in common usage that has since been replaced with the term micrometer. A micron, or micrometer, is one millionth of a meter, or about 1/25,000th of an inch.

middle/side microphone—A stereo microphone incorporating a cardioid element facing forward and a bidirectional element facing out the sides of the microphone. The combination of the middle element and the separate halves of the bidirectional element create the left and right channels.

near-coincident pair—Stereo microphone placement in which the two microphones are placed one above the other in a horizontal position, facing the sound source. With the midpoint of the mic bodies serving as the rotation point, one is aimed at the right side of the sound source, the other at the left side.

noise—Electrical noise, which appears as hiss in an audio signal, measured in negative dB. The larger the negative figure, the lower the noise level.

off axis—Outside of the centerline of a microphone's directional pattern, usually measured in degrees.

off-axis coloration—The change in the frequency response and sensitivity of a micro-

phone as it is turned away from a sound source and aimed in a different direction.

omnidirectional—A microphone pattern that allows the microphone to pick up sound from all directions equally.

overload—The point at which a microphone stops functioning under extremely high sound-pressure levels.

pattern—The term used to describe the directional characteristics of a microphone.

phantom power—Power supplied to a condenser microphone from a source such as a control board, portable mixing board, or other outside source through the microphone cable.

polar frequency response—The frequency-response curve of a microphone measured at various points in the microphone pattern.

pop filter—An acoustic foam filter within a microphone, used to prevent popping plosive sounds from reaching the microphone element.

popper stopper—A fine mesh screen placed a few inches off the face of a microphone to prevent popping plosive sounds from reaching the microphone element.

preamplifier—A voltage multiplier used to boost the weak signal of a microphone to a usable audio level.

prosumer—Prosumer equipment is equipment that offers many professional features but is not built to rigid professional standards. It is generally priced in between consumer and professional-level equipment.

proximity effect—The closer you move to a directional microphone, the more bass it appears to have.

ribbon—A member of the dynamic class of microphones; the ribbon uses a thin ribbon of metal as the sound pickup element.

rubber ducky—A flexible radio antenna made from silicone-based rubber products that can be bent and flexed without damage to the antenna coil contained within.

sensitivity—An electrical measurement in either dBV (decibel volts) or millivolts that tells what the audio output of the microphone will be at a given sound-pressure input level.

shock mount—A device designed to hold a microphone and isolate it from vibrations that might enter the microphone body and cause undesirable sounds.

shotgun microphone—A microphone designed with a long tube in front of the microphone element to increase the microphone's direct-to-reverberant sound ratio.

sound—Acoustic energy traveling through a medium such as air or water.

spaced pair—Stereo microphone placement in which two microphones are spaced a distance apart following the three-to-one rule: three feet of separation for each one foot of distance from the sound source.

spit screen—A fine mesh screen placed a few inches off the face of a microphone to prevent popping plosive sounds and spit from reaching the microphone element; same as a popper stopper.

super-cardioid—A heart-shaped microphone pattern with maximum sensitivity at 0 degrees and maximum rejection at 180 degrees. Super-cardioid microphones are even less sensitive to the sides than a cardioid microphone.

transient response—How a microphone reacts to transients, or sounds, with a fast attack that trails off slowly.

TRS connector—A one-quarter-inch-diameter connector with the tip as positive, the ring as negative, and the sleeve as shield or earth ground.

T/S connector—A one-quarter-inch-diameter connector with the tip as positive and the sleeve as negative and shield or earth ground.

unbalanced cable—A microphone cable or line that only has one positive conductor, with the shield acting as both the negative and the shield.

unidirectional—A generic term for a directional microphone, meaning one direction.

UHF—Ultra High Frequency, a band of frequencies assigned to television channels 14 through 83; 14 through 69 are also assigned to wireless microphones.

VHF—Very High Frequency, a band of frequencies assigned to television channels 2 through 13 and to wireless microphones.

windscreen—An acoustic foam cover for the head of a microphone, used to block wind outdoors.

XLR connector—A balanced microphone connector, sometimes referred to as a Cannon Connector, after the man and the company that invented it. A connector in which there are pins or sockets for the positive, negative, and shield, or earth ground.

X-Y stereo configuration—Stereo microphone placement in which the two microphones are placed one above the other in a horizontal position and aimed in either a coincident or near-coincident manner.

Control, Mixing, and Monitoring

HIGHLIGHTS

To the uninitiated, an audio control board looks pretty terrifying with all the knobs, switches, faders, and meters packed into a compact space. Although a control board may appear intimidating at first, it is a lot easier to learn and operate than you think. Generally, a station staff member trains new operators and takes them through the station's control board operation. With some hands-on experience you will get over your fear quickly. As one of my mentors in broadcasting said as I stood looking at my first 24-channel broadcast console, "This isn't rocket science; it's radio!" Still, operating a console requires hand-eye coordination, pre-planning, and some creativity and skill.

The reality is, running an on-air control board is the simplest task a show host has. The difficult work is planning your show, following the station format, and creating a fresh, innovative, relationship with listeners. The same applies to production. The operation of the hardware and software at your disposal is relatively easy. The tough part is creating the script, selecting music and sound effects, and learning how to communicate with your audience. Remember, despite all of the hardware you have to work with, the primary goal is to communicate messages to listeners. The control board is simply one tool used in the creative process.

Broken down into their modular components, audio control consoles are easily understood since they all do basically the same thing. In fact, once the basic theory of operation is understood, you will have the skills necessary to sit behind just about any control board and figure it out operationally.

Operational Theory

Understanding the Different Sections of a Console

An audio control surface performs three basic functions—amplification, routing, and mixing. Audio first enters the input section of the control board from microphones, recorders, or other sources, at either a mic or line level. The first stage of the control board *amplifies* the various audio inputs to a standardized level for use within the control board.

Using *routing,* or assignment switches, the operator determines the audio's path through the control board. The audio is eventually routed to the output section, where it is sent to recorders, audio processors, or broadcast transmitters. At the same time, the audio is routed to the monitor section of the control board so that operators and talent in the control room or studio can hear the project on monitor speakers or headphones.

Mixing is the process of using the various volume controls to balance or blend the audio from the numerous sources and achieve the sound the production person or producer desires. Mixing occurs at several stages in the control board and is finalized in the master section with the master output volume controls. Mixing also involves adjusting playback levels in the monitor section that feeds the monitor speakers, headphones, and intercoms, in both the control room and the studio.

Breaking down a console's functions into amplification, routing, and mixing makes it much easier to understand. These three functions occur within the input, master, output, and monitoring sections of the console.

Types of Audio Control Consoles

There are five popular types of audio control boards or consoles. **On-air** and **production consoles** are two different types found in radio stations. **Virtual consoles** exist within digital audio workstations, with some being used in on-air applications. **Portable mixers** are used for live remote radio broadcasts and sporting-event coverage. Although less common in radio production, **large-format mixing desks** are found in recording studios and in production houses that specialize in custom audio production for the media. Regardless of the console type, they all operate on the same universal principles of amplifying, routing, and mixing across the input, master, output, and monitoring sections of the console.

On-Air and Production Consoles

Broadcast audio control consoles for radio come in two variations that are as different as night and day—on-air consoles and production consoles.

On-Air Console Overview

On-air consoles are designed for controlling a number of audio sources, including microphones, CD players, digital audio storage systems for commercials and music, radio networks, and so forth.

An on-air console's only real role is to route and control the volume levels of all the sources, eventually sending them to the broadcast transmitter. The key design element of an on-air console is simplicity and ease of operation under pressure. In effect, the console designer tries to prevent operator errors with the layout

and design of the console. The true role of an on-air console is not creativity, but control.

Production Console Overview

A production console is just the opposite of the on-air console; it is designed for creativity. Production consoles have many more features and signal-routing abilities. These include individual channel equalization, the incorporation of outboard gear such as echo and reverbs through auxiliary audio sends and returns, and the ability to mix audio in three dimensions including width, depth, and height. Naturally, to be able to perform all of these functions a production console has more controls and metering.

The Impact of Digital Consoles

Both on-air and production consoles can be either analog or digital, the difference being that in a true digital console all inputs are from digital sources, the audio remains in the digital format in the console, and the console's digital outputs are fed to digital recorders, audio processors, or transmission equipment.

Digital consoles are available in two different physical styles. The first is a console that appears to be a traditional analog console with the same simple, familiar knobs and controls. Each knob and fader has an assigned function, or knob per function (see Fig. **4.1**). The only difference is that the console's internal components and the audio moving through the console are digital. This type of digital console requires no retraining on the part of the operator. In fact, the operator might not even know he or she is using a digital console. Typically, this is the type of digital console found as an on-air console and is simple and easy to operate.

Figure 4.1

Although this appears to be an analog console, it is digital! This type of digital console requires no retraining on the part of the operator. In fact, the operator might not even know he or she is using a digital console. Typically, this is the type of digital console found as an on-air console and is simple and easy to operate.

The second type of digital console is the "any-switch-can-be-anything-any-day" console. The heart of the console is an on-board microprocessor (computer) used to set up the console and assign the input and output functions to each of the console's switches and faders. The channel assignments, switching setup, and functions can be changed at any time, using the console's on-board microprocessor. Literally, any input, output, or function can be assigned to any channel or control; it's like moving checkers on a checkerboard (see Fig. **4.2**).

Each operator sets up, or programs, the console the way he or she prefers, rearranging console configuration to suit the operator's particular needs. The operator saves the configuration in the console's memory under his or her name or on a removable flash memory card. At any time the operator can recall the settings and reset the control board to that operator's original preferences. This type of digital console requires much more attention to detail and is usually found in production studios.

A digital console allows each operator to set up, or program, the console the way he or she prefers, rearranging the console configuration to suit the operator's particular needs. The operator saves the configuration in the console's memory. At any time the operator can recall the settings and reset the console to his or her original preferences.

On-Air Consoles in Depth

Most radio stations have already installed, or are in the process of installing, upgraded audio consoles. The new consoles are needed to meet competitive and consumer demands for high-quality audio and digital broadcast transmission requirements. On-air consoles are generally custom-ordered to meet the station's specific control room needs. This is easy to do since most consoles are made up of a number of different modules and individual channel strips and can be ordered in just about any configuration a station engineer desires. Prices for on-air consoles, such as the example in this chapter, start in the $10,000 range and rise quickly, depending on the features that

are ordered. Most radio stations operate in what is termed the **combo mode**, meaning that the talent serve as their own engineer, running the control board and other elements of their show.

The easiest way to understand a console is to break it down into components, looking at just one channel strip at a time, top to bottom. The digital on-air console chosen as an example has the appearance of an analog console. It has twelve identical channel strips; if you know how to operate one, you know how to operate all twelve, and if you know how to operate twelve, you can operate twenty-four (see Fig. **4.3**).

Selecting the Channel Input

At the top of the first channel strip, located on the left side of the example console, is the channel input selector (input section). This switch lets you choose between the two inputs feeding this particular channel, labeled A and B from the factory. For clarity and ease of operation, most stations have custom labels made indicating the actual radio station source, such as a CD player. Depending on the model, some console channels have as many as four different inputs to select from. After choosing an input to the channel, the next step is to use the output section of the channel strip and assign where you want the channel's audio to go after the level has been adjusted with the fader.

The Output or Assignment Section

Traditionally, on-air consoles have two main **buses** (common outputs) to which audio is assigned or routed, program and audition. The program bus generally feeds audio to the

Channel Input Selector

Output Section

INPUT

PGM   AUD

AUX1   AUX2

ASSIGN

Cue Switch

CUE

Unity Gain Position

Fader

Channel On/Off Switch

Figure 4.3

The easiest way to understand a console is to break it down into components, looking at just one channel strip at a time, top to bottom. The digital on-air console chosen as an example in this chapter has the appearance of an analog console. It has twelve identical channel strips; if you know how to operate one, you know how to operate all twelve.

radio station transmitter. Any channel with this button depressed is routed to the transmitter. The audition bus is an entirely separate circuit and is used to preview, or audition, audio on the studio monitor speakers without putting the audio on the air. The audition bus can also feed recorders, so that while the program bus is feeding the transmitter, the audition bus can be used to record a telephone call or other program elements.

The example console has two additional buses that audio can be assigned to, auxiliary one and two (again, see Fig. **4.3**). The outputs of these two buses can be sent anywhere the operator needs the additional audio feeds. For example, the auxiliary (aux) one bus might feed the telephone system so that talk-show callers can hear whatever console channels are assigned to that bus. The second auxiliary bus could be used to feed a station's **IFB (interruptible foldback** system) so that the on-air talent can talk to, or feed, an on-air signal to the remote talent's headphones during a live remote or sports broadcast. Using the example console, it is possible to route the signal from the channel to four separate places simultaneously, if necessary.

Listening In Cue

Continuing down the channel strip, the next button is the cue button. Cue is an isolated bus routed to a separate amplifier and speaker so that you can listen to a channel to preview music or check microphones before you put them on the air. When a channel is placed in cue, its signal cannot go over the air; cue is a part of the monitoring section of the console. Most cue speakers are small, crummy-sounding speakers placed in an odd location in the control room, such as behind the operator or under the desk the console is sitting on. The cue speaker might also be mounted in the con-

trol console. If an operator makes a mistake and inadvertently leaves a channel in cue that is supposed to go on the air, the odd sound from the tiny, crummy cue speaker alerts him or her to the error.

Consoles do not always have a cue button; instead, they may have "click-cue" faders. Click-cue faders, when turned all the way down, go one more notch and snap, or click, into the cue circuit.

Faders and Level Control

Often, instead of faders or level controls, the term **"pot"** is used. Pot is the abbreviation for the word potentiometer, the technical term for a volume control. Other terms for the volume control include attenuator, gain control, or just plain volume control.

There are basically two types of pots, rotary and faders. Rotary pots are round volume knobs that are turned in a clockwise/counterclockwise manner to raise and lower the volume. Faders are volume controls that require more space to operate, sliding a knob along a short linear scale. They are sometimes referred to as linear faders.

Looking back at the example console shown earlier, the fader slides along a linear scale to raise and lower the channel's audio volume. At about three quarters up the scale there is a simple dot or line with no numbers beside it. This mark is the **unity gain** position. Unity gain is an optimum audio level near 100 percent modulation and is preset by the station's engineer. This makes it very easy to run audio levels on the console. Later in the chapter, metering is discussed in detail.

Below the fader is the channel on/off switch. The switch can also be used to trigger remotely start/on and stop/off devices such as a CD or minidisc player or other digital playback source.

Monitoring Your Work

The monitor section controls what you hear in the control room monitor speakers and headphones. Monitoring levels should be set to a comfortable level in the control room. Keep in mind that your job is not to stand and listen to music, your job is to produce a radio show. Most beginning radio operators are surprised to find out how little music they listen to or even remember hearing during their show. A simple rule of thumb is to listen at an "office" level. You want to hear what is on the air, but you do not want it to dominate your control room since you are going to be doing other things in the control room while the music is playing, such as taking phone calls and talking to other staff coming and going from the control room.

Using our original example console (again, see Fig. **4.1**), there are multiple monitor inputs to select from on the monitor channel strips located on the right side of the console. In addition to the program, audition, and auxiliary buses one and two, often there is a cue and an external input. The external input is for an off-the-air monitor, referred to as an off-air signal. Any one of these sources can be listened to in the control room monitor speakers or headphones without affecting what is going on the air. Simply select the source and turn up the monitor speaker or headphone volume.

On-air talent use headphones to monitor with when they are talking on the air. The reason for this is that the moment the on-air microphone is turned on, the monitor speakers were muted (turned off) by the control board to prevent the **feedback** (the deafening howling sound that public-address systems sometimes produce) that would occur if the sound coming out of the monitor speakers were picked up by the control room microphone, fed back through the control board and broadcast transmitter, and back out of the monitor speakers into the microphone again in a vicious, screeching, never-ending circle.

Automatic muting of the monitoring speakers is a universal feature of broadcast control boards. Production control boards do not always have the feature and the operator has to turn the monitor speakers down manually before using the studio microphone.

A common beginner's error is listening to the program bus (what is coming out of the control board going to the transmitter) and not the actual air signal after it has been broadcast. When working in an on-air control room, your default monitor is always the actual air signal so that you are the first to know if there is a signal-quality problem or the station goes off the air. Many an operator has been embarrassed beyond belief when a station manager or chief engineer frantically entered the control room and the operator did not know the station was off the air. A station can go off the air for any number of reasons, including power outages, storms, lightning strikes, and so on. The point is, in an on-air control room, you should always listen to the off-the-air monitor.

On the right side of the example console, just before the monitor strip, is a telephone caller section. The operator can control the audio levels and monitor multiple telephone callers at once, ideal for talk shows or taking requests.

An additional feature of many consoles is an assignment switch for the console metering so that the meters can display any one of the audio buses, such as program or audition.

On-Air Operational Tips

Control consoles are pretty straightforward with regard to their functionality; they are all basically the same. The key to being able to handle any console is not to learn just the knobs and faders of one console but to understand the overall operational principles that have been discussed in this chapter, which you can then apply to all consoles. As an operator you are going to have to learn to "walk and chew gum at the same time" so that you can talk on the air and operate the console without really thinking about it. Given a little experience, operating a console is like riding a bicycle; they all have pedals and handlebars. The trick to smooth operation often lies in simple things that can make the job of the operator easier.

The first rule of working in a studio is never, ever, to take drinks, food, or lighted cigarettes into a control room. Sugar-saturated liquids and electricity do not mix. A soda spilled into a control board can cause thousands of dollars worth of damage and take the station off the air, costing thousands more in lost advertising revenue. Food is a real problem as crumbs find their way into equipment and greasy, sticky fingers leave fingerprints on control boards, computer keyboards, and computer touch screens. Cigarette smoke leaves a film on switch contacts and sensitive digital equipment, eventually causing equipment failure.

Although you might not get the final say in a console's layout, the operator's perspective is important. Talk to your station's operations director or engineer. From an operational standpoint, similar console inputs should be grouped together and logically arranged to assist the operator. We read left to right, so it is not unusual for a console to be laid out from left to right. For example, what is the most important input on the console? Your microphone is usually on pot 1. That is followed by any other microphones in the studio or adjoining studios. From this point on it is up to the engineer and the operations staff as to how the control board is laid out.

The simplest consoles to operate are those that have been laid out ergonomically, or in relation to the studio and operator. For example, if the CD decks are located on the left side of the console, locate the CD deck pots on the left side of the console, too. If the screen and computer keyboard for the music and commercial hard drives are located to the right, locate the pots for these to the right of the console as well. You don't want an unmarked mystery console; make sure your console is clearly marked as to the function of each channel strip, input, and output. The marking should be clear enough that someone who has never been in your studio can read the labels and figure out what is where on the console. This makes training new operators easier and makes it easier for part-time operators who may not have learned all of the "oh yeah, that's on that pot" locations.

As a side note, never mark or doodle on a console. Consoles are expensive. If you want to see an engineer get ugly, write on his or her console. We laughed pretty hard one day when our engineer caught an operator writing on a console and returned to the studio to write his name across the operator's forehead with a permanent marker. The operator got the message.

With regard to accepted operating procedures, follow some simple suggestions to avoid problems. Leave all of the pots you are not using closed, or down. This eliminates the chance of something you don't want to go on the air making it there, and it also reduces any noise that may be present in the source. When opening a mic, turn the mic on and then raise the level on the pot. Likewise, when closing a mic, lower the level and then turn the pot off. This avoids the noise of the switch getting on air and makes a smoother transition from the music to the acoustic environment of the studio.

Figure 4.4

As an operator, it is *your* responsibility to control the audio levels from the control board. Set too low, your station sounds weak on the air; too hot, or loud, and the station is distorted. Monitor your levels in accordance with your engineer's instructions. Typical readings should average 80 to 100 VU (volume units).

One of the biggest mistakes new operators and production people make is relying on their ears to tell how loud or soft a signal is. Studio monitor speakers *do not* allow you to judge audio levels accurately, since the speaker's volume can be adjusted up and down to compensate for low- or high-level audio. Always rely on the console meters to judge audio levels (see Fig. **4.4**). Metering is discussed in depth later in this chapter.

Most consoles are set up by the station engineer to run the pots at unity gain, or the three-quarters-open position. At these settings you should be seeing a reading of 80 to 100 VU (volume units) on the console's meters. As an operator, it is *your* responsibility to control the audio levels from the control board. Set too low, your station sounds weak on the air; too hot, or loud, and your station is distorted on the air. Monitor your levels in accordance with your engineer's instructions. The term for watching the levels and adjusting levels or gain as necessary is called "riding the gain."

Production Consoles in Depth

An on-air console is primarily designed for the control of playback levels. A production console is just the opposite; it is designed for creativity and manipulation of the audio in three dimensions within the stereo sound plane.

The three dimensions of sound include height, width, and depth. Using frequency equalization, or EQ, creates *height*, or a position for a sound either above or below various frequencies, sometimes referred to as "carving a hole" (see demo CD, cut 27). Using the panoramic control (pan) and panning sound sources from left to right, placing them at a given point within the sound image, creates *width* (see demo CD, cut 28). Reverbs and delays create a feeling of *depth* to sound, positioning it either at the forefront, close to the listener, or in the distance, depending on the timing of the effect (see demo CD, cut 29).

Production consoles vary greatly in price depending on the number of channels and the features offered. Consoles start at around $1,000, with prices going up proportionally for the various makes and models based on the number of faders and features.

For the purpose of definition, a production console has up to 32 faders and is available off the shelf, meaning that one can be ordered from a dealer and you can get delivery in a couple of weeks or sooner. Custom consoles with over 32 faders are classed as large mixing desks and are out of reach for most radio stations, as they can easily cost half a million dollars or more (see Fig. **4.5**). Generally, such large consoles are only found in recording studios or custom production houses.

However, as noted before, a high price does not necessarily mean the best console for a

Figure 4.5

Large mixing desks are usually custom designed for a particular studio and are out of reach for most radio stations, as they can easily cost half a million dollars or more. This particular console has 32 faders and 96 digital inputs. Generally, such large consoles are only found in recording studios or custom production houses.

particular job. The needs of the job must be matched to the functionality of the console. The example console in this chapter can meet the needs of a radio station or small production/post-production company and costs less than $1,500 (see Fig. **4.6**).

The In-Line Layout

Production consoles are typically in-line consoles. Each channel strip contains input and output routing, monitoring, equalization, and master output section controls. Each strip has individual inputs and outputs and can operate somewhat independently of the rest of the console. For example, a microphone can be plugged into a channel, and a direct output of that channel can be sent straight to a digital recorder, without the channel strip ever being routed to the master output section of the console. About the only limitation to a production console's flexibility is your imagination and creativity in routing signals.

The number of input channels, number of submasters, and number of master outputs is used to identify the production capability of a console. A $16 \times 4 \times 2$ console has 16 input channels, 4 submasters, and 2 master outputs for stereo. Submasters are used to group together a number of input channels so you can control them with one fader or a stereo fader pair.

Although models and name descriptions vary among manufacturers, most production consoles have many of the elements used in the chapter's example.

Patch Bay

Trim Control

Auxiliary Sends

Equalization Controls

Pan Control

Faders

Assignment Switches

Auxiliary Returns

Meters

Monitor Section

Master

Submasters

Figure 4.6

An excellent production console does not have to be expensive. This 16-channel console costs less than $1,500 and offers a number of professional features. It is quite popular with radio stations and small production/post-production companies.

Figure 4.7

A patch bay is a place to patch together, or route, signals in and out of a system. Patch bays are comprised of a jack field (female connectors) with system inputs and outputs on the jacks. Patch cords connect the jacks together, allowing the operator to route audio through the system easily.

The Input Section

Patch Bays and Routing Switchers: Getting Audio from Here to There

A patch bay is a place to patch together, or route, signals in and out of a system. Patch bays are comprised of a jack field (female connectors) with system inputs and outputs on the jacks. Using patch cords to connect the jacks together, the operator can route audio through the system easily. Often a patch bay is mounted in an equipment rack in the production room (see Fig. **4.7**).

A routing switcher is a microprocessor-based electronic patch bay to which all of the audio inputs and outputs have been wired and in which they have been assigned an input or output number. Using small terminals connected to the main router, you can route audio into your control board by simply punching in the source's number on the remote terminal. The router is mounted in an equipment rack in the engineering area of the radio station, with terminals located at each of the on-air or production control boards (see Fig. **4.8**).

In the case of the example console, it has a built-in patch bay on the back for convenience (again, see Fig. **4.6**). Either mic or line-level sources can be plugged into the console through the XLR or TRS connectors. The console's XLR connectors have 48-volt phantom power available that can be turned on and off, as needed, for condenser microphones.

Input Gain Staging

After a source has been plugged into the console, the first step in console setup is to gain stage the input. Before a signal reaches the input of the console preamplifier it typically passes through a trim, or volume, control. The trim control is usually at the top of the channel strip and is used to match the input level of the mixer to the output level of the source. Setting the trim level is very important in getting the best signal-to-noise ratio and so that you do not overload the console input and cause distortion. On the example console, the overload light next to the channel strip's fader comes on if the input to the channel is too high and the channel begins hard clipping. This is an immediate indication that you need to lower the trim level. Some consoles have a switchable pad instead

Figure 4.8

This routing switcher control head has two outputs that can be routed into a control board, A and B. Using the Input Select knob, you dial the input you want to route to your control board and then press the Take button and the connection is made.

of a trim control to boost or lower the audio input in fixed steps.

Channel Assignment and Routing

On the right side of each fader is the channel's routing, or assignment, switches that control where the audio from the channel goes. In this particular case, the choices are to send the channel's audio to the left/right channels of the main mix, to submasters one and two, or to submasters three and four.

Submasters one and two are a stereo pair of left (1) and right (2) channels. Likewise, submasters three and four are a stereo pair of left (3) and right (4) channels. Odd-numbered submaster channels are usually left channel and even-numbered submaster channels are usually right channel in a stereo mix.

Above the channel assignment switches is another assignment switch, labeled "solo." A solo assignment switch works independently of the other assignment switches. When a channel is placed in solo, all of the audio from the other channels is muted. The solo channel becomes the only channel that can be heard in the headphones or control room monitor speakers. Solo is handy for critically checking a channel or channels of audio.

Above the fader is the mute button, which is not an assignment switch per se. A mute button does the same thing as turning the channel fader to zero: it silences the output of the channel, regardless of how it is assigned or routed.

Controlling Audio Levels

Level control is accomplished with a linear, or sliding, fader. When the fader is drawn to the bottom of the linear scale, the fader is closed and does not allow any audio to pass from the channel strip. As with on-air consoles, there is a unity gain position marked at about three-quarters of the way up the linear scale on the fader. Provided the input trim on the channel has been properly adjusted, this should indicate the optimum level to work with. If the input level is too low, you may hear noise creeping into the signal due to the poor signal-to-noise ratio. If the level is too high, there's a good chance of hard clipping and audio distortion. The overload light (OL) next to the fader on the channel strip comes on if the channel begins hard clipping. In both cases, the input trim level needs to be adjusted (either up or down). It is best to follow a specific console manufacturer's guidelines for setting optimal trim levels.

Panoramic Control

The **pan** (panoramic) **control** permits the sonic positioning of a channel between the left and right stereo channels and works in conjunction with the left/right and other assignment switches. For example, if the left/right assignment switch is chosen to send the channel to the main stereo output, then turning the pan control to the far left or right places the audio on the left or right output channel. The same applies to the submaster one and two and submaster three and four assignment switches. Leaving the pan control in the center positions the sound equally between the left and right stereo channels, creating a mono, or single channel, feed. By carefully listening to the monitors, you can literally move a sound to any position located between the left and right speakers.

Shaping the Sound: Equalization

Usually, the EQ section of the channel strip is located above the pan pot. Equalization is the electronic process of altering a signal's frequency response by boosting or cutting certain frequencies (sophisticated bass and treble controls). Most consoles have equalization that is divided into three frequency bands: low, mid, and high. The example console provides up to fifteen decibels of boost or cut at 80 Hz for the low band, fifteen decibels of boost or cut at 12 kHz for the high band, and a sweepable (adjustable) midrange. Since the human ear is most sensitive to midrange frequencies, the midrange on the example console is adjustable from 100 Hz to 8 kHz and has fifteen decibels of boost or cut at the selected frequency.

Briefly, EQ is used to sweeten or correct minor problems with a mix and is covered in depth in chapter 6. Properly used, EQ can make a valuable contribution to a recording; improperly used, EQ can easily ruin a recording or project. Unless you have had specific training in this area, you would be wise to leave these controls set at their center, or neutral, positions.

Audio Filtering

In addition to EQ, many consoles have **high-pass filters** at around 75 Hz to eliminate very-low-frequency rumble and noise that may be present in a recording situation. High-pass filters allow only those frequencies *higher* than a specific frequency to pass the filter. Likewise, a **low-pass filter** is one at the high end of the frequency spectrum that allows only frequencies *lower* than a specific frequency to pass. On the console used as an example in this chapter, the manufacturer has chosen to simplify these often confusing terms by calling the filter that cuts everything below a specific frequency a low-cut filter. It is located just below the trim control at the top of the channel strip.

Unless you are recording a pipe organ, kick drum, bass guitar, synthesizer, or building rumble, or trying to record an earthquake, there is really not much below 75 Hz that contributes anything musically. The advantage to using a high-pass filter on sources other than those just listed is that when you do want to boost the low end it sounds much cleaner and tighter. This is because the high-pass filter has already eliminated the muddy sounding low-end rumble, leaving just cleanly recorded bass to work with.

Auxiliary Sends and Returns: Connecting Outboard Gear

Above the EQ controls are auxiliary (aux) send controls. An auxiliary send is an additional output from the individual channel used to send the channel's audio to an outboard signal processor or recorder, or to be used for a separate mix. An aux send taps into the audio on the channel and feeds the like-numbered auxiliary bus output. In the case of the example, each channel has six aux-send buses and is capable of sending the channel's audio to six different locations outside the mixer.

Naturally, if you use the aux send to route audio to an outboard signal processor, such as a reverb, you need a way to get the processed signal, with the reverb, back to include in the mix. This is accomplished using an aux return input to the console and the aux return level control (located on the upper right side of the example console) to assign the aux return to the main mix (again, see Fig. **4.6**). An unaltered audio signal being sent to an outboard processor is called a **dry signal,** and the returned signal, with the reverb or effect added, is called a **wet signal.**

There is one other feature of the aux sends that adds to their functionality. Aux sends have the option of tapping into the channel's audio before or after the fader. In the pre mode, an aux send taps into the audio before the fader, EQ, pan, and assignment switches. This provides a signal straight out of the pre-amp, which the console operation cannot affect in any way. A "post-aux" send taps into the audio after the fader and before the pan and assignment switches. This provides a signal over which the fader has level control. The pre-select switch is located below the aux 2 send on each channel strip.

Metering: Being Able to See Audio

Why You Must Watch the Meter

I mentioned this earlier in the chapter, but it's worth bringing up again: one of the biggest mistakes new operators and production people make is to rely on their ears to tell how loud or soft a signal is. Just as pilots are taught to rely on their instruments, you have to learn to rely on your audio meters to verify actual audio levels. Otherwise, you will crash and burn like a pilot in a storm. Production studio monitors *do not, cannot, and will not* allow you to judge audio levels accurately, since the speaker's volume can be adjusted up and down to compensate for low- or high-level audio signals.

Many a production person, with speakers blaring, has said "it sounds fine to me," only to be asked by the production director to look at the control board meters, where the audio level is barely registering. Proper audio levels are adjusted by *FIRST* observing the meters and setting the audio level, and then adjusting the monitor speakers to a comfortable listening level. Always refer to the meters to observe or set levels. Failure to rely on audio meters has ruined many a commercial and program.

VU Meters

Metering the audio in any console is a challenge. The problem lies in developing a mechanical (or other) device to represent accurately the audio, which is constantly varying as a quantity. In 1939, during the early days of radio, Bell Labs, NBC, and CBS agreed on a standard method to measure audio levels called the VU, or volume unit. The volume unit is an electrical measurement to indicate audio level in relation to human hearing and

Figure 4.9

A VU meter has two scales; the upper scale shows volume units listed from –20 VU, through 0, to +3 VU. The lower scale is the percent of modulation. At levels above 0 VU, distortion and clipping are likely.

how we perceive the loudness of sound. A VU meter is essentially a calibrated voltage meter through which the audio passes, with a mechanical needle moving back and forth to indicate the voltage or audio level.

The meter has two scales; the upper scale shows volume units, listed from –20 VU, through 0, to +3 VU. Typically, the meter's scale above 0 VU is red. The red area of the meter indicates levels that are likely to cause distortion and clipping. The lower scale is the percent of modulation (see Fig. **4.9**).

The word modulation means change. Modulation is measured in percentages; it represents the percent change in the audio signal. Zero percent modulation is no change, or no audio. In theory, 100 percent modulation is the maximum change that can occur without damage to the audio signal. Beyond 100 percent modulation, the audio distorts at some point; eventually, it hard clips.

The two different scales on the VU meter are calibrated so that –20 VU is equal to 0 percent modulation and 0 VU is equal to 100 percent modulation. Signals that indicate below –15 VU, or about 20 percent modulation, are considered too weak to be of any practical value. At the opposite end of the scale, audio driven past 0 VU, or 100 percent modulation, is "into the red" and in danger of distorting and clipping. Audio that is driven so hard that it pins the needle to the far right, past +3 VU, is called "gone," in that it consists of nothing but distortion and hard clipping. (Aside from the problems this causes in the audio itself, such abuse can make the needle stick or damage the meter.) VU meters display *average* audio levels, since it is physically impossible for the meter's needle to track accurately the instantaneous audio level changes in the signal.

To combat transients and instantaneous audio peaks that can surprise anyone, manufacturers build **headroom** into the console. Headroom is the difference between the normal operating levels and the point when distortion (clipping) starts to occur in the console. Because of this safety net, it is OK to allow *occasional* peaks into the red area of the VU, since there is some headroom before actual distortion occurs.

A production person has to keep in mind that although it is fine to push the limit sometimes in analog recording, pushing the limit in digital recording with a VU meter will certainly get you into trouble. This is because the VU meter only shows *average* levels and cannot physically move fast enough to show instantaneous audio peaks, which can cause digital audio to break up. A good guide to follow when recording digital audio using a VU meter is to keep average levels at about –10 VU, to allow enough headroom for transients and instantaneous audio peaks that might occur. Digital recording techniques are discussed in detail in chapter 5.

Peak Meters

VU meters are preferred in the United States. In Europe, the peak program meter, or ppm, is

Figure 4.10

A VU meter only displays average audio levels, whereas the peak meter above displays signal peaks, or the absolute maximum signal level present. A peak meter is well suited for digital recording because it indicates the maximum signal level so that digital overloads, or splatter, can be avoided. Unlike the VU meter, the peak meter is calibrated only in decibels.

the preferred method of metering audio. Although the VU meter displays only average levels, the peak meter displays the signal peaks, or the absolute maximum signal level present. This is the kind of meter best suited for digital recording, because by indicating the peak signal levels it allows you to avoid digital overloads, or splatter. Unlike the VU meter, the peak meter is calibrated only in decibels (see Fig. **4.10**).

Electronic Bar-Graph Metering

Any VU or peak program meter that depends on a moving needle to indicate levels is at a distinct physical disadvantage from the very start. It is limited by the laws of physics as to how fast the needle can go in one direction, stop, and instantly reverse. Liquid crystal, plasma, and LED (light-emitting diode) displays do away with the bouncing needle; they rely on an electronic display that reacts virtually instantly (see Fig. **4.11**).

An LED meter has a row of LEDs arranged in a vertical or horizontal pattern. As the signal passes through the meter, the LEDs range from green to red. The green LEDs indicate an acceptable audio level and the red LEDs indicate an overload. Each LED is marked on either a VU or peak scale. An LED meter can be quite accurate.

An LCD (liquid crystal display) or plasma display is basically the same as a laptop computer screen. The meter is a graphic display and can indicate VU or peak program levels. Many larger consoles with plasma displays offer a programmable selection of VU, peak program, or both types of metering simultaneously (see Fig. **4.12**).

Hearing Your Work: The Monitor Section

It is critical that you be able to hear your work accurately. The monitor section of a control board provides you the controls to do just that. The one control that can get you into the most trouble is the monitor volume control for either the headphones or monitor speakers.

Many beginners like to work with the monitors "cranked" (nearly loud enough to tear

Figure 4.11

A bar-graph LED meter has a row of LEDs (light-emitting diodes) arranged in a vertical or horizontal pattern. Unlike the moving needle of a standard VU meter, an LED bar-graph meter can react instantaneously to changes in the audio signal and can be extremely accurate.

As with an on-air console, assignment switches on the monitor section determine what audio source is sent to the monitor speakers and headphones. Using the example console (again, see Fig. **4.6**), the operator can choose to listen to audio from submaster pair one and two, three and four, or the main mix. The operator can also choose to monitor the return feed from a digital recorder, in other words, to listen to the audio *after* it has been recorded in real time to ensure it has been properly recorded.

All of these controls are overridden any time the solo switch is depressed, and the selected solo channel, or channels, appears on the monitors exclusive of any other sound.

The Master Section: Controlling the Final Console Output

Mastering is the final stage of audio production. It involves tweaking and making adjustments to the mix so that it sounds exactly as you, or the client, wants it to. During a mastering session the project is listened to critically. Final editing adjustments are made, the mix levels are fine-tuned, and the left/right stereo balance is adjusted to deliver the overall sound picture you are shooting for.

The master section of the console consists of the submaster and master faders. Submasters are used to group together channels that the operator wants to control with one fader or a stereo pair of faders. As an example, in a recording studio five microphones on a drum set are mixed using five different console channels, one channel for each microphone. All five channels are then assigned to the same submaster stereo pair so that the stereo fader can raise and lower the overall level of the entire drum set. In turn, each submaster is assigned to the right- or left-channel master in a stereo mix.

your clothes off). Big mistake. Learn to monitor your work at lower levels. Your listeners are not listening on studio monitors and certainly not at the levels you can listen at. And although it may seem easier to hear everything in the mix at louder levels, a good rule of thumb is to mix at a low level to make sure that everything in the mix can be heard clearly at that level. Most importantly, the voice needs to stand out above the mix.

Figure 4.12

An LCD (liquid crystal display) is basically the same as a laptop computer screen. The meter is a graphic display and can indicate VU or peak program levels. Many larger consoles with plasma displays offer a programmable selection of VU, peak program, or both types of metering simultaneously.

In the case of the example console, each of the sixteen channels can be assigned to one of the four submasters and each of the four submasters can be assigned to either the left or right master output faders. The master faders control which audio finally leaves the console and enters the recorder or some other device.

Console Automation

By now, the question may have occurred to you: if there are more than just a few faders on a console, how in the world can one person handle all those faders simultaneously during a mix?

Console automation is an advanced feature that is generally found on digital and some larger analog consoles. Automation digitally records the physical movements of each channel strip's controls, including the movement of the fader, mute, pan, EQ, filters, solo, and so forth. In the automation write mode, as you adjust each channel's level, a microprocessor records the control board movements you are making and translates them into stored computer data. If you don't get a perfect mix the first time, you can go back and do it again, rewriting or re-recording the automation for that particular channel over and over until you are happy. In the read mode, the automa-

Figure 4.13

Digital audio workstations use virtual audio consoles as a part of their operating software. Virtual consoles look and function similarly to their physical counterparts. The primary difference is that a virtual console is controlled by a keyboard, a mouse, or an outboard control surface.

tion plays back the audio and all of your recorded control movements that go along with the music.

This "one channel at a time" method of automation is how producers are able to create complex mixes involving numerous tracks of music, sound effects, dialogue, and other audio. There is nothing more incredible than watching a console literally come to life with all of its controls and faders moving on their own during the automated playback of a complicated mix. Automation is also a feature of digital audio workstations that is covered in detail later in chapter 5.

Virtual Control Consoles

Digital audio is nothing more than computer data. As such, it is quite easy for a digital audio workstation to record, mix, and edit digital audio. Digital audio workstations use virtual audio consoles as a part of their operating software (see Fig. **4.13**). Virtual consoles look and function similarly to their physical counterparts. The primary difference is that a virtual console is controlled by a keyboard, a mouse, or an outboard control surface.

An outboard control surface is a physical representation of software controls on the computer screen. Some operators prefer to use keyboard shortcuts, others a mouse or trackball, and some prefer the control surface to run the software. It is a matter of personal choice.

An outboard control surface is a physical representation of what is on the computer screen (see Fig. **4.14**). Move a control surface fader up and down and the corresponding fader on the computer screen moves up and down. Some operators prefer to use keyboard shortcuts, others a mouse or trackball, and some prefer the control surface. It is a matter of personal choice. Virtual consoles within digital audio workstations are commonplace in recording and production studios.

A logical extension of a virtual console is to use one to replace the physical console in a radio or television studio. It is not difficult for a computer to emulate all of the functions of a broadcast console. Physical control is with a keyboard, mouse, trackball, or touch screen.

Virtual consoles offer a number of functional, operational, and cost-saving advantages. The biggest obstacle to the use of virtual consoles in radio control rooms is operator training. Those who are accustomed to a physical control board tend to be set in their ways and not easily swayed to change. People new to the industry tend to accept virtual consoles and find them easy to use (see Fig. **4.15**).

Portable Mixers

Overview

Size does not matter. Portable field mixers are the smallest of all of the audio control consoles and, despite their very compact size, offer many of the same features and audio quality as do much larger control consoles. Although often referred to simply as "mic mixers," most field mixers offer a choice between mic or line-level inputs. Portable mixers can be either mono or stereo.

Two of the several major advantages portable mixers offer are that they are small and that they are built like tanks. Most are housed in steel or machined aircraft-aluminum enclosures. Portable mixers are able to run for several hours off internal battery power or can be plugged in with a **wall-wart** power supply. On long remote broadcasts, where AC power is not readily available, techs often power portable mixers

Figure 4.15

Although this studio has a standard radio console, it also has a virtual console that is operated by a touch screen. Notice that all of the faders on the control board are turned down. The biggest obstacle to the use of virtual consoles is operator training. People new to the industry tend to accept virtual consoles and find them easy to use.

Portable mixers tend to be expensive because of all of their advanced features and their small size. Prices for a quality portable mixer, such as the stereo example used in this chapter, start at about $1,900 and go to over $4,000, depending on the number of inputs and features (see Fig. **4.16**).

The Portable-Mixer Input Stage

Using our example portable mixer, audio enters through the switchable mic or line-level-balanced XLR inputs on the left side and is routed to the preamplifier, whose output is controlled by a pot. Although many portable mixers have sliding faders, the most compact portable field mixers use rotary pots to save space.

At the pot you have two sets of choices. The first concerns frequency: either the frequency response of the signal is left flat, or a selector switch rolls off (turns down) the frequencies below 150 Hz. The roll-off switch is located to the lower right of each pot and is marked with a flat line for flat frequency response and a line that drops off to indicate the roll-off position. The roll-off feature can be particularly useful in a location where there is a lot of low-frequency background noise and rumble you don't want to muddy your recording.

The second choice you can make at the pot concerns the sonic placement of the microphone within a stereo image. The pot's pan control, located directly above each pot, allows the pot's input to be assigned to the left channel, to the right channel, or to remain in the center channel for a mono signal. If the three channels offered are not enough mixing capability, two of the mixers can be linked together by a bridging cable that connects the two, providing six channels to mix with.

with deep-cycle marine batteries that are similar to car batteries. Additionally, most professional mixers can provide 48-volt phantom power for condenser microphones.

Portable mixers are used extensively in radio for remote broadcasts from sponsors' businesses, sports broadcasts, and major breaking news stories. Because the mixers have so much built-in flexibility, about the only limitation to their use is the producer's imagination.

Tone Generator Switch

Peak Limiter
On/Off Switch

Slate Marker Button

Pan Control

Mic or Line-Level Output

Headphone Jack

Mic or Line-Level Inputs

Power On/Off Switch

Frequency Roll-Off Switch

Headphone Monitor Switch

Master Level Control

Rotary Pots
(volume controls)

Figure 4.16

Portable mixers are very compact and offer many of the same features found on larger consoles. Mixers are used for station remotes, sportscasts, and for location news coverage.

The Portable Mixer Output Stage

When audio leaves the pot, it is routed to the master output-level controls. To save space and keep the mixer as compact as possible, a "knob within a knob," located to the left of the meters, is used to control the left- and right-channel master volumes so the stereo pair can be evenly balanced. The master output levels are routed through the meters and finally to the mixer outputs. The left and right outputs on the right side of the mixer can be switched between balanced mic or line level, depending on what equipment the mixer is feeding.

Additional Features on Portable Mixers

Tone Generator

Other features of portable mixers include a 1 kHz tone generator to send a reference tone

to recorders or any other devices connected to the mixer output, so that all of the equipment can be adjusted to operate at the same audio level. On our example (again, see Fig. **4.6**), pulling out the pot one control knob activates the tone generator, and the level is adjusted using the pot.

Slate Marker

A **slate** button at the upper right corner of the meter on the example mixer generates a one-second-long 400 Hz tone and activates an electret-condenser microphone, the slate mic, built into the front of the mixer, which feeds directly to the mixer output. The operator can slate the take, in other words, record important identifying information about the take on the recorder for later reference. Another use of a slate mic is to feed an intercom system so that the field producer can talk with the main control room operator during a live remote broadcast.

Limiter

Located to the lower right of the master volume control on the example mixer is the limiter switch, labeled PEAK/LIM (again, see Fig. **4.6**). A limiter acts as an automatic volume control to prevent overload. If the audio level suddenly spikes too high, the limiter turns it down to a safe level. This feature is intended to help an operator avoid hard clipping, or distorted audio, due to transients and sudden level changes. The operator has the choice of switching the limiter on or off.

The Portable Mixer Monitoring Stage

Location monitoring is usually done with a pair of headphones plugged into the headphone output (on the right side of the example mixer). The headphones can be switched to monitor the left channel only, right channel only, left plus right channel (mono), or stereo. Normally, a radio station sets up a public address system at live remotes and plays the station's air signal directly from a radio. However, in some unusual circumstances, such as when you are outside your station's signal coverage area, it is customary to feed the mixer output to the public address system so that listeners can hear playback of the broadcast.

Monitors

While you are on-air, and during the production process, as we already mentioned in talking about the monitor section of the control board, you have to be able to hear accurately what you are working on. Monitor speakers are the preferred method for studio work, and headphones are the choice for studio talent and location work. For remotes, however, radio stations often use portable monitor/public address speakers.

Monitor Speakers

It has already been established that there is no such thing as the best microphone; likewise, there is no such thing as the best monitor speaker. Just as you try to select the best microphone for a given job, an engineer tries to select the best monitor speaker for the job. The audio chain, including the microphone, preamplifier, control console amplifier, audio processor, digital recorder, and speaker amplifier—even the speaker cable—all depend on the monitor speaker to change electrical energy back into acoustic energy that you can hear as sound. Although you probably will not get to choose the monitor speakers used in your radio station, or where to place them in your studio, you should be familiar with how speakers function so that you are more able to judge your work accurately.

One of the very first pieces of equipment budgeted for in building a studio, and one that often gets a good portion of the budget, is the monitor-speaker system. The speakers are the direct link to your ears. Just as the microphone was critical in capturing the sound, the speaker is even more critical in playing back the sound; it is imperative that you accurately hear what you have recorded.

Most radio production studios work with a single set of **near-field monitors** or speakers. Near-field speakers are bookshelf-sized and are extremely accurate in their sound reproduction (see Fig. **4.17**). They are designed for

Figure 4.17

This production studio has a single set of near-field monitors or speakers. Near-field speakers are bookshelf-sized and are extremely accurate in their sound reproduction. Near-field monitors are designed for smaller rooms, where the producer sits closer to the speaker.

smaller rooms, where the producer sits closer to the speaker. Some stations also use a set of small, full-range, speakers to emulate the "at work" or "in car" listener's environment. Such small speakers are often referred to as "cubes" because the speaker cabinet is shaped like a small cube measuring just a few inches on each side.

In addition, extremely critical production people often take test mixes on CD to the parking lot and listen to them on several different car stereos. By using different monitor speakers, a production person is able to judge how the end product is going to sound to the consumer.

How Monitor Speakers Work

Chances are you are never going to build a set of speakers, but you should be familiar with how they work and understand the terms associated with them so that you can better judge the accuracy of a speaker. A microphone is the start of the audio chain, and the monitor speaker is at the end of the audio chain. Interestingly, both microphones and monitor speakers are transducers that change one form of energy into another. In the case of a monitor speaker, it converts electrical energy into acoustic energy (see Fig. **4.18**). In simplest terms, a monitor speaker is a giant dynamic microphone

Front Speaker Suspension

Speaker Terminals with Flexible Wire to the Voice-Coil

Speaker Cone

Permanent Magnet Structure

Voice-Coil

Voice-Coil Dust Cover

Rear Suspension

Metal Frame

Figure 4.18

Microphones and monitor speakers are both transducers that change one form of energy into another. In the case of a monitor speaker, it converts electrical energy into acoustic energy. In simplest terms, a monitor speaker is a giant dynamic microphone working in reverse.

working in reverse. Just like microphones, monitor speakers are judged by a set of specifications and how they sound to your golden ears.

A speaker typically features a bowl- or dish-shaped speaker cone that comes in various sizes, depending on the application. Attached to the back of the speaker cone is a coil of wire suspended within a large permanent-magnet structure mounted on the back of the speaker. When audio is sent to the speaker, the voltage enters and travels through the speaker coil. When a coil of wire is charged with electricity, it becomes an electromagnet, and when two magnetic fields are placed near one another, one of two things happens—the two either attract one another or they repel one another. As the magnetic field of the speaker coil pushes away from the speaker's permanent magnet, the speaker cone moves forward, setting air molecules in motion and creating compaction. When the speaker cone moves backward, it reduces air pressure, creating rarefaction. These cycles of back-and-forth movement of the speaker cone correspond to the analog electrical waveforms and cause the speaker to create sound waves.

Woofers and Tweeters

As you learned in chapter 2, different frequencies have different properties and sound wavelengths. It is very difficult, if not impossible, to design one speaker assembly that can reproduce all of the frequencies equally, or with a flat frequency response. By dividing the audio frequency spectrum into different bands and directing the audio to different speaker designs within the same cabinet, the frequency response of a monitor speaker can be made much more accurate. The individual speakers within a speaker cabinet are referred to as **drivers.**

The simplest division that can be made in a speaker is between bass and treble, or the low end and the high end of the frequency spectrum. The low end of the frequency spectrum, or bass, requires more power and a larger physical structure to create the long, low-frequency wavelengths. These larger, more powerful, speakers are called *woofers.* Practical woofers range in size from six to fifteen inches in diameter, with permanent-magnet structures that can weigh more than fifty pounds (see Fig. **4.19**).

The high end of the frequency spectrum, or treble, requires much less power and a smaller physical structure to create the high-frequency wavelengths. These smaller, less-powerful, speakers are called *tweeters.* Practical tweeters range in size from three-quarters of an inch to two inches in diameter, with much smaller magnet structures than woofers. Tweeters can be dish- or bowl-shaped, like the woofer, or they can be just the opposite, and be shaped like a dome; it's the designer's choice (again, see Fig. **4.19**).

Both the woofer and the tweeter are typically housed in the same speaker cabinet, with the tweeter located above the woofer on the speaker face. The size of the speakers varies greatly, based upon the decibels of sound pressure that the designer wants them to be able to reproduce. Bigger is not always better, though. As an example, using exotic materials such as titanium, carbon fiber, or other synthetic materials for the speaker cone, designers can produce an incredibly strong and physically small monitor speaker. The smaller, stronger drivers can handle large amounts of power and generate over 105 decibels of sound pressure.

The Crossover Network

The number of drivers within a single speaker cabinet identifies the type of speaker system.

Figure 4.19

The larger, more powerful, speaker is called a woofer. Practical woofers range in size from six to fifteen inches in diameter, with permanent-magnet structures that can weigh more than fifty pounds. The smaller, less powerful, speaker is called a tweeter. Practical tweeters range in size from three-quarters of an inch to two inches in diameter, with much smaller magnet structures than woofers.

A two-way system has a woofer and a tweeter. A three-way system has a woofer, tweeter, and a midrange driver to handle the middle frequencies (see Fig. 4.20).

Dividing the audio from the amplifier to send it to the appropriate driver within a speaker is the job of the crossover network. A crossover is an electronic circuit that splits the audio frequencies and routes them to the proper speaker, so that the bass goes to the woofer and the higher frequencies go to the tweeter. The actual frequency that is used as the dividing point is called the crossover frequency.

The crossover that divides the frequencies can be passive or active. A **passive crossover** network is comprised of fixed-value electronic components. The crossover frequencies are fixed and cannot be changed. A passive crossover is located within the speaker cabinet.

An **active crossover** network allows the user to change the crossover frequency to suit his or her tastes or particular acoustical needs by adjusting a knob or electronic control. An active crossover requires electrical power and can be mounted within the speaker or as an outboard piece of rack-mounted gear.

Figure 4.20

The number of drivers within a single speaker cabinet identifies the type of speaker system. A two-way system (left) has a woofer and a tweeter. A three-way system (right) has a woofer, tweeter, and a midrange driver to handle the middle frequencies.

Self-Powered Monitor Speakers

A traditional monitor-speaker setup feeds a signal from the control board to an amplifier and through speaker cable to the monitor speaker. **Self-powered** monitor **speakers** are self-contained monitors that include the power amplifiers mounted on or within the speaker cabinet.

Powered speakers have specially designed amplifiers matched to each of the drivers in the speaker. For example, in a two-way speaker system, there is an amplifier for the woofer and a separate one for the tweeter, or bi-amplification. In a three-way system it is tri-amplification.

An advantage of the powered monitor speaker is that the amplifier power ratings are matched to each specific driver. Most professional studio monitor speaker systems use bi- or tri-amplification.

Monitor Speaker Placement and Stereo Imaging

Ideally, monitor speakers should be at the mixer's ear level and should be centered in front of the mixing position at the console. Where should you sit in the studio to get the most accurate stereo image from your monitors? Stereo uses two channels of audio and two matched speakers to create a lifelike

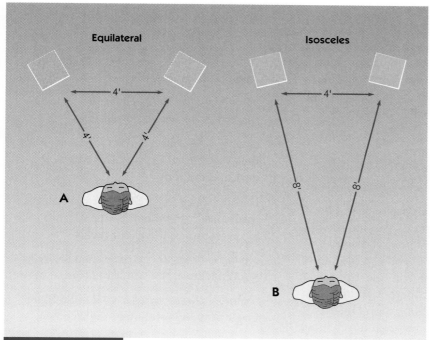

Figure 4.21

For a tight space, use a simple equilateral triangle as a guide (A). If the speakers are four feet apart, then the ideal listening position is centered between the two speakers, four feet from each, forming the triangle. For a wider overall sound field, double the distance between the two speakers to the mixing position (B). Using example A, if the speakers are four feet apart, then a wider sound field is centered between the two speakers, eight feet from each, forming the stretched, or isosceles, triangle found in example B.

sound field comprised of width and depth. As you learned earlier in this chapter, panning sound sources from left to right and placing them at a given point within the sound field creates width. Reverbs and delays create a feeling of depth to sound, positioning it either at the forefront, close to the listener, or in the distance, depending on the timing of the effect. Equalization can give height to a sound by placing it above or below other sounds.

For a tight space, use a simple equilateral triangle as a guide. If the speakers are four feet apart, then the ideal listening position is at a point equally distant from both speakers, four feet from each, forming the triangle (see Fig. 4.21). Ideally, the speakers are angled inward and focused directly on the listener. The only drawback to this position is that the proper stereo image appears only in a very narrow area and the mixer can easily move out of the sweet spot just by turning his or her head. If more than one person needs to listen to this setup, the speakers should be angled outward to enlarge the sweet spot.

For a wider overall sound field, double the distance between the two speakers to get the distance from the speakers to the mixing position. Using the preceding example, if the speakers are four feet apart, then a wider sound field is eight feet from each, forming a stretched, or isosceles, triangle (again, see Fig. **4.21**). This position is not as sensitive to the movement of the mixer as is the simple equilateral triangle.

Suggested Activities

1. Seek out the different types of portable mixers and control boards you have available to you as a part of your class work. Spend time with each. While speaking into a microphone, route it from the input to the output using the different audio buses available. On production control boards, route the microphone through the channel assignments to the submasters and masters. Likewise, experiment with the different monitoring options that you have.
2. Find an example of as many different kinds of audio meters as you can and do a comparison of how they display your voice. Which do you prefer, mechanical meters or LED meters?
3. With a pair of stereo speakers, experiment with listener placement using an equilateral triangle and an isosceles triangle placement. Which gives you the best stereo image in your listening environment?
4. Arrange for tours of a radio station, television station, and recording studio to see firsthand what the different types of control boards and mixing desks look like and how they are used in the different facilities. Ask ahead of time if they will let you bring a reference CD that you are familiar with so that you can play a track to hear on their monitors.

Web Sites for More Information

For information about:

- *monitor speakers and placement of monitor speakers*, visit www.genelec.com
- *on-air consoles for radio and television*, visit the Wheatstone Corporation at www.wheatstone.com
- *portable mixers*, visit Shure at www.shure.com and Professional Sound Corporation at www.professionalsound.com
- *production consoles for radio and television*, visit Mackie at www.mackie.com
- *recording studio consoles*, visit Solid State Logic at www.solid-state-logic.com

Pro Speak

You should be able to use these terms in your everyday conversations with other professionals.

active crossover—A powered speaker crossover network with adjustable crossover frequencies.

bus—A common point in an audio device into which several inputs feed and are joined together.

combo mode—When the on-air radio talent serves as the show's engineer as well, running the control board and other elements of the show in addition to announcing.

driver—An individual speaker within a speaker cabinet; each driver consists of a moving-coil transducer that converts analog electrical energy into acoustic energy.

dry signal—An original, unprocessed audio signal being sent from an audio console to an outboard audio processor, such as a reverb or delay unit.

feedback—A condition that occurs when a microphone is left open near a monitor speaker, creating a loud howling or whistling sound. The microphone picks up the amplified sound from the speaker and sends it back through the system, regenerating the signal over and over.

hard clipping—An audio condition in which the audio is driven beyond distortion to the point that the edges of the sine waves start breaking up.

headroom—The additional capacity of an audio device to handle level increases above average working levels to protect from transients, overload, and distortion.

high-pass filter—A filter that blocks audio frequencies below a specific frequency, allowing those frequencies above the specified frequency to pass.

interruptible foldback (IFB)—A type of intercom or communications system that allows the control board operator or producer to talk to the talent.

low-pass filter—A filter that blocks audio frequencies above a specific frequency, allowing those frequencies below the specified frequency to pass.

near-field monitors—Smaller monitor speakers placed very near the mixing position, often at the front of the console.

pan control—Panoramic control, a sonic positioning control that allows the input to a mixer channel to be assigned to the left channel or the right channel, or to remain in the center channel for a mono signal.

passive crossover—A crossover network comprised of electronic components whose values are fixed, with the audio requiring no electrical power to pass through the network.

pot—Pot is the abbreviation for the word potentiometer, which is the technical term for a volume control.

self-powered speakers—Speakers that have amplifiers built into them so that an audio feed from a mixer or control board can be fed directly into the speaker.

slate—The radio equivalent of the beginning of a scene in a television or film shoot, when someone holds a slate, or "clapboard," in front of a camera with the production name, scene number, take number, roll number, director, producer and date, to identify the material later. In radio, this is done audibly, with a slate mic, so that a production person can identify the audio cuts.

unity gain—A gain of one; the position on a fader at which the ideal operating level of 0 VU (volume units) occurs. A device with unity gain does not raise or lower the volume, or gain, of a signal.

wall-wart—A self-contained power supply for running portable equipment. It plugs directly into the wall and down-converts 110 volts AC to a DC voltage.

wet signal—A processed audio signal that is returning to a control board after audio processing such as reverb or delay.

CHAPTER 5

Basic Concepts in Digital Recording

HIGHLIGHTS

Recording in the Digital Domain

Digital Audio Workstations:
Using a Computer as a Recorder

Project Backup and Storage

The Digital Recording Process

Digital Recording Media

Suggested Activities

Web Sites for More Information

Pro Speak

We live in an analog world, a natural world in which all of the sounds that we perceive are made up of sound waves. But since Harry Nyquist's early work at the Bell Labs in the late 1920s, the theories behind digital audio have been based not on nature's sound waves but on binary mathematical principles developed in the 1700s. In fact, Nyquist was so far ahead of the game in the 1920s that his theory could not even be tested until the invention of the transistor in 1947!

Although analog audio is fairly simple and remained relatively unchanged for more than fifty years, digital audio changes as fast as hardware and software developers can come up with new gear to help make the production person more efficient. Because of its incredible scalability and flexibility, digital audio is more technically involved. After all, we're talking computers and data. However, the basic principles of digital audio apply across a broad spectrum of equipment and production techniques. In this chapter you are going to get to work with the raw audio from a multitrack studio recording session. The music was especially written and recorded for this chapter so that you could learn about recording, storing, manipulating, transporting, and delivering digital audio.

Recording in the Digital Domain

In earlier chapters, you learned the basics of how to select a microphone, place it, cable it, and route it through a preamplifier into the control board. The next stage in the production process is to learn the basics of the digital recording process.

Recording

The first step in recording involves routing the signal into a recorder and "laying down," or recording, the various tracks. The primary goal of recording any sound is to find the sweet spot with the microphone that most accurately captures the essence of the live sound; technically, you're after the best signal-to-noise ratio. Likewise, if you are recording music CDs, sports broadcasts, or a news or public affairs program, your goal is to capture the sound at a good usable level. As we pointed out in chapter 4, it is critical in digital recording that you rely on your VU or peak meters to adjust the recording levels.

During the initial recording session, your only goal is to capture the sound accurately; editing, mixing, and final mastering are done later, in post-production. As a radio production person, most of the time you are going to be a one-person band serving as the recording engineer, mixer, and mastering engineer. Occasionally, you might receive help from the production director with fine-tuning or tweaking a mix, to ensure that a commercial or program captures the essence of what the client wants.

A word of caution is in order if you are new to digital recording. When audio is fed into a digital recorder, it's important to make the best use of the recorder's available dynamic range. A recorder's dynamic range is measured in decibels and extends from the softest sound to the loudest sound the recorder is capable of recording. Set the recording level too low, and background noise and hiss become noticeable. Set the recording level too hot (loud), and the signal overdrives the inputs, resulting in hard clipping and seriously distorted audio. In a worst-case situation, the audio splatters and drops out.

The input audio level should register as high as possible on the meters without caus-

Figure 5.1

It does not look like much signal level, but a good rule of thumb for recording *digital* audio is that the average audio levels should be at about −10 on a VU meter, so that the audio peaks present in the signal have the necessary headroom to record without driving the recorder into hard clipping.

ing clipping or driving the meters into the red. A good rule of thumb for recording digital audio is that the average audio levels should be at about −10 on a VU meter, so that the audio peaks present in the signal have the necessary headroom to record without driving the recorder into hard clipping (see Fig. **5.1**).

Digital audio workstations **(DAW)** have two recording modes, nondestructive and destructive. In the nondestructive mode, each time a track is placed into record, the DAW automatically labels and saves the previous recording prior to the start of the new recording. In other words, nothing is erased; you can keep recording takes over and over until you are satisfied, and should you desire to, you can return to any one of the earlier saved takes. Destructive recording is just what the name implies; each time a track is placed into record, any previously recorded material on that track is recorded over and is lost or destroyed.

When you have completed either type of recording (nondestructive or destructive), always "safe" the recorder, locking it out of the record mode, so there is no chance of the recorder being accidentally enabled and recording over your work. Multitrack recorders let you do this on a track-by-track basis as you work on a project.

Editing

If there is one incredible feature of digital recording that just seems to jump out at you, it has to be the ease with which one can edit. Editing is the ability to cut, paste, and copy audio, just as you would do with a word processor for a paper or any other piece of writing.

What makes digital audio editing so attractive is that not only do you get to listen to the audio to pick an edit-point, but you can see the audio waveform displayed on the DAW (see Fig. **5.2**). Although we depend on our ears to hear, most people (even musicians) rely on sight as their primary sense. Using the visual display, it is possible to zoom in or out on the waveform and select the particular point to make the edit, right down to a point within a single sine wave (see Fig. **5.3**).

DAW editing, as opposed to recording, is known as nondestructive editing, because although you may be cutting, pasting, and copying on the visual display, absolutely nothing is physically happening to the original audio on the hard drive. The audio is never physically cut or moved about on the hard drive. Manipulating the visual display is how you write the computer commands that tell the hard drive what audio segments to play back and in what sequence. Of course, just as with every other edit function on a computer, if you make an error while editing prior to saving the session, there is always the Undo command on the menu bar.

Mixing

Mixing is the art of adjusting the audio levels of each of the recorded tracks and blending them to create the sound picture you or the client is seeking. Although it may seem a bit unusual, most production people already have some vision in their heads of the final

Figure 5.2

Although we depend on our ears to hear, most people (even musicians) rely on sight as their primary sense. The visual display is used to examine the waveform and select a particular point to make an edit or some other adjustment to the audio. *Adobe product screen shot reprinted with permission from Adobe Systems Incorporated.*

mix or sound they want, before they sit down at the console to mix a project.

In its most basic form, mixing involves five elements, with the most primary being balancing the playback-volume levels of the various tracks in the recording. This is often referred to as *balance*. If you are doing a voice-over-music commercial and adding a few sound effects (SFX), you have to balance the levels of the music, sound effects, and voice so that the voice is prominent. Sound effects are mixed to be either in the foreground or in the background, depending on how critical they are to the commercial.

A second aspect of the mix is the *sonic panorama*, or placement of the tracks. In a stereo mix, some tracks are left channel and some right, and a few may end up at various positions between the left and right channels.

As you mix and blend the sound from the various tracks, you may notice that some sounds seem to get lost and others dominate the mix, but neither can be corrected with simple level changes. *Equalization* (EQ) is used to correct and enhance constructively the frequency range of the mix to make it brighter, bigger, clearer, and so forth. And whereas anyone can adjust the controls on an equalizer, it takes training to EQ a mix properly. EQ is addressed in detail in the next chapter.

Dimension, or space, is something that should ideally be captured in the original recording, using natural room ambience or reverb. However, when that quality is not pres-

Using the visual display, it is possible to zoom in or out on the waveform and select a particular point to make the edit, right down to a point within a single sine wave. *Adobe product screen shot reprinted with permission from Adobe Systems Incorporated.*

ent in the original recording, there are a number of tools, such as electronic reverb, echo, and delay, which can be used to give the recording life and add depth to the sound field. See the next chapter for more details on dimension.

The *dynamics* of the mix refers to the difference between the softest sound and the loudest sound. Typically, though, as a part of the mix, dynamics processing techniques such as **compression, limiting,** and **gating** are used to control the dynamics and to increase the average audio level, making the mix sound louder. Just like EQ, dynamics processing can enhance a recording but, if improperly applied, can also seriously degrade a recording. Dynamics processing is discussed in depth in the next chapter.

An additional component of mixing is automating the mix, using the digital audio workstation's or control board's microprocessor to record your individual track-by-track adjustments and to control all of the functions previously described in this section simultaneously during the playback.

As a general rule, it is an excellent idea to save your mix prior to mastering. Some people save the original tracks as one file and the mix of those tracks as another. By saving these as separate files, you make it easy to come back to the project at a later date and modify it.

Mastering

Mastering is the last stage of audio production and involves the final tweaking and adjustments to the mix. Generally, the focus of a mastering session is critically listening to the project and making any final editing adjustments, fine-tuning the mix, confirming the left/right stereo balance, ensuring that the frequency response is relatively flat, and checking the overall sound picture.

For the average commercial produced in a radio station, the mastering process is pretty simple, since most clients tend to listen more for creative content than for audio quality. In fact, most local clients are satisfied to approve their radio commercials by listening to them over the phone.

A good rule of thumb prior to mastering a large project or a commercial for a major client, however, is to go ahead and burn a test CD of your project to listen to. With the CD, you are prepared to listen critically to the project, take detailed notes, and return to the DAW to make adjustments in the audio tracks. Many production people and mastering engineers go through this cycle of burning CDs and adjusting the mix several times until they and the client are happy with the project.

When completed, the final project is likely to end up in a number of locations. Using a local radio commercial as an example, one copy is transferred directly into the radio station's main server for on-air playback, another copy is burned to CD to be given to the client, and a third copy of the commercial might be transferred digitally or burned to CD for other radio stations running the client's ads in the same market. Finally, the production person might burn the entire project DAW data file to CD as an archive copy. (Clients often ask to reuse a commercial they liked from several months ago, with just one minor change. Having an archive copy makes it a simple matter of reopening the master and making the re-

quested changes, saving a lot of valuable time and money rather than recreating the commercial from scratch. Likewise, news people often want to extract audio clips from earlier programs that have long since aired.)

Digital Audio Workstations: Using a Computer as a Recorder

Digital audio is based on converting an analogous sound wave into binary numbers. Once the audio has been transformed into data by the analog-to-digital (A/D) converter, the possibilities for recording, storing, manipulating, transporting, and delivery are limitless. As you will learn in this chapter, virtually any device that can process computer data can be creatively used to record, store, and play back digital audio. A question that arises when considering a computer for a digital audio workstation is whether the computer should be a Windows or Mac-based platform. (Which is better, chocolate or vanilla ice cream?) The correct answer is: the platform that the software was optimized for and that you feel most comfortable working with. Because of the variety of equipment in the marketplace, many production people are dual-platform literate, understanding and operating both major computer operating systems.

Current-model computers, regardless of whether they are desktop or laptop models, can either serve as a digital audio workstation right off the shelf or be quickly and inexpensively modified to do so. It is simply a matter of matching the basic hardware to the requirements of the software.

Production studios are centered on a DAW (see Fig. 5.4). A full-featured DAW is a virtual

Figure 5.4

Production studios are centered on digital audio workstations (DAW). A full-featured DAW is a virtual studio within a computer. This studio features a DAW on the right with twin monitors for easier viewing of all of the DAW controls and editing functions. The monitor on the far left is for the radio station's central audio server where all "on air" production is stored.

studio within a computer. In addition to the basic recording and playback software, a DAW often features software referred to as digital signal processors **(DSP)** or "plug-ins." A plug-in is a software-based audio processor such as a reverb, echo, delay, or dynamics controller. A popular plug-in used in radio production is time compression and expansion. This plug-in digitally rearranges the audio to stretch or compress the length of an audio cut. If a commercial is produced and ends up being 62 seconds, sometimes it is simply a matter of digitally processing the commercial and compressing the time line to 60 seconds. This is done with no change in the pitch of the voices or other artifacts that the listener can

hear. Pitch shift is another popular plug-in with announcers (men and women), allowing them to slightly lower the pitch of their voice for a rounder, fuller sound.

One feature of DAWs that some people find disconcerting is that the computer's keyboard, mouse, or trackball controls everything. Whereas some operators are quite comfortable using these controls, others feel more comfortable touching real faders and knobs. The solution is a control surface that interfaces with the software (see Fig. **5.5**). Move a fader on the control surface, and the software's corresponding fader moves; turn the knobs and the software's knobs turn. This kind of interface is often referred to as a knob-per-function user

Figure 5.5

A digital audio workstation control surface provides a physical interface with the software. Move a fader on the control surface, and the software's corresponding fader moves; turn the knobs and the software's knobs turn. This kind of interface is often referred to as a knob-per-function user interface and makes the software easier to record and mix with.

interface and makes the software much easier to record and mix with.

An additional advantage of a computer-based DAW is networking with other workstations through a local area network **(LAN).** For example, a radio station might have two production rooms and a newsroom, each with a DAW. All three computers can be networked together to share files, as well as be networked to the station's main server. When a commercial or news story is produced, it is instantly accessible in the main control room or anywhere else in the radio station.

Broadcast stations within regional or national groups share files using wide area networks **(WAN)** or through broadband Internet services, via file transfer protocol **(FTP).**

Computer-Based Hybrid Devices

In addition to computers, computer-based hybrid devices offer production people a steady stream of new creative tools and recording media. A hybrid device is one that combines the technology and functions of two or more distinctly different devices into a related third device.

An excellent example of a hybrid device is a "studio in a box," featuring a digital multichannel control board incorporating software and a hard drive for recording and storing audio (see Fig. **5.6**). Digital signal processors (DSP), such as reverbs and echo, are included, along with a compact disc player/recorder. Audio never has to leave the box during the entire production process. In the example, at least four separate devices are combined to form a new device that is literally a studio in a box. Hybrid devices are incredibly compact, portable, and powerful tools.

Another powerful hybrid medium is the **DVD-A** (DVD-Audio), which combines digital audio with a DVD, resulting in an ultrahigh-quality 5.1 surround-sound audio format that nearly doubles the fidelity of a standard CD.

Digital Audio Workstation Software

Something that you should keep in mind as you review the array of digital audio workstation products on the market is that creativity

**Figure 5.6

A "studio in a box" is a digital multi-channel workstation incorporating a hard drive and software for recording and storing audio. A compact disc player/recorder and digital signal processors (DSP), such as reverbs and echo, can be included. Audio never has to leave the box during the entire production process. In the example, at least four separate devices are combined to form an incredibly compact and powerful tool.

does not come out of a box from a software or computer company. Creativity comes from you and from those you surround yourself with. Sure, having good tools helps, but don't think for a moment that just because you have all the latest bells and whistles on your computer you are suddenly more creative. Nothing could be farther from the truth. Your focus must first and foremost be on communicating the message: on creating a great commercial, news, sports, or public affairs program for your radio station. As your creativity requires, use the tools at your disposal, but don't use them just because they are there and you can.

There are a number of software products available for turning a computer into a DAW. For the most part, each company has tried to seek out a particular price-point and niche market for itself. The commercial music industry has a favorite DAW hardware/software combination; broadcasters, in turn, have a number of broadcast-specific software products, designed for everything from live studio work to full station automation. Many broadcast systems even interface with traffic and billing systems to schedule and play back commercials, promotional announcements, and station identification announcements.

Figure 5.7

In addition to software, each DAW product requires some type of physical interface to get the audio in and out of the system. These range from the sound card that came with the computer to outboard digital audio converters costing thousands of dollars, like the ones above. In most cases, the software provider specifies a specific type of converter.

In addition to software, each DAW product requires some type of physical interface to get the audio in and out of the system. These range from the sound card that came with the computer to outboard digital audio converters costing thousands of dollars (see Fig. **5.7**). In most cases, the software provider specifies a particular type of converter.

With the large number of DAW software products on the market, it is well beyond the scope of this text to attempt to cover all of them. As is usually the case, two major products have found significant acceptance in their respective industries: Adobe Audition and Pro Tools.

Adobe Audition

At three hundred dollars, Adobe Audition is a powerful and inexpensive digital audio workstation software. Adobe Audition requires a Windows platform—which brings up an interesting point. Radio broadcasters, as a general rule, operate their stations based on the Windows platform. This includes everything from the traffic and billing software to sophisticated computer-controlled transmitter operations. Why this preference developed over the years may have to do with radio embracing computers in the early 1960s for the tedious tasks of scheduling each day's commercials and preparing program logs. The early punch-card systems came from Big Blue—IBM—and thus the tie to Windows, the personal computer platform made popular by IBM. (If you have never heard of a computer that used punch cards made of paper to store data, look the subject up on the Web. It is a fascinating topic.)

Adobe Audition is a typical, intuitive, Windows point-and-click program with a fairly short learning curve (see Fig. **5.8**). If you have any experience at all with computer recording, chances are you will skip the instructions until you hit a roadblock. The software enables your computer to record up to 128 tracks of audio and supports the highest digital audio sampling rates, depending on how your computer is configured. In addition, Adobe Audition features over 45 digital signal-processing (DSP) effects such as echo, reverb, and a variety of other audio processors.

With Adobe Audition's large number of tracks and ability to support high sampling rates, your first thoughts might be about running out of hard disk storage space. From a practical standpoint, though, digital audio workstation storage space is not usually a problem. It is the hard drive speed (measured in rpm, or revolutions per minute) and RAM (random access memory) that limit the sampling rates and the total number of tracks that can be recorded and played back simultaneously. This is where the "reading the manual" part comes in, configuring a computer to optimize the use of the particular software.

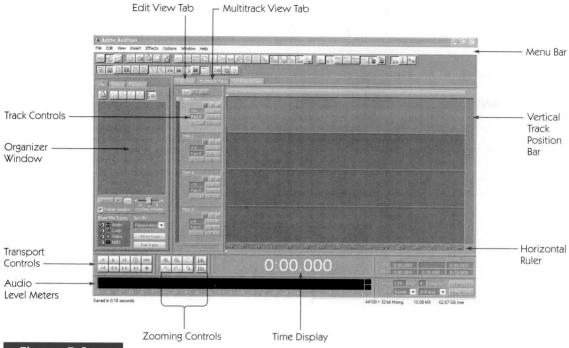

Edit View Tab — Multitrack View Tab

Menu Bar

Track Controls

Organizer Window

Transport Controls

Audio Level Meters

Vertical Track Position Bar

Horizontal Ruler

Zooming Controls   Time Display

Figure 5.8

In the multitrack view, Adobe Audition represents a virtual recorder (digital audio workstation) that can be used to record, play, edit, and add audio processing to a maximum of 128 tracks (depending on how your computer is configured).

Adobe product screen shot reprinted with permission from Adobe Systems Incorporated.

Adobe Audition does not require the purchase of any specific analog-to-digital audio hardware for the software to function. It works with the sound card that came with your computer. However, to interface with professional audio equipment and to take full advantage of the software, it is advisable to add a professional sound card with either balanced analog inputs and outputs or digital inputs and outputs (more on that later in the chapter) or both, depending on your specific needs. Such sound cards, depending on the number of inputs and outputs, range in price from $300 to $1,200.

Due to the intuitive nature of the software, the fact that it is Windows-based, and its rela-

tively low cost, Adobe Audition is popular with broadcasters. Some of the largest broadcast groups in the United States, including Clear Channel Communications, use Adobe Audition. Internationally, even the BBC uses Adobe Audition.

Producing a Project with Adobe Audition

Before you continue on in this chapter, if you have not done so already, install the Adobe Audition software that came with this textbook on your personal computer. Read the instructions that came with the software and

Edit View Tab — Multitrack View Tab

Menu Bar

Organizer Window

Vertical Audio Ruler

Horizontal Ruler

Transport Controls

Audio Level Meters

0:00.000

Zooming Controls

Time Display

Figure 5.9

In the edit view, Adobe Audition is a single waveform editor that can be used to record, play, edit, and add audio processing to mono or stereo tracks. From the edit view, tracks can be transferred to the multitrack view. *Adobe product screen shot reprinted with permission from Adobe Systems Incorporated.*

become familiar with the product. There is a lot of excellent information in the Help menu. This textbook also came with a CD of production music that you will need for this section of the chapter if you wish to follow along. One of the music selections is a traditional blues progression (see music CD, cut 1, Blues Mixed) and features not only the final mix of the music but the five raw individual studio tracks that were used to create the selection (see music CD, cuts 2–6). What is unique about these five tracks is that any one of them could be used by itself behind a project. Additionally, any two or more tracks can be mixed together to form a new musical selection. In all, just by mixing and matching the five tracks the way they are,

more than thirty new versions of this blues progression can be produced; with variations in level, audio processing, and editing to each of the tracks, the possibilities are limitless!

Adobe Audition has two main views or workspaces; the multitrack view (again, see Fig. **5.8**) and the edit view (see Fig. **5.9**). When you open Adobe Audition, you typically see the multitrack view; in essence, you are looking at a 128-track virtual studio. If not, click on the small Multitrack View tab at the top left of the multitrack display area or press the F12 key on your computer keyboard. The Multitrack View tab and the F12 key allow you to toggle back and forth between the two workspaces. There are also two small buttons located directly below File and Edit on the menu bar to switch back and forth between the two views. One button has a single waveform (edit view) the other has three waveforms (multitrack view).

In the multitrack view, Adobe Audition permits you to record, edit and mix, and sonically position (pan) each track between the left and right channels. Depending on your computer's configuration, Adobe Audition allows you to use up to 128 tracks of audio on a project. In the edit view, Adobe Audition is a single waveform editor that can be used to record, play, edit, and add audio processing to mono or stereo tracks.

Recording with Adobe Audition

There are three ways to record material into Adobe Audition. Normally, when taking material such as production music from a CD, you want to digitally extract, or "rip," the audio directly from the CD into the program. For live recording, or to record material from a CD being played back in real time, use the analog or digital inputs on your computer sound card.

To use the audio cuts from the Music CD included with this text, click on the "Copy" command by each cut on the Music CD and save the cut to a convenient location on your computer. From the edit view of Adobe Audition, click on File and on the drop-down menu select Open. The Open Window appears and you can select your saved file. When you click on the audio file to open it, the file appears on the left side of the Adobe Audition screen in the File Organizer Window and as a waveform in the edit window.

The only thing left to do is to move the audio cut you just opened into the multitrack view. Click on the Multitrack View tab and then click on the file in the organizer window and drag it to the track where you want to

place it (see Fig. **5.10**). Once in the track, you can position the file by placing the cursor on the audio waveform and right clicking and dragging, usually to the left or start of the track. You also can right click and drag the file to any track you wish. To play the file, use the play button or use the space bar on your keyboard to start and stop playback.

To "rip" the music from a regular CD, place a CD in your CD drive and in the edit view, click on File and on the drop-down menu select Extract Audio from CD. The Extract Audio from CD window appears (see Fig. **5.11**). In the Device window select the CD drive you placed the music in. A list of the cuts appears in a window labeled Source Selection. Highlight the track you wish to rip into Adobe Audition and click OK just below the highlighted track. The Extracting CD Digital Audio window opens and shows you the ripping progress. When finished, the audio file appears on the left side of the screen in the File Organizer Window and as a waveform in the edit window. The only thing left to do is to move the audio cut you just "ripped" into the multitrack view. Click on the Multitrack View tab and then click on the file in the organizer window and drag it to the track where you want to place it (again, see Fig. **5.10**). Once in the track, you can position the file by placing the cursor on the audio waveform and right clicking and dragging, usually to the left or start of the track. You also can right click and drag the file to any track you wish. To play the file, use the play button or use the space bar on your keyboard to start and stop playback.

For convenience, you may want to change the track name by clicking on the track number and highlighting it. Type in any name you wish to use to identify that track; you can change it as many times as you wish. If you have the track exactly as you want it, lock the track for play only by clicking on the waveform to highlight it. On the Edit drop-down menu select

Figure 5.10

Once you have moved the audio into the track, you can position the file by placing the cursor on the audio waveform and right-clicking and dragging, usually to the left or start of the track. You also can right-click and drag the file to any track you wish. To play the file, use the play button or use the space bar on your keyboard to start and stop the playback. *Adobe product screen shot reprinted with permission from Adobe Systems Incorporated.*

<u>Lock for Play Only</u>. This prevents you from accidentally placing the track in record.

Now is a good time to save your work, before you start editing. On the menu bar, click on <u>File</u>, and on the drop-down menu, select <u>Save Session</u>. When you are working on a project it is a good idea to save your work often, as a power outage or computer problem could otherwise wipe out all of your unsaved work.

Editing with Adobe Audition

Once you have a track recorded, the next step is to trim or edit each end of the track so that the music starts and ends cleanly. To demonstrate,

we are going to edit the very beginning of the track to remove any dead space or noise, so that the music starts instantly on playback. In the edit view, place the playback cursor (dashed vertical yellow line in the track area) over the area you wish to edit by clicking on the small yellow triangle at either the top or bottom of the yellow playback cursor and dragging it to the location near where you want to make an edit (see Fig. **5.12**). Now you are ready to zoom in on the area using the zooming controls located just to the right of the transport controls (see Fig. **5.13**). Adobe Audition offers you eight control buttons to zoom in or out on the area. The upper left button in the group is used to zoom in horizontally. Each

Figure 5.11

The <u>Extract Audio From CD</u> window permits you to select the CD drive you wish to rip the audio from. Highlight an audio cut under the <u>Source Selection</u> and press OK to rip the audio into the edit view. From the edit view, the audio cut can be moved into the multitrack view for mixing into a project.

Adobe product screen shot reprinted with permission from Adobe Systems Incorporated.

time you click the button you zoom the view in closer. The upper right button is used to zoom in vertically (again, see Fig. **5.13**). Notice that as you zoom in vertically, you change the size of the track (see Fig. **5.14**).

To edit the beginning of the music, place your mouse's cursor at the point where you wish to make the edit, then click and drag the cursor to the left, highlighting the area you want to remove (see Fig. **5.15**). If you don't manage to highlight exactly the area you want the first time, just place the cursor anywhere on the track, click once, and the highlighting will disappear. Keep trying, and once you have highlighted the area you want to edit out, press the delete key on your keyboard to remove the area. (Any time you have an "oops" and have removed too much, or made any other kind of error, all you have to do is go to the <u>Edit</u> drop-down menu and use the <u>Undo</u> command.) Although this example of editing was done in the edit view, the same process can be used in the multitrack view.

With the beginning trimmed, you are ready to edit the end of the musical cut using the same technique. Once that is done, record at least two more tracks of the music so that you are ready to move on to mixing.

Mixing with Adobe Audition

If you laid down more than a couple of tracks and tried to play them back, you probably noticed that they were all playing at the same

Figure 5.12

This audio cut has some blank space before the music begins. To remove this area, start your edit by placing the playback cursor (dashed vertical line in the track area) at the start point of the edit. The cursor can be positioned by clicking on the small triangle at either the top or bottom of the playback cursor. Click on the line and drag it over the area you want to edit, highlighting the proposed edit. *Adobe product screen shot reprinted with permission from Adobe Systems Incorporated.*

level and it was hard to tell what in the world was going on. Mixing is the art of adjusting the volume and sonic position of each track, or blending the sounds from the tracks together. Adobe Audition makes this easy with controls on each track.

Place your cursor into the gray track-control area below the <u>Lock</u> and <u>FX</u> buttons on the track you wish to adjust, then right-click on the area. The <u>Track Properties</u> window opens (see Fig. **5.16**). On the left side of the window, there is a vertical fader starting at the closed position (–102 dB) and going through +18 decibels. This adjusts the playback volume of the track, and you can set it wherever

you like, keeping in mind that the 0 position is unity gain and going past that can cause distortion. Should you wish to mute all of the other tracks and listen only to this track, press the <u>Solo</u> button.

You can sonically position the track with the horizontal fader, or pan control, at the top of the window. Moving it all the way to the right or left positions the track in the right or left channel of a stereo pair of speakers. Leaving it in the center positions the sound in the center, between the two stereo speakers.

Adjust all of the properties of each track individually until you have blended the tracks the way you want them. When you are satis-

Zooming Controls

Figure 5.13

The audio track above shows little detail and is hard to see. The zooming controls are located just to the right of the transport controls. They permit you to change the waveform view so as to display more detail with greater accuracy. *Adobe product screen shot reprinted with permission from Adobe Systems Incorporated.*

fied and ready to burn your project to a CD, you will need to save your work as a two-track stereo mix. This is done by using the <u>Mix Down to File</u> function located under <u>Edit</u> on the menu bar. <u>Mix Down to File</u> creates a two-track stereo file that includes all of the un-muted tracks and all of the waveform properties you used such as volume, pan, EQ, and so forth. Once mixed down, the stereo file can be burned to CD or distributed electronically to other users. The mix-down process is sometimes called "bouncing" to disk.

Naturally, there are many more controls, shortcuts, and adjustments that can be made in Adobe Audition. After this basic introduction, you are ready to explore the software using the excellent Help menu and your own trial and discovery process.

Pro Tools

Pro Tools is the de facto professional recording standard for the music recording industry and television/film production/post-production industry. It is also beginning to see use in larger radio markets. The software is available in both Mac and Windows versions, with the industry preference leaning toward Mac-based systems. Due to the versatility and scalability of the software and hardware, Pro Tools has a steeper learning curve than many other products on the market.

Figure 5.14

Adobe Audition offers you up to eight control buttons to zoom in on an area of your audio track. The upper left button in the group is used to zoom in horizontally. Each time you click the button you zoom in closer, displaying more detail. The upper right button is used to zoom in vertically. The view above is the same audio cut from Figure 5.13 that has been zoomed in for a closer inspection. *Adobe product screen shot reprinted with permission from Adobe Systems Incorporated.*

There are several versions of Pro Tools, ranging from a consumer version to a full professional package. Pro Tools is scalable from the standpoint that the on-screen interface remains essentially the same from the entry-level product through the top-of-the-line software. Once the entry-level product is mastered, you should be able to adapt quickly to the extensive features in the professional versions (see Fig. **5.17**).

Pro Tools software/hardware starts at around $500 for a two input/output analog-to-digital converter and a software package for your computer that provides up to 24 tracks to record, edit, and mix with. A complete professional software/hardware package supports up to 192 channels at sampling rates of up to 192 kHz at 24 bits. Larger Pro Tools professional systems start at around $10,000 plus the cost of the required computer and hardware configuration. Pro Tools features several digital signal processors. There is an extensive array of additional commercial plug-ins for the software, including everything from microphone preamplifiers to dynamics processors.

Whereas Adobe Audition opens with a virtual transport and is in a near ready-to-record mode, Pro Tools requires you to create your own custom work surface. Each operator selects the transport and software features to suit his or her particular project and personal preferences. The software settings are easily scaled to the

Figure 5.15

The silence at the start of this audio cut was highlighted by clicking and dragging the cursor over the area. Once you have highlighted the area you want to edit out, press the delete key on your keyboard and the area is removed. *Adobe product screen shot reprinted with permission from Adobe Systems Incorporated.*

project at hand, allowing you to work with only the features you need. Pro Tools also manufactures a number of control-surface interfaces, allowing the operator physically to work with as many as 24 faders at a time (see Fig. **5.18**).

Producing a Project with Pro Tools

Although not as intuitive as Adobe Audition, Pro Tools comes with a well-documented manual. Beginners should spend some time studying the manual to understand better Pro Tools' capabilities and the numerous options it offers producers. Regardless of the system, it is necessary to install and configure properly the analog-to-digital hardware and software before use.

Pro Tools has three work areas, the mix window, the edit window, and the transport window or controls. The *mix window* displays the Pro Tools virtual console. The console features individual channel strips with a fader for playback level control, mute, pan, solo, and record-enable buttons (again, see Fig. **5.17**). Automation controls are located just above this group of buttons. At the top of each strip are the insert buttons for activating audio processing plug-ins. Below them are the audio sends for routing audio to external devices or to any one of the internal audio bus paths. You can create as many channel strips as you need for your project, up to the limit of the particular system you are working on.

Figure 5.16

On the left side of the <u>Track Properties</u> window there is a vertical fader starting at –102 dB, or closed, and going from 0 through +18 decibels, that adjusts the playback volume of the track. The 0 position is unity gain and going past that can cause distortion. The track can be sonically positioned with the horizontal fader, or pan control, at the top of the window. *Adobe product screen shot reprinted with permission from Adobe Systems Incorporated.*

The *edit window* displays the recorded audio waveforms on each track (see Fig. **5.19**). Additionally, there are a large number of edit controls for functions such as zooming in/out and cutting and pasting the waveform. Across the top of the window are the available timebase rulers, including minutes and seconds, bars and beats, tempo, and meter. To the right of the edit window is the regions list that includes a listing of every audio segment (region) that has been recorded, imported, or created by editing. Items in the list can be dragged onto any available track in the edit window to work with.

The *transport window* features the controls to operate the system and can be configured to suit your particular needs (see Fig. **5.20**). The primary control buttons, from left to right, are

the online indicator, return to start, rewind, stop, play, fast forward, go to end, and record. When activated, the online control to the far left allows the playback of an audio cut to be started by an external device if your machine is so configured.

In addition to the primary controls, seven MIDI (musical instrument digital interface) controls can be added to the transport when composing and recording music. Likewise, there are a number of time displays and clock options that can be configured as a part of the transport (again, see Fig. **5.20**).

Recording with Pro Tools

Just as with Adobe Audition, there are two ways to record audio using Pro Tools. CD

Output Selector
Input Selector
Panoramic Control
Record, Solo, and Mute Buttons
Fader
Transport Control
Channel Strip

Figure 5.17

Pro Tools is scalable from the standpoint that the on-screen interface remains essentially the same from the entry-level product through the top-of-the-line software. Each operator selects the transport and software features to suit his or her particular project and personal preferences. The software settings are easily scaled to the project at hand, allowing you to work with only the features you need. The mix window above is configured to record and play back eight tracks of audio.

audio can be digitally "ripped" into the system, or you can record material from a CD or any other source by playing the material back in real time and using the analog or digital inputs of the system. Pro Tools uses two different methods of ripping audio from digital sources, one for Windows-based systems and one for Mac-based systems. Since you are working with the text's production music CD and we don't know which Pro Tools system you have access to or what operating platform, we can't walk you through the ripping process. You will need to play the CD back in real time and record the music or, if you elect to rip the music in, refer to your specific Pro

Tools operating system manual for the correct procedure.

After starting Pro Tools, you should be in the mix window view. If not, on the menu bar click on Windows and on the drop-down menu select Show Mix. You should see the mix window and the transport controls (see Fig. 5.21). To create the tracks, or channel strips, that you want to work with, click File on the menu bar and on the drop-down menu select New Track. In the window that appears, enter the number of tracks you wish to work with and click Create. Since the blues progression has five tracks, you can start with five and add more if you need to.

Figure 5.18

A control surface allows an operator to handle physically the controls illustrated within the digital audio software. Pro Tools has a number of control-surface interfaces, allowing the operator to work with as many as 24 faders at a time, as shown above.

The bottom of each channel strip is labeled audio 1, 2, and so on. You can change the label by double-clicking on the label and entering a new name in the window that appears. The names can be changed as many times as you wish.

To prepare a channel strip to record, click the channel's input selector and a drop-down menu will appear, listing the system inputs (see Fig. **5.22**). Select the appropriate audio input for your system. Likewise, you need to select the channel's output, or where you want the audio to go during playback (see Fig. **5.23**). Clicking the output selector causes a drop-down menu to appear listing the system outputs. Select the appropriate output for your system. You now have routed audio into and out of each channel strip.

To record the first track, click on the channel's rec button and place the channel into the record mode. The button turns from gray to red, indicating that the channel is ready to record. To place the transport into the record mode, click on the button to the far right of the transport, changing it from gray to flashing red, indicating that the transport and a channel, or channels, are ready to record (see Fig. **5.24**).

Adjust the input level either at the source or on the control board feeding Pro Tools. Click the play button, and the transport clocks begin rolling, indicating that you are recording. After recording track one, click the stop button on the transport to stop the recording. Before you play back, click the rec button again to take the channel out of the record mode so you don't accidentally record over the track

Zooming Controls

Edit Controls (cursor selection)

Timebase Ruler

Audio Waveform

Regions List

Transport Control

Figure 5.19

The edit window displays the recorded audio waveforms on each track. Additionally, there are a large number of edit controls for functions such as zooming in/out and cutting and pasting the waveform. Across the top of the window are the available timebase rulers, including minutes and seconds, bars and beats, tempo, and meter. To the right of the edit window is the regions list that includes a listing of every audio segment (region) that has been recorded, imported, or created by editing.

later. If you wish to lock out the <u>rec</u> button so that it takes two steps to put the track back into record, consult your manual, as the procedure is slightly different for the Windows and Mac versions of the software.

To play the track back, click on the return-to-start button, turn up Pro Tools on the control board, and press play. You can also use the space bar on the keyboard to start and stop playback. If you are happy with the track, now is a good time to save your work, *before* you start editing. On the menu bar click on <u>File</u>, and on the drop-down menu select <u>Save</u>.

When you are working on a project it is a good idea to save your work often, as a power outage or computer problem could wipe out all of your unsaved work.

Editing with Pro Tools

When the first track is recorded, the next step is to trim the ends of the track so that the music starts and ends cleanly. For demonstration purposes, we are going to trim the beginning of the track to remove the dead air or noise so that the music starts instantly upon

Figure 5.20

The transport window features the controls to operate the system and can be configured to suit your particular needs. The primary control buttons, from left to right, are the online indicator, return to start, rewind, stop, play, fast forward, go to end, and record. When activated, the online control to the far left allows the playback of an audio cut to be started by an external device if your machine is so configured. © 2004 Avid Technology, Inc. All rights reserved.

playback. To get to the edit window, go to the menu bar and click on <u>Windows</u>; on the drop-down menu select <u>Show Edit</u>. The audio waveform you recorded is displayed under the timebase ruler (see Fig. **5.25**). A waveform is referred to as a "region" in Pro Tools.

The tool bar across the top of the window has a number of controls for viewing and editing the waveform. Starting in the upper left corner are the edit mode controls. With the <u>Shuffle</u> mode selected, when an edit is made, the edited ends of the audio snap together automatically. In the <u>Slip</u> mode, the two ends of

an edit remain where they are and you can click and drag the audio regions wherever you like.

The next group of buttons to the right are the zooming controls used to magnify or re-size the audio waveform (again, see Fig. **5.25**). To zoom in horizontally, click the right zoom button until the view you want is displayed. To zoom out, use the left zoom button and click until the view you want is displayed. To zoom in vertically, click on the small button with the large waveform indicator. Likewise, to zoom out vertically, click on the small button with the small waveform indicator. Below the zooming buttons are five preset zooms numbered 1–5. Selecting one of these snaps the view to one of the preset zoom views. To change the size of the track, click on the track height selector and a drop-down menu appears with the available sizes ranging from mini to jumbo (again, see Fig. **5.25**).

Pro Tools uses two cursors in the edit window. The first is a solid black vertical line that moves horizontally across the waveform as you play back the audio. This is the playback cursor and indicates the exact point of playback as it moves. The second cursor is the edit cursor and is a blinking vertical line that only appears in the track in which you place it using the <u>Selector</u>.

To edit the beginning and end of the musical cut, there are two tools to choose from, the <u>Trimmer</u> and the <u>Selector</u> (again, see Fig. **5.25**). To trim the beginning of the waveform with the <u>Trimmer</u>, first select the <u>Slip</u> edit mode. Click on the <u>Trimmer</u> button, and move your cursor into the start of the waveform. Notice that the cursor has turned into a [cursor. Click and drag the <u>Trimmer</u> to the right; as you do, notice that you are trimming the unwanted noise and blank space (see Fig. **5.26**). When you release the <u>Trimmer</u>, the audio is trimmed to that point. The same procedure can be used for the end of the waveform, with the <u>Trimmer</u> automatically turning into a] cursor at the end of the cut. Should you make an error and trim too much, click <u>Edit</u> on the menu bar and on the drop-down menu select <u>Undo</u>.

The second tool you can use to edit a waveform is the <u>Selector</u> (again, see Fig. **5.25**). With the edit window still in the <u>Slip</u> mode, click on the <u>Selector</u> button and highlight it. Moving the cursor into the waveform changes the cursor into the shape of an I. Place the I at the start of the audio waveform, and click and drag it to the left, highlighting the area to be removed (see Fig. **5.27**). If you don't highlight the exact area you want the first time, place the cursor anywhere on the screen outside the waveform and click once, and the highlighting will disappear. Try again.

With the area you want to remove highlighted, press the delete key on the keyboard. The area is removed, leaving a space between the start of the audio and the start of the track. Click on the <u>Grabber</u> button located on the tool bar to activate the <u>Grabber</u> function (again, see Fig. **5.25**); as you move the cursor into the waveform, notice that the cursor is now the shape of a hand. Click on the track, and you can now slide it to the left or right, positioning it exactly where you want it. (Remember that, had the edit window been in the <u>Shuffle</u> mode when you hit the delete key, the waveform would have automatically snapped to the start of the track.) Anytime you are editing and have removed too much or made an error, all you have to do is go to the <u>Edit</u> drop-down menu and use the <u>Undo</u> command.

After trimming the beginning, you are ready to edit the end of the musical cut using the same technique. Once that is done, record

Figure 5.23

After selecting a channel's input you need to select the channel's output, or where you want the audio to go during playback. Clicking the output selector causes a drop-down menu to appear listing the system outputs. Select the appropriate output for your system.

at least two more tracks of the music so that you are ready to move on to mixing.

Mixing with Pro Tools

To get back to the mix window, go to the menu bar and click on <u>Windows</u>. On the drop-down menu select <u>Show Mix</u> (again, see Fig. **5.17**). Before you mix anything, make sure that all of the individual channel strips are out of the record mode. Just as you did with Adobe Audition, use the channel strip faders to adjust the audio levels from each channel to achieve the sound you desire. Just above the faders are the pan controls to position sonically the

audio from each channel in either the right or left channel. When satisfied with your project, you can save it to disk and bounce a stereo copy for burning to CD or electronic distribution.

As you have no doubt noticed, Pro Tools has many more controls, shortcuts, and adjustments with which to work. Generally, Pro Tools offers the user a number of different options to perform each task. Although this is handy, it does increase the learning curve necessary to take full advantage of all of the available options. However, with these basics, you are ready to understand the additional Pro Tools features by working with the software and manual.

Channel Strip Record Button

Transport Control Record Button

Figure 5.24

To place the transport into the record mode, click on the button to the far right of the transport, changing it from gray to flashing red, indicating that the transport and a channel, or channels, are ready to record.

Portable Digital Audio Recording

Portable digital audio recording lends itself to developing some very creative solutions, ranging from simple minidiscs, to laptop computers with DAW software, to specialty products designed to solve specific recording needs. Such products include high-quality flash card and portable real-time CD recorders that make digital location recording very affordable for even small radio stations and producers (see Fig. **5.28**). After returning from a location, the audio can be quickly downloaded into a DAW either by inserting a flash card into a docking port or by ripping a CD into the DAW software.

Both Adobe Audition and Pro Tools can easily be set up on a laptop computer for field use, which has many practical applications. For example, a laptop with newswriting software and Adobe Audition makes an incredible mobile news facility. The newsperson splits the computer's display, with the DAW on one side and the news software on the other. While recording the city council meeting, the person can be writing his or her story at the same time. Editing audio cuts is easy and fast. When it is time to feed the story, the reporter reads the copy and plays back the audio cuts, all from the same laptop. By adding wireless Internet service to the laptop, the reporter becomes a virtual newsroom.

Audio
Waveform
Movement
Controls

Zooming
Controls

Trimmer

Selector

Grabber

Figure 5.25

The edit window graphically displays the recorded audio waveforms. A waveform is referred to as a "region" in Pro Tools. The edit window has an entirely different set of controls than the mix window, offering the operator the opportunity to edit and manipulate the waveform easily.   © 2004 *Avid Technology, Inc. All rights reserved.*

Project Backup and Storage

Backup

It will happen, and it is nothing new. No matter how hard you try or how careful you are, you are going to lose a project at some point in your career. A digital audio tape (DAT) can stretch or a hard drive can crash. It's Murphy's Law: If something can go wrong, it will! Having a backup plan and being prepared for the inevitable is the key to saving your neck. Always plan for the worst and hope for the best!

If you are working with expensive studio talent, the last thing you want to tell an announcer after a great take is that the

Trimmer

Trimmer
Positioned
to Edit

Figure 5.26

To trim the beginning of the waveform with the <u>Trimmer</u>, first select the <u>Slip</u> edit mode. Click on the <u>Trimmer</u> button, and move your cursor into the start of the waveform. Notice that the cursor has turned into a [cursor. Click and drag the <u>Trimmer</u> to the right; as you do, notice that you are trimming the unwanted noise and blank space. When you release the <u>Trimmer</u>, the audio is trimmed to that point. The same procedure can be used for the end of the waveform.

recorder bought the farm. In a radio station you can usually move to another studio, but on location there is no other studio to move to. This applies particularly to live location events such as a concert, presidential speech, or important station event. The solution is simple: run two recorders simultaneously, your best recorder as the primary and another one as backup. Should the primary fail for some reason, you still have captured the event, or take,

on the backup. A good use for older portable analog cassette machines is as a backup to a primary recorder. Even in the worst case, you still have something on tape.

A true backup, though, is a copy of a project on another medium. Archival project backup can be done with a computer-tape backup system, with DAT, or by burning the project to CD, **DVD,** or DVD-A. Another effective and sensible way to back up projects is with a hot-

Audio
Waveform
Movement
Controls

Selector

I Cursor

Figure 5.27

Another tool you can use to edit a waveform is the <u>Selector</u>. With the edit window still in the <u>Slip</u> mode, click on the <u>Selector</u> button and highlight it. Moving the cursor into the waveform changes it into the shape of an I. Place the I at the start of the audio waveform, and click and drag it to the left or right, highlighting the area to be removed.

swap hard drive that is easily removed and stored in a secure location (see Fig. **5.29**). For maximum safety, you should back up to two different media, such as a hot-swap hard drive and a CD, keeping each in a separate, secure location.

Thanks to the reliability of the present generation of hard drives, many DAW users are lulled into a false sense of security. Keep in mind, though, that a hard drive, unlike a CD or DVD, is an electro-mechanical device and it *will* fail at some point.

The backup also serves another valuable purpose. When archived by the production person, it is a backup in case anything happens to the original, including getting lost by a shipper or being accidentally erased from a hard drive or destroyed by someone else in your department.

Figure 5.28

Portable digital audio recorders include products such as high-quality flash card and real-time CD recorders. Digital location recording is very affordable for even small radio stations and producers.

Project Storage

Each production person usually has a particular file or folder in which he or she stores projects on a main server or a local DAW hard drive. Given time and a large number of projects, such as radio commercials and/or long-form news and public affairs programs, storage space can become a problem.

Uncompressed digital audio takes up lots of hard-drive space. For example, each minute of CD-quality stereo audio (44.1 kHz, 16 bit)

consumes about 10 megabytes of storage. Bump the sampling rate up to 96 kHz at 24 bits, and the same minute of stereo audio gobbles up nearly 34.5 megabytes per minute. Stereo audio sampled at 192 kHz, 24 bits, takes up a monstrous 66 megabytes per minute. At some point, your computer's hard drive is going to fill up. (As a side note, many broadcast and production facilities limit server space and require staff to archive on a regular basis, deleting finished projects from the main server.)

Figure 5.29

An effective and sensible way to back up projects is with a hot-swap computer hard drive that is easily removed and stored in a secure location. This drive unlocks with the black handle and slides out for safe storage.

There are many creative solutions to solving storage problems, including DAT and CD file copies, along with personal hot-swap hard drives. Another solution for backup is commercial data-storage space. Some stations and studios have found it cost-effective to rent computer data-storage space from outside companies, just as people do with all their stuff at the U-Store-It.

The Digital Recording Process

Now that you know what some of the possibilities are in digital recording, the question is: how? What are the processes, components, and media that make it possible? From this point on, it may sound as though we are talking about computers rather than radio equipment. The reality is that a digital audio workstation is a computer emulating a physical piece of equipment, and by its very nature it is more technically involved.

The process of digital recording begins with signal acquisition, either from a microphone or a digital signal source, such as a control board or playback device like a CD player. Analog audio uses mic cables and wires to transfer audio from one piece of equipment to another.

Digital audio, though, requires unique cabling systems designed to handle computer data rather than analog audio signals. Getting the audio from point A to point B is where we start.

Digital Inputs and Outputs

Digital audio is transferred from one piece of equipment to another using standardized data-transfer protocol (methods) over twisted-pair wire, coaxial cable, or fiber-optic cable. The data is transferred at very high frequencies, similar to a video signal. Digital audio cable has the same appearance as analog mic cable, a twisted pair of conductors surrounded by a shield, but that is where the similarity ends.

Because of the very high frequency at which the data is sent, the cable's impedance (resistance to the flow of electricity) has to be higher than that of an analog cable, and cable quality is critical, especially for long runs. Typically, digital audio cable can be run a maximum distance of anywhere from 350 to just over 1,000 feet, depending on the quality of the cable. Cable manufacturers specify the maximum working distances of their particular brand of digital cable.

What makes things a little confusing is that common XLR microphone cable connectors are used for both analog and digital audio cables. In a facility where analog and digital

Figure 5.30

Some digital audio connectors look identical to their analog counterparts. From left to right, a SPDIF connector, a fiber-optic TOS link connector, a locking BNC connector, and an AES/EBU XLR connector.

equipment is mixed, engineers typically use a different color cable or clearly mark cables as digital. Digital audio quality is seriously affected if routed over an analog cable, and in some cases it can result in complete loss of the digital signal.

To simplify the transmission of digital audio signals, several industry standards have been adopted to help eliminate confusion and to make the production person's job easier. However, keeping track of all the standards requires attention to detail on your part.

AES/EBU Digital Audio Protocol

The Audio Engineering Society and the European Broadcast Union jointly established the AES/EBU professional protocol for transfer-

ring digital audio. The standard uses a balanced cable and sends two encoded audio channels (stereo) within a serial data stream on the cable. A serial data stream breaks down each audio sample's digital words into the individual bits (binary digits), sending them one bit after the other down the line. The receiving equipment reassembles the bits into the original digital words at the proper sampling frequency, and finally into audio, using a digital-to-analog converter (D/A).

The standard AES/EBU audio cable connector is the familiar XLR connector (see Fig. **5.30**). For long cable runs exceeding 1,000 feet, coaxial cable (similar to that used for the cable TV hook-up in your home) is used. The standard connector for AES/EBU digital audio coaxial cable is a locking **BNC** connector (again, see Fig. **5.30**).

Sony/Philips Digital Interface Audio Protocol

The Sony/Philips Digital InterFace, or **SPDIF**, is the consumer version of the AES/EBU standard. Commonly found on CD players and other digital equipment, it uses small-diameter, lightweight, coaxial cable with an RCA phono connector on each end for connecting equipment together (again, see Fig. **5.30**).

A **TOS link** fiber-optic cable can also be used to send SPDIF audio over short distances (again, see Fig. **5.30**). Fiber-optic cables have fewer inherent data errors than coaxial cables, and they have the potential to deliver higher audio quality. Typical consumer TOS link cables are generally no more than 15 feet in length. Most consumer electronic devices have both RCA phono and fiber-optic SPDIF inputs and outputs.

Firewire

Firewire was developed by the Institute of Electrical and Electronics Engineers (eye-triple-e) to transfer data between computers and external components using a special cable and data transfer protocol. Firewire is a popular method of connecting DAW control surfaces, external hard drives, and external analog-to-digital-audio converters to computers. A Firewire cable can also provide electrical power to external devices, making their connection to the computer a simple one-cable operation. Two of Firewire's biggest advantages are that it is fast, handling up to a gigabit of data per second, and that the cables can be as long as 300 feet (see Fig. **5.31**).

USB

Universal Serial Bus (USB) is another popular means to connect digital audio components to a computer. Each end of a USB cable has a different connector to facilitate ease of connection between equipment (again, see Fig. **5.31**). Many digital audio devices such as MIDI (musical instrument digital interface) controllers, portable hard drives, and outboard audio effects processors have USB connections. Virtually all computers have USB connections, and many have USB connectors on the computer's front panel for easy access. A USB cable can transmit data at speeds approaching 500 megabits per second and provide electrical power to external components. USB cables are limited to about 15 feet in length (USB does not support long cable runs like Firewire does).

Digital Audio Interconnection

Professional equipment using AES/EBU digital audio inputs and outputs has either XLR or locking BNC connectors; some equipment features both types of connectors. Consumer equipment using SPDIF digital audio inputs and outputs has either RCA phono jacks or TOS link fiber-optic connectors, or both, to interconnect with other equipment.

Some equipment is designed to interface with just about any digital audio source. Such equipment has a variety of connectors including AES/EBU XLR connectors, AES/EBU BNC coaxial connectors, SPDIF RCA phono connectors, SPDIF TOS link fiber-optic connectors, and a Firewire or USB connector. No wonder the back of some equipment appears so confusing. A number of prosumer and professional control boards and individual pieces of audio equipment are designed in this manner, allowing them to interface with virtually any digital audio source.

Figure 5.31

Firewire and USB are two very popular means to transfer data between computers and external components. The cables can be recognized by their distinctive connectors. The connector on the left is a Firewire connector; the one on the right is a USB connector. It is physically impossible to plug one into the other accidentally.

Digital Sample Rates and Clock Synchronization

Sample Rates

As you learned in chapter 2, the first step in digital recording is the analog-to-digital (A/D) conversion. The analog waveform is sampled, and each sample is converted into a binary number. The number of samples taken per second (sample rate) and the length of the digital word (bits) directly affect the audio quality. By their very nature, sampling and bit rates are rather technical; however, unless you are exporting audio to some other facility or media, the chances of your needing to know

the many different sampling rates are pretty slim. It is when you want to take a project outside your studio that the sampling and bit rates become important.

So that professional equipment is compatible, the AES/EBU established preferred sample rates, depending on the application. A sampling frequency of 48 kHz is recommended for the recording, processing, and exchange of digital audio. However, there are some exceptions. A sample rate of 44.1 kHz is recognized for consumer audio applications such as the CD. For high-quality audio applications, such as in a recording studio, 96 kHz is the recognized sampling frequency. Finally, for on-air broadcast signal transmission applications, 32 kHz is the present recognized sampling frequency.

Professional broadcast equipment often is sample-frequency agile, meaning the sampling frequency is selectable depending on the intended use. As an example of how sample rates are used, a CD has a fixed sample rate of 44.1 kHz at 16 bits; DVD audio has a sample rate of either 48 or 96 kHz at up to 24 bits. Minidiscs are recorded at 44.1 kHz at 16 bits, and professional DAT recorders can be switched, having 32, 44.1, or 48 kHz sample rates at 16 or 24 bits.

As a final note about sample rates, once hardware and software is established and operating properly in your studio, it is rare that you would ever need to adjust sample rates. In fact, doing so will most likely result in either recording or playback problems within the studio.

Clock Synchronization

You have seen the spy movies where all the spies stand around and synchronize their watches so they can all be on time to catch the bad guy. The same thing has to happen when multiple pieces of digital audio equipment are interconnected. The digital clock in each piece of equipment has to be synchronized with the ones in other pieces of equipment.

When a serial digital audio signal is sent to another piece of equipment, each sample's digital words are broken down into their individual bits and the bits are sent one bit after another down the line. The receiving equipment reassembles the bits into the original digital words at the proper sampling frequency and into audio using a digital-to-analog converter (D/A).

The data streams also contain additional information that tells the receiving equipment the signal's sampling frequency and where each sample begins and ends. This is called a self-clocking signal, since the signal includes information that keeps the sampling frequency and bit stream synchronized during the audio transfer.

Just as with the spies, someone has to keep the master clock for everyone to synchronize to. When two digital devices are connected together, one of them keeps the time or maintains the master word clock (a digital word is comprised of data bits) so that all of the digital words and bits arrive in synchronized order. One piece of equipment serves as the master and one, or more, as the slave.

Since the word clock, or synchronization signal, is already built into the AES/EBU and SPDIF signals, the process happens automatically most of the time. The recording equipment, such as a CD recorder, looks for the word clock at its input and synchronizes itself to the digital source feeding it. The source serves as the master, and the CD recorder becomes the slave. A master clock is also referred to as an external clock, and a slave clock is regarded as an internal clock. If two digital devices are connected and neither has an external, or master clock, the equipment receiving the digital audio does not know where the samples begin and end or how to put the bits back together into digital words. In other words, the two pieces of equipment can't communicate with one another, and the audio just becomes random computer data and is lost.

Normally, when a number of digital audio devices are connected together, one is set as the master and the others are slaves. Another way to synchronize the equipment is with a separate master clock (house clock) that feeds all of

Figure 5.32

DAT is a popular recording format designed specifically for digital audio. DAT machines have been popular for location recording in television and film production. The tiny tape cassette looks similar to a videocassette, containing tape that is only 3.81 millimeters wide. DAT never really caught on in radio stations.

the equipment in the radio station a single, synchronized, master word-clock signal.

Digital Recording Media

Once a signal has been converted into binary numbers, the recording process involves storing the data on magnetic, optical, or magneto-optical media, just as you would store any other computer data. The stored data represents audio that can be played back, edited, mixed, processed, and eventually mastered to the final product.

Magnetic Tape

High-quality magnetic tape is a suitable medium for digital audio recording. Of the three popular digital tape formats, one was designed specifically for audio and the other two are adaptations of existing videotape formats. All of these magnetic tape formats are contained in cassette shells, because the tape requires special care in handling. Just touch-ing the tape with your bare hands can cause a loss of quality, as the natural oils on your skin contaminate the recording surface. The tapes are also sensitive to dust and variations in heat and humidity.

Due to the high frequency of the data being recorded and the considerable bandwidth required, digital audio tape recorders use a recording mechanism similar to that of a videotape recorder.

Digital Audio Tape

DAT is a popular recording format designed specifically for digital audio. DAT machines have been popular for location recording in television and film production (see Fig. **5.32**), but DAT never really caught on in radio stations. The tiny tape cassette looks similar to a videocassette, containing tape that is only 3.81 millimeters wide (a little less than a quarter of an inch). Depending on the sampling frequency, it can record up to two hours of digital audio. The sampling frequency of most DAT machines is user-selectable at 32, 44.1, or 48 kHz.

Figure 5.33

DTRS uses Hi8 eight-millimeter-wide videotape as the recording medium. Machines designed for this format typically have eight tracks to record on and can be linked with other DTRS machines if more tracks are needed. Hi8 tapes have a maximum recording time of 113 minutes.

DAT delivers excellent digital audio quality; however, because DAT uses a flexible-magnetic-tape medium, there are some drawbacks. DAT is susceptible to signal loss due to dirt and dust contamination or excessive humidity. Professional DAT machines have warning systems to protect the tape from excessive humidity. DAT tapes are very difficult to erase, and sometimes even rerecording on them does not completely erase the tape. Long-term storage of DAT tapes requires a temperature- and humidity-controlled atmosphere.

Digital Tape Recording System and Alesis Digital Audio Tape

The digital tape recording system **(DTRS)** and the Alesis digital audiotape **(ADAT)** are two videotape-based recording media designed for modular digital multitrack (MDM) tape recorders. Unlike DAT machines, DTRS and ADAT recorders use videotape and record in what would normally be the video portion of the tape. DTRS and ADAT machines are most popular in the semi-pro and professional music industry; occasionally, radio stations have one or the other.

DTRS uses Hi8 eight-millimeter-wide videotape as the recording medium (see Fig. 5.33). Machines designed for this format typically have eight tracks to record on and can be linked together with other DTRS machines with a synchronization cable. In fact, up to sixteen DTRS machines can be linked together, providing the user with 128 tracks to record on. The only drawback is that there are sixteen tapes in sixteen machines working together. More commonly, two or three machines are linked together to create 16 or 24 tracks. Hi8 tapes have a maximum recording time of 113 minutes.

ADAT is the registered trademark of the Alesis company. An ADAT MDM recorder uses an S-VHS-format videotape (similar to VHS) to record eight tracks of audio (see Fig. 5.34). The ADAT machine has many of the same characteristics as the DTRS machine, in that there are eight tracks to record on, and the

Figure 5.34

An ADAT MDM digital recorder uses an S-VHS-format videotape (similar to VHS) to record eight tracks of audio on. Several machines can be linked together for up to 128 tracks.

machines are easily linked together with synchronization cables, allowing up to sixteen machines to be linked together for 128 tracks.

In addition to the standard Hi8 and S-VHS videotape formats that can be used with these media, tape manufacturers specially formulate tape in these formats for digital audio recording. ADAT technology is utilized by Alesis, Fostex, and Panasonic; DTRS technology is used by Sony and TASCAM.

Magnetic Hard Drives and Solid-State Memory

Computer hard drives are an ideal storage medium for digital audio due to their ability to store and retrieve quickly large quantities of data. CD-quality digital audio data requires just over 10 megabytes of hard disk space for each minute of stereo audio. At the opposite end of the spectrum, recording-studio quality 96 kHz, 24-bit audio requires nearly 34.5 megabytes for each minute of stereo storage.

Fixed Hard Drives

A fixed hard drive is mounted within the computer or server being used as a digital audio workstation. A hard disk used for digital audio recording needs to access large amounts of data very fast and often records and plays back continuously for several hours on end, a much more demanding duty cycle than what is asked of a typical office-computer hard drive. It is important that the appropriate hard drive be selected and that it be configured for the specific tasks it must perform. Many digital audio software and computer manufacturers specify particular makes and models of hard drives to use with their software. It is important to consult with them prior to adding or changing a system drive.

Hard drives have increasingly gotten larger as the cost per gigabyte of storage steadily goes down. Drives of 180 gigabytes are common and offer more-than-ample storage capacity for audio projects. However, bigger is not always better. Since a large hard drive has such a wide area to search, it takes more time

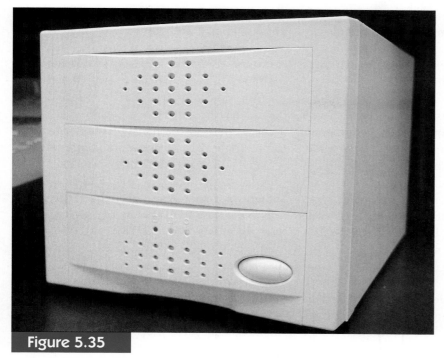

Figure 5.35

Modular hard drives are referred to as stand-alone drives, since they are
either rack-mounted or set on the console. Several drives can be stacked or
added to a computer to enhance greatly its storage capacity.

to retrieve your project and can slow down search and playback times.

Large hard drives are often partitioned, or divided, into smaller sections, which are then given separate drive numbers even though they are all physically located on the same magnetic disc. For example, a 120-gigabyte drive might be divided into six 20-gigabyte segments. The hard drive then only has to work in, and search, one small section of the disc at a time. Drive speed, or how fast the disk spins, also affects how quickly the data can be accessed and retrieved, and it also determines the maximum sample rate and the number of tracks that can be recorded simulta-

neously. Typically, the minimum hard-drive speed for audio applications is 7,200 rpm.

Modular or Portable Hard Drives

Modular hard drives are referred to as stand-alone drives, since they are either rack-mounted or set on the console and connected to the computer (see Fig. **5.35**). Several drives can be stacked or added to a computer to enhance greatly its storage capacity. In addition to normal use for storage and playback, a stand-alone drive is sometimes used as a mirror drive running in synchronization with the primary drive and recording everything the primary drive records. Should the primary drive fail, the mirror drive seamlessly takes over.

Another popular type of modular drive is the hot-swap drive mounted in a pull-out tray (again, see Fig. **5.29**). The drives are called hot-swap because they can be removed and plugged in without restarting the computer. These drives are portable and allow each production person to have his or her own. When not in use, the drive is removed and stored in a secure location. Hot-swap drives also allow facilities with more than one workstation to move huge amounts of data (over 200 gigabytes) around the facility by simply removing the drive from one computer and taking it to another. Hot-swap drives are excellent for backing up critical files, since the drive can physically be removed and stored in a safe location.

Another type of modular drive is a portable hard drive. Such drives are small and self-contained. Most are powered by the Firewire or USB cable that connects them to the computer. Apple's popular iPod has its own built-in display, offers up to 40 gigabytes of storage space, and supports a number of Mac and Windows audio storage formats. The iPod is smaller than a pack of cigarettes and weighs less than a couple of CDs.

Memory Cards and Solid-State Media

For a newsperson, nothing is more aggravating than to get a great interview, only to find that the recorder bought the farm because a tape got tangled in the machine, or just that being bounced around in a news vehicle for months on end finally proved too much for the machine. It's a fact of life: mechanical things break.

Portable recorders that do not have any moving parts are popular for fieldwork in radio. Such devices use removable solid-state memory cards or sticks available under a number of commercial names, including memory sticks or flash cards. Referred to as flash recorders, they are capable of storing over an hour and a half of CD-quality audio on a single card. Using data compression, a gigabyte memory card can store over three days of audio (again, see Fig. **5.28**). An added benefit of a flash recorder is the ability to remove the flash card or memory stick, insert it into a port attached to a DAW, and transfer the audio instantly to the workstation for editing or playback.

Another unique device for storing audio is a USB "keychain drive." The drive is a little bit smaller than a pack of gum and contains a memory chip having up to a gigabyte of data storage space. The drive is plugged into the USB port on the front of a computer and can be loaded with audio, carried on your keychain, and plugged into another computer and downloaded. Depending on the audio storage format, a "keychain" can easily hold an hour or more of audio and can be used either as a temporary backup or to transfer commercials from one studio to another in your station. (A popular place to carry a "keychain" drive is actually around your neck, on a media badge holder.)

Optical Discs

With the development of the CD in the late 1970s and its commercial release in the early 1980s, the world adopted a new standard in music playback. The plain old CD is the standard to which most other digital recording is compared. With the advent of the DVD and its many formats, optical storage has advanced to a point that is overwhelming to many because of the numerous format options that are available. Although higher sampling and bit rates are attainable with the **Super Audio Compact Disc (SACD)** and variations on the DVD, the CD is the de facto optical recording and storage medium, as well as the benchmark for consumers and the media.

Compact Disc

There is a reason the CD is so popular. It has excellent audio quality, the machines for recording and playback are inexpensive and easy to operate, and the medium itself costs only pennies per disc. Virtually every desktop computer is equipped with a CD recorder of some type, giving individuals as well as professionals the ability to capture and create quality recordings. You knew the medium was universal when your mother started burning discs to play in her soccer wagon.

A CD is a clear polycarbonate (tougher than regular plastic) disc that holds up to 700 megabytes of data, or up to 80 minutes of 44.1 kHz, 16-bit stereo audio. (The history of the original size and audio capacity of the CD is a quirky story. Mr. Norio Ohga, president of the SONY Corporation and a former classical vocalist, decreed that the new technology had to be able to play Beethoven's Ninth Symphony in its entirety, without interruption. So the original length of a CD was 74 minutes.) The laser that records and plays the disc looks up through the disc from below.

There are three layers of material on top of the disc that make it possible to record and play back audio (see Fig. **5.36**). The first layer is a heat- and photosensitive organic dye; this is where the information is stored. When a tightly focused laser beam is aimed at the disc

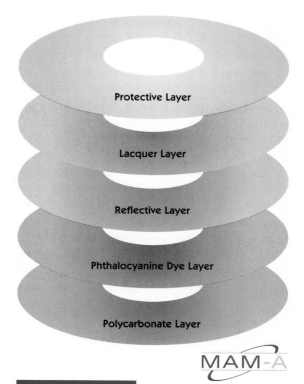

Figure 5.36

A CD is comprised of several layers. The laser reads from the bottom up, through the clear polycarbonate disc. The data is stored in the dye layer, which is the first layer of the disc. During playback, the next layer up, the reflective layer, reflects the laser beam so the data can be read by the CD player. The final lacquer layer seals the dye and reflective layer. The protective layer is to prevent scratches to the top of the disc.

during the recording process, it burns or blackens a tiny oblong area called a pit. On top of the dye is a layer of gold or silver that, wherever there is no pit, reflects the laser beam back off the disc to be read by the recorder/player.

During playback, a less-powerful laser is aimed at the disc, and it reads the reflections of the shiny flat areas and the darkened pits, respectively, as ones and zeros. If the laser's reflected signal changes (it sees a blackened pit), the binary value is read as a one. If the reflection is constant, it is read as a zero.

The third layer, on top of the gold or silver, is a coating of clear lacquer extending all the way over the inner and outer edges of the CD to seal the materials onto the disc. Once sealed, the disc's label is printed on top of the lacquer.

With regard to the gold or silver reflective layer, the gold is projected to last about three times longer than silver. One major manufacturer estimates that a silver-based CD can last one hundred years, versus three hundred years for the gold disc. Although the gold obviously has long-term advantages over the silver, for short-term use the less-expensive silver is more than adequate. Discs that have a blue or yellow cast to them are silver discs in which the dye color is apparent.

Super Audio Compact Disc

An SACD is a multilayer disc capable of storing an incredible amount of audio. The SACD format is a joint product of Sony and Philips and looks identical to a regular CD, but that is where the similarity stops. A hybrid SACD provides the opportunity to have not only regular CD-quality stereo audio but also the same audio in 5.1 surround sound piggy-backed on the disc as well.

An SACD is able to store all of this audio because it uses Direct Stream Digital (DSD) encoding developed by Sony. DSD uses a sample rate 64 times the sampling rate of a regular CD (2.8224 mHz or 2,822,400 samples per second) and uses only one bit, as compared to a CD's 16 bits. Due to the incredibly high sampling rate, the DSD is, in theory, better able to

track and reproduce accurately an analog sine wave. Present CDs play in an SACD player; however, SACDs must be specifically formatted to play in a regular CD player. There are three variations of SACDs available, with a capacity of up to 8.5 gigabytes of data, allowing them to store up to six channels of 5.1 surround sound. The SACD format offers some interesting possibilities as it is being further developed.

Digital Versatile Disc

The key word in DVD is versatile. A DVD can be used for a number of different types of audio and video storage. Most people are familiar with video DVDs they buy or rent that have a movie with surround sound. But that is not the only use of a digital versatile disc. In fact, all of the versatility that is available is almost too much for a person to keep track of. A DVD's storage capacity ranges from a one-sided, one-layer disc with 4.7 gigabytes of data capacity to a two-sided, two-layered disc with a total capacity of 17 gigabytes.

Video DVDs feature surround-sound audio capability and have about seven times the audio capacity of a regular CD. Unlike CDs, which have a fixed sampling frequency and bit rate, a DVD accommodates a number of different sampling and bit rates, depending on the intended use. However, the audio storage space is limited. As the audio quality goes up, the number of channels goes down. Using a 48 kHz, 20-bit sample rate enables a DVD to store 133 minutes of six-channel 5.1 surround sound. Increasing the sample rate to record-studio mastering-quality audio (96 kHz, 24 bits) leaves only enough storage space for 133 minutes of two-channel (stereo) audio.

Digital Versatile Disc—Audio

Take a DVD and strip off the video, and you are left with a huge amount of storage space. Thanks to the additional space, a DVD-Audio (DVD-A) provides the opportunity for significantly higher audio quality than a video DVD. Using higher sample and bit rates, a DVD-A can duplicate the quality of original master recordings made in a recording studio.

Because of its large storage capacity, the DVD-A offers scalability. A producer has a number of options with regard to audio quality, the number of the audio tracks, and the sampling rates and bit depths that are used on a particular project. Other information can also be added to the disc, including text or lyrics, still pictures, video sequences, and other nonmusical information such as web links to the producer's web site.

Although the DVD-A does not have the same market penetration in the consumer and professional fields as the CD does, it certainly is seeing acceptance and its professional uses are being explored. Its two biggest advantages are its extensibility as an open technology that can store a number of different audio formats and its scalability, since the producer decides the number of channels to work with, sampling rate and bit depth, and digital encoding method. DVD-A discs play in DVD and DVD-A players; they cannot play back in a regular CD player.

As a comparison, a one-layer DVD-A is capable of holding 400 minutes of standard CD-quality stereo audio or 74 minutes of high-quality (96 kHz, 24 bit) six-channel 5.1 surround-sound audio. Taken to the extreme, the DVD-A is capable of storing 74 minutes of 192 kHz, 24-bit stereo audio. The higher sampling rates of 96 and 192 kHz are identical to

what is used in recording studios to record and master music.

Magneto-Optical Discs

Minidisc

A magneto-optical disc is a recording and playback method that uses both magnetic and optical technologies. A common magneto-optical format is the minidisc (MD). The minidisc was originally intended for the consumer market, to replace analog cassette tape. Although it didn't find favor with consumers in this country, who opted to burn CDs, broadcasters and production people picked up on its compact size, excellent digital audio quality, and portability, preferring the minidisc over analog audio cassettes. Portable machines fit into a shirt pocket and produce excellent recordings that can be played back in professional rack-mount decks. The minidisc has also found favor in semi-pro recording situations, with an available multitrack format.

The minidisc cannot identically match a CD's audio performance. However, its low-noise, low-distortion, digital-quality audio is so close to that of a CD that most people cannot tell the difference. Minidiscs, just like CDs, have a table of contents recorded on the disc, listing the number and lengths of the recordings, making it easy to locate instantaneously any point on the disc, something not possible with cassettes. This further enhances the minidisc's capabilities with regard to program production or news use. Professional minidisc recorders interface with computer keyboards for editing, whereas small portable machines rely on pressing a sequence of buttons on the machine to edit or name tracks.

Figure 5.37

A common magneto-optical format is the minidisc (MD). Minidiscs are popular with broadcasters for news and field recording due to their excellent audio quality and portability. This particular minidisc recorder is only slightly larger than the minidisc itself. Set up with a microphone and some converter plugs for patching into equipment, this machine can go just about anywhere to record quality audio.

The disc itself is about two and one-half inches in diameter, enclosed in a small cartridge (see Fig. **5.37**). The polycarbonate disc is coated with a layer of magnetic material on one side. When inserted into a recorder/player, the disc is sandwiched between a laser below and a magnetic head above. The recording process involves heating a microscopic area of the disc to 400 degrees Fahrenheit with a laser. Just as the spot begins to cool, the magnetic head above the disc polarizes the spot with either a north or south polarity that represents either a one or zero in binary numbers, similar to the pits on a CD. The usage span that has been claimed for the minidisc is one million recordings.

Playback on a minidisc uses the same laser, but at a lower power setting. The laser reads the reflected light off the polarized magnetic material. Using data compression, the minidisc holds up to 80 minutes of stereo audio or 160 minutes of single-channel audio (monaural).

Suggested Activities

1. With the help of your facility engineer, trace the audio signal path through your production facility from the microphone to the final mastering medium (such as a CD). Is the path digital or analog? If digital,

what kind of signal path is being used in the facility, AES/EBU or SPDIF, or a combination of both?

2. You will have to collect a number of different recordable media for this activity. Work in a team if necessary. On your DAW, record either a live voice track or someone playing an instrument. Master to as many different media as you can round up (CD, DVD, DAT, ADAT, DTRS, and minidisc; analog tape, too, if you still have it around) and then critically listen to each. Hear any differences? Which of the media did you prefer working with?

3. If you have not done it already, visit the Adobe Audition web site (www.adobe .com) and take a look at the software and other products to see what is available to turn your computer into a DAW.

4. Visit the digidesign Pro Tools web site (www.digidesign.com) and explore the many different versions of Pro Tools available.

Web Sites for More Information

For more information about:

- *Adobe Audition*, visit www.adobe.com

- *American Engineering Society Digital Audio Standards*, visit www.aes.org

- *digital audio cable*, visit www.canare.com

- *how CDs are made*, visit www.mitsuicdr.com

- *how commercial music CDs are manufactured and other questions about CDs*, visit www .roxio.com/en/support/discs/index.html

how DVDs are made and how they function, visit www.dvdforum.org

- *Pro Tools*, visit www.digidesign.com

Pro Speak

You should be able to use these terms in your everyday conversations with other professionals.

ADAT—Alesis digital audiotape is a digital audio-recording system that uses S-VHS videotapes to record up to eight channels of digital audio. S-VHS stands for Super VHS. It was developed by JVC to offer better quality than the VHS format.

BNC—An unbalanced coaxial cable connector with a bayonet-type locking system invented by Paul Neill and Carl Concelman, thus the name Bayonet Neill-Concelman. Typically found on video and digital audio cables. The center conductor of the cable is connected to a pin, and the shield is connected to a barrel surrounding the pin. A rotating ring outside the barrel locks the cable to any female connector.

compression—An audio processing technique in which the highest audio peaks are automatically turned down, reducing the dynamic range of the audio signal in a direct ratio to the audio input level; a form of automatic volume control.

DAW—Digital audio workstation is the term generally applied to a computer-based digital recording system that incorporates the ability to record, store, manipulate, transport, and deliver digital audio products.

DSP—A digital signal processor is a device for the manipulation and modification of audio signals, such as reverb, delay, or dynamics processing.

DTRS—Digital tape recording system that uses Hi8 videotape as the recording medium, with the capability to record eight channels of digital audio.

DVD—The digital versatile disc is an optical storage medium that offers a number of both audio and video storage formats. Depending on the format, a DVD can store data on both sides of the disc, two layers deep.

DVD-A—A digital versatile disc that contains only audio.

FTP—File transfer protocol, a system for exchanging computer files with another computer, using the Internet as opposed to the World Wide Web.

gating—An audio processing technique that acts just as its name implies, as a gate. When audio is above a preset level, the gate allows it to pass. When the audio level drops below the preset level the gate closes, blocking the background noise.

LAN—A local area network is a computer interconnection system for sharing data between or among computers within a company or media facility at one location.

limiting—An audio processing technique that automatically controls audio levels that approach a preset maximum audio level. When the preset level is reached, the audio is turned down so that it does not exceed the preset level.

SPDIF—Sony/Philips Digital InterFace is a standard digital-audio-file-transfer format using 75-ohm coaxial cable.

Super Audio Compact Disc (SACD)—A joint product of Sony and Philips that uses a two-layer, CD-sized disc to reproduce both 5.1 surround sound and standard stereo using Direct Stream Digital encoding, which is a one-bit system with a sampling rate of 2,822,400 samples per second.

TOS link—The name given a system of fiber-optic cables and connectors developed by Toshiba and used for the transmission of SPDIF digital audio.

WAN—A wide-area network is a computer interconnection system for sharing data among computers within a company or media facility at multiple geographic locations.

CHAPTER 6

Audio Processing

HIGHLIGHTS

An Introduction to Audio Processing

A chocolate cake is pretty good by itself, but with a thick, rich layer of dark chocolate-fudge icing, the cake is irresistible. It excites our taste buds and creates an insatiable desire for more. It's the same thing with a good piece of production. Add audio processing that complements the original work, and suddenly the production comes to life, demanding the listener's attention. Audio processing is the icing on the cake to our ears.

Audio processing is used either to help correct a problem or to add a unique artistic signature that sets a recording apart from the competition. Why do those announcers on national commercials all have the little-extra-something special about the bottom end of their voice (see demo CD, cut 30)? If you play a musical instrument, have you ever listened to a CD and wondered how in the world the musician on the disc got that sound out of that instrument? The answer to these questions is: audio processing.

To this point, most of what you have learned with regard to audio production is basic science. In this chapter you begin to merge the science with your talents and abilities. Audio processing is not an exact science; it is mostly based upon artistic taste. There are no charts or tables that list exactly how much echo to add to a piano recorded in a studio so that it sounds like it was recorded in a four-hundred-seat concert hall. Your skills in this area develop from listening, observing, and reading about how others work, along with your own experimentation. There is one finite aspect of audio processing that you should be very clear about. A bad recording is a bad recording: Garbage in equals garbage out. No amount of audio processing can turn a bad recording into a good recording.

There are three primary types of audio processors: dynamics processors, frequency equalizers, and dimensional processors.

Dynamics Processing

The traditional recording technique is a simple process. Select the hall or studio with the best acoustics. Select the best pair of stereo microphones for the job; one for left channel, one for right. Audition the musical group, taking care to place the mics in the **sweet spot** of the studio or hall to achieve the desired direct-to-ambient sound ratio. Have the musicians play their loudest musical passage, and set the recorder input levels at about –10 VU, leaving adequate headroom. Start the recorder and do not touch the input-level controls until the group is finished. If you have done everything correctly, the recording likely sounds very natural, with a wide dynamic range from the softest to the loudest sound. This is a timeless recording technique for jazz and classical music that highlights the subtle nuances of the music, just as they occurred in the live performance. The very same basic recording technique can be applied to recording an announcer in your production studio.

Unfortunately, we live in a very noisy world, and listening to such traditionally recorded material is difficult in a car, office, or when jogging, because the quieter passages get lost in the ambient noise that surrounds us. This is one of the reasons producers turn to audio processing to tweak, or tune up, a recording or radio signal and make it more commercially viable.

As a general rule, dynamics processors are the first ones used to improve or alter a recording. A dynamics processor changes the dynamic range of the program material, either reducing or increasing its dynamic range. Dy-

Figure 6.1

A compressor enables you to control sounds, such as vocals, that have a wide dynamic range. By reducing the dynamic range, the overall level can be increased. A compressor is the most basic tool used for processing. If a studio has only one audio processor, count on it being a compressor. In the view above, the audio on the left has been compressed while the audio on the right remains uncompressed.   *Adobe product screen shot reprinted with permission from Adobe Systems Incorporated.*

namic processing includes compression, limiting, expansion, and gating.

Compression

Successful recording and mixing techniques require producers to develop a unique sound image that stirs emotions and draws attention to a project. The project must stand out from all of the other material in the marketplace if it is to be successful.

A compressor is an automatic level control that reduces an audio signal's dynamic range by turning down, or compressing, the loudest audio peaks. By reducing the high-level audio peaks, the producer can then raise the overall average level without the peaks causing hard clipping. For example, if a compressor is used to lower the level of the loudest audio peaks by 6 dB, then the average level can be raised 6 dB, producing a louder, more uniform audio signal. The compressed audio peaks still sound loud, and because you have turned up the average level of the audio by 6 dB, the softest sounds are now also louder (see Fig. **6.1**). A compressor enables you to control sounds, such as vocals, that have a wide dynamic range. A compressor is very effective at making an announcer sound louder and making his or her voice dominate anything it is mixed with (see demo CD, cut 31). Even a whisper, when properly compressed, can dominate a commercial or promo and although loud, can still sound like a whisper (see demo CD, cut 32). A compressor is the most basic tool used for processing. If a studio has only one audio processor, count on it being a compressor.

How Compressors Work

When audio is fed to the compressor input, it decides whether the audio is above or below an adjustable **threshold,** set in decibels below 0 VU. If the audio is below the threshold, the compressor does nothing. If the audio rises above the threshold, the compressor reacts, turning down the level. How quickly the compressor reacts to the incoming audio is the **attack time,** measured in milliseconds (thousandths of a second).

The compressor reduces the audio level of the signal based on an adjustable gain ratio that compares the input level of the compressor to the output level. For example, with the ratio set at 3:1, when the audio rises above the threshold, every 3 dB of audio input produces only 1 dB of audio output. When the audio drops below the threshold, the compressor releases control of the audio and it returns to normal. How slowly the compressor releases control of the audio is the **release time,** also measured in milliseconds. Once the audio peaks are compressed, the overall level can be raised using the compressor's gain control.

The procedure for adjusting a compressor is pretty straightforward. The first adjustment is the **compression ratio,** or how much the audio will be turned down. Ratios of between 3:1 and 6:1 produce natural-sounding level control (compression) that is not generally noticeable. Excessive compression ratios produce dull-sounding recordings because the dynamic range is reduced to the point that there are no loud or soft passages—it's all one

fixed level, producing lifeless-sounding production and causing **listener fatigue** (see demo CD, cut 33).

The second set of adjustments on a compressor is the attack and release times (see Fig. **6.2**). Start with a fast attack time of 1 to 1.5 milliseconds and a release time of 350 to 500 milliseconds. You want the compressor to take action quickly and to release slowly, so that it is not noticeable. However, depending on the sound you want to achieve, you can start with the slowest attack time and the fastest release time, delivering a very punchy sound, one that jumps out at you. Announcers love this kind of effect as it makes their voice sound bigger and gives it more impact.

An indicator of excessive compression is "pumping" or "breathing." This is caused by improperly adjusting the attack and release times so that the millisecond the audio is sensed the compressor kicks in and dramatically lowers the level. The moment there is a pause in the audio the compressor releases and the background noise rushes up, producing breathing, or a pumping sound, as the audio fluctuates up and down. This is a very annoying effect (see demo CD, cut 34).

The third adjustment is the threshold: slowly turn down the threshold control of the compressor until the compressor meter reads 3 to 6 dB of compression on the loudest audio peaks (again, see Fig. **6.2**).

Since the compressor is turning down the audio, the compressor's meter reads the opposite of a VU meter. The needle, or indicator, sits at the right side of the meter at 0 and pulls back to the left, showing the decibels of audio reduction. After compression, to compensate for the reduced audio level, use the compressor's gain control to boost the final output to the desired level.

These basic compressor settings are just that, a place to start. With each different proj-

Left Channel

Threshold Adjustment

Compression Ratio

Compressor Output Level

Right Channel

Attack Time Adjustment

Release Time Adjustment

Figure 6.2

If a radio station has only one audio processor in production, it is likely a compressor/limiter. The versatility of such a device allows you to create a number of unique effects and improve the sound of audio tracks. The controls labeled above are used for compression.

ect and brand of compressor, the settings are going to vary depending on the effect you want. Some compressors have a broader range of adjustment than others. As you will find with most audio processors, the best way to learn how a compressor works is to experiment with it. Feed it an audio signal and see how many different ways you can make the audio sound.

Limiting

A limiter is basically a compressor with a gain ratio in excess of 10:1; some go as high as 100:1. A compressor can be adjusted to act as a limiter, and many compressors are sold as compressor/limiters (see Fig. **6.3**). Where the compressor's output is always a ratio in relation to its input and varies, however, the output of a limiter is fixed. Limiters are like a brick wall through which the audio peaks cannot pass, regardless of the audio input level (see Fig. **6.4**). Once you hit the limiter's predetermined level, it really doesn't matter how

much you turn up the input, the audio output level stays the same.

Limiters are used to prevent hard clipping and to increase average audio levels. Compressors and limiters are often used in production to make sure that each piece of production that leaves your studio is at the same maximum level. This makes the commercial sound louder and makes it easier for the jocks to do their job, since they don't have to be on guard constantly for commercials that are too loud or too soft. Limiters have similar controls to a compressor and are set up and used in a comparable manner (see demo CD, cut 35).

Expansion

An expander is the opposite of a compressor. A compressor reduces a signal's dynamic range, and an expander increases, or restores it, after compression. An upward expander makes loud audio segments even louder, and a downward expander turns softer audio segments down. Upward expansion is unusual

Left Channel   **Right Channel**

Threshold Adjustment

Compression Ratio

Compressor Output Level

Attack Time Adjustment

Release Time Adjustment

Limiter Adjustment

Figure 6.3

A limiter is basically a compressor with a very high compression ratio; some go as high as 100:1. Limiters are used to prevent hard clipping and to increase average audio levels. On this model, the limiter control is called the "stop level." In other words, you set the maximum audio level and no matter how much you turn up the input, the output will not exceed your preset maximum level.

since there are so many other ways available to make audio louder. A downward expander, though, is used to lower background noise.

A compressed audio signal has a reduced dynamic range, and the average audio level has been increased or made louder by several dB. When the average level is increased, the softer passages and background noise level are also made louder. Loud average levels normally mask any background noise until a soft passage comes along and the noise suddenly becomes apparent.

A downward expander functions like a compressor in reverse and turns down the background noise during the softer passages, making the audio appear to have a wider dynamic range from the softest sound to the loudest sound. An expander works well to turn down the studio or background noise present when an announcer pauses between words. An expander has a threshold and a variable ratio setting similar to those of a compressor, except that the ratios are reversed (see

Fig. **6.5**). The expander reacts to the audio when it drops below the threshold, and instead of a 3:1 compression ratio (for example) the expander might have a 1:3 expansion ratio (see demo CD, cut 36).

Gating

A gate is a dynamic processor used to reduce background noise. Just as its name suggests, a gate normally remains closed until the audio reaches a predetermined threshold, at which time it opens, allowing the audio to pass. When the audio level drops back below the threshold, the gate can either lower the audio to a preset level or close the channel completely, blocking any background noise.

Sometimes referred to as noise gates, gates are used to open and close audio channels automatically to reduce unwanted background noise (see Fig. **6.6**). Noise gates can also be used to create special effects, such as shortening the reverb or delay time on a recording.

Figure 6.4

Limiters are like brick wall through which the audio peaks cannot pass, regardless of the audio input level. The audio on the left has not been processed. The audio on the right is passing through a limiter adjusted to prevent audio peaks. Once the audio hits the limiter's predetermined maximum level (in this case, –17 dB), it really doesn't matter how much you turn up the input, the audio output level stays the same. *Adobe product screen shot reprinted with permission from Adobe Systems Incorporated.*

Figure 6.5

A downward expander functions like a compressor in reverse and turns down the background noise during the softer passages. An expander is an excellent tool to turn down the studio or background noise present when an announcer pauses between words. The expander shown at the far right of the figure is a component in a microphone preamplifier/processor.

As the audio fades out and drops below the preset level, the gate reduces the audio level or closes, muting the channel (see demo CD, cut 37). Noise gates have thresholds, attack and release times, and ratio settings. Just as a compressor can be adjusted to become a limiter, an expander can be adjusted to become a noise gate.

Figure 6.6

Sometimes referred to as noise gates, gates are used to open and close audio channels automatically to reduce unwanted background noise. As the audio fades out and drops below the preset level, the gate reduces the audio level, or closes, muting the channel. In the example above, when the audio falls below –20 dB the gate closes. Likewise, the audio has to rise above –20 dB before the gate will reopen. *Adobe product screen shot reprinted with permission from Adobe Systems Incorporated.*

Although still widely accepted, gates do not see as much use as they once did because automated consoles and digital audio workstations are capable of easily opening and closing faders, eliminating unwanted background noise just as effectively as a gate.

Frequency Equalization

The telephone company was the first to use frequency equalizers to compensate for signal losses over early telephone lines. Audio production equalizers are really frequency unequalizers, since they are generally used not to make all frequencies equal in strength but to boost or cut specific frequencies to make sounds stand out or blend into the background. Equalizers are primarily used to shape the frequency response and tone of a recording. The industry term for equalization is simply EQ.

Of all the audio processors, EQ is the one that requires the most skill and training to use. It is also the group of audio processors that is most often abused, usually due to a lack of knowledge about the purpose and power of EQ. The first rule of EQ is that if you are not sure what to do, DON'T, and leave it alone.

A graphic equalizer gets its name from the physical layout of the controls on its faceplate. Because each frequency band has its own slider, more than one can be used simultaneously. Raising the slider up boosts the frequency, and lowering it cuts a frequency. When adjusted, it is easy to see the pattern the faders have created, giving a visual, or graphic, reference of the frequency response created.

The second rule of EQ is that if you have been working on the project for any length of time, walk away and go have lunch, let your ears rest and flush the project out of your head. When you come back to the project you are starting with rested ears and a fresh perspective. Pros sometimes give serious projects twenty-four hours before they come back to do the final EQ.

There are three basic reasons to EQ a track. The first reason is to make an instrument or voice sound clearer, or to achieve more clarity in the overall sound. The second reason is to add size and make an instrument or a vocal bigger or larger than life. The final reason is to make all of the elements in a mix fit together by adjusting the frequencies surrounding each voice or instrument so that it has its own space, so to speak, or its own distinct frequency range.

Regardless of how careful a production person is, there are some sounds that for one reason or another blend well during a project mix, some that may stick out, and still others that may seem to disappear. EQ is subjectively used to make things sound brighter, clearer, bigger, and sometimes **fatter.** Other terms used to describe signals before or after EQ include **muddy, crispy, tinny, hollow,** and **bright** or **dark.** Of all the audio processors, EQ is the one that requires the most skill and training to use.

There are two popular types of equalizers, graphic and parametric.

Graphic EQ

A graphic equalizer gets its name from the physical layout of the controls on its faceplate (see Fig. **6.7**). It consists of a series of slide faders vertically arranged side by side. Each fader represents a particular fixed frequency (center frequency) and a small band of frequencies just above and below the center frequency, called the bandwidth. Observed on an oscilloscope, the center frequency is at the top of a curve surrounded to the left and right by the rest of the bandwidth (see Fig. **6.8**).

Although the number of frequency adjustments varies from equalizer to equalizer, the frequencies are based on third-, half-, and full-octave intervals. A full-octave EQ usually begins near 50 Hz, with the succeeding filters at 100 Hz, 200 Hz, 400 Hz, 800 Hz, and 1,600 Hz,

Figure 6.8

Each fader on a graphic equalizer represents a particular fixed frequency (center frequency) and a small band of frequencies just above and below the center frequency, called the bandwidth. Observed on a display, the center frequency is at the top of the curve, surrounded to the left and right by the rest of the frequency bandwidth. The display is indicating that the center frequency is 120 Hz and the bandwidth extends from 90 Hz to 150 Hz.

and going all the way up to 12,800 Hz. For finer adjustments, a half-octave or third-octave EQ is used. Most equalizers have between ten and fifteen frequency bands.

The midposition of each slider is 0. Raising the slider up boosts the frequency, and lowering it cuts a frequency. Because each frequency band has its own slider, more than one can be used simultaneously. When adjusted, it is easy to see the pattern the faders have created, giving a visual, or graphic, reference of the frequency response created (again, see Fig. 6.7). The only drawback to a graphic equalizer is that the center frequencies and bandwidths surrounding them are fixed, and you are limited to working with the equalizer's preset available bands.

Parametric EQ

A parametric EQ has a series of adjustable frequency controls with additional adjustable parameters; thus the name parametric. A parametric equalizer provides much more control

and precision than does a graphic equalizer in selecting a specific center frequency and bandwidth to boost or cut. A parametric EQ has as many as eight controls on its face that let you select a center frequency for adjustment (see Fig. **6.9**). With the frequency selected, the user then adjusts the amount of boost or cut for the selected frequency.

A third adjustment allows you to select the bandwidth surrounding the center frequency. This adjustment is called "Q," or quality factor. The higher the Q value is set, the higher and sharper the peak is around the center frequency of the bandwidth. The lower the Q value is set, the wider and smoother the bandwidth peak is around the center frequency (see Fig. **6.10**). The end result is an equalizer that has continuously variable frequencies and bandwidths.

Filters

Filters are the components of an equalizer used to boost or cut the center frequency and the bandwidth on either side of the frequency. Filters, though, can serve another valuable purpose. A filter can be set to block certain frequencies while at the same time allowing others to pass. Filters are used to remove unwanted sounds, including everything from pops and clicks to building and traffic rumble. There are three types of filters.

A **high-pass filter** (often called a low-cut filter) blocks all of the frequencies *below* a preset frequency and allows those higher than the preset frequency to pass unaffected. As an example, high-pass filters are found on a lot of microphones to roll off or attenuate all of the frequencies below 75 Hz. This gets rid of most building rumble from air conditioners and traffic vibrations (see demo CD, cut 38).

A **low-pass filter** (often called a high-cut filter) blocks all of the frequencies *above* a preset

Figure 6.9

A parametric equalizer offers maximum flexibility. The user selects the frequency, the bandwidth surrounding the frequency, and the amount of cut or boost for the frequency. The end result is an equalizer that has continuously variable frequencies and bandwidths.

Figure 6.10

The "Q" factor determines the bandwidth on a parametric equalizer. The frequency curve on the left has a center frequency of 120 Hz boosted 10 dB. Note the sharp peak and that its narrow bandwidth extends only 90 Hz to 120 Hz. The curve on the right has a center frequency of 2.5 kHz boosted 10 dB. Its wide, smooth bandwidth extends from 650 Hz to 10 kHz. The higher the Q value is set, the higher and sharper the bandwidth peak. The lower the Q value is set, the wider and smoother the bandwidth peak.

frequency and allows those lower than the preset frequency to pass unaffected. As an example, a low-pass filter might be used on a vocal to eliminate room noise and hiss occurring in the studio above the vocal (see demo, CD cut 39). A human voice typically has no usable frequencies above 10,000 Hz. By cutting those frequencies above 10,000 Hz you are cleaning up the track and eliminating the possibility of picking up another sound source you don't want in the recording.

Another kind of filter is a **band-pass filter.** This filter establishes a low and a high cutoff frequency and allows the band of frequencies in between to pass unaffected. A band-pass filter is usually used to isolate a sound or correct a problem with a track.

Finally, there is the **notch filter** that is just as its name implies. A very narrow frequency band is blocked, allowing the frequencies above or below the notch filter to pass unaffected. A notch filter is typically used to eliminate a specific sound such as a click or pop or the rumble of a building air conditioner (see demo CD, cut 40).

De-essing

Between the frequencies of 6 kHz and 8 kHz is an annoying vocal quality known as sibilance. Sibilance refers to the hissing sound people make when they say words with the *ess* (s) sound. Some people have little or no sibilance when they talk; others, however, create a very annoying *ess* sound that is a cross between a hiss and sizzle.

A **de-esser** is a specialty compressor that has an adjustable frequency range so that the frequency of the sibilant *ess* can be determined and attenuated with very narrow bandwidth compression. A threshold is set, and when the *ess* sound goes above it, compression kicks in and the *ess* is de-emphasized. De-essers have to be adjusted to each particular person to be effective (see demo CD, cut 41).

Guidelines for Using EQ

Generally you start the EQ process in the mid-range, keeping in mind that in most cases it is better to *cut* frequencies than to boost them. This is particularly important between the frequencies of 250 Hz and 10,000 Hz. Humans are most sensitive to the frequencies around 5,000 Hz. Boosting the frequencies in this range too much (and it does not take a lot) can turn a mix into a harsh or hard-sounding mix. For example, if your mix sounds muddy, cut some of the lower frequencies, between 100 Hz and 300 Hz, by a few dB rather than cranking up the midrange or high end, which could cause harshness in the mix.

If your project has a nasal sound to it, try cutting in the 250 Hz to 1,000 Hz range. If a vocal or an instrument sounds too punchy, or it stands out above the rest of the mix, try cutting a few decibels between 2.5 kHz and 4 kHz. If you are trying to make things sound better, CUT. Only if you are trying to create a different sound for effect should you boost.

When it comes to the bass in a project, listen to some commercial music mixes carefully. You will likely find that the bass has *not* been boosted but rather filtered and compressed. Using a high-pass filter, everything below 40 Hz has been rolled off. There are two reasons for this. One is that, although there is sound energy below 40 Hz, it is only the frequencies from 50 Hz to 100 Hz that most people perceive as bass. The other reason is that most car and home speakers don't reproduce these low frequencies anyway, so by rolling off these low frequencies, the bass that remains appears cleaner and better defined. Rather than boosting the EQ in this bandwidth, use a multiband compressor to increase the average level and give the bottom end some punch.

The high frequencies have the ability to give your mix a clean, open sound. If you compare your mix to a commercial CD and it sounds a little flat in the upper end, this is not a serious problem. Use a parametric EQ with a center frequency between 12 kHz and 15 kHz with a low Q setting (wide smooth curve). Don't overdo it; compare your project to similar commercial projects. Last, but not least, don't be afraid to roll off the upper end of your project smoothly (above 15 kHz) by 3 decibels. Listen carefully, and you will find many commercial CDs on which this has been done to create a smooth tonal balance.

The sounds below 250 Hz and above 12,500 Hz constitute exceptions to the cautions and guidelines given here. You can play a lot with the extreme upper and lower frequencies without ruining the mix, so feel free to adjust to your acoustical taste, but do still keep in mind that a little bit of EQ goes a long way.

Earlier we said that there was no chart in the world that could tell you exactly how to equalize or process sound to achieve a specific result and that you had to use your ears and your knowledge of music to make these decisions. The EQ chart at the top of page 187 can be used as a very basic guideline, but it certainly is not specific (see demo CD, cut 42).

Finally, listen critically to your mix and keep in mind that you cannot cut or boost something that is not there in the first place.

Dimension

Every sound you hear is a combination of the original sound and how the sound reacted to the environment it was in. Dimension processing adds perceived size or depth to a recording. Introducing a time delay in the form of echo, reverb, or a chorus effect creates dimension. The artificial delay creates the impression that the listener is in a larger

Frequency Range	Description	Acoustic Effect
20–80 Hz Sub Bass	felt more than heard; creates a sense of power	Rumble zone; too much sub bass makes music unclear and sound muddy.
80–250 Hz Bass	fundamental notes of the rhythm section and drums; bottom end of guitars	Too much makes things sound boomy or muddy.
250 Hz–2 kHz Low Mids	the bottom end of most instruments and their low-end harmonics	Boosting 500–800 Hz makes things sound flat and hard; 1–2 kHz improves intelligibility, but be careful or it will sound like a tinny car horn.
2–4 kHz Mid Highs	human ear is most sensitive to this range, which contains speech-recognition sounds	Too much boost in this area causes listener fatigue. If a mix sounds harsh, cut here first.
4–6 kHz Presence	clarity of the mix, vocal definition including articulation and breathiness	Boosting makes music seem closer, but be careful—too much boost creates a biting sound.
6–16 kHz Brightness	brightness and clarity come from this range	Boosting creates sizzle, vocal sibilance; a little boost in this region adds an open airiness.

space by simulating natural-sounding repetitions of the original signal that normally occur in a venue like a concert hall or stadium. Short delays are normally associated with small spaces, and longer delays with large spaces. A simple rule of thumb in using a dimensional processor is to imagine yourself in an acoustic space and what it sounds like, and then try to recreate the sound you are hearing in your head, around you in the studio.

Good candidates for dimensional processing are recordings made in a **dead studio** or location, one that has little or no natural ambience, echo, or delay. Dimension is also used to mask the mixing or blending of two or more audio sources together.

Echo, Slap Delay, and Doubling

Echo, slap delay, and doubling are the simplest forms of introducing depth into a recording. An echo or delay uses one or more repeats of the original signal to create the effect. Delay-effects processors have input- and output-level controls and a control, referred to as the delay time or delay length, to adjust the time delay in milliseconds (see Fig. **6.11**). Such controls may be individual knobs on the face of the equipment or appear as a part of a

Figure 6.11

An electronic reverberation unit recreates the acoustic environment of a number of different spaces, from a small room to a large concert hall. Most come with numerous preset effects and also let you create your own new effects and place them into memory.

menu on a small screen. Slap delay is generally a single repeat of the sound with a delay of over 35 milliseconds (see demo CD, cut 43). When adding this effect to a music bed it is a good idea to adjust the repeat time in relation to the beat, or tempo, of the music. By matching the music's beat, the delay adds to the music rather than fights it by being out of tempo with the music.

A feature of many delays is a feedback control. A feedback control does exactly what its name implies; it feeds the delayed signal back into the delay input so that a delay of a delay is created. The higher the feedback setting, the more delays are created (see demo CD, cut 44).

A single slap delay of less than 35 milliseconds is called doubling, since it creates the impression that there are two of whatever you are applying the delay to (see demo CD, cut 45).

Reverberation

Reverberation, or reverb, is different from delay in that it is a complex combination of multiple, randomly mixed delays designed to simulate a specific acoustical space such as a large concert hall, sports stadium, or small intimate room. A distinguishing characteristic of reverb is that, as the repetitions of the signal slowly drop in intensity, the number of repetitions increases.

Reverb has three distinct purposes. The first is to create an aural space, to trick the brain of the listener into believing that he or she is in a particular listening environment. Most reverbs are infinitely adjustable; the space can be adjusted to taste to enhance the production. The second use for reverb is to make a sound appear bigger, fatter, or deeper. The selection of the space and the decay time affects this. And the third purpose for reverb is to be able to use a pan control to position an audio signal between the left and right sides of the stereo image—for example, you could put an instrument in the left channel and let the reverb trail off into the right channel, creating a huge space. Remember that audio being sent to the processor prior to the addition of reverb is called dry, and when the audio is returned from the reverb after processing, it is called wet.

The adjustable parameters for a reverb include an input-level adjustment, delay or space adjustment, and decay time (again, see Fig. **6.11**). The delay or space adjustment regulates the size of the acoustic space that the reverb creates, from a small, tight room to a football stadium (see demo CD, cut 46).

The decay time control sets the length of the effect. Smaller reverbs and shorter delays make things sound bigger. To create these effects, reverb decay times should be under a second and delays should be 100 milliseconds or less. These are maximum settings, and you will likely find that shorter decay and delay times work as well or better, particularly if the recording is stereo (see demo CD, cut 47).

Likewise, longer reverb decays and longer delays push the sound further away from the listener. This begins to happen at around 100 milliseconds of decay or delay and really kicks in at over 200 milliseconds. If the decay or delay is too long and too loud, the track just sounds far away and is not very interesting.

Reverb can be used to bring a track to the front, closer to the listener, or blend it into the background, moving it away from the listener. For example, say you have a dry piece of music for a commercial and a dry announcement or vocal track that you want to mix together. To make the voice stand out from the music, leave the announcer dry and wet down the music (add reverb); the announcer moves forward and dominates the mix (see demo CD, cut 48).

If the reverse is true and you want the music to stand out and the announcer to be in the background, leave the music dry and wet down the announcer (see demo CD, cut 48).

A third option is to blend the two together, with equal amounts of reverb on each. This typically happens when a dry announcer track is being laid down over a production music bed that has some reverb. In this case, the voice stands out in front until you add some reverb to the voice, blending it with the music.

Chorus, Phase Shifting, and Flanging

Chorus is an electronic effect that modifies the sound of a voice or instrument to simulate a group of vocalists or instruments. For example, one vocalist is processed to sound like a group of three; a violin becomes a convincing-sounding string section.

The chorus effect is based upon tricking the listener into thinking there are several of something instead of one. When you are seated in front of a musical group at a concert, the acoustic environment modifies the sound that you hear by introducing time delays. Sounds naturally bounce off the floor, ceiling, walls, furniture, and so on, and each arrives at your ears at a slightly different time. If you remember from an earlier chapter, this shift in time is called a phase shift. The acoustical environment also introduces slight shifts in the pitch of the instruments.

Using an adjustable time delay of between 20 and 35 milliseconds creates a chorus effect. The distinguishing difference between the chorus effect and delay or reverb is that in the chorus effect, the length of the delay is randomly varied, introducing phase shifts that simulate what naturally happens in an acoustic environment. The random phase shifts also cause slight variations in the pitch of the sound. This creates the impression of several of the same signals arriving at your ears at various times. This effect is then mixed back into the original signal, causing one of something to sound like a group (see demo CD, cut 49).

The same processor that creates a chorus effect can also create a phase-shift effect. A phase shift creates the illusion of a swooshing motion in the music, sounding like the mid and high frequencies are being swept through frequency equalization (more on that later in the chapter). Adjusting the delay time of a chorus processor from 1 to 3 milliseconds creates a phase-shift effect (see demo CD, cut 50).

Flanging is a more dramatic phase-shift effect. It is used in the recording industry on vocals, keyboards, guitars, bass, and drums. The flanging effect is created by adjusting the delay time of a chorus processor to 10 to 20 milliseconds of delay. Although flanging is a digital electronic effect today, famed guitarist

Les Paul is said to have created the flanging effect using four reel-to-reel tape machines. Listen to the Beatles, Jimi Hendrix, and many other artists of that era to hear examples of the original flanging effect (see demo CD, cut 51).

As with most audio-effects processors, the best way to learn the processor is to feed it some audio and start experimenting with the controls, to learn firsthand all of the unique effects that you can create.

Re-amping

Re-amping is one of the oldest audio effects that can be created. It is used to simulate a natural-sounding environment. The process is so simple many people overlook it. Take an audio signal and play it back through an amplifier and monitor speaker in the studio. Place a microphone, or pair of microphones for stereo, in the studio and rerecord the track using the ambience in the studio to create a variety of effects, depending on how far the microphone is placed from the speaker. By experimenting with the placement of the speaker and microphone, you can create some unique acoustical effects. Try placing the speaker facing away from the microphone and recording the sounds that have bounced off a studio wall. There are no rules to re-amping and no expensive audio processor; that is what makes it so much fun to try. The effect that you create is unique to your studio, speaker, and mic placement (see demo CD, cut 52).

Broadcast Audio Delay

Broadcast audio delay is not an effect; it is an extremely valuable audio processor used in the radio industry. During live talk shows or telephone conversations with listeners it is critical that the caller not be put on the air live, since the broadcaster is responsible for anything that the caller might say. Indecent and obscene language can bring heavy fines from the FCC. A single word can cost a station thousands of dollars and put your job in jeopardy.

Typically, broadcasters use a seven-second delay on listener calls or talk shows. If someone says something the producer thinks is objectionable, whether it is objectionable language or a libelous remark, the producer has seven seconds to delete the language by pressing and holding a "dump" button. When the dump button is released, the processor then automatically plays catch up and restores the seven-second delay (see Fig. **6.12**).

Broadcast delays go into and out of delay very smoothly. During the opening of the show, while the host is talking, the digital audio processor begins introducing delay over a few seconds so that by the time the first caller is taken there is a full seven seconds of delay. This is called ramping up to delay. At the end of the show, when the announcer is wrapping up the program, the producer deactivates the delay and the unit ramps down from a seven-second delay to real time.

The listeners are not aware of what is going on until they call the show and are told by the producer to turn their radio down so that they don't get confused while talking and then hearing their own voice over the radio seven seconds later.

Normalizing

A normalizing processor is included on most digital audio workstations. It corrects the problems associated with a track that has been

Figure 6.12

A broadcast delay does exactly what the name implies; it takes live audio and delays it a preset time (typically seven seconds) so that in the event of inappropriate language the producer or operator has a few seconds to dump the offending audio so that it never reaches the air. Note the DUMP button on the right side of the unit.

recorded with too little amplitude (volume) or too softly. The processor analyzes the audio and searches for the highest and lowest peak levels to determine the dynamic range of the signal. With this data, the processor raises the overall volume level of the track while maintaining the signal's original dynamic range. Normalizing allows a producer to select the percent of modulation to be applied to the signal (see Fig. **6.13**). If one hundred percent is selected, the highest audio peak occurs just before hard clipping (see demo CD, cut 53). Normalizing, though, is not a substitute for recording at the proper level to begin with.

Normalizing can also be used to match the audio level between two different audio segments that you want to join together seamlessly. You can match existing audio levels in a track or session by first using the processor's gain-analyzer function to determine the maximum peaks in the existing audio tracks. After analysis, adjust the processor accordingly and normalize the new track to match the original track's level.

Most professional recording engineers prefer a properly recorded track with good levels to normalizing. With that said, the exception to the rule is in radio, where program directors want maximum modulation to achieve a sound on the air that jumps out at the listener. In essence, radio production directors want it loud, and normalizing a commercial or station promotional announcement to one hundred percent modulation will certainly do that.

Voice Processors

Voice or microphone processors are designed to be the first stage after the microphone in the audio chain. Designed primarily for broadcasting and voice-over work, voice processors are designed to "punch up" the talent's voice, giving it a unique quality and making it stand out. The thing to keep in mind is that a voice processor can make a good voice sound dynamic and exciting. A voice processor is not capable, though, of

Figure 6.13

A normalizing processor corrects the problems associated with a track that has been recorded with too little amplitude (volume) or too softly. Normalizing allows a producer to select the percent of modulation to be applied to the signal. The audio on the right side of the window has been normalized to a maximum level. Normalizing, though, is not a substitute for recording at the proper level to begin with. *Adobe product screen shot reprinted with permission from Adobe Systems Incorporated.*

Figure 6.14

Voice processors are actually a combination of a number of processors in one convenient box. A typical voice processor includes a high-quality mic preamp with phantom power for condenser microphones. This processor also includes a compressor, expander, de-esser, equalizer, and limiter.

magically turning a mediocre voice into a great voice.

Voice processors are actually a combination of a number of processors in one convenient box. A typical voice processor includes a high-quality mic preamp with phantom power for condenser microphones. Following the mic preamp are a compressor, limiter, de-esser, expander, noise gate, and high-pass/low-pass and band-pass filters. Some voice processors include a multiband parametric EQ and are offered with reverb (see Fig. **6.14**).

Basic Voice Processor Adjustments

The first stage of a voice processor is typically a microphone preamplifier. A preamplifier features an input level control and a trim pad to match the output level of the microphone to the input level of the processor. Additionally, most professional voice processors have 48-volt phantom power for condenser microphones. Start by adjusting the input level so that the preamplifier is seeing an incoming signal of 80–100 VU from the microphone (see demo CD, cut 54).

The preamp section is usually followed by a compressor (gain reduction) to limit the variations in the levels of the voice that occur in normal speaking. As discussed earlier in the chapter, a good compression ratio to start with is from 3:1 to 6:1. These lower ratios reduce the transients in the voice without reducing the dynamic range of the voice too much (to avoid making it sound flat and without life). After the voice is compressed, use the compressor output control to raise the average level of the voice back up to 80–100 VU (see demo CD, cut 55).

Keep in mind that when you compress a voice to reduce its dynamic range and then turn up the average level, you also turn up any electrical noise or ambient studio noise. To reduce or eliminate the unwanted noise, most voice processors offer a downward expander. A downward expander works in just the opposite way from a compressor, and instead of making loud sounds louder it makes quiet sounds quieter. Set the threshold of the expander at the point below which you want the expander to close and silence the signal. Then adjust the amount of expansion you want (see demo CD, cut 56).

A de-esser removes sibilant *ess* sounds that can be quite annoying. De-essers are frequency-specific compressors. (We have discussed them already under Frequency Equalization in this chapter.) By setting a high compression ratio and then adjusting the frequency-range control, the specific frequency causing the problem can be found and completely removed in most cases. However, it does have to be adjusted for each person (see demo CD, cut 57).

Most voice processors have a frequency equalizer, and unless you have specific training in EQ it is wise to leave this alone or seek the help of others if there is a serious problem with the frequency response of the person's voice. As discussed earlier, more harm than good can be done to a signal through improper EQ.

Many voice processors offer adjustable high and low filters. Typically, the low filter is set at 80 Hz, since there really is not that much sound energy in the human voice below this. In addition, this part of the frequency range is where most building rumble and vibration occur, so eliminating the audio below 80 Hz provides a cleaner-sounding bottom end to the audio. Likewise, adjustable high-pass filters allow you to adjust how much audio above 12 kHz is used. There is very little vocal energy above 12 kHz, and eliminating these unused frequencies eliminates hiss and noise in a signal. By rolling off or eliminating these two frequency ranges, the audio appears cleaner (see demo CD, cut 58).

The last section in a voice processor is the peak limiter. If you remember from earlier in the chapter, this is the device used to adjust the maximum audio level. The limiter is useful in preventing an overload of the output stage and in setting the maximum audio level (see demo CD, cut 59).

The only remaining control on the preamplifier is the output level adjustment, to match the input level of the control board or recorder the preamp is feeding an audio signal to.

Figure 6.15

An effects processor is capable of creating literally thousands of special audio effects in addition to the hundreds of effects that come preprogrammed with the unit. Newly created effects can be saved for future use. An effects processor can create everything from reverb to sophisticated phase shifts and repeating effects.

There is no chart or list of the exact settings for voice processors and what works with what kind of voice. By careful experimentation, an announcer can determine the right combination of settings to reinforce his or her radio voice.

Digital voice processors are computer-controlled and can store up to 100 different announcer presets, so that each announcer's voice can be maximized. Before announcers go on the air, they select their preset number, and the processor recalls all of the settings for that particular voice.

expansion, tremolo, vocal harmonizing, laser blasts, video-game-sounding electronic weapons fire, vibrato, random pitch shifting and panning, "Max Headroom" stutter, complete reversal of words and phrases, and sweep tones, just to name a few of the thousands of effects available on some processors.

These are very powerful and elaborate tools, and they provide the production person with a valuable edge in creative audio work in commercials and creative productions (see demo CD, cut 60).

Effects Processors

To a production person, an effects processor is the equivalent of a dump-truck load of Legos to a six-year-old. This digital microprocessor (computer)-based audio device is capable of creating any sound or effect you can imagine by manipulating audio through advanced digital algorithms. Effects processors can be used to combine multiple effects and create unique new sounds, storing them in the processor memory to be easily recalled (see Fig. **6.15**).

Effects include endless variations on reverb, slap delay, echo, chorusing, flanging, phase shifting, pitch shifting, time compression and

Broadcast Audio Processing

Listeners are a little smarter and a little more sophisticated than many people realize. The first thing that usually catches listeners' attention as they scan through the frequencies on their radio is the music or show itself. Once they have located the show they like, they focus on the station's presentation. Is it loud enough so that it can easily be heard in a car or over the office chatter? Does it sound great on their car or home system? Many cars have rather sophisticated audio systems straight from the factory. Is it a unique sound that

Audio processing often is the reason a listener chooses one radio station over another, even though both play the same music. Digital broadcast audio processors offer the program director and engineer an incredible array of multiband digital signal processing (DSP) including sophisticated compressors, expanders, limiters, gates, filters, and EQ to customize the station's sound.

complements the music and is easy to listen to for long periods of time? Of course, listeners are not consciously asking themselves these questions, but programming research has shown that each is a reason a listener will select another station. Just as important as the music itself is the audio processing the station applies to the music.

Radio stations process all program audio before it is sent to the transmitter. Originally, the reason for on-air processors was to control audio levels so they didn't overload the transmitter and distort the on-air sound. Now, though, digital broadcast audio processors offer the program director and engineer an incredible array of multiband digital signal processing (DSP) including sophisticated compressors, expanders, limiters, gates, filters, and EQ to customize the station's sound. Select any song and listen to it on ten different radio stations, and it will sound ten different ways. Audio processing is often the reason a listener chooses one radio station over the other, even though they both play the same music (see Fig. **6.16**).

Broadcast audio processing is based on a psychoacoustic musical image created by the program director in conjunction with the station engineer. As an example, a classic rock station understands that a lot of its listeners turn up their radios and listen at louder-than-average levels. The processing has to be adjusted so that the audio peaks in the rock music don't cause distortion on a car or portable radio. An urban hip-hop station, to take another example, has to have a clean, loud, distinct bottom end; muddy bass is not tolerable to a serious hip-hop listener with a high-wattage sound system in his or her car. The bass has to have a solid punch to it. Finally, a light rock station that targets at-work listeners adjusts its processor so that the station sounds good on small, portable radios that are not turned up very loudly.

As a production person, you should consult your program director and station engineer on how far you can take audio processing in your work with programs and commercials. Broadcast engineers prefer that you leave the frequency response as flat (as even throughout the frequency spectrum) as possible on your projects and use only slight amounts of processing to correct minor problems. Because all on-air audio will be processed again when it goes through the broadcast processor, there is the possibility of heavily processed production causing listener fatigue or creating a **tune-out** factor.

Webcast Audio Processing

Putting an audio signal on the web would appear to be a pretty simple task at first. Tap into the on-air audio someplace in the radio station and feed it to a computer hooked up to the Internet. Sources range from a spare FM radio to an auxiliary output from the station's broadcast audio processor. Sending good-sounding audio to the Internet is not that simple, though.

The first problem that broadcasters encounter is the fact that, unlike for the radio station, there are no FCC-mandated technical standards for transmitting the signal to the listener's receiver via the web. A person listening on a dial-up phone modem hears audio very differently than someone who's connected on a high-speed cable modem. Because webcasters don't know what kind of computer and Internet connection their listeners are using, they typically prepare audio based on "the average site visitor" so that as many people as possible will be able to hear the webcast.

The second problem a webcaster encounters is the fact that it is not easy to jam all of that digital-audio data down a very narrow pipeline to the listener. CD-quality audio (44.1 kHz, 16 bit) guzzles more than 10 megabytes of data per minute. Most consumers using plain old telephone service **(POTS)** have an average dial-up connection speed of around 30 kilobits per second. A webcast of a four-minute CD-quality song would take approximately four hours to reach a listener at that speed. Either the pipe has to be bigger or the amount of data has to be reduced.

The audio processing required to originate a good-sounding webcast is as technically involved as the on-air broadcast processor. The first step is the use of an Internet audio processor, as they are very different from their broadcast counterparts. Microsoft, RealNetworks, and QuickTime all feature the sophisticated data-compression algorithms necessary to send audio over the Internet. The compression algorithms analyze the digital audio and discard those inaudible frequencies (data) not critical to the musical quality and to which our ears are not sensitive. Because some of the data is discarded, causing a slight loss in audio quality, this is known as lossy compression.

As a general guideline, audio production intended for the Internet needs to have a very good signal-to-noise ratio. The frequency response should be left flat, and high- and low-pass filters should be used to eliminate those audio frequencies above and below what the Internet will easily transmit. Heavy compression and limiting should be avoided, as most commonly used Internet audio processors do not work well with audio that has been heavily processed.

Suggested Activities

1. Try feeding a plain voice track and a stereo music track through the compressor that is included with Adobe Audition. (You can also use a compressor in your radio production studio, if you have one.) Spend an hour adjusting the gain control, threshold, and attack and release times to see how many different sound treatments you can create from the same tracks. Afterward, see if you can adjust your compressor to act as

a limiter. Experiment with establishing maximum levels.

2. Using the different dimensional-effects processors that you have access to in Adobe Audition, record one track each with echo, reverb, and slap delay. Can you tell the difference among them all by listening? Now try chorus, phase shift, and flanging. Again, can you tell the difference by listening?

3. Record two separate tracks, one a dry voice track and one a dry stereo music track. Using reverb, bring the voice to the front of the recording and then place the voice behind the recording. What challenges or difficulties did you encounter?

4. Record a short musical selection using Adobe Audition. Experiment by using the different filters, or bands, on a graphic EQ and see how many ways you can change the spectral balance of the music. Can you make any instruments seem to disappear or to stand out from the rest?

   Now experiment specifically with cutting frequencies to make things come to the front.

   Repeat the experiments with a parametric EQ to see how it differs in operation from the graphic EQ. Which gives you the most control?

Web Sites for More Information

For more information about:

- *broadcast audio processors,* visit Orban Audio Processors at www.orban.com or Omnia Audio Processors at www.omniaaudio.com

- *echo, slap delay, doubling, and reverberation,* visit Lexicon at www.lexicon.com or tc.electronics at www.tcelectronics.com

- *effects processors,* visit Eventide at www.eventide.com

- *streaming audio on the Internet,* visit Real Networks at www.realnetworks.com/index.html, Apple's QuickTime at www.apple.com/quicktime/products, or Microsoft's Media Player at www.microsoft.com/windows/windowsmedia/distribute.asp

- *voice processors,* visit Focusrite Audio Engineering at www.focusrite.com/index2.html or DBx Professional Products at www.dbxpro.com

Pro Speak

You should be able to use these terms in your everyday conversations with other professionals.

attack time—The fixed or adjustable length of time it takes for an audio processor to sense the presence of audio and react to the audio, measured in milliseconds.

band-pass filter—An audio filter that has a high and low cutoff frequency, allowing only the frequencies in between to pass unaffected.

bright—A sound rich in high frequencies.

compression ratio—The fixed or adjustable ratio of the input to the output of an audio compressor.

crispy—A sound with extended high-frequency response, like the sizzle of crisp bacon frying.

dark—A sound that is the direct opposite of bright; dull with a weak high-frequency response.

dead studio—A studio or a location that has no natural reverberation or echo.

de-esser—A specialty compressor that has a variable frequency range used to reduce sibilant *ess* sounds in speech between 6 kHz and 8 kHz.

fatter—A sound with a good, solid, low-frequency response with emphasis in the 100 to 300 Hz range.

high-pass filter—An audio filter that has a preset cutoff frequency, allowing those frequencies above the cutoff frequency to pass; those below the cutoff frequency are blocked. Sometimes referred to as a low-cut filter, a term more descriptive of what the filter actually does.

hollow—A sound that has a mid-frequency dip similar to when you cup your hands around your mouth and talk.

listener fatigue—A condition brought on by misadjusted audio processing, causing the listener to become consciously, or sub-consciously, tired of listening to a musical selection or radio station.

low-pass filter—An audio filter that has a preset cutoff frequency, allowing those frequencies below the cutoff frequency to pass; those above the cutoff frequency are blocked. Sometimes referred to as a high-cut filter, a term more descriptive of what the filter actually does.

muddy—Muffled-sounding audio, not clear, with too much reverb at the lower frequencies.

notch filter—An audio filter designed to eliminate a very narrow bandwidth of sound, creating a notch in the frequency. Generally used to eliminate unwanted sounds.

POTS—A telephone company term for Plain Old Telephone Service, or a dial-up hard-line telephone connection.

release time—The fixed, or adjustable, length of time it takes for an audio processor, such as a compressor or limiter, to return a signal to its normal level after processing, measured in milliseconds.

sweet spot—The physical location in a concert hall or studio where there is the least phase cancellation of live sound and where the direct-to-ambient sound ratio is in proper proportion.

threshold—When used in relation to an audio processor, an adjustment that sets the audio level at which the device will become active and begin processing.

tinny—A sound that has an almost telephone-like quality to it. A very narrow-band sound that sounds as if it were coming through a tin can or over a telephone.

tune-out—Any psychoacoustic element of a radio station's signal that is annoying to the listener. Often referred to as a tune-out factor.

CHAPTER 7

The Art of Sixty-Second Story Telling

HIGHLIGHTS

Production as a Part of the Sales Process

Turning a Sales Order into a Working Commercial

Record-Keeping and Archiving

Suggested Activities

Web Sites for More Information

Pro Speak

Regardless of the medium—radio, television, film, or the web—nothing goes on the air without the help of a production person. Production people transform the ideas and concepts that come from salespeople and clients into commercials. These sixty-second messages are really short stories about how the listener benefits from the products and services offered by the advertiser. (Occasionally, advertisers may choose to use a thirty-second commercial, depending on what goals and objectives they have for their advertising campaign.) Ideally, a commercial is so well-crafted that it motivates people to take some form of action. There is only one measure of success when it comes to a commercial: Did the client's store traffic and retail sales increase?

Radio and television commercials may appear to be two entirely dissimilar media. However, a well-crafted television commercial is a radio commercial with pictures. A good television commercial does not depend upon the images alone to deliver the advertising message, it depends on a combination of the audio track and the images. The most effective television commercial has an audio track that can stand alone as a radio commercial. During a commercial break, when the audience gets up to go into the kitchen and get a soda, the commercial is still effective because the audience can hear it. These stand-alone audio tracks are often used on radio because they have the ability to trigger visual images in the radio listener's mind. The visualization of a television commercial while hearing it on radio is called **image transfer.**

Although many major market operations employ writers and continuity directors (responsible for writing all the commercials), many others do not. There are times when you yourself will need to put together a commercial. Here's a real-life lesson: A salesperson shows up at 4:30 on a Thursday afternoon with a sales order for several thousand dollars from a major client (big car dealership). The copywriter has gone home early because of illness. The commercials need to start running at six o'clock tomorrow morning. What are you going to do? Tell the client, "We're sorry, our copywriter went home sick, so we can't take your thousands of dollars today and you'll have to wait until tomorrow afternoon to start your schedule of ads"? Events like this are the reason you need to be able to assemble a commercial on your own.

A note about commercials: before you go any further in this chapter you must rethink a word that may be in your vocabulary. Production people do not produce **spots.** When you dribble marinara sauce down the front of your shirt or blouse while eating spaghetti, you produce a spot. Dry cleaners remove spots. The fact is, salespeople DO NOT SELL, and clients DO NOT BUY, spots. Clients buy well-crafted solutions to their marketing problems that help them increase store traffic and retail sales. You produce ads, or commercials, that are a critical part of the client's sales process and marketing plan.

Production as a Part of the Sales Process

Commercial production is one of the final steps in the selling process. Although the client may have signed a contract for airtime, until a commercial is produced to go on the air, the order is incomplete and cannot start. Often, the client sees the production service itself as a valuable resource that the radio station offers. This is particularly true when the client is planning on using **dubs** for advertising schedules on other stations.

Why Advertising Works

Advertising is not difficult. But somehow, in all that is written and said, many people forget the simple formula that is the basic premise of advertising. Successful advertising consists of four components: the right product, at the right price, at the right time, aimed at the right target audience. When the four components are brought together, the result is a chain reaction of events culminating in increased sales for the client. Change any one of the four variables in the formula, though, and the advertising will not work nearly as well, if at all.

Here's a story about some hardware stores in Florida that were trying to sell lifetime-guaranteed twenty-five-foot garden hoses in the summertime—the price, $49.95. A chain of three hardware stores had two pallets of these things that had been gathering dust in their warehouse. The stores decided to try radio advertising. They thought that if they put commercials on the radio, people would somehow magically snap up the hoses. The radio salesperson reminded store management of the formula. A garden hose in Florida is a "got-to-have" item, the right product. The summertime is the right time. The radio station's target audience included 35-to-64-year-old homeowners, the right target audience. The price, though, was a problem. Who buys a fifty-dollar garden hose? The salesperson convinced hardware store management to do a half-price promotion and sell the hoses at fifty percent off (they were still making a buck). The ads started on Wednesday, and on the following Monday all but two of the hoses were gone. The right product, the right price, the right time, the right target audience; it's not rocket science.

AIDA, an Opera about Success

Regardless of how well-produced a commercial is, just putting an ad on the air will not instantly generate sales increases. Regardless of the medium used, there are four stages in a successful advertising schedule leading to increased sales. There are a number of variations of these stages. You can remember them by thinking of the opera AIDA. AIDA, in this case, stands for Awareness, Interest, Desire, and Action.

Awareness

First, a potential customer has to be made aware of a business. Depending on the schedule of ads, this can take some time. Can a single ad in the Sunday paper accomplish this? Can five radio ads on Friday do the trick? Can one ad each night during the evening news on TV create awareness? Regardless of the medium, the faster a business wants to build awareness, the more ads the business will have to run. As an example, radio salespeople typically recommend a *minimum* of fifteen ads per week to accomplish the kind of results and sales increases that an established radio advertiser expects. A new advertiser, though, might have to increase that number of ads proportionately to develop the consumer's awareness of his or her business before potential customers can be moved along in the buying process.

Interest

Before customers can be moved to buy a product, they have to be interested in the product itself. Their curiosity needs to be aroused. To develop this interest, the advertiser shows or tells the listener what the product does. What problem will the product solve for the customer? What kinds of satisfaction will the customer receive from it? What kind of benefits will the product provide the customer? It is important to remember that the focus needs to be on the benefits the product provides to the consumer. Until sufficient interest is developed in the product, the consumer is not ready to move to the next stage of the buying process.

Desire

With product awareness and consumer interest established, the advertiser can focus on developing a desire for the product. This is the stage at which the advertiser tells the consumer how good the consumer will look wearing, using, or being seen with the product. The advertiser appeals to many of the consumer's most basic desires to look good, smell good, be safe, be successful, have esteem, prestige, self-fulfillment, and so forth. The advertiser can do this by appealing to the consumer's most basic wants, needs, and desires.

Action

This is the final stage of the buying process. The advertiser asks for some type of action on the part of the consumer. To quote some well-worn clichés, "Don't miss this once-a-year event." "Act now and save thousands." "So you don't forget, send before midnight tonight." Customers go where they are invited and do what they are asked. The advertiser must ask for some type of action on the part of the consumer.

What's In It For Me? (WIFM)

Have you ever met someone who did nothing during the first five minutes of a conversation except tell you how great and wonderful they were, the things they owned, and the people they associated with? If you are like most peo-ple, you probably started looking for an easy getaway from this egocentric bore.

That is exactly what happens to a commercial when the advertiser spends sixty seconds telling the audience how great his or her business is. Who cares? Customers don't care about a business for its own sake. What customers care about is as old as the ages: "What's in it for me?" (WIFM). If they spend their money with the advertiser, what will they get in return?

Another element of a commercial that can be a real turn-off for the consumer is the use of the advertiser's industry terms and jargon. Although this may impress another business, the consumer has no idea in the world what the business is talking about and, frankly, does not care (see demo CD, cut 61).

The focus of a successful commercial is *not* on the advertiser but on how the products offered by the advertiser will solve the consumer's problems and meet the consumer's needs, wants, and desires. This does not mean that the advertiser is not important. It means that the advertiser has to learn to think from the consumer's point of view (see demo CD, cut 62). Remember, WIFM: What's in it for me?

The Salesperson/Client Relationship

As a production person, you are going to be working with very valuable property: commercials. A commercial has a real cash value based on the time invested by the salesperson and everyone else who processes the commercial, including the production time you yourself are going to invest in creating the commercial.

As a production person, you need to be sensitive to the fact that a commercial is a collaborative effort among the client, the salesperson, and you. Notice that the salesperson is between you and the client. Beginning with the salesperson, everyone employed at the radio station depends on your work for his or her income. In a small market, a monthly schedule of a hundred commercials at $10 per commercial is $1,000. The salesperson earns $150 (a fifteen percent commission) on the sale, and the station nets $850. In a larger market, those ten-dollar ads are suddenly $175 each, the client is spending $17,500, the salesperson's commission is $2,625, and the net to station is $14,875. You should be aware that people become very sensitive when money is at stake.

As a production person, you should follow your company's policy regarding any direct contact you have with the client. Usually, the salesperson will want to handle all communications with the client, and rightfully so, since you may not be aware of where the client/salesperson is in the buying process. As a general rule, it is not a good idea to get between a salesperson and a client. Channel all your communications with the client through the salesperson. This includes having the salesperson call the client for ad approval or take the client a copy of the ad on CD. As simple as it may sound, one of the last steps in the buying process is the client's approval of the ad before it goes on the air. Usually, only the salesperson is prepared to handle the client's questions and concerns at this critical time in the sales process.

There are times when a salesperson may ask you to have direct contact with a client (because he or she has a scheduling conflict, or for some other reason). You should talk with the salesperson beforehand and find out exactly what he or she wants you to do and say. If the client asks you any question you don't know the answer to, politely refer the client back to the account representative. To sum it up, don't try and go around the salesperson to the client.

Turning a Sales Order into a Working Commercial

Why You Need to Create Great Commercials

A client said yes, a salesperson wrote a broadcast order, traffic has scheduled a start date, and a production order gets dropped on your desk (see Fig. **7.1**). The success of the radio station is now on your shoulders. No kidding.

There are two reasons you need to create great commercials. Firstly, a bad commercial fails to help the client generate anticipated sales increases. Successful radio advertising is based upon solving client marketing and advertising problems through increased store traffic and retail sales. Radio's success is dependent on helping a client build his or her business with radio advertising so that the business becomes a regular advertiser. If a commercial fails, it fails the business that bought it and the radio station, and the station has lost a repeat customer.

Secondly, you need to create a great commercial because bad ones are *dangerous* to the station's audience ratings. During a television show, commercial breaks can be filled with bad commercials. The audience still watches the show, but when the commercials come on viewers have the option to get up and leave the room, returning when the commercials are over to watch their show. Regardless of whether or not the viewer watches the commercials, the television show still gets good ratings. Radio, though, is different. A commuter stuck in a car during morning rush-hour

WRPC Production Order
104.1 FM *Classic Hits*

Client Number: 88-9679
Date: 5/29
Salesperson: Jim Underwood
Client: Carolina Furniture Outlet
Client Contact: Rick Green
Address: 2617 Hendersonville Road
Phone #:   555-5011   **Fax:** 555-5165
E-mail: rickg@spiderlink.net   Web site: www.cfoutlet.net
Start Date: 5/24   **Start Time:** 0600
End Date: 5/30   **End Time:** 1700
Client approval due date: 5/22 Time: 3:30 PM
How many different commercials? 2
Length: 60
Who Writes Copy? Continuity _**X**_ Salesperson ___ Production____

Specific Production Requirements

(Staple additional information to this order if needed)

Client wants an aggressive car dealer sound to commercial. Really Hard Hitting.

Please see if Jeff will do the voice on this.

Make sure you mention the phone number 4 times, 2 at front of ad and 2 at end.

Client wants to approve music before you do production.

COPY ON ATTACHED SHEET

Produced by: _____   Date: _____   Time: _____

Salesperson notified on: Date: _____   Time: _____

Music cuts used: _____

SFX used: _____

Figure 7.1

A production order is the first step in producing a commercial. Note the amount of information on the sample above. The production order also tracks who produced the commercial and what music and sound effects were used to create it. Many stations now use "online" or web-based production orders so that everyone connected with the sales and production process can follow the order.

traffic when a bad commercial comes on has only one option. The driver can't get up and leave the car, so he or she changes the station in search of something better. Every listener is valuable. Losing listeners causes ratings to drop. As ratings drop, so does the station income. Poorly produced commercials are just as responsible for the loss of listeners as are bad jocks.

Let's look at the steps involved in creating a great commercial.

Brainstorming

The process of creating an award-winning commercial begins with brainstorming. Brainstorming is a wonderful part of the creative process, because it triggers people's imagination and brings out innovative ideas. All you need is a piece of paper or a marker board and a quiet place to think. As you think, write down all your ideas. Nothing is too silly, too stupid, or too off the wall. At this stage in the process go for the preposterous, push the limits, be a little daring, and don't be critical or make any judgments regarding your ideas. Just write them down. The goal is quantity—come up with as many ideas as possible for the ad.

Build on the ideas by grabbing anyone nearby and soliciting his or her ideas. People tend to play off one another, and the more people you have, the more imaginative you can be in coming up with creative solutions to meet the client's needs.

Brainstorming does not have to be a long, drawn-out process. Allow fifteen minutes, focused on the project at hand. Focused means NO interruptions: close your door, take the phone off the hook, shut off your instant messenger, and tell anyone who knocks on your door to go away. You're brainstorming.

Refinement

In the refinement stage, you evaluate what you have written down. Start the refinement process by using the guidelines that the salesperson and client have established for the commercial. These guidelines are your filter. Read the ideas you have on paper aloud, since this may trigger more new ideas from you or someone on your team. Group similar ideas together and see if anything begins to take shape. Combining a new idea with one you already have could be the key to a dynamite commercial. As you filter the ideas, some may be tossed out as too off the wall, and that is fine, since the purpose of the filtering process is to narrow your options and focus in one direction or another.

Selecting a Style

As a part of the refinement process, you are likely to come up with an idea about a possible style for the commercial. Some might argue that selecting a style has to come before refining the ideas. But they depend on each other. Which came first anyway, the chicken or the egg?

In this respect, the process originates with you. Do whatever you are most comfortable with. Refine the ideas, select a style, in the order that makes sense to you.

There are five broad categories of commercial styles. Nevertheless, these categories can and do overlap.

Dialogue and Narration, with and without Music

Commercials can use plain language very effectively, whether it's one person talking the whole time or two or more people acting out a scene together. Spoken commercials like this can be kept entirely plain, with no musical effects whatsoever, or they can be enhanced with production music.

The most basic commercial features a single person talking for sixty seconds (narration). On its face, this may seem like a very dull and boring approach. But consider this: when you go into a car dealership to talk to a salesperson, do they play the company's theme music and jingle beds while they are trying to talk to you? Nope!

In spite of this, just about every commercial on the air has music, sound effects, and multiple voices. After a while, with two or three ads to a **stop-set,** the commercials begin to blend together and sound alike to the listener. A narration commercial (one person) or a commercial in the form of a dialogue between two people can be very effective at capturing the audience's attention and standing out from other commercials.

One of the most effective commercial approaches is a business owner voicing his or her own commercial. Not only does the commercial stand out because it is just narration, it stands out because it is not a slick-sounding professional voice. As a real person and a known quantity in the community, the business owner has a great deal of credibility. People will tell the owner, "I heard you on the radio." These are some of the most powerful words a business owner can ever hear.

A dialogue or narration commercial can also use music, in addition to the talking, to reinforce ideas and themes. Music can add a powerful element to a commercial, providing nonverbal cues to many emotions that people experience. The tone of the music provides a cue to the audience ranging from upbeat and positive to the opposite end of the spectrum, very serious. Listen to the variety of music cuts on the music CD included with this text and you will experience a variety of emotions that can be used to enhance a narration-type commercial.

Production music is purchased in the form of music libraries that are either bought outright or leased. Production libraries feature thirty- and sixty-second-long cuts of music that are copyright-cleared for commercial broadcast purposes. (It is a violation of the copyright laws to edit and use popular general-release music behind commercial material, unless you have paid for the right to do so. Aside from the copyright aspect, using popular music behind a commercial causes the audience to focus on the music rather than on the dialogue in the commercial.)

Customized music can provide another advantage for a client. Custom music beds and jingles become a client's signature, so that every time the music airs, the audience immediately associates it with the client.

Testimonials

Many business owners feel that the best advertising is word-of-mouth advertising. This is good for radio commercial sales, since a radio station has the biggest mouth in town.

Word-of-mouth advertising is testimonial advertising. Using a business's customers to tell listeners why they should shop at a particular business is very convincing. As an example, restaurants use this commercial style very effectively, featuring customers telling listeners why they like the restaurant and what their favorite dishes are. With the right mix of people, the customers can voice the entire commercial. The only downside to this type of commercial is that it takes more time to produce, since it involves location recording and selective editing.

Product Comparisons

Many business owners want to go head-to-head with their competition and compare products and prices. One school of thought on this approach says never give the competition your airtime; another says: if you have the advantage, push it.

Comparative advertising can be effective with products and services that the listener needs and that have high brand loyalty. If a small independent grocery store wants to challenge a big chain store, they can use price and product, demonstrating that they have the better buys on specific "need" items.

Lifetime Experiences

The lifetime-experience style of commercial involves using talent that mimics people in the listener's life. Real-life situations are used to show how a business can solve problems or make life easier for the listener. People tend to relate to people like themselves, and so this type of commercial can be very effective.

Lifetime-experience commercials must be carefully written and developed so that they are realistic and believable. Otherwise, they appear hokey and not very credible. The same applies to the talent in the commercial; the speakers have to be believable so that the audience identifies with them. Although announcers have good voices, often they make poor actors. You may have to reach outside the announcing staff to voice a believable lifetime-experience commercial. This is particularly true when you need the voices of older adults or children.

Humor

Humor can be a great selling tool; it can also be a commercial's downfall. Humor has to be well done to be an effective and persuasive advertising style. Just like with anyone telling a joke, the message has to keep the listener's interest and attention until the punch line, and it has to provide some real entertainment for the listener.

Humor requires care so that you entertain, rather than offend, listeners. It is best to stick with generic themes that apply to lifetime situations such as family, children, and friends. All of these people have similar lifetime experiences that you can base humor on. Keep in mind that what you may think is a scream, your audience may not find funny at all (and vice versa).

More than anything, humor is an exaggeration of life. If you stick too close to real life, then it is unlikely that anyone is going to laugh. It is when you step on the line or push the envelope that things begin to get funny.

Always, though, keep in mind that your goal is to entertain and not to offend. Try out your ideas on people before putting them before the client, and listen carefully to the responses.

Putting Words to Paper

This is not a chapter about writing but rather how to assemble a commercial, how to put the pieces and parts together. Here are seven things to keep in mind when assembling a commercial.

The Target Audience

Contrary to popular belief, commercials cannot force anyone to buy anything. Most consumers are motivated to buy something only because the product or service offered solves a problem they have, or at least think they have. A focal point to keep in mind as you write a commercial is WIFM: What's in it for me? Keep the ad focused on the benefits that the target consumer is going to receive or the value that the consumer is going to get from the product.

Almost every business is number one at something and wants to toot its own horn. And yet, although customers are drawn to businesses they perceive as leaders, that is not the customer's primary concern. Customers are not so interested in the business itself; they want to know how the business's products and services can solve their problems. Focus the commercial on the target audience, not on the advertiser.

Some consumer problems are easy to identify because they are based on need. As an example, people get hungry and have to shop somewhere for food. Consumer problems that are more difficult to pinpoint are those based on desire or want. (For instance: the first major purchase many college students *want* to make after leaving college is a new car. The kind of car they can (or cannot) afford is going to depend on the job they get right out of college.)

The client and salesperson must identify the target audience. Who is the business trying to reach? Who are you supposed to be talking to? What kind of problem are you trying to solve for the target audience? The answers to these questions include demographic as well as psychographic information. Demographic information includes quantifiable data such as the fact that a target audience includes married couples, 25 to 54 years old, with a combined income of $75,000 per year, and 1.2 children. Psychographic information about this couple includes the information that they prefer country music, eat out two times a week, buy one CD a month, rent four DVDs a month, and like domestic beer. The more information you have, the more effective your commercial can be.

The Objective

A schedule of ads, or a campaign, has to have an objective to succeed. Why is the client running these ads? This information is determined by the salesperson working with the client. The overall campaign objective involves solving a specific marketing problem that the client has.

After determining the overall campaign objective, the specific purpose of the ads themselves can be identified. What does the client want each commercial to do? Before you start writing, finish this sentence in clear and concise language: "This commercial's specific purpose is . . ." Any given commercial should be focused on solving only one advertising objective or purpose. Trying to accomplish multiple objectives within the same ad dilutes the message and makes it difficult for the listener to follow. If necessary, create more than one ad and rotate the ads in an appropriate schedule so that each ad gets the proper **frequency.**

As a part of the commercial-creation process, write the overall campaign objective and the specific commercial objective, or purpose, on the copy. Some stations use copy forms to define objectives and strategy more clearly and to help keep the writer "on message" (see Fig. **7.2**).

One purpose, besides its specific purpose, that every commercial has in common is to establish the name of the business in the listener's mind. This is done through a three-step process: repetition, repetition, and

WRPC Production Copy
104.1 FM *Classic Hits*

Client Number: 88-9679   **Date:** 5/29   **Salesperson:** Jim Underwood
Client: Carolina Furniture Outlet   **Client Contact:** Rick Green
Address: 2617 Hendersonville Road   **Phone #:**   555-5011   **Fax:** 555-5165
E-mail: rickg@spiderlink.net   Web site: www.cfoutlet.net
Start Date: 5/24   **Start Time:** 0600
End Date: 5/30   **End Time:** 1700
Client approval due date: 5/22 Time: 3:30 PM
How many different commercials? 2
Length: 60
Overall campaign objective: To establish Carolina Furniture Outlet as THE only store in Western

North Carolina that is a true manufacturer's outlet. The only direct-from-the-factory manufacturer's

furniture outlet.

Specific commercial objective: Move overstock dining room sets in a 12-hour one-day-only

monster sale.

COPY

Attach additional copy sheets as needed.

Figure 7.2

Excellent commercial copy is important to the success of an advertising campaign. The copy form above repeats much of the information on the production order so that it is always in front of either the writer or the producer, making it easy to check vital client information and due dates. Like the production order, many stations prepare copy online for easy access and editing.

repetition. The client's name needs to be mentioned at least four to six times in a sixty-second commercial. Instead of using words like "we" or "our" when referring to the business, use the client's name, and use it often, throughout the ad (see demo CD, cut 63).

A Few Phrases to Eliminate from Your Vocabulary

Before you ever start to write a commercial, you need to eliminate some of the following words and phrases from your vocabulary. They are overused, trite, clichéd, and meaningless. They are junk words with no real meaning, which waste your client's valuable time. These are just a few of the junk phrases that show up over and over in commercials.

- That's right . . .
- You, the customer . . .
- So hurry on down to . . .
- So you don't forget . . .
- Call right now . . .
- This is a limited edition that won't last long . . .
- For storewide savings . . .
- We service what we sell . . .
- Our friendly and knowledgeable staff is here to serve you . . .
- Where our service makes the difference . . .
- Plus, you'll save . . .
- With prices too low to mention . . .
- Come see us today . . .
- For all your [insert product here] needs, see . . .
- Conveniently located at . . .

- They're going fast and won't last long . . .
- Drive a little and save a lot . . .

Start listening critically to radio commercials. You will quickly find out that there are even more useless phrases that need to be trashed. Sixty seconds is not much time; learn to edit your copy, and don't waste your client's money. Remember, the goal is to create copy that increases store traffic and retail sales.

Opening the Commercial

Time is money when it comes to creating a commercial. Although the entire length of the ad may be sixty seconds, the reality is that you have only eight to ten seconds to catch and hold the listener's attention at the beginning of the commercial. This can be done through a variety of ways, including definitive statements such as:

- This weekend, say good-bye to your old clunker and drive off in a new Subaru for only $129.95 a month, at Ridgemont Subaru.
- This week, Wild Bill's Thriftway Store has over $20 in special in-store coupons to help you save on your groceries.
- Would you like to own a new home for what you're currently paying in monthly rent? The First Bank of Eldon can show you how, with First Bank's low-interest, no-down-payment home loan.

Notice that each of the above targets a listener's needs, wants, and desires. An ad can also be opened with a startling question, an unusual statistic, an example, a comparison, a quotation, a survey result, or a simple story. Do something different, be creative, and get the listener's attention. In opening the commercial, remember the short amount of time you have and stay focused on consumer benefits.

The Price and the Product

If you take nothing else from this chapter, remember this: Above all else, every commercial must mention price and product. This is not an option. If the commercial does not have a price and a product, you are not writing a commercial. A commercial without price and product will not produce increased store traffic or retail sales for the client.

Stop and think about it for a moment. Every car dealership in the world can tell you it has the lowest prices, easiest financing, an award-winning service department, friendly salespeople, no-hassle pricing, a convenient location, years in business, prices too low to advertise, and so forth. So what! The *only* thing that distinguishes one car dealership from another, or any business from any other business, is price and product.

Marketing research has shown time and time again that although consumers are loyal to a particular brand, they hold little loyalty to a particular retailer. When it comes time to buy, the retailer with the low price wins. If you don't think this is the case, ask yourself this question: "Where do I shop?" Complicating matters, the Internet has made it easier than ever for a consumer to determine not only a fair market value for a product but also its wholesale price as well. If the product is not available locally at the right price, consumers will drive to a nearby city or purchase the product online.

When presenting the price and product in a commercial, the price needs to be as consumer-friendly as possible. Ask yourself, "What would attract me?" For example, an ad for a

cable television company featured the company's premium package of channels, which were regularly $61.95 a month, on sale for only $51.95 a month, plus free installation. You save $10.00 per month. Pretty impressive, huh? But the company wasn't selling any packages because the thought of paying over $50.00 per month (over $600.00 per year) for television was still enough to scare customers away.

To solve the problem, the ads were rewritten using a price-comparison technique. The $51.95 monthly cost breaks down to about $1.70 per day. The comparison could have been made with anything, but the choice was made to compare this to the cost of food. The ad copy read:

> A buck seventy a day won't even buy your lunch at a fast-food restaurant, but it *will* buy you CableVision's Gold Deluxe package, with 105 channels of incredible television *and* 12 channels of HBO and Cinemax. Which would you rather have every day, a greasy hamburger or quality entertainment for the whole family?

Based on the results from this one campaign, the local cable company changed its whole marketing strategy. This type of approach is what I like to call "baby steps." Just like a baby, you walk the consumer through the buying process, one little step at a time. Car dealerships use this technique every day. Advertise a car for "only $26,995" and it will sit on the lot. Advertise the same car for "$250 down and only $227.51 a month" and it will sell. A consumer cannot afford to spend $27,000 for a new car, but he or she can afford $227.51 a month.

With respect to "percentage off" sales, they mean nothing to a consumer. As an example, a client wanted to advertise lawn furniture at "thirty percent off their already low, low, price." In effect, the client was saying "blah blah blah blah blah" to the listener. Instead, tell the listeners they will "Save $50 this weekend on an outdoor table and four chairs." In another instance, a 105-year-old family-owned department store had long experience with an annual founders'-day sale. Each year, the store closed for the afternoon before the start of the sale to mark down the prices in the store. Their radio and print ads said things like "save $14.00 on men's Dockers slacks." The store-owner said that his family had learned quite a long time ago that a percentage of nothing is nothing, and that customers understand money, not percentages.

Here are two sample pieces of copy for a furniture store:

This Saturday is super savings day at Hallmark Furniture. Save 15 percent on select Hallmark leather sofas and love seats! Leather three-way recliners are 20 percent off! Relax tonight in your new Hallmark sofa or love seat with Hallmark's interest-free financing!

This Saturday is super savings day at Hallmark Furniture. Save $200 on select Hallmark leather sofas and loveseats, starting at only $799. Save $175 on Hallmark three-way leather recliners, starting at only $599. Relax tonight in your new Hallmark sofa and love seat for just $28.95 a month, with Hallmark Furniture's interest-free financing.

Which of the above clearly communicates price and product? A critical part of creating a successful commercial is considering how the consumer evaluates the cost of the client's product. You have to present the price to consumers in terms they understand, making it appear more affordable from the consumers' point of view (remember: WIFM).

The Call to Action

Ask and you get, don't and you won't. A business has to ask, or invite, customers to shop with them. As a part of the commercial, the client has to tell consumers what the client would like them to do or ask consumers to take some action that will result in a sale for the client. This is the stage where it's easy for the clichés highlighted earlier in this chapter to show up if you're not on the alert. Avoid them!

Combining a product benefit with a call to action works well. Be creative. Here's an example: "Don't fight bugs in your home any longer; call Acme Pest Control today at . . ." Another example could be: "Schedule your free Acme Pest Control home inspection at acmepestcontrol.com."

Closing the Commercial

A good wrap to a commercial is very important. In just a few words all of the elements of the commercial need to be tied together into an easy-to-remember message for the audience. The wrap, or closure, should reinforce the purpose and advertising objective of the client (see demo CD, cut 64).

Most businesses want to end their commercials with their address, phone number, and web address. This block of information can take up a significant amount of time and needs to be very well written if the audience is going to remember it.

A business address has to be reduced to the simplest of terms so that it can be easily remembered; not many people can write well while they are driving, jogging, or listening in the shower. Eliminate long strings of numbers and use landmarks instead to create an address that can be remembered. Which is easier to remember: "5-6-8-7-9 West State Road 107" or "Highway 107, across from Danny Lenn Subaru"? (Other ways to give an address include using an intersection as a reference point or saying that the business is just past, or near, a major landmark.) People expect a business to have a large sign they can see if they get close enough, so generic addresses work well. The goal is to keep the address as short and simple as possible.

Phone numbers take up a lot of valuable time, five to seven seconds for a local number if it's repeated and longer for ten- or eleven-digit toll-free numbers. A business often includes its phone number just because all the other businesses have included theirs. The reality is that most phone numbers serve no real purpose in an ad and just take up valuable time. Before including a phone number, ask if it is really necessary. Do you ever hear a phone number in a McDonald's commercial?

On the other hand, a florist who has telefloral services or a beauty shop that takes appointments needs to include the phone number. If a phone number is used, it should be easy to remember. Have the announcer combine the last four numbers in the telephone number into two groupings, such as 555-53-86. This makes it simpler for someone hearing the ad to remember the number. Fifty-three, eighty-six is easier to remember than 5-3-8-6 (see demo CD, cut 65).

Businesses that have e-commerce web sites need to include the web address in their ad. As an example, car dealerships encourage customers to make online service appointments, golf courses let players schedule tee times, and so on. Just like the phone number, the web address must be simplified. Long web addresses with underscores, hyphens, and dashes DO NOT work verbally. Since there is only one World Wide Web, drop the www from the web address (it takes a couple of seconds just to say w-w-w). People understand what to do when they hear "schedule your service appointment on the web at mountainchevy.com" in a commercial.

However you simplify the business's contact info at the end of the commercial, remember to keep the closing strong, memorable, and structured to reinforce the client's objectives.

Record-Keeping and Archiving

Throughout the commercial production process, it is important to keep accurate records and copies of all of the information related to the commercial, including the production order, original script, and an archive data copy of the DAW file.

The production order is a record of what you've done and how you did it. Usually there is a place on the order to record when the client approves the written copy and when the client approves the final production before it goes on the air. It is important to keep production notes as to what you do and how you do it, either on the production order or on the copy itself. These notes should include the track numbers and content along with a listing of the music bed and sound effects sources used to create the commercial.

Clients often develop a liking for a specific ad because it significantly increases their store traffic and sales. It is not unusual for a client to ask a salesperson to update last year's big blowout bonanza ad because it worked so well. The client won't be able to remember the exact wording or the music that was used, just that it was the best ad the business had ever run and management wants to run it again. With complete records, it is easy to recreate the ad or make changes to the original. Most stations have policies regarding how long a commercial can be stored on a hard drive and, when it's time, how to archive creative materials. Such materials are kept in active client files, sometimes for as long as two years.

The best rule of thumb when it comes to record-keeping and archiving is to leave an information trail that is accurate enough so that a complete stranger can pick up the file and re-create the ad. Not that a stranger is going to do that, but the chances of your remembering exactly what you yourself did to produce an ad, a year after the fact, are very small.

Suggested Activities

1. Look up a listing for a pet store in the Yellow Pages. Round up two friends and brainstorm a commercial for the pet store based on the information in the listing. Spend no longer than fifteen minutes writing down your thoughts. See if you can come up with more than twenty different ideas.
2. Select and record five radio or television commercials off the air. Carefully listen to the commercials and see if you can pinpoint the target audience, advertising objective, and specific purpose of each commercial.
3. Using the commercials you recorded in #2, see if you can figure out the style of each.
4. Using the commercials you recorded in #2, see if you can figure out the wrap to the commercial.

Web Sites for More Information

For more information about:

- *books on radio advertising,* visit the National Association of Broadcasters at www.nab.com
- *creativity,* from one of the most creative people on the face of the planet, visit www.danoday.com
- *why radio advertising works,* visit the Radio Advertising Bureau at www.rab.com

Pro Speak

You should be able to use these terms in your everyday conversations with other professionals.

dubs—Slang for the word duplicate, a term used for a copy or copies of an original.

frequency—The number of times a radio ad airs during a given period of time.

image transfer—When an audio track from a television commercial is used as a stand-alone radio commercial, causing the radio listener to visualize the images of the matching television commercial.

spot—Slang term for a radio or television commercial. Don't use this word. Although advertising salespeople call them spots, clients typically think in terms of ads or commercials.

stop-set—A break in a station's music programming, composed of a jock talking, commercials, and promotional announcements.

CHAPTER 8

Producing Commercials, Promos, and News

HIGHLIGHTS

Talent

Production Pre-Planning

Production

News Production

Suggested Activities

Web Sites for More Information

Pro Speak

Typically, when we think of production in a radio station we think of commercials, station promotional announcements, and the imaging elements that give a radio station its personality. And in fact, this is the bulk of what is involved in radio station production.

From a production standpoint, commercials, station promotional announcements, and public service announcements are all basically the same. A commercial is produced for a station client, a promotional announcement is produced for the station, and a public service announcement (PSA) is produced on behalf of a nonprofit organization, but the core production elements of recording, editing, and mixing are the same for each. When we refer to commercials, throughout this chapter, please think commercials, promos, and PSAs.

News is a different critter and gets its own special section at the end of the chapter. But even there, keep in mind that many of the core elements of production with regard to recording, editing, and mixing are all the same basic production skills, just used in a slightly different manner.

Talent

What in the world is talent? Simply, talent is a person's inherent, distinctive ability to do certain things a little better than other people do. Some people explain talent as God-given; others attribute talent to learned behavioral patterns or skills. It really does not matter how a person comes by talent. Some people appear to be naturals, whereas others work hard to build skills in a particular area. Talent is also a generic term used to describe announcers.

Whether they are talented or skilled, one of the pitfalls production people face in their day-to-day work is turning out "formula" production. Call it falling into a rut, or turning

out the "same old, same old." This is especially true in consolidated markets, where a production person typically has a more diverse and heavier workload. The individual may be producing work for five to seven different radio stations. Give any experienced production person the name, address, and phone number of a business and three items with price and product, and he or she can likely ad-lib sixty seconds for you based on clichés and meaningless verbiage. It won't be pretty, but it is a commercial, and if scheduled properly it stands a chance of working.

Of course, the time may come when you are backed into a corner and are forced to resort to a formulaic work product. When this author was a general manager, I had a standing house rule ("house" being the radio station). In an emergency, we would process a sales order and have the commercial on the air in an hour or less, using formula-type production. I can't tell you how many times a car dealership called in near cardiac arrest, because a newspaper had screwed up a big weekend ad or a competitor had under-priced the dealership, and the client wanted to use the flexibility of radio to correct the situation NOW. Once the emergency commercial was on the air, though, the salesperson and production had to revamp it and bring the commercial up to station production standards. That was the house rule.

To remain fresh, talented, and skilled, production people need to stop from time to time to evaluate their work and the production process, from the creation of the script forward. This evaluation can involve anything from a lunch away from the station to attending an industry seminar. Anywhere you can talk freely and objectively evaluate your production process with others will work. Evaluation should be a constant, ongoing process. If nothing else, use a simple form of self-evaluation on a daily basis. Ask yourself at the end of each day what you did that day that was great. Likewise, ask yourself if there was anything you could have done better, and what you could have done to make it better. Regular evaluation is a valuable resource for news and public affairs producers as well.

Production Pre-Planning

Before going into the studio, take a moment to plan out what you are going to do and how you are going to do it. This does not have to be a lengthy process. Keep in mind that studio time is valuable, especially in a multistation complex.

Script

Regardless of whether you or the continuity coordinator wrote the script for a commercial, review it before you go into the studio. Believe it or not, people do make mistakes, and before you spend time on a project you should make sure you are working with good copy. Do the names, telephone numbers, and addresses in the script match up with the production order? A simple error caught at this point saves everyone time and trouble at some point in the future.

Check pronunciation and look for any new or unusual words you, or the talent, may not be 100 percent sure how to pronounce. If you find something you are not familiar with, ask the continuity coordinator or salesperson how the word should be pronounced. Sometimes it's the simple words that will jump up and bite you. As an example, a pronunciation that comes up frequently in the furniture business is a "suite" of furniture. Is the word "suite" pronounced like a man's suit of clothes, or it is pronounced "sweet"? The dictionary's pre-ferred pronunciation and what the furniture store wants may be two different things. In this case, after confirming with the salesperson, you go with what the client wants.

Look for any phrases that require special attention, such as the client's slogan. Sometimes the client has a particular way he or she likes the slogan to be read, with emphasis placed on certain words. A car dealership, for example, uses the slogan "Nobody, but Nobody beats a Mountain Jeep Deal." The client insists that the talent read the first "Nobody" quickly, and that "but Nobody" be stretched out, with a lot of emphasis on the second "Nobody."

Check the script's timing by reading the script aloud and timing it with a stopwatch. How long is a sixty-second commercial? Sixty seconds. When it comes to timing, you also need to be aware that many stations use computer live-assist systems to play back the ads in the stop-sets. These systems are adjusted so that the ads in the stop-set play back to back, and often the system overlaps the ads by a fraction of a second. Check with the production director or the station's engineering staff to see what the overlap is. If a station is using a common overlap of 750 milliseconds, that means that during the last three-fourths of a second, the ad is being faded down and the next ad is starting. The end result is that your voice track must be finished at fifty-nine seconds or the end of the voice track will be clipped off by the live-assist system as it fades the ad.

Technical Considerations and Track Layout

After previewing the script, you should have a good idea of what is going to be required to create the commercial. The first question to get out of the way is whether or not you have everything in-house to complete the project.

Have you got the voice talent, sound effects, and music to produce the commercial? Are there any production elements, like a client-supplied jingle, or music bed, that you still need in order to complete the project? If the commercial is a simple dialogue (voice-only) commercial, then all you need is the voice talent and you are ready to go.

Of course, if you are producing an ad for a car dealership you might be asked to do a little more. For example, the dealership may be required to use a manufacturer-supplied music bed, to which the dealership wants to add synthesizer rips, called laser blasts, to emphasize price points. The dealership might also like to overlap the announcer's voice on top of itself with reverb and close the commercial with the eight-second tag line from a custom jingle the dealership has purchased.

As a part of studio prep, make a quick track count and see where you stand. For the car dealership's commercial, eight tracks are required to complete the project in stereo—two tracks for the manufacturer's music bed, two tracks for the client's eight-second custom jingle tag line, two tracks for laser blasts, and two tracks for the voice talent so that the voice can be overlapped. Most digital audio workstations (DAWs) have that many tracks and more, but you just need to consider the track count to make sure you are covered.

As a part of preparing to go to the studio, figure out how you want to group or lay out your tracks. There really is no set rule, except to try and keep it as simple as possible. The best track layout is the one that works for you. Don't ask me why, but this author's personal habit is to lay down (record) the voice tracks to the left, or top (depending on software), of the DAW monitor screen, starting at track one. Music tracks get set to the far right, or bottom (again depending on software), of the DAW monitor screen. The sound effects (SFX) usually end up on the tracks in between the voice and the music. Regardless of how you lay out your tracks, though, you need to have a plan in mind before you go into the studio. It is at this stage that you can take a production/track layout form and begin designing the commercial (see Fig. **8.1**).

Music Selection

The time to make general music and SFX decisions is before you go to the studio. To avoid tying up a studio, most people use the computer on their desk or a small boom box with a CD player to audition music and SFX.

Before considering music, consider the lack of it. In chapter 7, plain voice and dialogue commercials were discussed as being very powerful at communicating ideas. Some commercials really do not need, nor should they have, music behind them. When a friend is talking to you about the big sale at the electronics store, does he play music in the background? When a man and woman are talking about wedding plans, do they stop and play music in the background so they can talk? Nope.

If you think you just have to have music in the background of a straight voice, or dialogue, commercial, try this test. Go ahead and mix a track of music you like with the voice track. Play it back and listen critically to the commercial, then immediately play back the commercial without the music bed. Does the commercial message suddenly sound like it's missing something? If it sounds like it lacks something without the music, then you were right: You know the music is adding something to the commercial. But if the commercial message still sounds good without the music, drop the music.

WRPC PRODUCTION CREATIVE CONCEPTS

Client Number: 88-9679
Date: 5/29
Client: Carolina Furniture Outlet
Salesperson: Jim Underwood
Length: 60 _____ 30 _____
Date due for approval: 5/22

Production music bed used: _____

SFX used: _____

Any special music or SFX you created for this ad? _____

Track 1: _____

Track 2: _____

Track 3: _____

Track 4: _____

Track 5: _____

Track 6: _____

Track 7: _____

Track 8: _____

Track 9: _____

Track 10: _____

Track 11: _____

Track 12: _____

Use reverse side for more tracks.
Complete form online or attach to completed production order.

Figure 8.1

A production track-layout form helps you to pre-plan your work before you go into the studio. It also serves as a record of what you did, should you have to re-create a similar commercial for the client at some time in the future.

The best music for a commercial is something written and scored specifically for the commercial, something that appeals to the commercial's target audience, and that matches the tempo, mood, and style of the commercial. If you are fortunate enough to live in a larger metropolitan area, there are likely to be a number of talented professionals who can quickly score sixty seconds of music for a very reasonable fee. Such fees will depend on a number of factors. For example, who owns the music and retains the copyright: the composer, client, or the radio station? Is the fee a one-time-use fee, with additional fees to be paid whenever the client uses the music again? Or is the music an outright one-time purchase, where the radio station or client pays for it and it is the property of one or the other in perpetuity? Some radio stations negotiate quantity discount rates from these independent producers, making the cost even more affordable for the client. (Typically, the client pays for any additional costs associated with a custom music bed, even if the costs are folded into an annual contract or commercial rates.)

The next best thing to custom music is a music library. Very likely, most of the music for your commercials and station promotional announcements is going to be selected from a production music library. Production music libraries consist of sixty- and thirty-second cuts of music that are copyright-cleared for commercial use. Some libraries include ten- and fifteen-second cuts as well. Production libraries come in a variety of music formats, tempos, and styles, fitting just about every business and mood. Most libraries include news, sports, and public affairs theme music as well. A small production music library has been included with this text for your class projects, including news and sports themes (see Appendix).

Music libraries are created and sold by music production companies that specialize in production music and jingles. These libraries offer music to fit numerous radio formats. A music library can be acquired on a market-exclusive basis, meaning that the production company will only sell a format-specific library, such as classic rock, to one station in the market. However, the company will sell that same library to a number of stations across the country on a market-by-market basis.

There are three ways a station acquires the rights to production music. Firstly, a station can buy the library outright, with market exclusivity, for a one-time payment. Prices for libraries purchased in this manner range from the hundreds to the thousands of dollars, depending on the number of cuts and the quality of the library. Secondly, a station can lease a library for a monthly fee, never owning the CDs in their possession. The advantage of a leased library is that it is updated on a regular basis, and you get fresh music to work with, exchanging older CDs for new ones. A third way, and the least common way to get a library, is on a **"needle-drop basis."** This is a pay-as-you-go situation in which the station initially pays nothing for the library. Each time the station uses a cut from the library, it has to report the usage to the music production company and pay the fee for that cut. (The term "needle-drop" comes from the early days of radio, when record players had a replaceable phonograph needle, or stylus, and a payment was made for each drop of the needle onto the record.)

Clients sometimes request a popular song as the background to a commercial. It is not possible to use commercially released songs behind commercials. In virtually all cases, it is a violation of the copyright held by the music's owner. When you hear and see national and regional ads with popular songs used behind them, additional rights fees have been paid to the music's copyright holder. (An exception to this rule is when your station is promoting a music concert and you use the band's own music behind the ad for their concert.)

As far as selecting the music for the commercial, there are a few more considerations to take into account. Firstly, your program and production director are going to require you to use music that complements the station's format. You can't have music that goes counter to the format. For example, if your station is a light-rock station, you will not select something with a heavy-metal sound to it. Conflicts like this are usually avoided through the careful selection of the production music library in the first place, but don't be surprised if you occasionally see a production CD with a cut labeled "not for air" on the liner notes.

Secondly, consider the commercial's pacing and energy level. You are looking for a piece of music that will appeal to the commercial's target audience and complement the announcer's timing and energy level. The music is not the star of the commercial. The music is backing up the announcer and needs to remain in the background, assisting the announcer to reach the target. Often, the music influences how the talent reads the copy. If you select something too fast and intense, it appears as though you are trying to push, or rush, the announcer along. Likewise, selecting something too slow, with a weak energy level, drags the announcer down.

Thirdly, consider the emotional level, or appeal, of the commercial. Music is a very powerful emotional tool; use it wisely. Select just the right track for the commercial and you can greatly enhance the commercial's impact. Choosing music is often a trial-and-error process as you look for the track that fits just right with the commercial. What you are looking for is a piece of music that complements and reinforces the commercial to help reach the target audience, all without calling too much attention to itself. You want to affect listeners, but you don't want them to know it is the music doing it. You want the focus to be on the dialogue of the commercial message; the music stays in the background.

Fourthly, consider the client's business type. Try to match the music style and tempo, or pacing, to the business. A bank is going to get an entirely different music bed than a car dealership or a fast-food restaurant will. A

commercial for an Italian restaurant needs something that sounds like an Italian restaurant. Again the trial-and-error process comes into play, trying cuts of music until you hear the one that causes you to say, "That's it!" Of course, for effect, you can also try going one-hundred-eighty degrees from what you think the music should be. For example, try putting classical music behind a local Dairy Queen Halloween commercial for hot dogs. Bach's Toccata and Fugue in D Minor, which is rather scary, makes a convincing background for Dairy Queen's Hallow-weenies!

Fifthly, you have to consider the client's request, or lack of request. Clients sometimes ask for a specific style or type of music and, just as often, clients leave it up to the salesperson to select something that fits with the commercial. The ultimate music decision is going to rest with the client, and it is a good idea, if possible, to run the music by the client first for approval before producing the commercial.

Sound Effects Selection

The purpose of a sound effect in a commercial is to give the listener an audible cue to what is going on. Depending on how sound effects are used, they can either add to your commercial and enhance the message, or they can detract from your work and make the message difficult or impossible to understand. It's a balancing act. Use too few sound effects, and the listener misses the point of the commercial. Use too many, and the listener misses the commercial message entirely (see demo CD, cut 66). When it comes to the use of sound effects, less is generally more.

There are three ways to use sound effects to enhance a commercial. The first is as background continuity, to set the stage for a commercial. For example, if you have a dialogue between two people who are supposed to be hiking in the mountains, an outdoor background with birds would set the stage for the ad. Other examples for different contexts include street sounds, sports crowd noise, babbling brooks, and chirping crickets. Background continuity is just that, nondescript background sounds. Background continuity is sometimes referred to as a secondary sound effect. Nothing in the background should stand out and draw attention.

A second use for sound effects is as foreground continuity. Foreground continuity is a sound effect that supports the dialogue or the event that is being depicted in the commercial. For example, if an ad for a tire store talks about you having a flat tire, you need a tire blowout with the flop, flop, flop of the tire as the car comes to a stop. Foreground sound effects are sometimes called primary sound effects, as they give the listener important clues to what is happening.

The third use of a sound effect is as punctuation to the dialogue or action in the ad. This is an effect that has to occur at precisely the right moment or the ad does not work. For example, an ad for a cell phone company uses a single cell phone ring to punctuate each price point in the ad. A beer company depends on the sound of a pop-top and the fizz of opening a beer at just the right moment. Timing is absolutely key for sound effects used as punctuation.

Of course, there are also commercials with very little dialogue and are composed mostly of sound effects. (These are just the opposite of the ones described above, in which sound effects merely support the dialogue.) In this case, the sound effects have to carry the commercial; they have to be clear, simple, and definitive. This is not easy to do, since you are depending on the listener to figure out what is going on. Such ads require a lot of extra work and trial-and-error experimentation to find just the right mix of sound and dialogue. It is always a good idea to test this type of commercial on a number of people to make sure they understand the ad, before it goes on the air.

Specific Sound Effects

One class of sound effects that you should try to avoid entirely is realistic-sounding police and fire sirens, or for that matter any realistic-sounding emergency alert effect, as a primary sound effect. Although this can draw immediate attention to your commercial, it can potentially cause confusion on the part of in-vehicle listeners and distract them from what they are doing.

There is one sound effect that scares everyone to death. It is so stark, startling, and abrupt, that many are afraid to use it in a commercial. Silence. Famed radio commentator Paul Harvey will hold the title "Master of Silence" forever. His pauses while delivering commercials and news copy dramatically punctuate and enhance his stories. Three to five seconds of silence sounds like an eternity on radio and can really make a point.

Talent Selection

Voice talent is what makes a commercial. The talent becomes the actor in the "theatre of the mind" story you are creating. As a production person, you need to develop a sense of what talent you have available within the radio station and what they are capable of doing with their voices. Most production people, as they review a script, are mentally casting station staff members in the various roles in the commercial. However, it is important to note that jocks with great voices are not necessarily going to be great actors for your commercial projects.

When selecting the voices for your commercials (in other words, casting), go for character and style first and voice quality second. Network with everyone you meet, because someday you are going to have to reach outside the radio station for a child, an elderly person, or an ethnic personality to do an accent or role in a commercial. Remember, too, that there is a distinct difference between an announcer and an actor. It is not how the person's voice sounds but what he or she can do with that voice that makes a person an actor.

Every commercial has a personality, character, or attitude to it. Your goal in selecting the talent is to reflect and enhance the commercial's character. As simple as a plain voice, or dialogue, commercial might seem, it can be the most difficult to cast because you have to match the speaker's personality to the commercial. There are male and female speakers who specialize in sounding warm and fuzzy, firm and authoritative, relaxed and easygoing, full of energy and upbeat, or even a touch goofy, but still with some credibility, just to name a few of the styles available. A key to the commercial's success is your ability to match the right vocal character and qualities to the commercial.

In the pre-planning stage, select the talent you need to complete the commercial and set a time for them to record, or cut, the tracks. With a multitrack DAW, keep in mind that the talent can cut their tracks anytime they are available and you can come back to the tracks later to produce the commercial. As an example, a station produced a series of commercials for a high-end jewelry store chain that involved a six-year-old girl and the chain's owner talking about Christmas and Hanukkah gifts. The little girl was brought in first and recorded her lines. The store owner came in a week later and, listening to the little girl, recorded his responses to the little girl's lines. The voice tracks were recorded in September and mixed and edited in October; no one believed the two had never met.

However, you need to be aware that you don't always get to pick the talent for your projects. There are several instances in which station staff are assigned or outside talent brought in to work on a project. Most production directors rotate station talent on commercials so that voices don't get overused or scheduled back-to-back in stop-sets. Sometimes a client even provides the talent for the commercial, as in the case of the previously mentioned jewelry ad, and in most cases the salesperson works to try and accommodate the client's wishes.

Another aspect of talent selection is a talent fee. Who gets a talent fee and who does not varies from market to market and even within stations. Most often, a station's on-air announcers do not receive talent fees for in-house work, but they do receive a fee when a commercial is used on another station in the market at the client's request. In larger markets, it is not unusual for the talent to belong to a labor union. AFTRA, the American Federation of Television and Radio Artists, is the most prominent union in the broadcasting field. SAG, the Screen Actors Guild, also represents some on-air talent. Radio talent working at a union station work under a local and national contract and must be paid accordingly.

As a word of caution, any time people are brought into the station as outside talent, be sure they sign a talent release authorizing the station to use their voice. This is particularly important when working with children. Depending on the state, you might need the parent or guardian's permission to use the child's voice or likeness in a commercial even if the child is not identified by name.

Scheduling Studio Time

The last stage of the pre-planning is to schedule your studio time to complete the project. Each facility has its own policy about studio time; don't be a studio hog. In simplest terms, use the studio for the actual work of creating the ad. The key to making maximum use of your studio time is first: to know what you want before you go into the studio, and second: to know how to create it with the equipment you have to work with. Do not be afraid to ask questions of others or to observe others while they work. Most people are more than happy to assist you when you ask for their help, and watching others is a great way to pick up tips and software shortcuts.

Production

It is time to gather the script, music, sound effects, and talent and head to the studio. When you stop to think about it, radio production is absolutely incredible. Where else can you create something so powerful that it actually motivates people to do something they would not otherwise do? Radio is particularly satisfying because it is such a cost-effective and creative medium, cheaper than print, television, or film.

Recording

This is really the easiest step in the commercial-production process. You pre-planned what was going onto each track of the DAW; now it's time to record each element of the ad as cleanly as possible on a separate track, or tracks in the case of stereo music and some sound effects. You don't have to do things in real time because you can digitally edit the project later. You are working in a medium that allows you to rearrange every-thing, including time, so the order in which you record the tracks is immaterial.

Recording Talent

We are in the communications business, but sometimes we forget to communicate with those right around us. We just assume they know. In working with talent, let the announcer have the script early so that you can answer any questions he or she may have. Give your talent a general feel for what it is you are looking for. If you want an upbeat read with excitement in the voice, tell the announcer. He or she cannot deliver what you want without your guidance. As an example, one producer of an ad for a Florida retirement community had an almost twenty-minute-long discussion with the announcer doing the voice-over ahead of time about the read. The producer emphatically explained he did *not* want a typical commercial read on the script. He wanted from-the-heart sincerity, just as if the announcer were talking to her own parents, trying to convince them that this retirement community was the right place for them. Tell your talent what you want; it saves a lot of time in the studio.

Ideally, you would like the talent to give you a clean read, without errors, since this saves editing time later. Don't be afraid, though, to ask the talent for two or three reads of the copy, even when they have given you the read you want (see demo CD, cut 67). In fact, try asking the announcer to read the commercial however he or she would like to read it, and encouraging the talent just to have fun with it. Not every paragraph of every read is going to be perfect. As the talent gives you that second and third read, you may hear individual sections from the various reads that you want to mix and match in the final edit. Be aware, though, that some talent finds it hard to read more than one paragraph at a time without a screw-up. That's fine—that's why digital editing was invented.

Don't ever let anyone you are working with gloss over screw-ups with the infamous words that editors hate: "Don't worry; they can fix it in post" (meaning post-production). Even with digital editing, there are some things that cannot be easily changed. Listen carefully to the talent as he or she reads your copy take-to-take, making sure that the announcer maintains the same distance to the mic, vocal level, intensity, and pacing. Also, follow the announcer's read with the script, making sure it is word-for-word. By doing so you make it easier to edit the voice track later.

This should go without saying, but after each track is recorded to your satisfaction, save your work and check playback to make sure it is OK. When you have completed recording all of the tracks; back up the project. Editing and mixing of the project can always be redone, but if you inadvertently lose a voice track, the talent is going to charge you to return and cut it again.

Recording Music

The music for your commercial has likely been recorded in stereo, on CD, by a composer/producer, or come from the station's production music library. Depending on your DAW software, you can either play the CD back in real time to record it or drag and drop the audio file from the CD into your project. If you are using multiple cuts of music, say different cuts for the open and close of the commercial, you'll need a stereo pair of tracks for each cut of music you are recording. Following your multitrack layout pattern allows you more easily to edit and mix the music later.

Recording Sound Effects

There are three sources for sound effects: a sound effects library, "foley," or go out and get it yourself. A sound effects library is just like a music library. It is a huge collection of copyright-cleared sound effects on CD that is catalogued and easy to find. Sound effects libraries range from a simple set with basic "door creaking" and "dog barking" kinds of sounds to the BBC Sound Effects Library, which includes just about any sound you can imagine from around the world. Often, sound effects are combined or mixed to produce just the right effect that the production person is looking for.

The second source for sound effects is foley. Jack Foley was a movie sound effects editor at Universal Studios for over thirty years who pioneered the creation of synchronous sound effects in the studio for film. The process of creating sound effects and matching them to dialogue is named after him. (Ironically, after all those years on the sound stage, there is no known recording of his voice.) A true foley effect is created in a studio and recorded. For example, you are producing a commercial about a wedding. A couple is celebrating a wedding announcement with a bottle of champagne. You need the sound of the cork popping out of the bottle. You have a choice: You can either open a real bottle of champagne (not always practical), or you can place your index finger in your mouth and pop it out to make the sound. Foley is about using things and objects to create sound effects in the studio.

The third source for sound effects is to go out and record them. Sometimes the needed sound effect is so unique that there is no substitute for getting the sound itself. For example, a station was producing a commercial for a tourist railroad that featured a historic steam locomotive. The ad called for the sounds of *the* steam engine in the background. A generic steam engine from a sound effects CD was out of the question because railroad enthusiasts *know* what the various types of steam engines sound like. A bogus-sounding steam engine would have cost the railroad customers. Armed with a minidisc recorder and condenser microphone, the production person spent about an hour with the locomotive, even recording the train's historically correct steam whistle (see demo CD, cut 68).

Sound effects are like talent in that they can be recorded at basically any time and edited later. The goal is to get a good, clean recording. Most primary sound effects, like a phone ringing, are recorded on a single channel (monaural) to be close to the dialogue in the sound field. Background sound effects, such as street sounds, are often recorded in stereo to broaden the sound field.

Editing

Editing is the art of digitally cutting, pasting, and assembling the elements of a commercial in the specific order, or time line, that you desire. It is often referred to simply as "cutting."

Editing Talent

When you work with good talent, you often get a great take in which every word is pronounced properly, the inflection in the voice is right, and the timing is dead on. Listen to the entire take carefully. Listen for the quality of the presentation, how the dialogue flows, and the impact and overall impression the track creates. If you are satisfied with the take, then leave it alone. If not, move on to editing the voice track.

Editing allows you to move lines around within a commercial and to cut and paste dialogue within the ad. When working with multiple voices, you have the control to edit voices as tight (close together) or loose (far apart) as you want. By adjusting the space between sentences, and sometimes between words, you have the power to make the commercial sound very natural. You can even overlap voice tracks and make the talent sound as if they are conversationally overlapping the ends of the sentences, as people do when they are talking to one another (see Fig. **8.2**).

It is a good idea, as previously suggested, to record several takes of the talent while they are in the studio. Assuming that you did not get any one perfect take, select what you think is the best take and use that cut as your basis for building a better track. With the track selected, listen carefully to all of your other takes (see demo CD, cut 69). You may find a sentence, paragraph, or even a word, that is better in one of the other takes that can be edited into your original.

When editing dialogue, you have to use great care in making sure to match the vocal intensity, tonal qualities, audio level, and pacing of the original track you are cutting to; otherwise the audio edit won't match, which is quite noticeable. You also need to make sure that when a talent's phrases are edited together, the person's speech flows in a natural pattern.

Understand that when you edit a voice track, you do so at your own risk. With nondestructive digital editing this is not too much of a problem. However, even with nondestructive editing, if you spend thirty minutes editing, only to have to start over again, you have wasted valuable time. It is possible to do a perfect job of editing and still screw up a commercial. A person may cut and paste a voice track until each individual element within the commercial sounds just right, only

Figure 8.2

Editing allows you to move the announcer's lines around within a commercial and to cut and paste dialogue within the ad. In the example above, voice tracks one and two are very slightly overlapped to make the talent sound as if they are conversationally overlapping the ends of their sentences, just as people do when they are talking to one another. *Adobe product screen shot reprinted with permission from Adobe Systems Incorporated.*

to listen to the entire sixty-second voice track and have the overall impact and presentation fall flat. Early in the author's broadcasting career I edited a person who spoke broken English. I did a perfect job of taking out every pause, "uh," and stammer. One problem, though: in my zeal to make this person speak perfect English I forgot to leave in any breath sounds. The person spoke for sixty seconds without taking a breath! The words were in perfect sequence, but the natural flow of the person's speech pattern was completely off and it sounded very unnatural.

While editing, another thing to keep in the back of your mind is that the final voice track has to be slightly shorter than sixty seconds. If you are cutting a dialogue commercial, then you can take it right up to your station's time limit. If you are using a music background, try for a voice track that is fifty-seven to fifty-eight seconds long. The two to three seconds left over gives you a second or so at the start of the commercial and a second or so at the end of the commercial for the music to establish and to fade out, respectively.

Editing Music

Music editing is an art, and the interesting thing is that when it is done well, no one even notices the editor's work. There are four basic ways to approach the music track of your commercial. The first is to create a commercial and send it to a composer and have him or her score and produce a custom piece of music to appeal to the target audience and to fit the commercial. If you have the time and the budget to work with, this produces outstanding results because the music is written to match the tempo and style of the ad by surrounding and reinforcing the dialogue and sound effects. The music can even punctuate lines and elements in the commercial.

If you don't have the budget for a custom music cut, there is a way you can make your commercial sound as if the music were custom-scored for it. Select the music first and write the commercial to fit the music. You will need a stopwatch to time the breaks in the music where you want to put copy. Your talent will have to hit those timing marks as he or she reads each segment of the voice track to make it fit with the music. In essence, you are working backwards. If this is done with just a little bit of care, no one will ever know the music wasn't custom-scored for the ad.

The third way to add music to your commercial is to create all of the elements of the commercial as previously discussed. Then select a cut, or cuts, of music from your production library that fits the commercial. You can also select something that is close enough that it can be edited to fit. Depending on how familiar you are with your music library, selecting an appropriate music cut could take a few minutes. In any case, don't spend more than thirty to forty-five minutes trying to select music. If you have not found anything after this amount of time, you need to ask yourself whether the ad really needs the music or not. (Another option is to select a couple of cuts of music and edit them together to fit the ad.)

A fourth option is to use a commercially available music loop CD or loop service to create your own musical track. The music CD bundled with this text includes two-hundred-fifty music loops. "Looping," as it is called, can produce some interesting pieces of music (see demo CD, cut 70).

Even when you have found just the right piece of music, you are going to want to clean up the cut. A commercial is sixty seconds long. How long is your music? Chances are it is not exactly sixty seconds long; even in production libraries, you find cuts that range from fifty-eight to sixty-two seconds. You can easily correct this by loading the cut into your DAW and using a time-compression-and-expansion plug-in to adjust the music track length to exactly sixty seconds.

Working with production music, you will discover that much of it is written so that it can be easily edited. Production music typically has well-defined intros and extros with a bed in between. You may be happy with a cut but want to chop off the first two seconds before the downbeat. You may want to clip the end of the music, ending it on a more definitive downbeat instead of a fade. Then again, there may be two cuts of music you want to blend together, creating a third cut of music that fits the commercial.

Editing music on a DAW allows you to use hard cuts (butt cuts), butting the ends together, or overlapping cross fades to make an edit (see Figs. **8.3** and **8.4**). A trick to mask, or hide, edits is to apply a small amount of reverb or delay to the music track. Reverb is also handy for smoothing out the end of a music cut that has been cut to a hard downbeat. The reverb adds a few milliseconds of fade, making the music appear to trail off naturally.

The simplest form of music editing is to use two cuts of music in an ad. One typically leads

Figure 8.3

A hard cut, or butt-cut, edit is when two audio clips are joined together end-to-end as shown above. This is fairly easy when there are clear indicators of where to cut within the audio waveform, such as at the ends of words, sentences, and beats of music. *Adobe product screen shot reprinted with permission from Adobe Systems Incorporated.*

into the ad, and the other leads out of the ad. Keep things simple: use the first cut of music to open the ad and slowly fade it out at the appropriate spot. If this is done properly, the listener is unaware that the music is disappearing. Likewise, for the end of the ad, slowly fade up the second music cut and time it so that the cut ends when the commercial ends. Don't try to overlap the music. Leave a couple of seconds, or more, of silence between the two cuts.

(If you have little or no knowledge about music, then the following suggestions may not make much sense to you. If this is the case, seek help from someone with more musical knowledge before attempting to edit music.) When cutting music, it is easiest if you can

butt cut on the beat and match the two ends of the edit together as you cut seconds from or add seconds to a selection (again, see Fig. **8.3**). The beats are easy to see on the DAW monitor, which makes the job fairly simple. Only whole measures should be cut from or added to a selection (see Fig. **8.5**). Refrain from cutting or adding individual beats. Cutting or adding just a few individual beats to or from the music can really bother listeners, even though they probably won't know why the music sounds a little off.

Finally, when you are cutting two pieces of music together, they must be in the same key, or very close. If they aren't, the abrupt change in the musical key will be distracting

Figure 8.4

When a butt cut edit sounds too abrupt, it can often be smoothed out with a cross-fade edit. In the cross fade above, the top track is faded down at the same time that the lower track is faded up, one crossing over the other at the same time. This is an effective way of making a smooth-sounding edit or transition. *Adobe product screen shot reprinted with permission from Adobe Systems Incorporated.*

to listeners and draw attention away from the message and to the music.

Editing Sound Effects

With the voice and music tracks cut to length, the next step is to add any secondary and primary sound effects to the ad. A secondary sound effect is the background continuity, like street sounds, a sports stadium, or car-interior sounds. In editing the background continuity, keep in mind you don't want anything in the effect that stands out and draws attention to the background. For example, if you are using an outdoor background that suddenly has a

blue jay screeching loudly several times, the blue jay has to go. The background is just to give the listener an audible cue as to where the talent is located; it should not draw the listener's attention.

After the background continuity is established, record the primary sound effects, which are the foreground continuity. These are the effects that you want noticed; they establish action or movement in the commercial. For example, in a commercial for a lawnmower the typical homeowner is trying unsuccessfully to start his or her old lawnmower. The sound of a lawnmower failing to start is needed to support the dialogue. The purpose

Figure 8.5

When editing music it is best to edit on the beat. Track 1 above shows just one beat of a drum track. However, adding or cutting just one beat can really throw off the flow of the music. It is best to edit whole bars of music instead. Track 2 shows a complete bar of music consisting of four beats.

Adobe product screen shot reprinted with permission from Adobe Systems Incorporated.

of the effect is to support the voice track and the action in the commercial, but it should not overpower the voice track.

Sound effects that you are going to use to punctuate the commercial are added last. These are effects that are critical to the success of the ad, such as a phone ringing at the precise moment, a car starting, or the sound of a cash register to match the dialogue. These are effects whose placement is critical and should dominate all other effects. Again, the effect should complement the voice track but not overpower it.

Experiment with different placements of a sound effect just before, during, or after dialogue to see how it works. Also learn to experiment with the length of the effect and the effect's strength or intensity. Don't be afraid to shorten or stretch the length of an effect. What you are trying to create is an effect that complements and supports the dialogue in the commercial. Although it might be a great oversimplification, play with the effects until they sound like they belong in the commercial and sound real in your "theater of the mind."

Mixing and Processing

Until this point in the creation process, the concern has been recording good clean tracks and editing each segment of the commercial to fit within the sixty-second time frame. We have not been concerned with adjusting levels or using audio processing to enhance the audio. During the mixing process, audio levels are adjusted. The tracks are blended together by assigning the various elements to particular channels so that a stereo-sound field is created. Mixing and processing is when the commercial starts taking shape and suddenly comes to life.

Mixing

As you learned in chapter 4, mixing involves track assignments and audio-level adjustments to create a sound field or stereo image. For commercials, music and background sound effects should be mixed in stereo and everything else should be assigned to the center channel (monaural). Stereo music and background sound effects give the commercial a bigger, wider, fuller, stereo-sound field. Primary sound effects and any music used as a sound effect, such as a radio on in the background, are assigned to the center channel to make them stand above the background with the voice track.

On a two-voice commercial, as we've mention before, don't even think about putting one voice in the left channel and one in the right. The reason you don't do this is because, although it may sound cool in the studio, it will not sound that way on most car stereos. In fact, depending on where the listener is sitting in the car, it very likely will sound as if one of the voices is disappearing into the background. This acoustic effect occurs because a car interior does not provide the same acoustic listening environment that your studio does. Likewise, you need to consider the home or office listener who just wants background music. In those contexts, since a stereo has two speakers, one speaker might easily get put in one room and the other speaker in another room or office.

After making the track assignments, start mixing with the voice track first, since it is the most important element. Use the solo feature on your DAW to isolate the voice track and adjust the track's level to near-maximum. After the voice track, blend in the background and then the primary sound effects, one-by-one, listening to the mix after each is added. The background sound effects should be very low behind everything else. The primary sound effects are more important to the ad, and their levels should be adjusted to stand out more. If you are using a music bed, at the start of the commercial the music should establish at full volume for a second or so before fading down under the commercial copy. At the end of the commercial the music bed comes back up during the last second or two and ends the commercial.

Processing

As you learned in chapter 6, less is more when it comes to equalization and audio processing. Unless there is a problem that needs correcting, there is really very little processing to do to a commercial to make it sound better. There are some basics, though, that work on just about every commercial.

For the voice track, there are two things you can do to make it stand out. Firstly, mildly compress the announcer's voice track with three to five decibels of compression. This gives the announcer's voice a consistent level and allows you to raise the overall level of the voice track, making it appear louder. Secondly, apply a small amount of reverb to the voice track and match the reverb on the music or the background sound effects. This takes the **dead-studio sound** off the voice, giving it a more natural sound (see demo CD, cut 71).

Unless there is a problem with the voice track, avoid the temptation to equalize it. On occasion, a voice blends with the background sound effects. As discussed in chapter 6, rather than boosting a frequency in the voice to make it stand out, cut a frequency from the background sounds and carve an "equalization hole" for the voice to sit in. If needed, apply this same technique to any other problem you want to try to fix. With regard to equalization, always try to lower background levels to bring out a sound effect or voice track first, and when equalization is the only option, cut before you boost.

As a final note on processing, keep in mind that most engineering staffs have spent a lot of time adjusting the station's audio processor to obtain maximum modulation (loudness) and on-air presence for the station. Their adjustments are based on average program levels and frequency curves. Most engineering staffs request that you do not "over process" a commercial in an attempt to alter dramatically the overall equalization, intensity, or tonal quality of the ad. Such attempts often go counter to the station's audio processing and only result in your commercial not sounding as good as it should.

Monitoring

How you monitor, or listen, to the commercial, is important to the mix and audio processing choices you make. If you are working in a nice studio, you may be listening to a big pair of high-end monitors at a pretty good volume level. But how many of your listeners are going to be listening on similar speakers at similar levels? How you monitor a mix can make a big difference in what the listener hears when the commercial is played back on the air or over a web site.

Firstly, learn to mix at normal listening levels; only turn the monitors up loud when you need to listen critically to a quiet passage. Secondly, when you have completed the mix, listen to it at a normal listening level on a sound cube or a portable boom box with the tone controls adjusted flat. (A sound cube is a small monitor speaker designed to emulate a portable radio or car speaker.) Can you understand the voice track? Is it clear and above the background? Can you hear all of the sound effects clearly? If the commercial does not pass the sound cube/boom box test, then a remix is in order. As an alternative, make a copy of the commercial on a CD and run out to the parking lot and listen to the ad on a couple of different factory car stereos.

Agency- and Manufacturer-Supplied Commercial Material

Advertising agencies often supply radio stations and local clients with commercial material. This material can be one of two varieties. The first type of ad that an agency may provide a station is a commercial that is already produced and ready to air. This material is supplied on CD or by some means of electronic delivery, such as posting the audio file on a web site for you to download. When a station receives an agency ad in this format, all the station does is dub, or copy, the ad into the station's server system. The second variety of agency-supplied material is a script that still needs to be produced and must be produced by the station exactly to the agency's specifications.

A common variation on the pre-produced agency-supplied ad is a commercial that is almost complete but requires the addition of a local tag or insert to complete it. The agency may send an ad that has a blank space of ten to fifteen seconds in which the station is to insert local copy. The first of these "local insert" type ads is one that has the blank space at the end of the ad. At about fifty seconds, the agency voice is out, leaving ten seconds of background music, or sound effect, over which you put the local information the agency has specified (see demo CD, cut 72). This is called a **tag,** or "adding a tag."

The second type of local insert commercial is one that has the hole for the local copy in the middle of the commercial. This hole can range from ten to thirty seconds. Because the copy is going in a hole in the middle of the ad, this type of ad is known as a **donut** (see demo CD, cut 73).

Producing a tag or donut-type agency commercial is simply a matter of laying down the commercial on two tracks (stereo) and adding a third track for the local voice. The mix involves matching the local voice level and intensity to the already-produced agency material.

Always check the timing when you are working with agency materials. Agencies sometimes forget their stopwatches in hopes of getting just a little bit extra for their client. Pre-produced agency materials sometimes run a couple of seconds long, a couple of seconds they have not paid for. Agency-recorded materials are easily time adjusted with the time-compression-or-expansion feature of your DAW.

In the case of scripts, it is not out of the ordinary for a "sixty-second" script to read longer than sixty seconds. When written scripts read overtime, the salesperson needs to let the agency know that the script is long and needs a rewrite.

Client Approval

After the ad is produced and you are satisfied with the mix, it is time to play the ad for the salesperson and get his or her approval. Don't be surprised if the salesperson has questions or makes a couple of suggestions for change. After all, he or she is representing the client and is more familiar with the client's wants and needs.

The ad-approval process can take a couple of different forms. The salesperson may choose to call the client and, with your help, let the client hear the ad over the phone. This is how most ads get approved. On the other hand, the salesperson may choose to take the client a copy of the ad on CD and play it in person.

Either way, until the client approves the ad it cannot go on the air. Typically, clients who are more experienced with buying advertising are more likely to listen to their ad on the phone, whereas clients newer to the advertising-buying experience like to have a physical copy of the ad that they can play back for themselves and friends. As previously mentioned, if the salesperson is leaving the client-approval stage of the buying process up to you, ask the salesperson exactly what he or she wants you to do and what you should say to the client when you call on the phone.

Preparing the Commercial to Go On-Air

Once the client has approved the ad, the commercial is ready to go on the air. Depending on your station's physical layout, this generally involves moving the ad, as a data file, from the DAW in production to the main on-air server. Usually, this is a drag-and-drop procedure. In many station systems, the new file is placed in a folder on the DAW that the on-air server automatically checks every few minutes, picking up new production and transferring it to the on-air server. Or you might drag the commercial audio file from the DAW across the computer network to the on-air server folder where the commercial is to be stored for on-air playback.

If you are working with a local group of stations, this likely involves a LAN. In some cases it involves putting the commercial on a WAN server so that a number of regional stations within your company can access the commercial.

A less-sophisticated method for transferring audio from one radio station to another, but one that certainly works, is through standard Internet FTP (file transfer protocol). This involves logging into a computer via the Internet and either taking files from, or sending files to, the destination computer. FTP is discussed in detail in chapter 12.

Preparing the Commercial Archive: Backup

In chapter 7, backing up files was discussed in detail, and the points we made there certainly apply to commercial material. Files get corrupted, and computers crash. Each station has different procedures to follow. The best backup is one that is on a different medium from the primary work. If you created a commercial on a hard drive, then back it up on a CD and store it in a safe place. CDs cost only pennies and are easy to drop into a client's file.

You should do two kinds of backup if possible. Firstly, back up an audio copy of the final mix as the commercial aired. Secondly, back up a data copy of the individual audio files used to create the ad. These are the software files that hold the data that created your commercial. With a data copy, you can return months from now and open the commercial to change a price or edit an individual track.

Always back up your work. There is nothing more frustrating than to have a file corrupted or have someone accidentally delete a file, and it will happen. With a backup file, you grin like a Cheshire cat and save the day for everyone.

Duplication for Other Stations

As previously stated in this chapter, many clients value a radio station for the quality of its production. Clients often bump up their advertising buy on your station since you are the one producing a great ad and sending dubs to the other stations in the market. When a client asks you to make dubs of a commercial, it is a compliment to your work.

Typically, a copy of an ad for another station is posted on a web site for the requesting station to download, or the audio file is attached to e-mail and sent to the station. Occasionally, a salesperson may want to drop a hard copy of an ad at another station as a courtesy to the client or to the other station. This is especially true in a market in which one owner has several stations that may be located at different sites. Make a quality copy of the ad, or ads, on a CD and give it to the salesperson. Likewise, you will retrieve dubs from other stations and ad agencies electronically to prepare to go on the air. The key to a good, professional, working relationship with other stations and ad agencies is to deliver a quality product on time.

Documentation

As discussed in chapter 7, it is critical that you leave a trail of information regarding the work you have done on a project. Each station has different procedures to follow. Usually, though, a client file contains a completed production order with clear notes on anything special you did. In particular, note the sources for all of your music and sound effects. Better yet, a track layout for the ad helps someone in your department who might be the next person assigned to work on the account.

Many production people keep personal backup copies of all of their work. These can be handy not only for station purposes, but also when it comes time to produce a personal audition CD if you seek other employment.

News Production

It is not that often that production people produce newscasts or sound bites for the news department. News people are pretty independent and prefer to do their own thing when it comes to creating a newscast. However, news people do need good basic production skills in today's consolidated market structure. The days of the news person just writing copy and delivering the news are long gone. Today, news people write their own copy, gather their own sound, and edit and produce their own newscasts. And to some degree, technology is to blame for this.

Using software such as the WireReady system, news people can sit at a single computer terminal and receive their news service, such as the Associated Press, write stories, record and edit audio cuts, and embed those audio cuts into the copy (see Fig. **8.6**). They can retrieve data services and audio cuts from major news networks such as ABC, CBS, and CNN, and can handle their e-mail, all on one terminal (see Fig. **8.7**). When they step into the studio to do the news, newscasters read from a computer screen and play back the audio cuts embedded in the story by pressing a key on a computer keyboard. It is a paperless news operation and one in which all of the sound bites are stored as computer files on a hard drive. Even more incredible is that with a wide area network (WAN), the news stories can be shared with any other station in a market, region, or nationally, all on a mouse click.

Generally, about the only time production people are directly involved in the newsroom is when they are asked to assist in producing long-form public affairs shows or to help clean up a poorly recorded sound bite.

Newscasts

As previously stated, news people do need good solid production skills. Typically, they are recording and editing sound bites that have been received over the phone, from a television audio source for which they have clearance to use the audio cuts, the Internet, or location sound recorded in the field. The key element here is that almost all of their work is comprised of recording and editing voice recordings.

Digital audio production has raised some interesting ethical questions with regard to news reporting. How much do we edit and mix when it comes to news? With digital editing it is easy to lift sentences or quotes out of speeches or news events, completely out of context. It is easy to rearrange digitally the time line of an event or the order of a presentation. Likewise, it is possible to reduce the background noise behind a newsmaker to make him or her easier to understand, or conversely, it is possible to inject more background noise to make it sound the way you think the event should. A news person could use a recorded background to enhance a report (see demo CD, cut 74).

In addition to editing and mixing, there is the ability to use audio processors to enhance or detract from a person's voice or likeness. How far are you permitted to go with audio processing devices such as compressors, limiters, or EQ to make a sound bite more intelligible?

You may ask why these questions are being raised here in a production text, and the answer is simple: They have already been

Figure 8.6

Digital workstations make it possible for news people to sit at a single computer terminal and receive their news service, such as the Associated Press, write stories, record and edit audio cuts, and embed those audio cuts into the copy. They can retrieve data services and audio cuts from major news networks such as ABC, CBS, and CNN, and can handle their e-mail, all on one terminal. *Courtesy WireReady and GoldWave.*

raised in newsrooms across the country. Your station should have its own set of standards, which you are required to follow. Keep in mind, if the *New York Times* has had to deal with someone altering the news, the potential is there for it to happen anywhere.

Basic news production is recording sound and then editing that sound to length, so that it fits in a newscast. The same recording and editing skills required for producing a commercial apply to news. Although these skills make up the core of the news person's job, often considered just as important is the presentation style. Most stations design their news format and style of their newscasts around the station's target audience. Announcing style and newscast presentation are discussed in detail in chapter 9.

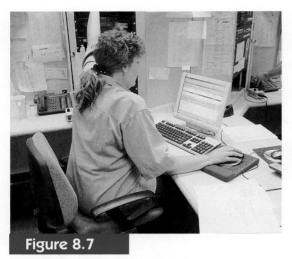

Figure 8.7

In a digital newsroom, the sound bites are embedded into the copy so that as a newscaster reads the story from a computer screen he or she can play the cuts by simply pressing a key on the keyboard. It is a paperless news operation and one in which all of the sound bites are stored as computer files on a hard drive.

Long-Form Programming

Long-form news programming is usually associated with public affairs programs or a major breaking story, such as a weather disaster. The news person most often needs assistance with the volume of work and the length of the project. Radio stations are required by the FCC to produce public affairs programs that serve the community interest. Most news departments rely on production staff to assist them as recording, editing, and mastering engineers. Usually, though, the news person wants to assist with editing the program to retain control of the program content.

Once produced, such shows are placed on a hard drive for airing. A backup copy should be made and given to the news person for safe keeping. News people like to go back and pull archival cuts from such programs. In short, as a production person you are going to be more an engineer than a producer when it comes to the news department, since they have the final judgment with regard to content, just as a commercial client does with an ad.

Suggested Activities

1. Sharpen your dialogue-editing skills by editing the random numbers one through ten on the demo CD, cut 75, into the proper sequence, allowing for a natural pause, or breath, between each number.
2. Using demo CD, cut 69, edit the sixty-second voice track to create a good, clean read. Remember to try to maintain the natural flow of the announcer's voice.
3. Using demo CD, cut 68, edit the raw sounds of the steam engine to make a sixty-second secondary sound effect or background continuity bed to go behind a commercial.
4. Select a thirty-second music cut from the production music CD that accompanies this text. Identify the intro, extro, and bed of the music. Try your hand at turning the thirty-second cut of music into a sixty-second cut of music by repeating measures of music from the music bed.
5. Select a sixty-second music cut from the production music CD that accompanies this text. Identify the intro, extro, and bed of the music. Try your hand at turning the sixty-second cut of music into a thirty-second cut of music by removing measures of music from the music bed.
6. Using three tracks of a DAW, create a commercial with a monaural voice track and stereo music bed; experiment with mixing the dialogue to fit the music bed so that the dialogue is dominant in the mix.

7. Record a two-person dialogue commercial with a background sound effects bed and three primary sound effects. Add mild compression to the voice tracks to make them stand out and some reverb to help them blend with the background sound effects. Mix the project.

Web Sites for More Information

For information about:

- *custom jingles and production music,* visit TM Century at www.tmcentury.com

- *Foley,* visit the Motion Picture Sound Editors organization at www.mpse.org

- *newsroom software,* visit WireReady at www.wireready.com

- *production music,* visit Network Music at www.networkmusic.com

- *sound effects,* visit Sounds Ideas at www.sound-ideas.com

Pro Speak

You should be able to use these terms in your everyday conversations with other professionals.

dead-studio sound—A studio is said to be a "dead studio" when there is little or no natural reverberation—the less reverberation, the more dead the studio.

donut—A type of agency-supplied commercial that has a hole in the middle of the ad for the insertion of local copy.

needle-drop basis—An old radio term used to describe paying for production music on a per-cut-used basis.

tag—A ten- to fifteen-second space at the end of an agency ad over which the local station puts copy.

CHAPTER 9

Communicating with the Listener: Announcing

The success or failure of a radio station is based on the ability of its announcers to communicate with one person—the listener. Not "all you guys out there," not "all our listeners," and certainly not "everyone out there in radio land." Regardless of whether it is production work or an on-air show, radio is about one-to-one communication between the announcer and the listener (see Fig. **9.1**). An on-air announcer's relationship with listeners is unique because, even though the two will probably never meet, a good announcer builds a lasting bond with the listener.

Entire semester-length announcing courses are offered by many universities. The focus of this chapter is not so much about announcing as it is about good communication skills and professional announcing practices. Many of the things discussed in this chapter relate to both on-air work and production.

Figure 9.1

An on-air announcer's relationship with listeners is unique because, even though the two will probably never meet, a good announcer builds a lasting bond with the listener. One of the simplest things an announcer can do to improve his or her delivery is to smile.

Communicating On-Air

Very few people know the amount of work that goes into creating a great on-air radio show. Most people have this image of a jock standing in a studio playing music and having a good time for four hours. On-air announcers just work four hours a day, don't they? Nothing could be farther from the truth. Creating a good show takes a lot of work before, during, and after the show.

Pre-Planning Your Show

A good show starts with pre-planning. Beginning jocks often ask "When should I plan my show, the day before or the day of my show?" The answer is: both and neither.

You should plan your show 24/7. Every waking moment, if you see something, hear something, or think of something that might work well on your show, write it down, take a picture of it with your cell phone and e-mail it to yourself, or find some other way to remember it. Keep a file of these things. As crazy as it sounds, you may think of a great New Year's Eve bit for your show, but in August. File it away in your BIF, your "Brilliant Idea File."

```
WRPC  Talk "Clock"

Morning Drive  6:00 – 7:00 a.m.

:03      Traffic and Weather (:60)

:06      Stop set # 1 (3:00)  Promo contest in second half of hour

:13      Traffic and Weather (:60)

:21      Stop set #2  (3:00)  Promo tomorrow's show and guests (if any)

:23      Traffic and Weather (:60)

:33      Traffic and Weather (:60)

:37      Stop set # 3  (3:00)  Morning Breakfast Bunch Giveaway/Promo afternoon drive
         Dinner for Two and A Movie Giveaway

:43      Traffic and Weather (:60)

:53      Traffic and Weather (:60)

:54      Stop Set # 4 (4:00)   Promo next 20 minutes, station ID at end of stop set
```

Figure 9.2

A talk clock is a listing of the mandatory things you are required to do and is a part of your show planning. Items from the talk clock are merged into your show planner.

Another often misunderstood aspect of pre-planning a show for new jocks has to do with keeping their show local. A lot of general managers and program directors instruct talent to "keep it local." Beginning jocks often think this means that everything in their show has to be from, or related to, the people and things in the station's physical coverage area. That's not really the case: If something is important to your listeners, it's local. For example, 9/11/01 was a national event; however, it affected every one of your listeners, and so it was also local. Anything that affects your listeners becomes a local event.

The Talk Clock

Formal planning of your show starts the day before, prior to going home. The main thing you'll have to plan is what to say and do in the stop sets during your show. A **stop set** is a break in the music or other programming during which you talk and play back commercials, promos, and so on. As the show host, you know when your stop sets appear and the length of each stop set (see Fig. **9.2**). The stop sets are listed on sheets of paper, sometimes called a show planner or talk clock, depending on your station. News, weather, traffic reports, contest promotional mentions, giveaways you have to conduct, and vertical promotional mentions are some of the common examples. Some of your stop sets will have to be taken up with things mandated by the program director (see Fig. **9.3**), and these are the first things to put on your talk clock, along with items that always happen at scheduled times. When all of the mandatory items are taken care of, you will know exactly how much time you will need to plan.

Read a Newspaper

If you remember how to write a commercial, you already know how to plan the remainder of your stop sets. Focus on the customers (listeners) and their wants, needs, and desires. What interests them? What is happening in their lives? It might be anything from a local Little League baseball team's regional tournament to traffic snarls due to road construction. You cannot overlook the local things that are important to your listeners. That is why you read (no, you CONSUME) the local newspaper each day before your show. Notice that I say the *local* newspaper. It is imperative that you know what is going on in your listeners' lives, so although you may want to read something like *USA Today* for ideas, read your local paper *first*. The local paper is a great source of show-prep ideas.

BIF: Brilliant Idea File

After you have checked out the papers, pull together the items in your BIF, Brilliant Idea File, and see if anything fits for tomorrow. It might be something that is timely or something going on somewhere else in the media, such as a major star or political figure who is going to appear on a talk show. What question would you ask that person if you were the host? Do you know a little-known fact about that person that you can share with your listeners?

Another kind of item you might have stored in your BIF is something from your life or the life of one of your listeners. For example,

> "I flew home to see my parents this last weekend and you would not believe what was in this lady's suitcase in front of me at the security checkpoint. Talk about embarrassing! What is the most embarrassing thing you have ever done in an airport?"

Often you can tie listeners' experiences into your show through current events or something that everyone has been through in his or her life. Holidays and seasons are a natural tie-in for a show: "Do you know where valentines came from?"

One Stop Set, One Thought

While you are putting your show together, there is something you always need to keep in mind, and that is: one stop set, one thought. Cover only one topic or thought per stop set. The reason is that you want listeners to be able to remember your really good material, and they can't do that if you are rambling all over the place from one topic to the next during a stop set. Pick one topic and stick to it.

Live Delivery

A live show is a lot of fun if you know what you are doing and where you are going. In other words, it is planned out. Live delivery

```
WRPC Show Planner                    Date _____

Announcer _____

HOUR 1

Contest Promo_____
Horizontal Promo _____
Vertical Promo_____
Giveaways _____


Top of hour (:55)

Stop Set 1:


Stop Set 2:


Stop Set 3:


Stop Set 4:


HOUR 2

Contest Promo_____
Horizontal Promo _____
Vertical Promo_____
Giveaways _____


Top of hour (:55)

Stop Set 1:


Stop Set 2:


Stop Set 3:


Stop Set 4:


Use reverse for additional hours.      Retain this sheet for 5 working days.
```

Figure 9.3

A show planner lets you plan what you are going to do in advance and when you are going to do it. Planning helps give structure to your show and helps avoid repetition or forgetting a critical promo or contest promo.

A live show is a lot of fun if you know what you are doing and where you are going. In other words, it is planned out. Live delivery has a certain spontaneity and excitement to it that keeps listeners intrigued.

has a certain spontaneity and excitement to it that keeps listeners intrigued, and careful planning enhances that and allows it to work. A live show lets you do a lot of things to attract the listener's attention, such as interacting with listeners by taking their calls, participating in station promotions, and pulling off stunts (see Fig. **9.4**). Quite bluntly, there is no substitute for the energy and enthusiasm of a creative, live show.

Part of what makes a live show so attractive to listeners is the unpredictability of the show. Where is it going today? Hopefully, you are not doing the same bits at the same time every day; that would be boring for you and boring for your audience. That's why you have a written show planner that directs the show

and provides you with a record of what you did, what worked, and what didn't.

Making the Human Connection

As a show host, one of the unique aspects of radio is that you are trying to develop a lasting relationship with someone you have never met, using only your voice. Not an easy task! Listeners have to know something about you before they can come to like you. The things you reveal about yourself on the air are a way to let listeners get to know you.

Listeners would like to feel that you are "one of us" at heart, and this can be something as simple as an on-air birthday party on your birthday or letting your listeners know your likes and dislikes when it comes to food, or talking about your relatives or pets on the air. Your listeners would like to know that there is some commonality between you and them, and the only way this can happen is through what you reveal about yourself.

In revealing this information you have to be careful not to put yourself above your listeners; you want to relate to them on a one-to-one level. I don't think I would brag about my big house, fancy car, house at the lake, or the lavish vacation I took. As a mentor of this author once said, you have to have some "humble." There are also some basic pieces of information I would not reveal about myself, such as my real name and where I live. Most air personalities in larger markets work with assumed names on the air for security purposes. I would also not reveal my religious beliefs or political affiliation. Although religion and politics make for some good discussion topics, they are also a great way to alienate listeners.

Knowing Your Audience

At some point before you start doing an on-air show or production work you need to sit down with the program director and become thoroughly familiar with the station's target audience. Who is the station try to reach? Production needs to be aimed at the station's target audience just like the announcer's air shifts are. Two types of information can help you to learn more about who you are trying to reach.

Demographic information is quantifiable data, such as a target audience's age range, the group's average income, whether or not people are married or single, how many children they have, or what geographic area they live in. Psychographic information is data about a group's lifestyle, such as eating out two times a week, taking two short vacations per year, renting four DVDs a month, and liking domestic beer. The more you know, the better you can relate to your listeners in your production work on the air.

Another aspect of getting to know your audience is becoming a local yourself. If you have just moved to the area, you need to become "a local" as fast as possible. You can do this through talking with other station employees and everyone you meet. The first thing to do is to get a map of the area and drive around, getting familiar with all of the local landmarks and roads. Find out how people get around town. Is there local public transit? What do the locals use? Are there any vehicles that are popular for one reason or another, such as four-wheel drives in a snowy mountain area? While you are driving around, locate the top industries and shopping areas in your community.

Find out about the local government and the school system. What kind of city and county government is there, and what is the hot button with the schools? Is it sports, the marching band, or academics? What are the local athletic teams? Who supports what sports?

Explore local foods. What are the regional favorites when it comes to restaurants, soft drinks, beers, and specialty items? Buffalo is known for wings, Memphis for barbecue, and Philadelphia for cheese-steak sandwiches. What does your new area like, or what is it famous for?

Another interesting area to find out about is the local critters. What kinds of animals are in the area and what kind of bugs drive everyone crazy? Florida, for example, is home to alligators and crocodiles. What is the difference between the two, and where do they live? What kind of snakes and spiders live in your area? Some areas are known for mosquitoes the size of Volkswagens. Is the area known for any-thing special like the annual "Possum-Trot Festival"? Critters can make for some interesting conversation.

Another area you should find out about is who the local heroes are. Who are the people that locals hold in high regard and to whom you should show proper reverence?

These are just a few of the many things you need to know to become a local. Don't plan on it just happening by osmosis over a period of time. The faster you become a local, the better you can communicate with your listeners.

Voice-Tracking Delivery

Voice tracking is recording your stop sets and letting a computer run your show while you do something else. It is the opposite of live delivery. Voice tracking has been around for some time; within the last couple of years, however, it has become "the" way of doing business throughout the industry (see Fig. **9.5**). Some broadcasters view voice tracking as simply a way to squeeze the costs out of radio and increase profits. Another way to look at it, though, is that voice tracking provides an opportunity to maximize staff and to give listeners better on-air talent, particularly in the smaller markets. In fact, it was the small-market operators who first embraced voice tracking in order to save money and be able to continue to operate their stations profitably.

It takes about thirty minutes to voice-track a four-hour show. A large-market announcer can do a live show and then comfortably voice-track shows for three other stations in smaller markets. The problem with voice tracking is the safety net. When you voice-track a show, there is no fear of failure—you are recording onto a hard drive. Make a mis-take, and you can re-record the stop set. Many announcers look at voice tracking as the way to do a perfect show with no mistakes. But in whose eyes is that really a perfect show? Record a stop set two or three times and just about every bit of whatever spontaneity there was is stripped away. The result is a lifeless "announcer in a can."

Listeners turn on a radio for fun and excitement and for the spur-of-the-moment things that happen. They want to hear someone on the morning team make a goof every now and then, and how the others on the team react to it. There is a certain level of danger in doing a live radio show, an edge that excites listeners, which can easily be lost in voice tracking a show.

Another related concern in voice tracking a show is that announcers have to be very careful not to let the show become just something they do every day before they work in promotions or some other department. Bluntly put, voice tracking is not as much fun as doing a live show. Sadly, some announcers see voice tracking a show as just another job they have to do before they get to go home.

The best way to combat the pitfalls of voice tracking and to do a really decent-sounding voice-tracked radio show is to do it "live to disk." In other words, cut the safety net. Do each stop set as if you were on the air and *do not* go back and re-cut a stop set unless you made a serious technical mistake that will affect playback. This way, you retain some of the freshness, excitement, and liveliness that listeners seek in a good show. It is not enough for listeners not to be able to figure out that you are voice tracking a show; that's not the point. The point is that listeners have to hear something in your voice and personality that keeps them coming back to hear you again every day.

Figure 9.5

Voice tracking is recording your stop sets and letting a computer run your show while you do something else. It has been around for some time; within the last couple of years, however, it has become "the" way of doing business throughout the industry.

Even more than a regular live daily show, voice tracking requires good solid preparation and a commitment on the part of the announcer to take possession of the show and be proud of his or her work.

Localizing the Delivery

Voice tracking a radio show, whether it is for your station or another, requires you to be "local." You have to become a local in the ways we have already discussed, even if you live hundreds of miles from the station you are tracking for. You can become a local through the information you have about the community and through the language you use. The moment your listeners suspect you are not real, not one of them, an outsider— you are toast.

Localization for a remote station can be accomplished through general knowledge of an area (maybe you worked or visited there once), daily faxes, e-mails, or even a web site the station sets up for the voice-tracking talent so the station can post community information. It's not the technology that is important, it is the information the jock needs to be local that is.

News Delivery

Unless you are working at a news/talk radio station, news does not get the airtime it once did, particularly on FM stations. The traditional five-minute newscast at the top of the hour and a minute-and-a-half or two-minute news headlines at the bottom of the hour are long gone on most stations. The concentration today is on short FM-style newscasts of two minutes or less, with four or five brief stories each, a couple of which have sound bites. Even news/talk stations have changed their delivery and approach to one that presents a full range of news in a minimal amount of time. Typically, in morning or afternoon drive the news is even shorter and more upbeat in tempo.

Another aspect to news on a music-based station is that often the morning- or afternoon-drive sidekick is the person responsible for the "news." Usually the news is little more than some quick rewrites out of the newspaper. Quite bluntly, it is not really news, since the stories are nothing new and the jock delivering it has very little news authority, believability, or credibility.

Although this might not be the first thing you think of, a good reporter or newscaster has to have a lot of energy and excitement in his or her voice to get and keep our attention. On most stations news needs to be upbeat, quick, and to-the-point to grab and keep a listener's attention. Just as with production or an on-air show, newscasters have to communicate one-to-one with listeners and, more than anything, tell them the story.

Credibilty and Authority

As already mentioned, a good, clean, two-minute newscast can have as many as five stories, with three or four of them including short sound bites. The delivery style has to be upbeat and authoritative to convey the importance of the information you are telling listeners, although not so authoritative as to sound pompous. The newscast is something special; it has to be, to interrupt the music. It does not need to be sugar-coated. To develop a credible and authoritative news delivery, eliminate the minute or two of "happy talk" that newscasters sometimes get caught up in with jocks just before or after the news. This drags down the pace, quality, and credibility of the news. On some stations, the chat-up almost sounds like the jock is apologizing to the audience for having to break for news. In effect, the jock is telling listeners, "We are going to do the news now, so if you want to try another station you have a few minutes to spend station surfing."

News should get a neat, clean introduction and start. If the stories are good and the presentation is upbeat, with an air of importance, you can hook the listeners and they hang with the station because they know that the news moves fast and gives them what they need to know. Following the news, jocks and newscasters often go through a typical "thank you" routine that jocks and newscasters go through at the end of the newscast. Like "happy talk," it is not necessary, and it distracts from the importance and quality of the news. When the news is over, it is over. Play the commercial or sweeper and move on.

In many respects, a news story is like a commercial, and the announcer has to sell it to the audience. This goes right along with the old adage that a commercial is a news story about a business. All of the basic communication tools discussed later in this chapter are used in a newscast. Reading ability is paramount. Pronunciation is critical. You have to articulate each word during a two-minute newscast or no one can understand you. Good newscasters and reporters read with a lot of vitality in their voices to let the listener know that they are on top of things. The vocal inflection you choose often varies from story to story, depending on the seriousness or importance of the story. The tempo of the newscast needs to be upbeat and is accomplished by reading copy at fifteen to eighteen lines per minute.

Nevertheless, you have to keep in mind that each station has its own style guidelines when it comes to the news, and it is your job to follow them. Regardless of the guidelines or style, though, the basics we've covered here still apply and can be used to develop a strong, credible presentation.

Sports Delivery

A sportscast is something that typically requires a lot of vitality and excitement. Just as you were instructed to look for the passion in a commercial, sportscasters need to look for the passion in sports. Sports fans are passionate about their teams and have clear likes and dislikes. Chances are, nothing you say is going to change a sports fan's biases toward one team or another, but you can certainly share a sports fan's excitement about sports and give that fan something to talk about with friends and coworkers the rest of the day.

Energy and Enthusiasm

More than anything, sports has to be upbeat and forward moving. You have to be enthusiastic. An interesting aspect of sportscasting is something called "home-town advantage" or bias. It is not at all unusual for sportscasters to give an edge to the hometown team in their coverage. They didn't lose the game last night; it was a hard-fought battle. Our team didn't just win the game, they steamrolled right over the Mud Hens.

One of the ways you can show your energy and enthusiasm is by the language you use.

You need to be speaking the same language your listeners are. Often words and terms develop locally that you need to incorporate into your sportscasts. You need to speak in an informed, yet conversational, manner. Your choice of words can play a big part in this. Get away from more formal words and use simple terms. For example:

- Sports figures don't express concern—they are worried
- Games are not lengthy—they are long
- Things are not similar—they are like
- A sports legend has never expired—they died
- Sports are not timely—they are fast, quick, or speedy
- There are no sports physicians—they are doctors

Nothing in simplifying the language is meant to dumb down the message; it is meant to make it clearer and easier to read and understand.

Inflection and tempo play big roles in sportscasting. Your presentation needs to move at about eighteen lines of copy per minute and you need to learn to use the full range of inflection in your voice. There is an international soccer broadcaster who became famous by the way he said "goooooooooooaaaaaaaaaaalllllllllll" when his team scored, stretching the word out for six to ten seconds. That is inflection!

With that said, there are going to be times in sports when things get very serious for one reason or another. It is during those times that a sportscaster needs to assume some of the persona of a newscaster. This occurs when a stock car racing driver is killed or an athlete is seriously injured or charged with a crime. And as previously mentioned

Figure 9.6

Often it is a good idea to involve an extra set of ears on a project. Producers and production directors can provide valuable input to a project. Really good producers and directors assume the role of the listener or client and see your work from the consumer's point of view.

with news, each station is going to have its own set of guidelines regarding the overall style of the sportscast it wants.

Working with Producers and Production Directors

On-air staff and production people often work with a producer or production director who provides guidance and a sense of direction to a show or commercial project. Typically, talent resists such input since "we know how to do our jobs."

The only problem to knowing how to do our jobs is that sometimes we get too close to the work and don't step back to take a critical listen. Producers and production directors can provide valuable input to a show or project (see Fig. 9.6). Really good producers and directors assume the role of the listener or client and see your work from the consumer's point of view.

Generally, when someone takes the time to give you input into your work, it is because they want to help you improve the quality of the product. Take the time to listen critically to your work from time to time and keep something in mind: You can always learn something from just about everyone.

An Announcer's Basic Tools of Communication

Your Voice

Of all the qualities it takes to be a good announcer, the most important has to be a personable sounding, natural voice. Whether you realize it or not, your voice is one of the key elements that you have used in building and shaping your personality, long before you considered a career in radio. One of the interesting things about radio is that listeners never get to see the nonverbal cues they otherwise depend on while communicating with others. Your listeners will never get to see your eyes, your facial expressions, or your body language as you do your job each day. Your voice is the only aspect of your personality that your listener has to judge you by.

The voice you have is the one you were born with. You didn't get to choose it. Although a few people still think that all male announcers have to have big, deep, rumbling voices and women have to have low, husky, sexy voices, that just isn't really the case. Listeners are looking for a friend and, quite frankly, very few people have friends that sound like that. Your natural voice, the one you use every day, is the one your listeners are looking for as a friend. And just as you can spot someone who lacks sincerity and is a fake, so can your listener. Radio is not about being someone else, it's about being you, and this is one of the most difficult things for a new announcer to master.

Although delivery styles will vary between a regular daily show, news and sportscasts, or production work, one thing remains constant: your voice. Just like someone who trains so he or she can be better at golf, tennis, or some other sports activity, you can train and improve your vocal performance for a variety of presentations and styles.

Developing Your Voice

Before going any further let's get something straight. There is an old radio legend that says if you want a deep voice, drink whiskey and smoke a lot of cigarettes. Nothing could be farther from the truth. Smoking irritates the vocal folds and does give a gravel-like quality to your voice, similar to what happens when you have a cold and your voice becomes deeper. The reality, though, is that you don't develop a great-sounding voice by routinely damaging your vocal folds, which is exactly what smoking and whiskey do. Politely put, this is about the stupidest thing you can do.

Your Natural Pitch

When it comes to your speaking voice, everyone has a natural pitch. You have had it all your life; you just may not have known what it was. Try forcing your voice above or below your natural pitch for any length of time and your vocal folds become tired; you start sounding raspy. Your vocal folds are complex muscles, and just like other muscles in your body, if pushed too far, they give out. To determine your natural pitch, without thinking about it, spontaneously say "mm-hmm" as if you are indicating it is ok, or you agree with something. You don't really say it as much as you hum it with your lips closed. From the "mm-hmm," begin speaking with a phrase you use often, such as "how are you?" at a normal volume level. The two should be very close in pitch because the pitch you hum in and the pitch of your speaking voice should match. If you are having problems hearing whether they match, try recording your voice and playing it back to yourself, or get someone else to listen to you.

If there is a significant difference in the pitch of your hum and your speaking voice, then chances are very good that you are pushing your voice either up or down, and that can strain the vocal folds. This often results in discomfort in the chest and throat. Anytime you experience such discomfort, you are exceeding the comfortable range of your voice.

Breathing and Breath Control

Your voice is powered by air being pushed past your vocal folds by your lungs and diaphragm. To be a good announcer, you need a steady supply of air so that you are not gasping for breath at the end of each sentence.

There is no magic trick for instantly learning breath control; however, with a regular training regimen you can build the muscle control necessary and learn to control your breath. It is not that you don't have enough air in your lungs; you just don't have the muscle control necessary for good breath control. Learning to breathe properly is the first step in expanding your versatility and vocal range.

How to Breathe

Everyone knows how to breathe, right? Not really. Some of us breathe pretty shallowly, meaning we don't use the full capacity of our lungs.

Here is an exercise to help you learn to use your available lung capacity. Standing upright, relax and place your hands on your abdomen (belly) and breathe in slowly and deeply, filling your lungs. You should feel your *lower* ribs and abdomen move out against your hands. The object is not to push your stomach out but to fill your lower lungs with air. As you slowly exhale, your lower abdomen and ribs should relax. During this process, keep your focus on your lower abdomen.

You want the power to come from the abdomen, where you have lots of muscles to do the job, not the chest. Do this deep-breathing exercise for one minute several times a day.

Breath-Control Exercises

There is a very simple exercise you can do to build your breath control and improve your speaking voice: "oohs" and "ahs." Six to eight times a day, while standing upright, relax and breathe out, eliminating as much air from your lungs as possible. Pause a few seconds with your lungs at rest and then allow your lungs to take in as much air as you are comfortable with. You don't really have to think about breathing in a lot of air; your body automatically does that all by itself.

With your lungs full of air, tilt your head back slightly and make the "ooh" sound, as in "ooh isn't that delicious," until you empty your lungs of air. Your goal is to make the "ooh" sound for thirty seconds. If you are like most people, you are not going to be able to do this the first time you try. The goal is to be able to do this for thirty seconds with ease and still have a comfortable reserve of air in your lungs. Thirty-five seconds is even better. Use a watch or clock, and no cheating.

For the basic exercise, do your first "ooh" until you empty your lungs, pause a moment, let your lungs refill with air, and repeat the exercise. Beginners should repeat this five times. As you develop muscle control, extend it to ten repetitions. Doing these ten repetitions five or six times a day, over thirty to sixty days, will help you improve your breath control. You are training yourself to regulate the flow of air from your lungs so that you have plenty of air to speak with. Each time you do the exercise, alternate from "ooh" to "ah."

When you can do the "ooh" and "ah" exercise for thirty seconds, try repeating the exercise and varying the volume level of your voice up and down, from soft to loud. This takes even more breath control and gives you more flexibility in your delivery.

By making the "ooh" and "ah" sounds, you are forcing all of the air from your lungs out through your mouth. Another benefit of this exercise is that it helps train the muscles in your throat to route the air that powers your voice through your mouth, not through your nose. Air that escapes through your nose creates a honking-nasal sound or overtone to your normal speaking voice that most people find annoying. (An easy way to check for nasality is to place your index finger lightly on the tip of your nose. Slowly say the alphabet. If you feel the tip of your nose vibrating on any letter, those sounds are coming out of your nose. The only two letters you *should* feel a vibration on are "m" and "n.")

A final benefit of the ooh and ah exercise is that after all of those oohs and ahs, you will have given your vocal folds a great workout. Over time, don't be surprised if your voice mellows or lowers a bit.

Another breath-management exercise is to take a small breath of air and say the number "one" at a normal volume. Take another breath of air and say "one," pause one second, and then say "two." Take in another breath for "one," pause, "two," pause, "three," and so forth. Adding one number at a time, see how far you can count using one breath. Over sixty to ninety days, build up until you can count to thirty or thirty-five on a single breath with a slight pause between each number.

Basic Communication Skills

It is one thing to have a great voice, and an entirely different thing to be able to communicate with others. Communicating with others using only your voice requires that you be able to read and that the words you read be audible, clear, and distinct. The basic communication skills include reading ability, pronunciation, and articulation. You should already be familiar with reading and pronunciation. Articulation is the way that you move your tongue, palate, teeth, and lips to form the different speech sounds.

Reading

The first aspect of reading is the process of comprehending a written message. Although we typically think of reading as requiring sight, those with impaired vision can read just as well using a number of methods, including finger reading to pick up raised Braille symbols. Comprehending written messages is at the core of reading, but that is just the first step in the radio communication process. Not only do you have to be able to read, you have to be able to translate the written message into spoken words so that someone else can understand the written message.

A large part of reading well for radio comes down to being able to read ahead of the words you are saying, in other words, reading several words ahead of your spoken words so that you have time to interpret the words, their meanings, and the punctuation. Each punctuation symbol translates into a vocal cue for you to pass on to the listener. Commas translate into brief pauses; periods indicate the end of a sentence and are about twice as long as a comma. Colons get a pause similar to a period, as do semicolons.

Most punctuation marks also provide a cue as to what you should do vocally to convey the punctuation to the listener. For example, a period indicates the end of something, finality. Typically, we finish sentences with a slight downturn in the tone and inflection of the voice to indicate the end. A question mark often causes a slight rise in the voice at the end of the sentence. Exclamation points signal us to be expressive, with some astonishment. Each of the punctuation marks can be a cue to one of the many effects that can be created by adjusting the tone and inflection of the voice up or down.

Reading and speaking simultaneously is a complex process and it is beyond the scope of this text to diagnose and offer a solution to all of the possible reading problems that each person might have. As a university student, if you are not an excellent reader, seek out help through your student support services department. Most universities have programs that can help you become a better reader.

If you are going to be in radio, learn right now to read copy out loud. Typically, when we read silently to ourselves, we mumble and leave out a lot of the expressiveness of our interpretation. This is why it is so important for those who desire a career in radio to read aloud. Reading also involves the pronunciation and articulation of each individual word. Slow reading is an old radio exercise to help you learn to read and pronounce each word separately and to give the proper vocal cues to the punctuation.

Slow reading works like this. Twice a day, block out half an hour and pick up some kind of reading material. It is not really important what you read; it could be a book, a magazine, a newspaper, or something else. In fact, reading different materials each time provides a good variety of different writing styles. For thirty minutes, read the copy out loud, pausing for one second between each word. Pronounce each word clearly and distinctly. Learn to read four to six words in advance of what you are saying.

This drives most people pretty crazy the first time or two they do it, but under no circumstances are you to speed up the tempo.

The benefit is that you hear each and every word, and as you do this in "slow motion" you are programming your mind to see the individual words, pronounce the individual words correctly, and to read the punctuation and interpret its meaning so that you can provide verbal cues to your listeners.

The benefit of slow reading for sixty to ninety days is that you become a better reader, pronouncing every word clearly and distinctly. This is called clipping your words. Over time, you will find that you can read copy with greater ease, since you have trained yourself to read ahead, recognize individual words, and pronounce each word separately. You will discover that you make fewer mistakes reading copy for the first time. Also, the overall quality of your presentation improves tremendously, as words that were once run together are now separated and are easily understood.

The first time you do this, you might want to find a quiet out-of-the-way place to do your slow reading, as it is quite annoying to other people. As you become proficient at slow reading, try reading different types of materials. For example, read the classifieds in the Sunday newspaper and add some style and emphasis to various words; experiment and have fun while building your reading skills.

Articulation

Articulation is the way that you move your tongue, palate, teeth, and lips to form the different speech sounds. Each of the vowels and consonants is formed using different muscular and skeletal combinations of the throat and oral cavity. Some typical potential problem areas include a tight or stiff jaw, lazy tongue, and lazy lips. Another problem that sometimes shows up is a person who talks too fast.

Figure 9.7

Open your mouth is a big, cheesy, ear-to-ear smile for vocal exercises and on-air delivery. Listeners can't see you so your voice has to carry the whole load when it comes to inflection and emotion. A big smile adds a whole lot of personality and friendliness to your voice.

Here are some basic exercises that can help you articulate words better.

Start by limbering up. Spread your lips in a big, cheesy, ear-to-ear smile and say "eeeee" several times (see Fig. **9.7**). Then open your mouth as wide as an airplane hangar and say "aaaahhh" several times. Finally, close your lips down and make the "ooh" sound. Repeat each of these several times to stretch and limber up your mouth.

To limber up your jaw say a series of words that requires you to open your mouth. Try saying the following words while exaggerating your jaw opening as wide as you can:

Hah, Yacht, Dog, Paw, Laugh, Yard, Dart, Tab, Huh, Tater Tots, Why, Dark, Load, Wiggle

A stiff or tense upper lip can cause articulation problems. Try saying "pity, Patty" several times in a row to loosen up, making sure to clearly pronounce the Ps and Ts. When you can do the exercise cleanly at a slow pace, try going faster, but be sure you are clearly saying the "p" and "t" sounds.

Your tongue needs articulation exercise to be properly directed to its proper place in your mouth for particular sounds. Try saying each of the following words with your tongue forward in your mouth, just behind your upper front teeth:

Disc, Tea, Nope, Table-Top, Tale, Tick-Tock, Deal, Naughty, Nice

Another exercise to limber up your tongue is to place your teeth fairly close together and make the sound of a rattlesnake by trilling your tongue.

Probably the most popular way to exercise your articulators is through tongue twisters. However, the goal with tongue twisters is not to see how fast you can say them but how well you can articulate each of the individual words. Some that I like are:

The skunk thought the stump stunk; the stump thought the skunk stunk.

The big black bug bled blue-black blood, and the other big bug bled blue blood.

Sarah sells seashells by the seashore sitting in her stick-shift Chevrolet. The shells she sells are surely seashells. As she sits she shifts and sits. Sarah, Sarah, sitting in her stick-shift Chevrolet.

Toy Boat, Toy Boat, Toy Boat.

Pronunciation

Pronunciation is the manner in which someone says a word. It is based upon the phonetic sounds of vowels and consonants. Pronunciation is also based upon regional peculiarities, accents, and dialects. Regional pronunciations of words are often the result of tradition rather than correct phonetic syntax. For example, go to the city of Cairo, Illinois, and pronounce the name of their city like the one in Egypt and you will get a funny look, because the one in Illinois is pronounced kay-row; with a long "a" sound. And in Missouri, there is a river called the Osceola (Oh-see-oh-la) River. In Florida, however, that same Seminole Indian name is pronounced Ah-see-oh-la. These are just two of thousands of examples of regional pronunciations.

When you arrive in a new area, be sure to enlist the help of the other station staff to find out what local expressions are used; which local community names, if mispronounced, are dead giveaways that you are an outsider; and any other regionalisms that are important for you to understand. Be sure you can pronounce all the high school sports teams' names, the names of local government officials, and the different neighborhoods or communities in the area. Even though news, as well as commercial copy, often comes with a pronunciation guide, ask someone whenever there is any doubt about a pronunciation.

Basic Communication Tools

With all of the previously discussed elements of your voice in place, including breathing, reading, pronunciation, and articulation, you are ready to begin to have some fun with your voice. As mentioned earlier, it is one thing to have a great-sounding voice, and it is another thing entirely to know how to use it. What follows are some basic tools and techniques you can use to become more than just a good-sounding voice. Inflection, tempo, vitality, phrasing, and volume are all elements of the creativity used to "sell the copy" to a listener.

Inflection

Speaking in the same tone of voice all the time and showing no expression or emotion is speaking in a monotone, meaning one tone. A monotone presentation does not work on the radio, unless it is for a character in a comedy bit on a show. The opposite of someone speaking in a monotone is someone speaking with inflection in his or her voice. Inflection involves changing the voice by adding emphasis to words through simple things like a change in pitch, pronunciation, the force with which a word is said, and variations in how you say words. It involves subtle changes in your voice to express emotion.

For example, how many ways can you find to say "I want you to come here"? You could say it in a deep, sexy whisper to attract a partner, or at the opposite end of the spectrum, you could say it like an angry father ordering his child to come to him, pronouncing each word loudly, separately, and with a lot of force and emphasis to give a feeling of power. In between, the possibilities are up to you.

It may sound crazy, but all the electronics and audio processing of radio strip your voice of some of its subtle, unique qualities. A good announcer works at being very expressive with his or her voice, through inflection, since the listener can't see any of the announcer's body language or facial expressions to get visual emotional cues. Although we use our ears to hear, interestingly, we normally use our eyes just as much to help us hear by interpreting body language and facial expressions. But in radio, your voice is the only real tool you have to reach your listener.

Figure 9.8

Reading a commercial is like telling a story to your best friend. Don't be afraid to use facial expressions or body movement to emphasize the story you are telling. When you focus on telling a story, your voice changes and you naturally add inflection and character.

There are three basic things to remember when you are doing an air shift or newscast or producing a commercial. The first is that you are talking to one person and one person only. Pick a particular person and speak to that person. Imagine a close friend, your best buddy, or a close family member. Speak directly to that person, as you would if he or she were sitting in front of you. By focusing on speaking to that one person, you naturally pick up some inflection in your voice.

The second thing that you have to get past is that you are not reading copy or lecturing to this person; you are telling your best friend a story. Concentrate and focus on telling that person the story. Communicate with the person as you would if he or she were sitting right there with you. Don't be afraid to use fa-

cial expressions or body movement to emphasize the story you are telling (see Fig. **9.8**). This method works just as well for news as it does for on-air work or recording commercials. Again, by focusing on telling a story to the person who is there with you, your voice changes and you naturally add inflection to your voice.

Finally, above all else, smile. I don't mean a little smirk; as I've said, I mean a big, cheesy, ear-to-ear smile (again, see Fig. **9.7**). And about the time you think you sound friendly, add just a little more. However, if you are reading news copy, you have to use your best judgment as to how to present each story. Some stories are deadly serious, and others are sometimes quite ironic in an almost humorous way. No matter what you are reading, though, keep in mind that your listener can't see you so your voice has to carry the whole load when it comes to inflection and emotion. A big smile adds a whole lot of personality and friendliness to your voice. As a result, a lot of your natural inflections make it through to the listener.

Here is a fun inflection exercise you can try. Take any sentence and imagine five or six different situations in which you could say that same sentence; imagine the emotion that would go along with each situation. For example, imagine saying to someone "Is it time to eat yet?" Say this as you would in the following situations:

- You are a six-year-old child saying it to your mother while she is preparing dinner.

- You are on a first date and have been waiting at a restaurant for nearly forty-five minutes for your food; you are asking the server if your meal is about ready.

- You have spent the entire day hiking in the woods and it is after six p.m.

- You are a teenager who missed lunch and you have to wait for your sister to get home before the rest of the family eats dinner.

- You are on a cell phone with your lover who is fixing a special dinner for your birthday, and you are already twenty-five minutes late getting there.

- Your partner bought your favorite chocolate-covered strawberries at the mall and you don't want to wait until you get home to try them.

Announcers often give a client two or three different reads of a commercial, trying out various inflections to see how it changes the commercial's meaning. Sometimes a producer may tell the talent just to have fun with the copy and try a couple of different reads. Over-

all, inflection adds personality and character to the copy's written words.

Tempo

Tempo is the speed at which you deliver the read on a project. Different projects require different tempos. A commercial for a romantic five-star restaurant gets an entirely different read than one for a car dealer's twelve-hour mega-sale. Even news and public affairs are presented at different tempos, depending on the situation. Learning to use tempo requires an overall sense of timing. Asked to do so, most experienced announcers can talk for exactly sixty seconds without looking at a clock. Likewise, he or she can look at a piece of copy and tell you if it is too long or short. This kind of timing comes with experience.

Another factor that contributes to tempo are the announcers themselves. Each announcer has a range of speed at which he or she can comfortably read and still maintain inflection and emotion in the voice. Some announcers can't even begin to approach anything closely related to a speed read, and, similarly, others have problems doing slow, intimate, reads. As with inflection, you should try to expand your versatility and the range of tempos that you are comfortable delivering.

The two extremes of tempo each come with built-in difficulties. A slow, intimate read means that every word you say can be heard and the articulation has to be razor sharp. Any defect, no matter how slight, is emphasized by a slow, intimate read. Often, mouth noise or the noise made by your lips and the saliva in your mouth become evident. An old radio trick to help with this is to eat an apple or sip some apple juice before you start. Apple juice does a good job of cleansing the mouth and reducing the excess saliva.

At the opposite end of the spectrum is the high-pressure car commercial in which the announcer is asked to cram sixty-eight seconds of copy into a sixty-second commercial by reading at a blazing speed. The difficulty with a speed read is getting each word out of your mouth in the first place. You have to do it so someone can understand what it is you are saying. Adding to the difficulty of a speed read is trying to keep any inflection or feeling in the voice.

One of the things you can do to help you learn to control tempo is the slow reading exercise explained earlier in the chapter. Slow reading lets you hear every word so that you can build pronunciation and articulation skills for those slow reads. It also helps to slow down those announcers who already have a fast natural tempo. By saying just one word at a time, you learn to pronounce the entire word, making sure you say things such as the "ing" or the "ed" on the end of words. As you practice slow reading, though, you may notice that over time you can speak faster if you want to, since each word comes out of your mouth as a separate, distinct word.

Vitality

When applied to announcing, vitality refers to the energy in your voice or the animation of your personality through your voice. Vitality is closely tied to inflection and, to some degree, tempo. Vitality is also a component in acting. Really good announcers can deliver a wide range of energy levels in their voice, from something soft and caring to a screaming NASCAR race commercial. Vitality is also a component in doing news. A newscaster needs a certain level of energy to the voice to let listeners know that he or she is on top of things, that there is an interest in making sure listeners are kept up-to-date. Sportscasters

need a much higher level of energy, because that is what sports broadcasting is all about—energy, excitement, and enthusiasm.

Radio announcers are similar to actors when it comes to delivering their personality to listeners. One of the interesting comparisons between announcers and actors can be made when actors get the opportunity to voice a character in an animated feature film. Most have remarked that creating and carrying a character with their voice is just as difficult as acting, if not more so. Again, this is because listeners don't get to see any of the body language that actors normally depend on to give viewers so many of the cues to their character.

The best way to develop vitality in your voice is to listen to yourself and to have others listen and critique you. Often you hear producers telling announcers to "kick it up a couple of notches." What they are asking for is a little more personality, a little more of you to come through. Another thing that helps an announcer to improve vitality is to find the emotion in a piece of copy. One of my mentors taught me that to sell the copy, you had to find the passion in it. You had to find something to love and bring it to the audience. In other words, find something in the copy that you have a love for or that the listener has a love for. Or pick something in the copy that you want to really move the listener with. For example, take a soft and soothing commercial for a health spa. Can you be passionate about a health spa? Let me put it this way: Can you be passionate about the incredible cuisine in the four-star restaurant, the total relaxation full-body massage, soaking in the hot tub, or the fact that you are going to be pampered for a three-day weekend? Maybe it is just going to be getting away from the rat race for three days. Now can you find something in those ideas that you could be passionate about or express a love for? Easily!

From the standpoint of presentation, the flip side is a raucous commercial for a NASCAR race. Can you be passionate about noisy stock cars? The smell of race gas, burning rubber, the roar of the engines, the great junk food, the excitement of the race itself, and the friendship of being with others who understand racing?

If you look, you can find some kind of passion in just about every piece of copy you are asked to read. You just have to take a moment to find it.

If you want to have some fun, take a copy of the Sunday want ads and pull out the classified section. Try reading aloud the ads from the cars-for-sale section. Find the passion in each ad. What point does the seller really think is important? Read aloud from the jobs section and pick out what each employer thinks is important; get passionate about it. Finally, turn to the situations-wanted section and read the ads there, looking for why each person thinks an employer should hire them. What are those job seekers passionate about?

Phrasing

There is an old saying that says you need to be able to walk and chew gum at the same time. The same thing applies to phrasing the words in a piece of copy. You need to be able to read copy and breathe at the same time. Breathing and phrasing go hand-in-hand. Ideally, you breathe at the natural breaks in the copy that are often indicated by punctuation. The copy writer affects your phrasing from the standpoint that he or she creates the sentence structure and the paragraphs. Different styles of writing present some interesting challenges. The flip side is when you write your own copy and tailor it to your natural breathing and phrasing patterns.

Copy that is written for a newspaper is entirely different from copy that is written for radio. Newspaper copy adheres to a completely different style of writing than radio copy. The newspaper is informational, whereas radio is conversational. Try reading a front-page story from your local newspaper aloud. Chances are it does not read well at all because the sentence structure and paragraphs are written to convey a lot of detailed information. A newspaper's journalistic style includes longer sentences and small details.

Radio copy is written from the perspective that we only have a short time to tell a listener a story, whether it is a news story or a commercial. The copy is written to convey the essential details or the big picture, similar to the way you might tell a friend about something. Radio copy typically avoids long, multisyllabic words and run-on sentences. It is purposely written to be read aloud to someone so that the announcer can tell listeners a story.

To phrase copy properly, you have to have a good supply of air to begin with, and you have to learn how to replenish that supply of air without gasping or making loud sucking noises. The way to practice this is to pick a favorite book or magazine and read the first twenty words or so from it. Look first for the punctuation or other natural places to pause in the copy; mark those places with a slash mark (/). Every time you reach one of those pauses while reading, allow your lungs to take in air naturally rather than sucking in air consciously to fill your lungs. Pace yourself, and don't speak so long that you allow yourself to run out of breath. It takes some time to develop the ability to pre-read copy, figure out the phrasing that works best for you, and deliver the copy's message. As an example, try reading and phrasing the following paragraph and see how you do:

It was a very cool, foggy, and breezy spring morning as the sun crested the mountain top and the hikers walked slowly along the Appalachian Trail, their packs heavily laden with provisions for the next two weeks of their solitary journey.

Just as you did to practice vitality, try reading aloud from a variety of sources, including a newspaper, magazine, and a book—even this textbook, for that matter. The more you practice, the better you will become at breaking a piece of copy down into phrasing that complements your style and accents the meaning of the copy.

Volume

How loud do you have to talk to be heard on the radio? Not very loud. We often associate the loudness of a person's voice with a number of emotions ranging from joy and excitement to extreme anger. Many think that the louder you are, the more forceful you are; the louder you laugh, the happier you are; and so forth. Sadness is often associated with a soft, weak voice. Although these are all typical reactions, actors learn early on that the secret to conveying many of these emotions is not actually loudness or softness but the emotion itself. Although volume plays a role in expressing the emotion, your control over the emotion is what is important.

An announcer uses a microphone in a studio. Rather than thinking of it as a microphone, think of it as your best friend's ear. Learning to control the volume of your voice is an important aspect of being an announcer. The only thing that happens when you shout into a microphone is that the microphone and associated equipment overload and distort. The end result is that the listener does not get the message. On the other hand, speaking too softly or whispering into the microphone causes the audio processing automatically to turn up the audio levels to the point that background and room noises become very evident.

Good announcers learn to express themselves with their regular speaking voice. You can make it sound as though you were shouting by changing your vitality and the inflection you are using. Likewise, you can make it sound as though you were whispering while still speaking at your regular vocal level.

Your Personality

Communicating with your listeners involves both the technical skill of announcing and learning to convey your personality and express yourself through your voice. As said earlier in the chapter, your voice is the only means you have to communicate with listeners; they will likely never see you in the studio. To be successful, it is vitally important that you learn to practice vocal skills and at the same time experiment and have fun with your voice. Learn to listen to yourself critically and to depend on others you trust for critical evaluation.

Developing a voice and personality does not happen overnight, it might take months of work to get to the professional entry level you want to achieve. One final thing to keep in mind is that developing your voice and personality is a continuing process that will follow you throughout your career.

Suggested Activities

These questions assume you already have a show of your own. If you don't, just imagine that you do, or, put yourself in the place of a show host you are familiar with.

1. Listening to other stations is a great way to improve your show. Listen critically to any

local radio morning show you want to and do a talk clock in reverse. In other words, track the station and chart what the jock or jocks are doing during each stop set. When are the stop sets each hour? How long are the stop sets? What do they contain? Do this for the length of the show. Track it over several days. See any predictable patterns or routines?

2. Log onto the web and see if you can locate any major-market radio stations that are streaming their signal. Carefully listen to the jocks and how they present and do things. See if you can find one or two stylistic things you could incorporate into your show.

3. Listen to a radio station, not for the music but for the commercials and promos. Record them if you can and then listen to them again and take each one apart. Take notes: What is different about their work from yours? See if you can find two things you like that they are doing and that you can incorporate into your commercial work.

4. Record yourself every time you are on the air and listen to yourself after you are off the air. Likewise, keep a copy of every commercial and promo you do. Then, listen to them a week later. Are they still as good as you thought they were when you produced them? What could you do to improve your work? In both cases, have someone you respect critique your work.

Web Sites for More Information

For more information about:

- *announcing, production, and being a great jock,* visit Dan O'Day.com at www.danoday.com

Pro Speak

You should be able to use this term in your everyday conversations with other professionals.

stop set—a break in the music or other programming during which you talk and play back commercials, promos, etc.

Promotion and Station Imaging

Creating a great-sounding radio station is much more than just playing a lot of music back-to-back. In fact, listeners don't really want to hear back-to-back music; they want to be entertained and to be a part of something. A really great radio station is based around creating an original **sound design** that sets the station apart from the rest of the competition. The purpose of the sound design is to give the radio station charisma and a personality—the same kind of charisma and personality that listeners seek in a good friend.

The production person is at the heart of any station promotion, imaging, or contest. You are the person challenged to bring the concept to life for the listener, to create a "theater-of-the-mind" event. In this chapter you are going to learn about two of the most important elements of creating a station's sound design: promotion and imaging. It is imperative that you understand the broad scope and purpose of station promotion and imaging so that you can do your job more effectively. You also need to understand how these two elements play a key role in programming and sales.

Station Promotion

There is an old media saying that if something is worth doing, then it is worth promoting. The key to a successful radio station is how the station promotes itself. An outstanding radio station has a continuing stream of promotions and promotional announcements, one after the other. Promotions include station events, contests, and public service. Promotions help create the positive, forward-moving image in the listener's mind that is required for a station to be successful.

The Purpose of Promotion

Stations use promotions to build **Arbitron** audience ratings by increasing the number of time segments **(dayparts)** during which listeners tune in and to extend the time those listeners spend listening to the station **(time spent listening).** A station also uses promotions to direct listeners to a specific daypart the station wants to build audience for, such as morning or afternoon drive time. Arbitron ratings are discussed in detail in chapter 14.

A well-designed promotion creates an awareness of the station and interest in the community beyond the station's **core audience.** Promotions help build a bond with listeners and enhance the station's image. A second major motivating factor behind station promotion is to generate sales revenue; 70 percent or more of station promotions are sales-driven (see Fig. **10.1**). Even a station's public-service events are often sponsored by businesses, for public relations purposes, on behalf of a charity or community-service organization. Building audience and generating revenue are the two overriding purposes of promotion.

Promotions require pre-planning for proper execution and to generate the visibility, publicity, and revenue the station seeks. A promotions-driven station plans major promotions as much as a year in advance. Concert promotions require three to four months of work. A simple appearance by a musical artist or concert ticket giveaway should be planned three to six weeks in advance. An effective promotions campaign includes a charted timeline from brainstorming the promotion concept, through pre-planning the event, to executing the promotion, and to the follow-up. In effect, promotion planning is preparing to go into a ratings war with your competitors. The promotions office and the production studio become the ratings war rooms.

Figure 10.1

A well-designed promotion creates an awareness of the station and interest in the community beyond the station's core audience. Promotions help build a bond with listeners and enhance the station's image.

A well-designed promotion plan of attack includes clearly stated overall objectives. You must be able to finish the sentence: "Our promotion will . . ." To achieve the objectives, the station must develop a strategy, or plan, that includes a detailed time line on a calendar. Finally, the station must develop specific tactics or methods to carry out the strategy. Promotion requires objectives, strategies, and tactics to have a maximum impact on the station's listeners and other radio stations.

A station committed to success works with a promotional marketing plan that targets and highlights the key elements in the station's programming that set it apart from the competition. The marketing plan includes positioning and branding the station.

Positioning the Station

Each station needs a clearly defined **positioning statement.** A positioning statement is a unique selling proposition, or slogan, used by the station to separate itself from the competition. Only one station in a market can own or dominate a particular position. Positioning requires the station to focus and specialize on a target audience.

A positioning statement is clear and includes definitive language about the station

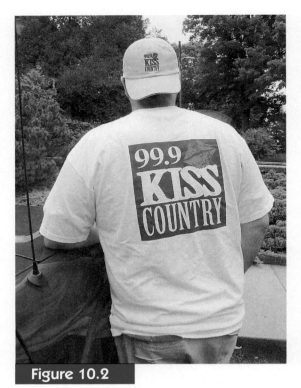

Figure 10.2

Although we wouldn't consider "99.9 KISS Country" to be a statement in normal language, it qualifies as a positioning statement on this T-shirt and hat. The radio station's dial position, music format, and signature logo are all easily identifiable at a glance.

The best positioning statement includes the station's dial position, the station's location, and the kind of music it plays. Short and simple is best. Examples of strong positioning statements include, "Fun Times and Great Oldies, Kansas City's 104 One," "St. Louis's Home for Rock N' Roll—99 Five," "Live 95 Five, Gainesville's Classic Rock Superstation." Each of these short positioning statements lays claim to a specific target audience in a specific geographical area. A casual listener scanning the dial instantly knows where the station is located, what kind of music it plays, and what the station's frequency is so that he or she can return or tell a friend.

Notice that two things are missing in each of the preceding positioning statements. First, the letters AM or FM. They are not needed. Second, the station dial position is simplified by removing the "point" from the sentence. No one outside the industry tells a friend, "I listen to 104 point 1 FM." Instead, they say, "I listen to 104—One." So why not speak to your listeners in the language they are using? Instead of saying 104 point 1, make it simply 104—One. (There are some cases where this will not work. For example, 90 point 5 would become 90—Five, and this is confusing, since there is a 95 on the dial. In this case, something creative should be done, such as calling the point a dot; 90 dot Five has a nice Internet-related high-tech sound [see demo CD, cut 76].)

Positioning statements evolve over time as stations seek to maintain their current market position and expand their listener base. This often involves a refinement of the station format or a change in the musical trends within a format. The goal is to maintain the current target audience and to add listeners through programming revision and updating of the positioning statement.

(see Fig. **10.2**). Broad, undefined positioning statements fail to differentiate a station from its competitors. "Your FM weather station," for example, is a particularly weak statement because every FM radio station has weather in one form or another. The other weakness is that a station does not need to remind people they are listening to FM. Maybe in 1965 it was necessary, but not today. Similarly, "The Valley's Best Music" does not tell the listener what valley or what kind of music is "best." Equally bad is "less talk, more music"; less of what talk and more of what kind of music, from what radio station?

Branding the Station

Branding is a part of the overall marketing plan and works in conjunction with a station's positioning statement. Whereas a positioning statement is tightly focused, branding encompasses the entire marketing effort of the station. Branding provides a clear differentiation from the other stations in the marketplace based on the station's overall identity and attitude, as defined by the listener. The station's brand should be aimed at making the listener feel as if he or she is part of the radio station.

A station's branding concept is not something the station dreams up and throws at the listener, hoping it will stick. Branding comes from the consumer, in this case the listener. A radio station has to go out and walk through the mall and talk to its listeners; it has to become involved with its listeners to learn their likes and dislikes about the station. A station needs to find out what the key elements are that listeners associate with the radio station.

In effect, branding is a promise by the radio station to provide a solution to a problem that the listener has. For example, if a listener is seeking a station with an upbeat lite-rock format and a super morning team, so that the listener does not fall asleep driving into work, that is a listener need, or problem, that a station can solve. If there is a large base of sports fans in a community, there is an opportunity for a sports-talk station to brand itself as the "sports authority" and serve the needs of rabid sports fans.

Branding comes down to two things, listener awareness and attachment. Everything, from the music on the station to the station's logo, should be aimed at making listeners and potential listeners aware of the station's positioning and branding. Attachment comes when the station provides a solution to the listener's needs and the listener adopts the station as "his or her radio station." In an ideal situation, listeners feel like they are a part of the station. The radio station needs to find a place in each listener's life. Once this occurs, an emotional bond is built.

Using listener-based information, branding should be applied to every form of "packaging" the radio station, including the station's positioning statement, logo, music, on-air personalities, contests, liners, sweepers, promotions, and public service (see Fig. **10.3**). Branding is all about top-of-mind awareness, so that when the ratings are being taken, the listener remembers the station. Using all of a station's unique qualities and variables, successful branding turns the generic product of "a radio station" into "my radio station."

Ultimately, it is not so much the branding as it is the relationship that develops between the listener and the radio station that is the most powerful. Branding creates a mental image or identity for a station that makes it instantly recognizable as a unique, one-of-a-kind individual. In a best-case scenario, the radio station reaches out beyond the station to form an emotional bond with the listener and become a part of his or her life.

Program Promotion

Every successful station seeks to promote itself and the uniqueness of what it is doing. Good station promos follow the station branding and positioning statements, tying all of the elements together. Promos highlight the station's music, contests, personalities, public service, and all of the things that the station does that benefit the listener.

Promos should be forward-moving (promoting the future) and make maximum use of the "theater of the mind" effect so that listeners develop visual images in their heads of

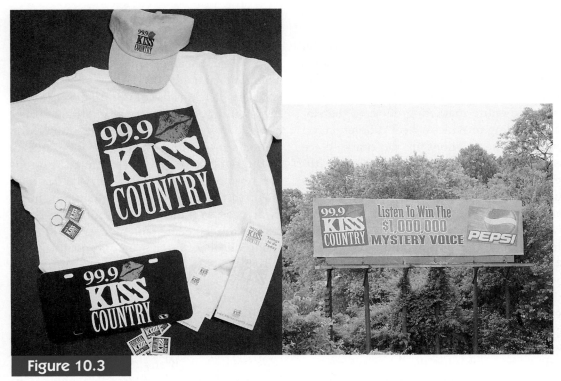

Figure 10.3

Branding is all about top-of-mind awareness, so that when the ratings are being taken, the listener remembers the station. This station uses the same logo and trademarks consistently, on everything from billboards to temporary tattoos (lower center).

what it is you are doing. They should be exciting, fun, dynamic, attention-getting stories about your station aimed at the station's target audience or demographic. A demographic group of people is identified based upon age, gender, income, and other quantifiable statistical information. Even if a station does not have a huge promotion budget, if it has a creative production person it can unleash a firestorm of promos that build the station's image, create excitement, and attract and help hold listeners (see demo CD, cut 77).

The fact is that a creative outside-the-box thinker with a good imagination and a production room can run circles around a station with a big promotions budget and little creativity. Promos are valuable, just as valuable as a commercial. Salespeople ask clients to sell their products on the radio. Likewise, the radio station needs to sell itself, and it should be its own biggest client.

Cross-Promotion

Promotions must have a purpose, with the most basic being to cross-promote, or promote another event or program on the radio station, to help build audience ratings. For example, every radio station should promote the next day's morning show twenty-four hours a day since it is usually a station's most-listened-to show. Each day, within an hour after the morning show is over, there should be a promo running about tomorrow's show, its features, and how great it's going to be. Sometimes cross-promotion extends to promoting an event such as special news or sports coverage of a major event on a sister station in the same market group (see demo, CD cut 78).

All jocks should be cross-promoting ahead to other dayparts on the station to build interest and maintain listenership. A station that is constantly cross-promoting ahead holds the listeners it has and develops a steady base of listeners across a number of dayparts throughout the week. There are two basic types of cross-promotion.

Horizontal Promotion

Horizontal promos are announcements that promote events, contests, and station public service on a day-to-day basis (see Fig. **10.4**). The previously discussed morning-show promos are a good example of horizontal promotion. You should always start promoting at least a day in advance. For example, promos for the weekend need to start on Wednesday and promos for the morning drive show on Monday need to start Friday, within an hour after the morning show is over, and run through the start of the show at 5 or 6 a.m. Monday. Like all other promos, horizontal promos should promote ahead on a day-to-day basis to a station event.

Vertical Promotion

Vertical promos are announcements that give a listener a reason to keep listening through the next twenty minutes, the next hour, and the next daypart or show (see Fig. **10.5**). Vertical promos create a lot of urgency when it comes to events or contests. When a jock promises to do something in the next twenty minutes, chances are a listener sticks around to see what happens, because twenty minutes is not that long. The reason jocks work with "the next twenty minutes" is that Arbitron ratings are based on quarter-hour segments. If a jock can get you to stay into the next quarter hour, he or she can potentially get credit for that quarter hour as well.

Jocks should constantly be promoting the next hour and the next daypart as well, and to some degree, there needs to be repetition of theme within vertical promos. As listeners join the station at various times, they need to be constantly brought up to date as to what is coming up in the next few minutes.

The Bad Promo: A Dangerous Situation

A station promo is as valuable as a commercial and should be given the same creativity and attention to detail in its production as the station's best commercial client gets. Sloppy production, at any level, is dangerous to a radio station, and here's why.

When people are watching a television show and the commercials come on, they have a choice. Viewers can either watch the commercials, or they can get up and go get another beer and some chips and then come back and collapse in their recliner to watch the rest of their show. Worst-case scenario, the commercial or promo fails to sell the product.

However, when a person is in his or her car driving down the road and a commercial or promo comes on the radio, the person has no other activity to fall back on besides listening to the radio. The only choice he or she has is whether or not to change stations. An interesting promo or commercial holds a listener's attention until the music returns, whereas a bad

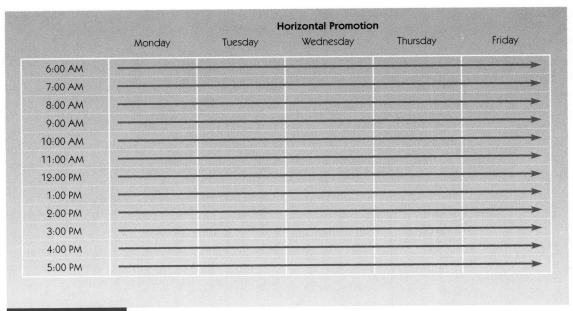

Figure 10.4

Horizontal promos are announcements that promote events, contests, and station public service on a day-to-day basis. Announcers should always cross-promote other dayparts on the station to build interest and maintain listenership.

promo or commercial sends the fickle finger of fate to press the next preset on the radio and change stations. On a radio station, a bad commercial or promo not only fails to sell the product, it costs the station listeners and Arbitron audience ratings. Bad commercial and promo production is just as responsible for a drop in station ratings as are bad jocks and poor music selection.

Station Imaging

The Purpose of Station Imaging

Station imaging consists of the live and recorded elements that are used between segments of a station's programming to tie every-thing together, creating a station's signature sound. Through a singular, consistent voice, imaging creates a mood, or tone, and establishes a texture for a radio station. Imaging can be a powerful audio marketing tool that constantly reminds listeners what station they are listening to and why they should continue to listen. Overall, imaging creates the public face of the radio station.

The Promotional Voice

If imaging creates the face of the radio station, then the promotional voice constitutes the features of that face. It is how listeners recognize that station. Station imaging requires a distinctive voice, a real powerhouse, to stand out and set your station apart from

Vertical Promotion

	Monday	Tuesday	Wednesday	Thursday	Friday
6:00 AM					
7:00 AM					
8:00 AM					
9:00 AM					
10:00 AM					
11:00 AM					
12:00 PM					
1:00 PM					
2:00 PM					
3:00 PM					
4:00 PM					
5:00 PM					

Figure 10.5

Vertical promos are announcements that promote events, contests, and station public service on an hour-to-hour basis. Announcers should always promote the next twenty minutes, next hour, and next daypart, or show, to create interest and build listenership. Combined with horizontal promos, a powerful promotional grid is formed, as above.

the competition (see demo CD, cut 79). The voice can be male or female—which is determined by the kind of image the station wants to create.

The promotional voice should not be someone on your station staff, and it is often outsourced to a professional voice talent (see Fig. **10.6**). In many cases, stations within a regional or national group, such as Clear Channel Communications, swap voices among the stations. The promotional voice should appear only on the station's imaging. It should never be heard as a jock on the station, it should never be heard on commercials on the station, and it should never be heard on another station in the market. The station's promotional voice is the personality of the station

and has a very special relationship with the listener.

A well-established promotional voice attracts attention because the listeners, whether they are aware of it or not, relate to the voice as a friend. They know that when this voice speaks, it is something special and deserves their attention. In effect, the voice is the radio station speaking directly to them. Even when listeners are not listening closely, the promotional voice catches their attention, either consciously or subconsciously.

There are two types of station imaging, liners and sweepers. With either of these types, the four keys to success are keeping the message simple and repetition, repetition, repetition.

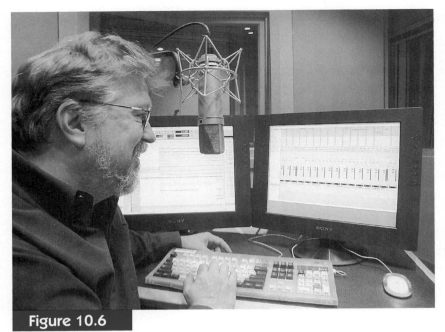

Figure 10.6

A professional voice from outside a market can make a big difference in the sound of a radio station. Because of their national exposure, professional voices often have great creative ideas for station imaging and branding. This particular voice is heard on more than 120 radio stations and on numerous national television commercials.

Liners

A liner is a dry voice (without music or sound effects) that promotes the talent, the music, or a station promotional event (see demo CD, cut 80). Liners keep listeners informed about what is happening and promote the station's branding and positioning statement. Liners help to create a sense of urgency; if the listener doesn't stay with the station a few minutes longer, something is going to be missed. Liners can either be recorded by the station's promotional voice or done live by the on-air talent. Some stations use a mix of live and recorded liners.

Sweepers

Sweepers are liners that have been produced to create the station's signature sound. Sweepers are designed to reinforce the music format and the station's attitude. A well-produced sweeper triggers an immediate listener response. Listeners instantly recognize the signature sound and their radio station (see demo CD, cut 81).

Some of the various elements often included in a sweeper are the promotional voice, sound effects, laser blasts, music elements that match the type and energy of the station format, and various effects created through audio processing. Depending on the station format, a sweeper can be as short as seven seconds or as long as twenty seconds. Although short in length, sweepers are full-blown multitrack productions and require excellent production skills to make an effective impression (see demo CD, cut 82). Typically, a satellite-formatted station is restricted to short, fixed-length time slots in which to insert local station sweepers, so timing has to be exact.

Sweepers are often designed and produced to make music transitions smoother between two dissimilar cuts of music. For example, sweepers are produced that transition from a fast-paced song to a slow-paced song and vice versa. There are any number of variations on transition sweepers, including sweepers to take the station from music into traffic, weather, or news (see demo CD, cut 83).

Station Identification: The Legal ID

Station identification is a legal requirement of the Federal Communications Commission. Radio stations must make station identification announcements when they sign on and off for the day and hourly, as close to the top of the hour as possible, at a natural programming stop set. Legal station identification consists of the station call letters, immediately followed by the station's city of license, for example: KOKO, Warrensburg or WWNZ, Orlando.

Once the legal obligation is met, the station is free to enhance the ID by including other cities the station serves or by adding a station positioning statement. For example, "Serving Altmonte, Mt. Dora, and Zellwood, we're WWNZ, Orlando." The station has to be careful that it does not make a false claim to serve a city that it does not. Also, be sure to check the station license for the correct call letters and city of license. (Contrary to popular belief, most stations do not have the letters AM or FM included as a part of their assigned call sign. Stations east of the Mississippi River use call letters starting with a W; those west of the Mississippi start with a K. Stations that went on the air prior to the call sign ruling many years ago, such as KDKA in Pittsburgh, Pennsylvania, or WDAF in Kansas City, Missouri, are allowed to keep their original call sign.)

Something as simple as a station ID can affect station branding and positioning if it gets in the way or sends a mixed message to the listener. Station IDs can be used to position the station, or they can be buried. The city of license will affect the station's choice here. For example, in the Orlando, Florida, market there are a number of radio stations that are licensed to smaller towns outside the Orlando **metro area,** but their signal coverage over the area makes them valuable broadcast properties. If a station boldly states that it is from Cocoa Beach, which is fifty miles to the east of Orlando, people in Orlando are not going to identify the station as an Orlando station.

Some stations prefer to give only the call letters and city of license, buried between two songs near the top of the hour, with little or no attention drawn to the ID, as is the case for many stations around Orlando and other major cities in a similar position. Another way to mask an ID is to include it creatively in a produced station sweeper so that it blends in and sounds just like all of the other imaging that is targeted at positioning and branding the station (see demo CD, cut 84).

Jingles

Jingles are positioning statements and station branding set to music and sung. They were once thought to be absolutely critical to a station's success. For many years, it was thought that a new package of jingles each year was what kept a station fresh and exciting. Today, jingles run hot and cold, depending on the format. A quality, custom, jingle package from one of the major studios can easily top the $5,000 mark (see demo CD, cut 85).

With jingles the question is not so much whether they work or not, but whether or not they fit, musically, with the format, positioning, and branding of the station. Although jingles can certainly be written to carry out positioning and branding, it is critical that they fit the format and sound design of the station. Some markets are jingle rich; others use very few, if any.

Image Placement

As a production person, you need to understand that listeners are going to hear the imaging you produce over, and over, and over, so it is imperative for you to do quality work. The placement of station imaging is a market- and format-based decision. Every station treats imaging in a different manner. A new station needs to hammer home the station's message and personality to an audience that is likely listening for the first time. In this case, the station needs to overdo it and constantly remind the listeners what station they are listening to and what the station does better than everyone else. Because the station is "burning," or using the imaging a lot, you are going to have to produce a steady stream of creative materials so that the station sound remains fresh.

Established radio stations use imaging to help keep the listeners they have, to hook new listeners, and to direct listeners to specific dayparts the station wants to build an audience for. The overall goal is to increase time spent listening to the station.

Station staff and listeners hear imaging in a completely different way. Jocks and production people hear every liner or sweeper played. Jocks get tired of liners and sweepers very quickly and often complain that the station is running too many. There is an old adage that applies to just about everything in radio. When the staff is sick and tired of a liner, sweeper, promotional announcement, or even a particular commercial, the audience is just beginning really to notice it. The audience does not listen for every liner, sweeper, or promo as the jock and production person does, and so they react differently to these programming elements.

Jocks should not be allowed to go into or out of a stop set without forward-promoting some aspect of the radio station with a liner or sweeper. Jocks should constantly be selling the station's signature sound and products with your production work. It is important for jocks to promote what is going to happen in the next twenty minutes, the next hour, or on the next jock's show. As previously stated, every jock on the station should also be cross-promoting the next day's morning show.

At a very minimum, a station should use a liner or sweeper once every quarter-hour. At the opposite end of the spectrum, a station running a tighter rotation of liners and sweepers might choose to run a series of two songs back-to-back, then a sweeper, then two songs, and so on.

Contest Promotion

Station contests are an extension of promotion. The goal of a contest is to cause the station's listeners to notice who they are listening to in the first place and to get them to listen longer, to increase their time spent listening. Another purpose of a contest promotion is to focus, or guide, listeners to a specific daypart the station wants to build an audience for. Creative production is what sells the contest or promotion to the listener.

A good contest is one that offers your target audience a prize it can relate to and would like to have. The prize has to be large enough to attract and hold a listener's attention. A six-pack of soda is not a very impressive prize, a new cell phone with a year's free service is. Of course, the universal prize every listener likes the best is cold, hard cash!

A contest has to be presented to listeners in a manner that is simple and easy for them to understand. Complicated contests fail every time because listeners have a hard time grasping all of the intricate rules. Such contests appear as though you are trying not to give away the prize. Your contest has to be winnable; you want to have a winner!

One of the simplest contests a station can play is Hi-LO. The station starts with a mystery cash jackpot. Listeners are invited to call the station at various times of the day and guess the jackpot. If they hit the exact amount in the jackpot, they win it. If they miss the jackpot amount, they are told that their guess was either high or low. Each time a listener misses the jackpot the station adds a fixed amount of cash to the jackpot, usually the station's dial position translated into dollars. For example, if your station is at 106.1 on the dial, you add $106.10 each time the jackpot is missed.

It will take about four days of play for your audience to figure out exactly how much is in the jackpot through the process of elimination. Listeners start keeping charts of the amounts guessed and the last four or five plays of the game are very exciting as they get within pennies of the amount and finally hit it. When the jackpot is won, you start with a new mystery cash jackpot and repeat the contest.

Contests require extensive pre-planning due to the prize elements and the legal requirements that must be met under both state and federal laws. Contests are detail-heavy events involving published contest rules, prizes that must be awarded, and sometimes insurance policies to cover an event in which listeners are going to be involved. Contests are planned as much as a year in advance to coordinate the timing of the contest with other events occurring in the market at the same time.

A contest promo is just like a commercial for a business—it needs to stick out and grab the listener's attention. Just like a commercial, the focus needs to be more on the listeners and the benefits they receive by listening to the radio station than on the radio station telling everyone how great the station is. The focus of contest promos should be on the question every listener asks: "What's in it for me (WIFM) if I listen to your radio station?" Contest promos have to be written from the listener's viewpoint, in simple easy-to-understand terms. Production people need to understand that contest promos deserve just as much attention as a station's best client—and maybe even a little more.

The Great Tease: Getting the Listener Interested

Before a station can have a contest, there has to be someone interested in participating. A key element to the success of a contest is the tease. Teases are the well-planned hints that personalities let "slip" on the air, the mysterious promos you created, and the promos that give the listener a clue as to what is going to happen, but still leave them guessing. The tease is planned in advance and carried out with precision, between the programming, promotion, production, and sales departments. Sometimes the tease starts as early as two weeks before the contest begins.

Occasionally, for competitive reasons, the tease is carefully planned so that only a select few within the station's promotion department really know what is going to happen. The station wants the element of surprise to thrill listeners and drive the competition absolutely nuts trying to figure out what the station is up to. Some stations go to the length of having the contest tease promos produced by a voice talent outside the market. The talent is required to sign a nondisclosure agreement stating that he or she cannot tell anyone what is being done, and the talent agrees to face serious legal action if he or she does tell.

Care has to go into the production of a tease. The goal is to get the listener's imagination working, trying to figure out what the station is up to. During the tease phase it is important not to raise the listener's expectations too high or in the wrong direction. The key to a successful contest promo is to tease the audience, generate interest, and get people talking about what it might be. Tease promos should always undersell the event, and the station should deliver more contest than promised during the tease.

Contest Promos

Once a contest is launched, a series of promos is required to support it. A contest's generic promos tell the listeners, in terms they can understand, who you are, what you are doing, and the benefits of listening to your station. Contest explanation promos explain who can enter the contest, how the contest works, and what a listener has to do to win. If a contest is complicated, and some are, the contest explanation should be broken down into a series of two or three easy-to-understand promos that rotate.

Contest promos use many of the same elements of regular station promos, with the exception that there is a prize, or prizes, to be won. Contest promos must create a sense of urgency, that the listener must listen to the radio station, and he or she must listen often, or he or she is going to miss out on a great prize. Just like station promos, contest promos can be designed as cross-promotional, vertical, or horizontal in nature. Contest promos encourage the listener to listen for the next twenty minutes, the next hour, the next day, or over the weekend for what is going to happen on Monday.

If a contest involves winning phone callers, every call should be recorded, and every winning call turned into a promo. When a winner hoots and hollers on the phone it translates into a promo that generates a lot of excitement about the contest. A winner's promo should be produced quickly so that it can be on the air within an hour and run throughout the day. Likewise, if contest prizes are awarded outside the station, such as at remotes, every winner should be recorded and the cuts used for promos to keep the excitement at a high level. Contest promos are the fuel that keeps the contest moving in a forward direction; they require creativity and fast work on your part.

Contest Post-Promotion

Once the new car, incredible vacation, or truckload of cash is given away, there are still a lot of promos to be produced. Contest post-promotion is just as important as the contest itself. Contest post-promotion should last at least five days after a major contest. Just like the promos that launched the contest, the post-promotion promos should stress the benefits the listener gains from listening and what the station is doing for the listeners. The station wants listeners to know who won the grand prize and how happy and excited the listener was to win. A great contest post-promo is one in which the winner tells listeners why they should be listening to the station.

Legal Requirements of Contest Promotion

As a production person, you should be aware that a station must comply with the rules and regulations promulgated by the Federal Communications Commission and the Federal Trade Commission, in addition to any applicable state laws regarding contests. In most cases, these rules, regulations, and laws are to prevent deceptive contest promotion and fraud in the awarding of the prize. Just the hint of fraud in a station contest can quickly turn into a public relations nightmare, costing the station listeners and revenue from advertisers. For this reason, approved contest promo copy prepared by the promotions director cannot be changed on a whim. They have carefully worked it out to satisfy all the legal requirements as well as the station's promotional needs.

Although you are probably not an attorney, you should be aware of general contest requirements and your state's laws in this regard. General contest rules and regulations are specified by the FCC and include:

> Licensees that broadcast or advertise information concerning a contest that they conduct must fully and accurately disclose the material terms of the contest and must conduct the contest substantially as announced or advertised. Contest descriptions may not be false, misleading or deceptive with respect to any material term. Material terms include those factors that define the operation of the contest and affect participation in the contest.

Further . . .

the (Federal) Criminal Code prohibits fraud by wire, radio or television, and violation of this provision may lead to Commission sanctions against FCC licensees.

Depending on the contest, certain legal disclaimers, such as the odds of winning the contest, may be required to be included in the promo. It's your job as the production person to weave these creatively into the promo. An innocent error of omission in editing the copy on your part could cost the station a fine or cause a contest to come under scrutiny.

Suggested Activities

1. Select three radio stations in your market and see if you can determine their positioning statement. Analyze the positioning statement and see if it accurately describes the station and what it does. Using the criteria found in this chapter, see whether you can develop a better positioning statement for any of the stations that more accurately describes the station.

2. Select three radio stations in your market and determine whether each is actively branding the station. If so, write a description of the station's branding concept and the "promise" the station is making to the listeners. Make a list of at least ten areas of the station's packaging in which the branding is carried out (billboards, T-shirts, etc.).

3. Select a station in your market and develop a new branding concept for the station, including a new positioning statement. Based on what you develop, write a package of fifteen liners for vertical and cross-promotion of the station's programming.

4. Using a calendar, develop a promotion time line for a concert promotion in which there are two station visits by the group, a contest to win twenty pairs of tickets, and a

grand prize of two front-row seats and VIP backstage passes, along with limo service and dinner with the group. Work backward from the last day of the post-promotion, to the concert, to the award of the grand prize, the award of the twenty pairs of tickets, the start of contest promos, the start of contest tease promos, and dates by which promos have to be produced.

5. Visit your State Attorney General's web site, or phone the office, and find out about the contest laws in your state. Are there any types of contests that are prohibited? Can you use alcoholic beverages as a prize in your state? Do you have to register a contest with the state, or post a bond with the state, to insure the award of the prize?

Web Sites for More Information

For more information about:

- *conducting contests and a strategy for successful contests,* visit Dan O'Day.Com at www.danoday.com

- *contest insurance and radio contests,* visit SCA Promotions at www.scapromotions.com

- *custom jingle packages,* visit TM Century at www.tmcentury.com

- *custom station imaging, liner, and sweeper services,* visit Autumn Hill Studios at www.jefflaurence.com

- *Federal Communications Commission Rules and Regulations regarding contests,* visit the FCC at www.fcc.gov

- *federal rules, regulations, and laws regarding contests,* visit the Federal Trade Commission at www.ftc.gov

Pro Speak

You should be able to use these terms in your everyday conversations with other professionals.

Arbitron—The primary radio audience measurement service. Arbitron ratings are often referred to as "the book," since the ratings are published in book form each quarter.

branding—A marketing plan that seeks to provide a clear differentiation from the other stations in the marketplace, based on the station's overall identity and attitude as defined by the listener.

core audience—The primary target demographic of a radio station.

daypart—A broadcast industry term that classifies a specific time period of radio listening. For example, 6 a.m. to 10 a.m. Monday through Friday is generally accepted as the morning-drive daypart.

metro area—A metropolitan city's area as defined by the U.S. Government's Office of Management and Budget, also generally accepted by the major rating services as a designated geographical area.

positioning statement—A unique selling proposition, or slogan, used by a station to separate itself from the competition.

sound design—The overall sound quality of a radio station that sets it apart from others.

time spent listening—An audience ratings measurement indicating the number of quarter-hour time segments the average person spends listening to a radio station in a given time period, such as a week.

CHAPTER 11

Fieldwork:
Taking the Station
on Location

HIGHLIGHTS

Location Planning

Remote Broadcast Transmission Methods

Producing Audio for Radio Remotes

Suggested Activities

Web Sites for More Information

Pro Speak

Location Planning

It's just plumb magic! Radio is filled with mystery. When listeners think that they are going to get a chance to see the magic of how radio is created, they are drawn to a location, much the way Dorothy in the Wizard of Oz was drawn to pull back the curtain and see the wizard at work. For a listener, there is always the surprise of seeing what the talent looks like for the first time (never what is imagined) and seeing the equipment that makes radio possible.

Radio routinely goes on location for commercial remotes from sponsors' businesses. These live broadcasts are an important part of promotion and sales. Stations also spend a lot of time on location producing local sports and news coverage. Regardless of whether it is a commercial remote, a sports event, or news coverage, a successful remote broadcast requires a lot of careful planning.

Promotion and Sales Location Planning

Unless a breaking news story is involved, most remote broadcasts are a joint effort of a station's promotion and sales departments. The reason a business hosts a remote is the excitement and increased sales that it can potentially generate. Stations do remotes for the promotional value, the chance to interact with listeners, and the revenue a remote generates for the station.

The promotion and sales department can even turn a public-service event, such as a dog-adoption day by the Humane Society, into a revenue-generating event. For example, a local business hosts a dog-adoption day, paying for the remote broadcast as a community service. The station gets to be associated with a high-profile community event (who doesn't like puppies?). The business gets increased traffic, sales, and tremendous public-relations value from the event (everyone loves puppies). The Humane Society gets a major promotion, free (they love puppy adoption!). This is an example of a win, win, win, situation.

Remotes do not happen by themselves. A lot of pre-planning is required on the part of everyone in the station. The planning usually starts in the sales department and is fine-tuned by the promotion department, or vice versa. The promotion department works in conjunction with the engineering department to make sure the remote is technically feasible. At some point, production is called in to produce ads for the client and station promotional announcements for the event.

Depending on how a station is structured, the person in charge of producing the remote varies. At some radio stations, the production person is charged with overseeing the technical, and sometimes the talent, side of the remote. Other stations send an engineer and a remote producer from the promotion department. In smaller markets, the talent may also be his or her own producer and technician.

Planning for a remote, from the sales department's perspective, takes place between the salesperson and the client to determine what the goals are for the remote. In some cases, the goal is not so much retail sales as it is making listeners aware of a new business's location, launching a new product, or promoting a grand opening. Salespeople tend to look at the remotes from the business side: What can the station do for the client? The client is looking at the remote asking, "What's in it for me?" The client wants to know if the station's listeners are the kind of people that buy his or her products. Is the station capable of generating increased traffic and sales and creating a positive impression on customers? During the negotiation process between the client and the salesperson, the salesperson may turn to the promotion department for ideas and input on how to make the remote a success.

Before any in-depth remote planning can take place, someone from either the sales or the promotion department should conduct a site survey of the client's business. The purpose of the survey is to check for things such as: Where can the station vehicle be parked? Is there adequate parking for listeners? Is there adequate electrical power? Where will the talent be placed? Where can station banners and other promotional materials be positioned? How early can the station get on the property to set up before the event? Depending on the station, the engineering department may do its own site survey to make sure a remote transmitter to send the signal back to the station can be accommodated. All of these little details are summarized on a site-survey form to assist in planning the event (see Fig. **11.1**).

Regardless of a remote's specific stated purpose, the promotion department also looks at a remote from the standpoint of creating an event, or a **"draw,"** for the client. The event aspect of the remote often involves contests, free station promotional items (T-shirts, etc.), product samples, free food, free soft drinks, **vendor involvement,** and products and prizes offered by the client.

The promotion department is in charge of making sure the station's positioning statement and branding are carried out at the remote through the use of the station vehicle, banners, staff attire, station mascot, and so forth. Remotes are unique in that the promotion department is charged with taking an ordinary day and turning it into something special. Some of the things involved in promotion planning for an event include:

- Station vehicle to be at the business, parked near the street to act as a billboard.

- Real-estate-sized yard signs directing listeners to the remote, if necessary.
- Station banners on the business or in front of the business.
- Presence of the station salesperson who sold the remote to act as the liaison between the client and the station staff during the event.
- Station promotion staff to coordinate the remote so that it comes off as planned.
- Station-supplied promotional items.
- Vendor-supplied promotional items.
- Business-supplied promotional items.
- Any necessary station, business, or vendor contest materials.
- Food vendors.
- Soft drink vendors.
- Station mascot, if applicable.

Depending on the size of the event, the preceding are just a few of the physical items and considerations that might be necessary. A final but crucial consideration is the business's regular customers. Have you physically laid out the remote to allow space for the business to do business? The worst of all possible scenarios is a business so jam-packed with listeners that sales come to a standstill.

All of these elements have to be coordinated in advance so that both the station staff and the business owner are aware of how the remote is going to be staged.

News and Sports Location Planning

Planning a remote with the news and sports departments presents an entirely different set of circumstances. The difference is that rather than the station creating the event, someone

WRPC REMOTE EVENT SPECIFICATIONS

DATE: 5-29
TIME: 10 am – 12 Noon
CLIENT: Carolina Furniture Outlet

Name of Event: Carolina Furniture Outlet Remote
Promo Start Date: Promo#: 3578 STARTS Mon 5-24
Account Executive: Mark Fox
Station Promotional Event: No
Booked Thru Programming: No
Logged Thru Traffic: Yes
Event Type: Live broadcast
Business Name: Carolina Furniture Outlet
Customer #: 88-9679
Business Contact: Jason Carter
Business Phone: 555-5011
Address: 2617 Hendersonville Rd
Directions: I-26 south to exit #42, left 2.8 miles, on the right
Copy Talking Points: prepared by client/will give to staff on arrival
Talent Requested: Josh Michaels
Talent Assigned: Josh Michaels
Remote Talent Fee: $325
Attire: Standard Station Attire (logo golf shirt/slacks)
Drinks: Yes
Drink Brand: any
Vendor Drink Trailer: Coca Cola ___ Pepsi _X_ Other ___ None___
Inflatable Station Logo: Yes
Contest Registration Box: Yes
Registration Box Info: Win A Car promo
Food: Yes, Subway party sub
Remote Prizes: T shirts _X_ Lisc Plates _X_ Key Chain ___ Ball Caps ___
Vehicle: Station Van
On-Site AC Power: Yes _X_ No ___
Overhead Power Lines: Yes ___ No _X_ If yes, note conditions below
Engineer: Tim Neese
Frequency: VHF _X_ UHF ___
Special: Client paying $175 extra for station mascot to appear.

NOTES:

Park station van next to street and use generator power.
Station banner's to go on store front.

Figure 11.1

A site survey is a good way for everyone associated with a station event to know what is going to occur and what his or her role is in the event. Site surveys are often posted in a password-protected area of the station's web site so that all of the departments of the radio station have easy access 24/7.

else creates the event and the station's role is to cover it.

Typically, news remotes involve a breaking story or disaster coverage from a major event. In any case, preparations for such events are often made far in advance even though the specifics cannot be known or planned for. As an example, many news departments have what are called "go bags" or "jump-and-run bags," intended for a reporter to pick up and go with. The cases contain a recorder, mic, **mic flag,** cables, spare recording media (minidiscs), telephone patch cords, and so on. Similarly, connections are set up in advance so that when a major weather system approaches, contacts can be called at other stations around the state and agreements made to exchange reports.

A news-talk radio station taking a talk show "on the road" is another form of news remote. To some degree, then, the talk show itself becomes a "mini-newsmaker." Such remotes involve both sales and promotion and are often treated as a regular commercial remote.

Although the rights to broadcast a sporting event may belong to someone else, the station's sales and promotion department will likely be involved in selling sponsorships and promoting the station's involvement. Sports remotes require a lot of planning from the standpoint of what the station would like to do and what the rights holder of the sporting event permits the station to do. This ranges from high school events to major national teams. For example, your station may not be permitted to broadcast a major sporting event because a national network has secured the broadcast rights. However, the rights holder to the event may permit the station to host a tailgate party in the parking lot prior to and during the event. With the support of the station's sales and promotion departments, a station can host a large remote and get a lot of mileage out of being associated with such a sporting event.

Even when a station is granted rights to broadcast the sporting event itself, there are generally strict guidelines as to what is permitted with regard to banners and station promotional items. The station and the rights holder must agree exactly on how the station is to promote and broadcast the event and what promotional activities are permitted during the event.

Another form of sports remote is taking a sports-talk show on location prior to a sporting event or featuring a major sports figure in a public appearance. Some sports-talk shows are produced entirely on location as a co-promotion with a business that serves as a co-host for the show. For example, the show is produced at a local sports-themed restaurant or bar on a regular basis. The business receives the benefit of people coming to see the show, and the station receives the visibility that helps to build audiences.

Depending on the radio station, the role of the production person is to prepare the promotional announcements and commercials, and possibly to serve as location producer or advisor to the promotion and sales departments on what is required technically to broadcast the event.

Remote Broadcast Transmission Methods

From a technical standpoint, the first rule of remotes is KISS: keep it simple, stupid. The key element to the success of any remote broadcast is using a simple, reliable, remote transmission system to return the program signal to the station and to have a backup for that system. Redundancy is our friend. Unlike with a studio broadcast, if there is a problem on location, you cannot dash down the hall to another studio and go on the air. In this section of the chapter we are going to examine remote systems, moving from the simplest to the most complex. Keep in mind, though, no matter how sophisticated the equipment, the goal is to put the talent's voice on the air. Always have a backup.

Plain Old Telephone Service (POTS)

In the beginning there was the telephone, and only the telephone. To this day, a telephone is the simplest and most reliable way to get someone on the air. The talent dials the station. The station uses a device called a **phone hybrid** to interface the telephone line to the station's broadcast equipment and put the call on the air: simple, but effective. (Although digital cell phones sound pretty good, from an audio-quality standpoint, they are at the low end of the scale.) Remember that the original goal is to put the talent on the air and, in a worst-case scenario, POTS can do just that. It has been the experience of this author that many, many sporting and news events have been covered using a telephone handset held like a microphone because the primary remote equipment failed at the last minute before a broadcast. It's not pretty, but it works. As a side note, many news and sports equipment bags contain phone cards for just such situations.

Phones lines are inexpensive, and there is a phone just about anywhere. Radio stations often use a POTS line in conjunction with a remote analog phone hybrid. The hybrid is just what its name implies, a combination of devices. A basic remote phone hybrid combines a telephone, telephone audio interface, audio mixer, and headphone amplifier (see Fig. **11.2**).

Phone hybrids plug into a standard telephone jack and accept microphone inputs. After dialing the station, the location talent speaks through the microphone just as if he or she were in the studio. By listening through headphones plugged into the hybrid, the tal-

Figure 11.2

A POTS hybrid is just what its name implies, a combination of devices. A basic remote phone hybrid combines a telephone, telephone audio interface, audio mixer, and headphone amplifier, as seen in the one above. These are ideal for news, sports, and remote broadcasts.

ent monitors the signal. During commercial stop sets in the broadcast, station personnel can talk back down the phone line to the talent, who hear the cues via the headphones.

Although the audio quality is limited to what you would normally hear over a phone, analog phone hybrids offer an easy and inexpensive way to get on the air from just about anywhere (see demo CD, cut 86). For further mobility, there are interfaces available that allow the connection of an analog POTS phone hybrid to a cell phone.

Plain Old Telephone Service (POTS) Codecs

For more than seventy years, most radio stations were content to rely on POTS, or some variation of POTS, to get a signal back to the

A POTS codec is a hybrid device combining a phone, A/D and D/A converters, a small audio mixer, and a modem. The codec physically connects to the POTS line, just like plugging in a modem or telephone at home. POTS codecs are extremely popular, since there are phones just about everywhere a radio station might want to do a remote. Shown above are the small location unit and the rack mount unit it interfaces with at the station.

radio station for a remote broadcast. Most often, the station was dialed and a small mixer or phone hybrid was used to send the audio back down the line to the station.

With the advent of digital audio, new technologies allow the transmission of digital audio on a POTS line using a **codec** at each end of the connection. POTS codecs are extremely popular, since there are phones just about everywhere a radio station might want to do a remote. POTS codecs are **duplex devices,** meaning that audio can be sent and received simultaneously.

A POTS codec is a hybrid device combining a phone, **A/D** and **D/A** converters, a small audio mixer, and a modem (see Fig. **11.3**). The codec physically connects to the POTS line, just like plugging in your computer modem at home. Often a business has a spare phone line (otherwise used for a computer or a fax machine) that can be made available for the sta-

tion to use. Sports stadiums usually provide **courtesy lines** for visiting stations. This avoids a costly line-installation charge from the phone company.

Once connected to a line with the remote codec, the technician dials the station codec's phone number. When the station codec answers, it sounds like a dial-up **ISP** connection being made. The two codecs link together and complete the digital connection. During the connection process, the remote codec's modem runs a test on the phone line to see what transmission rate it can use to send and receive data. Depending on the quality of the phone line, near-studio voice quality can be achieved (see demo CD, cut 87).

A POTS codec is a duplex device, meaning that it is capable of sending and receiving audio simultaneously on a single line, as already described (see Fig. **11.4**). The feature is often used to provide a remote announcer

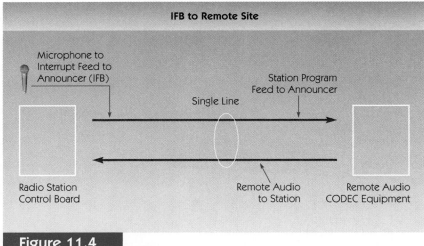

IFB to Remote Site

Microphone to
Interrupt Feed to
Announcer (IFB)

Station Program
Feed to Announcer

Single Line

Radio Station
Control Board

Remote Audio
to Station

Remote Audio
CODEC Equipment

Figure 11.4

A duplex device can send and receive audio simultaneously on the same line. While the announcer at the remote site is sending his or her broadcast back to the radio station, the radio station is sending the program audio back down the line (foldback) so the announcer can hear the broadcast. Using a microphone at the radio station, the producer can interrupt the foldback (IFB) to the talent and talk to the announcer in his or her headphones.

with an interruptible foldback loop (IFB). While the audio from the remote is going to the station, the radio station's program signal (IFB feed) is being sent back down the line from the station to the announcer's headphones. The reason it is called an interruptible foldback loop is that the producer back at the radio station can interrupt the program feed and talk to the announcer in his or her headphones. Typically, the program monitor is in one ear of the announcer's headphones and the IFB is in the other. Needless to say, it takes some practice to be able to talk on the air and simultaneously listen to cues in headphones.

POTS codecs are not without some potential disadvantages. Audio quality is entirely dependent upon the individual telephone line. While the codecs are connected, the elec-

trical properties of a telephone line can change, affecting the codecs' audio quality. In a worst-case scenario, the change could cause the codec to drop the call (hang-up). Another potential problem is that a POTS codec can introduce a delay of up to an eighth of a second in the audio during the analog-to-digital encoding/decoding process. An announcer monitoring the station in headphones hears his or her voice an eighth to a quarter of a second after speaking.

To prevent the announcer from hearing the delay, the station can send the remote announcer a station program mix, minus the announcer's voice. This is called a mix/minus feed, which is the program mix minus one or more audio sources. Most broadcast consoles are equipped to create easily a mix/minus

Mix-Minus Feed

Station Audition
Feed to Remote
Minus the Remote
Announcer Audio

Single Line

Radio Station
Control Board

Remote Audio
to Station

Remote Audio
CODEC Equipment

Figure 11.5

A mix/minus feed to an announcer at a remote broadcast is typically created by putting everything on the control board into both program and audition except the announcer's audio feed to the station, which is only put in program. Audition then has the radio station's entire signal (mix), minus the announcer's audio feed to the station. The announcer hears everything but his or her own voice.

feed for the announcer. A simple way to accomplish this is to route every channel on the control board *except* the remote announcer's channel to the program and audition buses. The announcer's channel is routed only to the program bus so it can go on the air. The audition bus is used for the announcer's monitor feed because it includes every channel on the control board except for the channel with the announcer's own voice. The announcer hears everything on the station except his or her voice (see Fig. **11.5**).

A major advantage of a POTS codec is that all you need to get on the air is a regular analog telephone line, available everywhere. POTS codecs are physically small, portable, and relatively inexpensive. Most have a small mixer built in that accepts microphone and

line inputs for additional equipment. The other aspect of POTS codecs that stations like is that they are simple to use.

Wireless POTS Codecs

If a station can use a plain old telephone service line to do a remote with a POTS codec, what is to prevent the station from plugging a POTS codec into a cell phone and using the same digital transmission technology?

The answer is: Quite a bit. The most typical method of transmitting cell phone signals causes the data to travel in bursts instead of a steady stream. Without the consistent reliability of a data stream coming from the cell phone, it simply is not feasible to send reliable, real-time, digital audio on a cell phone.

However, the good news is that cell-phone technology is changing rapidly. The Global System for Mobile Communications **(GSM)** was developed in Europe and is the worldwide wireless-telephone technology standard outside the United States. GSM has the ability to support high-speed, wide-bandwidth digital transmissions. The design goal for GSM is to be able to stream full-motion video and accommodate high-speed data transmission.

Currently, in the United States, GSM service is limited to larger metropolitan areas, but it is developing rapidly. This class of cell phone is known as a GSM 3G (third generation) phone. A GSM phone can accept a POTS codec interconnection and is capable of transmitting excellent quality audio. GSM is a moving target, in that as the service develops and becomes available, so will new generations of devices for portable, studio-quality, remote broadcasting.

ISDN Codecs

The use of an **ISDN** (Integrated Services Digital Network) line with an audio codec provides studio-quality audio for remote broadcasts. ISDN is a full-duplex service and simultaneously provides digital audio delivery in both directions. For example, during a sports broadcast the sportscasters can carry on a conversation with the in-studio announcer over the ISDN line while both are also on the air. This is accomplished by using one of the codec's audio channels in the send mode and the other channel in the receive mode.

An ISDN line is a specially installed dial-up line. An ISDN codec is capable of sending and receiving CD-quality audio over a single ISDN telephone line (see demo CD, cut 88). To link with another station or production facility, dial the phone number of the codec you want to connect to. When the link is completed, the audio feed can begin.

Portable ISDN codecs can also be used to send studio-quality audio from remote broadcasts (see Fig. **11.6**). Although there are ISDN-only codecs, many portable codec products incorporate both POTS and ISDN codecs. This provides a station the ability to do a remote virtually anywhere there is a phone line or digital ISDN line. As with the POTS codec, the remote audio is sent to the station and the return channel can be used for an IFB/program monitor.

A disadvantage of an ISDN codec is that it is slightly more complex to set up than a POTS codec. If a location does not already have a dial-up ISDN line, one has to be ordered. Depending upon the location, it can be expensive and take several weeks to get an ISDN line installed. Another disadvantage of ISDN lines is that some systems introduce delays of up to half a second in the audio during the encoding/decoding process. This requires a mix/minus monitor feed for the remote announcer as previously discussed. The major advantages of ISDN, on the other hand, are that it features rock-solid reliability, delivers studio-quality audio, and is the only choice for sending quality stereo audio to the station. ISDN is used extensively for sports broadcasting.

Which Is Best, POTS or ISDN?

Both types of codecs have distinct advantages and disadvantages. As to whether one is better than the other, that is a question that only your station engineer can answer, taking into consideration the specific situation in which the codec is going to be used. There really is no correct answer. In some respects, the industry has given broadcasters the answer by creating codec products that have both POTS and ISDN codecs in one portable, easy-to-use box.

Figure 11.6

A portable ISDN codec is used to send studio-quality audio from a remote broadcast back to the station. Pictured above are the remote codec (top) and its rack mount studio companion. This portable unit has both a microphone and line input.

The station can be ready for virtually any situation that might arise.

Remote-Pickup Units (Transmitters)

A remote-pickup unit (RPU), or transmitter, is exactly what its name implies. It's a small low-power transmitter used to send a radio signal back to the radio station.

RPUs are physically small and often have a built-in mixer, operate on AC line current, batteries, or 12-volt power from a vehicle. Rather than being called a remote-pickup transmitter, or RPU, these units are most often referred to by the brand name "Marti," even when they aren't of that brand. Marti Electronics (named after George Marti, who founded the company) is known for building what are universally termed "bulletproof transmitters" and receivers. It has been estimated that at least eighty percent of the radio stations worldwide use at least one of Marti's products. Martis just keep working and working. Don't be sur-

prised the first time you see a twenty-year-old Marti RPU in service at a radio station, just like the one pictured in this chapter (see Fig. **11.7**). The units operate in the VHF (very-high frequency) and UHF (ultra-high frequency) radio bands and deliver excellent-quality audio (see demo CD, cut 89).

At a remote, the transmitter is set up with the antenna aimed at the radio station's receiving antenna. Various antenna configurations and a direct line-of-sight to the station's tower can greatly enhance the range of the transmitter (see Fig. **11.8**). Many radio stations outfit the station van with a telescoping mast and twin-directional transmitting antennas. Under ideal conditions, such systems can transmit forty-five miles with near-studio quality. A Marti receiver at the station picks up the signal and feeds it to the control board. Unlike duplex codecs, a remote pickup transmitter is a one-way communications system, from the remote to the station.

Disadvantages of a Marti RPU are that several pieces of equipment are necessary to go

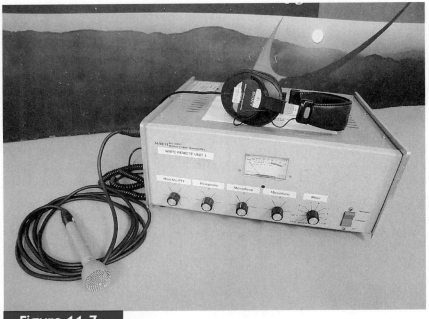

Figure 11.7

Marti remote pickup transmitters are legendary for their toughness and ability to just keep working. Don't be surprised to see a nearly twenty-year-old unit, like this one, still in service at a radio station.

on the air, including the transmitter, antenna cable, antenna mast, and antenna. Care is required in the setup to make sure the antenna is pointing in the correct direction (use a map and a compass if you need to). Sometimes buildings, structures, and the surrounding terrain can reflect, or block, the signal from reaching the station, in which case you have to move. It is always advisable to do a site survey and system test the day before a remote.

The advantage of a Marti is the ability it gives you to transmit excellent-quality audio from just about anywhere in your community on short notice. Another advantage is that the station is not depending on anyone, such as the phone company, to return the signal to the station. Marti transmitters are used extensively for remotes, news, and sports coverage.

The transmitters can be easily mounted in a station car for local "on-the-spot" news coverage. The Marti's functionality can be expanded beyond its built-in audio mixer by plugging a production mixer into either a line or mic input.

Basic RPU technology has been around a long time and most stations have, and continue to use, RPU transmitters because of the reliability, excellent audio quality, and the independence that they give a station to do a remote when and where it wants to without having to depend on anyone else.

Remote Pickup Safety

Each radio station's RPU system requires specific safety training. Safety practices must be

Remote-Pickup Transmitter Antenna Mast

Contest Entry Box for Broadcast

Equipment and Safety Checklist

Marti Remote-Pickup Transmitter

Speaker Stand for Public Address System

Roll of Gaffer's Tape

Small Generator

Safety Cones

Microphone and Cable

Figure 11.8

A remote broadcast van is a radio station on wheels. This van has everything to do a remote broadcast safely, including a portable generator to run the Marti remote-pickup transmitter.

followed when raising any kind of antenna mast near power lines. Several people have been *killed* by parking their station van under power lines and inadvertently raising the telescoping antenna mast into a high-tension line, sending thousands of volts of electricity into the remote vehicle and anyone touching it. This author once watched a competing radio station finish a remote broadcast at a music concert and attempt to drive off with the antenna mast still up. They were fortunate. The power line that they hit just sheared off the antenna mast, and no one was injured. You do not even have to have a remote truck in order to be in a dangerous situation. Imagine two excited radio sportscasters sitting on open aluminum bleachers, holding golf umbrellas, broadcasting a high school football playoff game in the rain. At their feet is an unprotected Marti transmitter plugged into 110-volt electrical power. In the excitement of the muddy, rough-and-tumble game, it might never occur to the broadcasters that either lightning or the 110-volt power feeding the Marti could kill them—and that's why safety training and safety consciousness are essential.

Satellite Telephone Service

When all else fails, or you are going into the boonies, there are several satellite-telephone technologies available to return a radio signal to a station. The only restriction is that you have to be able to see the sky to use a satellite (sat) phone. A number of different classes of satellite phones is available, and they are not as expensive as you might think. Sizes range from what appears to be an ordinary cell phone to a satellite uplink the size of a laptop computer.

A handheld sat phone uses either standard, land-based-cell-phone service or satellite phone service, depending on what is available (see demo CD, cut 90). The phone operates like a regular cell phone except that a "whip" type antenna is raised from the side of the sat phone for satellite service (see Fig. **11.9**). Satellite phone rates are as low as seventeen cents per minute, depending on the service plan. Just like a cell phone, a sat phone can be adapted to connect to an analog phone hybrid, allowing microphones and headphones to be interfaced with the phone.

At the opposite end of the spectrum, appearing similar to a laptop computer, are portable satellite uplinks. The uplink cover is raised at an angle and folding panels open to the left and right, forming the transmit/receive antenna (see Fig. **11.10**). A built in **GPS** locator tells the operator in what direction to aim the antenna to reach the nearest satellite. The uplink can be aimed at more than forty-five low-earth-orbit (**LEO**) satellites. The uplink is not only capable of transmitting a regular satellite phone call but also transmitting an ISDN digital audio codec signal, allowing broadcasters to send studio-quality digital audio back to the station. Typically, a mixer is plugged into the codec to create multiple microphone inputs.

Although sat phones may initially appear beyond the reach of the average station, a station does not have to purchase a satellite phone to be able to use one. Many companies rent sat

Figure 11.9

Satellite phones provide the opportunity for a radio station to go anywhere to do a remote such as on lakes, the ocean, and in the mountains. This phone has two modes of operation, land-based cell phone and satellite. The small antenna on the right is used in the cell-phone mode. When the angled antenna on the left is folded out and extended, the phone switches to the satellite mode.

Figure 11.10

A portable satellite uplink is a powerful tool for news, sports, or other live remotes. The uplink above is about the size of a laptop computer and is not only capable of transmitting a regular satellite phone call but also transmitting an ISDN digital audio codec signal, allowing broadcasters to send studio-quality digital audio back to the station. Typically, an audio mixer is plugged into the uplink to create multiple microphone or line inputs.

phones on a weekly or monthly basis, making the cost reasonable, even for a local station.

Producing Audio for Radio Remotes

Remember, the first rule of producing is still always KISS: keep it simple, stupid. There is not a single book, or list, in the world to tell you how to produce every remote you might possibly be assigned. There is, however, a simple system you can use to help you prepare for virtually any remote broadcast. There are three basic types of radio remotes: commercial, sports, and news, but you can use the same simple system to prepare for any of

them. The system is a simple, low-tech checklist that you create for any given broadcast, starting with the talent and following the signal path backwards to the radio station. Your list should have three elements: transmission, monitoring, and tools.

Commercial Remotes

Commercial remotes are, just as their name implies, remotes produced at a business with the sole purpose being to increase store traffic and sales. Below is a checklist for a basic commercial remote from a client's business, using a Marti RPU. Note that some items have backups, just in case Murphy's Law comes into play. Follow the signal path: the talent speaks into a microphone, the microphone needs a windscreen, the microphone sits in a mic clip, the mic clip attaches to a mic stand, the microphone needs a cable, and so forth.

Transmission includes:

1. Talent—two jocks.
2. Two dynamic microphones—one for each jock. (Should you choose condenser mics, be sure to take additional batteries or a backup power supply.)
3. Two *backup* microphones—one for each jock.
4. Two microphone windscreens—one for each mic.
5. Two microphone stands with mic clips—one for each jock.
6. Four microphone cables, length to be determined from site survey—one main and one *backup* for each jock.
7. One Marti transmitter/mixer for the mic cables to plug into.
8. Two six-outlet AC power strips, one main and one *backup* for the Marti transmitter and other gear (monitor) to plug into.
9. Two power cords to feed the power strips, one main and one *backup,* length to be determined by site survey.
10. Two antenna coaxial cables to go from the Marti transmitter to the antenna, one main and one *backup,* length to be determined by site survey.
11. One Marti antenna, directional or nondirectional, to be determined by site survey.
12. One Marti antenna mast, or stand, to be determined by site survey.
13. Cell phone for studio-to-site communications and as *backup* should the Marti fail.

Monitoring includes:

1. Three sets of headphones—one for each jock and one *backup.*

2. Monitor for jocks' headphones to plug into, either boom box or tuner, depending on site survey, and one *backup*—backup is always a boom box, regardless of what type of monitor the first one is.
3. PA system for guests (listeners' air monitor).
4. Two patch cables from jocks' monitor to feed PA system, one main and one *backup.*
5. Speakers (left and right) for PA system.
6. Speaker stands.

Tools include:

1. Two rolls of two-inch-wide gaffer's tape; never use duct tape.
2. Bag of assorted-length plastic wire ties.
3. Bag of patch cords and adapters, including headphone splitters, audio adapters (mini-to-¼-inch-phone and similar), headphone extension cords, etc.
4. One Leatherman tool or well-equipped Swiss Army knife.

All of the equipment on the preceding lists is required for a basic remote. How the gear is transported varies from station to station. If your station has a vehicle, some of the gear, like a Marti transmitter and antenna, may be permanently mounted in the vehicle.

A station vehicle serves two functions. It is a place to put your stuff, and it is a rolling billboard. With a built-in Marti, antenna mast, and power source, a vehicle also becomes a mobile operations center that serves as a base of operations for a remote. For example, instead of playing with lots of mic cables, mount two wireless microphone receivers in the vehicle and a receiving antenna on the vehicle's roof. With a handheld wireless mic, the jock then has the freedom to roam the store with the business owner, push price and product, and mingle with customers. Since everything is mounted in the vehicle, there are fewer wires and a much easier setup. The merchant, playing the station on his or her storewide system, provides the station monitor. Depending on the location and line-of-sight, professional wireless microphones have a reach of up to a thousand feet.

Prior to doing a remote with wireless microphones, it is imperative that you coordinate the frequency of the wireless microphones with any that might already be present at, or near, the location you are broadcasting from. This is particularly true of sports venues or other public facilities. Just like for everything else, don't forget backup microphones and mic cables, should the wireless fail.

There is a downside to using such a clean and simple set up. Listeners don't get to see any of the magic. No knobs, buttons, flashing lights, or bouncing meters. This is where you depend on the promotion department to pick up the slack with banners, decorations, and to create an air of excitement so that the focus is on the event and not on your hardware.

Regardless of whether your microphone is wireless or hard-wired, what pickup pattern makes the most sense for location use? If you want to give listeners a sense of being there with you, try an omnidirectional microphone. An omni works fine picking up sound from all directions in a controlled environment. However, if there is going to be significant background noise at an event, the omni becomes a problem. The omni picks up just as much noise as it does announcer, with the voice fighting just to be heard over the noise. When you know the background noise is going to be a factor, switch to a super-cardioid microphone and use the directional pattern to isolate the announcer and block the background

noise. Any ambience you desire can be added with a crowd mic adjusted to an appropriate level. For an in-depth review of microphone patterns, see chapter 3.

Sports Remotes

The process of making a checklist for sports remotes is the same as for a commercial remote. For sports remotes, start by first substituting broadcast headsets with attached microphones in place of the jock's mics.

A headset mic is ideal for sportscasting, allowing the announcer the freedom to move about and have his or her hands free to keep stats or take notes. A headset mic also helps keep the desk in front of the announcer free of wires and visual obstructions. A headset mic is usually highly directional, blocking out all but the announcer's voice. The headphones provide sound isolation so the announcers can hear each other clearly on the program or air monitor. The headphones also provide a convenient way to deliver an IFB signal to the announcers. Broadcast headsets are often wired so that one ear is the program feed and the other is the IFB feed, and they are usually wired with a volume control for the headset and a "cough" or "kill" switch so that the announcer can momentarily turn the mic off.

The use of headset mics requires the addition of a crowd microphone for ambience to make the listeners feel as if they are there. A crowd mic should be placed either in the press area, aimed down at the crowd, or on the sideline, aimed up at the crowd. A crowd mic gives a producer the ability to control the exact ratio of the announcer's voice to the crowd sounds. A crowd mic is normally mixed at a low background level to provide presence and follow the action. Crowd mics are also handy to open wide when the national anthem is played or "the crowd goes wild."

The method of transmission for sports remotes varies depending on the location. A station's RPU transmitter is often used for home games. Away games are broadcast on an analog POTS phone hybrid, a digital POTS codec, or a digital ISDN codec. Prior to the remote, it is necessary to determine what telco (telephone company) services are available at the sports venue, and whether there is a courtesy line available to use. Also, check to see if there is Internet access, dial-up or networked, so that a laptop can be used to check on sports scores from other events during the course of the game.

Most sports stadiums provide courtesy lines to dial your station's toll-free line or to call the station collect to get the game on the air. Another creative way a station can get a signal on the air is by using prepaid long-distance phone cards that the station has traded with a sponsor to pay for the call. If a courtesy line is not available, the appropriate POTS or ISDN line must be ordered from the local phone company. When ordering a line, be sure to allow plenty of lead time before the event. In some locations, an ISDN line can take four to six weeks to be installed. Most stations place all their phone orders in writing with the phone company several weeks before the start of the season.

Radio sports remotes are typically produced in monaural (one channel). However, if you are using a stereo ISDN codec you can add sonic width and depth to the game by replacing the crowd mic with a stereo mic (see chapter 3). Ideally, a stereo crowd mic should be positioned near the mid-field or mid-court line.

In addition to the headset and crowd mics, sportscasters often plug a portable recorder into a line input on the mixer to play back pre-game interviews. Some sportscasters use portable digital storage units, such as a 360 Systems Instant Replay or a laptop computer, to record, edit, and playback interviews (see Fig. **11.11**). Such devices can also be used to record the game for instant replays of the play-by-play action. To handle this many inputs, a small audio mixer is required to feed the codec's input.

Another popular addition to a sports broadcast is a wireless microphone(s) for courtside or sideline interviews. Here again, create a checklist for the wireless system, including frequency coordination, the microphone, receiver, batteries, and so on, and make it a part of your overall checklist. As a remote setup becomes more technical in nature, a field producer becomes necessary to accompany the play-by-play and color announcer.

Sportscasters often listen to an **off-air monitor** when they are within range of the station. On the road, depending on the method of transmission, the talent can be fed a mix/minus monitor signal from the station on the return side of the digital POTS or ISDN codec (again, see Fig. **11.4**). The station can also put the program on the IFB, interrupting the feed when the producer at the station needs to talk to the announcers in their headsets.

Just as with commercial remotes, there is usually someone at the station to act as a control-board operator to put the game on the air, play back commercials, and so forth. However, it's not necessary if the station is equipped with the appropriate computer server and software. Many stations use automation and live-assist systems that permit remote access via the Internet or a dial-up modem. With a laptop computer at the remote site, the producer logs into the station server and remotely takes over operation of

Figure 11.11

Some broadcasters use digital storage units, such as a 360 Systems Instant Replay or a laptop computer, to record, edit, and playback interviews (right side of picture under announcer's hand). Such devices can also be used to record the game for instant replays of the play-by-play action.

the radio station, producing the entire broadcast from the remote site.

A sports remote can be as simple or as complicated as the broadcast team wants to make it. Keep in mind that a low-tech written checklist, starting with the talent and working backwards to the station, makes sure you take what you need for the remote. You can even keep the list on a personal digital assistant, or PDA, retaining the lists for future reference should you ever return to that site. Physically observe each item that is packed for the remote and check it off the list, making sure not to forget the backups. Likewise, when it's time to leave a site, go over the checklist again to make sure everything you took to the remote comes back to the "house."

News and Special-Event Coverage

Back in the dark ages of pay phones and cassette machines, a reporter's best friends were a roll of quarters and an official telephone company "out-of-order" sign to tape on the closest phone to the event. When the event was over, you rushed to your out-of-order phone, peeled off the sign, and started feeding the phone quarters. Today, phone lines are almost a thing of the past. Most news remotes, or electronic news gathering **(ENG)** are simple, one-person jobs, and each reporter generally does his or her own work as both talent and technician.

News reporters have a number of effective, portable digital recorders to select from in order to capture sound. Options range from a minidisc to a sophisticated hard disk, flash memory card, or real-time CD recorder. Also, a number of recorders store audio on random access memory (RAM) chips. Smaller, lighter, laptop computers and specially equipped personal digital assistants (PDAs) are ideal ENG solutions featuring the ability to provide support for an entire location news operation, as discussed in chapter 5. If the laptop or PDA is equipped with a wireless Internet card, you can essentially take your entire newsroom on location.

The 2004 Presidential election coverage was a virtually wireless operation, with reporters using laptops, PDAs, and other digital recorders equipped with wireless technology. In some instances, candidates' speeches were available as digital audio files and could be downloaded instantly into laptops for editing and transmission to a station's newsroom. Audio cuts from speeches were converted to mp3 files and were either transferred over the Internet or attached to e-mails and sent to news editors. Another advantage of using a laptop for news gathering was that a reporter could archive a number of the candidate's entire speeches along with all of their edited audio cuts as a reference. Using wireless Internet technology, reporters quickly found themselves filing stories from rental cars and as they traveled on campaign buses and aircraft (although it must be noted that most wireless cards lose their Internet connection at an altitude of about five thousand feet). Combined with news-writing software and microphone, a laptop is an anytime, anywhere newsroom.

For the most part, the challenge in news recording comes in capturing the sound at its source. Usually, this involves interviewing the newsmaker. Occasionally, news people are asked to capture background sound such as sirens, chanting labor-union pickets, or some other easily identifiable sound that can help support a story. Most small digital recorders have built-in microphones; however, it is best to use a professional microphone plugged into a digital recorder. Save the built-in mic for a last-resort backup.

A news person can select either a nondirectional or a super-cardioid microphone for location recording. Remember that the omnidirectional mic captures everything, including the interview subject and any background noise present, which is fine in a controlled environment. On the other hand, a super-cardioid mic provides a great deal of control over what the microphone picks up and is especially useful if the news event is in a noisy location (see chapter 3). Some news people choose to be very selective and use a handheld hyper-cardioid shotgun microphone to isolate and pick up only the newsmaker. The whole microphone selection process for a news person comes down to what the person is comfortable working with and the quality level he or she desires.

For special-event coverage, such as a press conference or a major speech by a political figure, a **pool audio feed** is often provided. Pool feeds are created with a **breakout box** or a multiple outlet box **(mult).** A breakout box is a device that takes a single audio feed and, using amplifiers, splits it into multiple feeds at standard broadcast levels so that each member of the media receives a good clean audio feed (see Fig. **11.12**). Breakout boxes are provided by whoever is holding the press conference or special event to ensure that the press receives good quality audio.

An extension of the breakout box is a mobile wireless Internet terminal. Set up at a special event, the mobile terminal provides rock-solid wireless Internet access to as many as

Breakout, or pool feed boxes, are provided to ensure the press receives good quality audio at press conferences or special events. Sometimes called a "mult" box, a breakout box takes a single audio feed and, using amplifiers, splits it into multiple feeds at standard broadcast levels so that each member of the media receives a good clean audio feed. The box above can provide twelve feeds at mic level to the media.

150 reporters at once for a reasonable fee. During the 2004 Presidential campaign, some rates were as low as $20 per reporter per event. The cost to install telephone lines or digital ISDN lines could have been as much as ten times that high for each event.

Occasionally, a reporter encounters a situation in which there has been little preparation on the part of the group holding the press event, and the news person is asked to take a feed from the public address system. There are two ways of doing this. The first is simply to place your microphone in a direct line with the public address speaker, a few feet away so you get a good audio level. The second

method you can use is to tap directly into the PA system. A word of caution: Any time you take a direct tap off a public address system, you need to be aware that PA systems, especially inexpensive ones, are not noted for their outstanding audio quality. You may have to use your spare connectors and cords to rig a patch cord or figure out a way to get the signal from the amplifier to your gear. Look first for a headphone output on the front of the PA amplifier as a place to start, followed by a tape, or auxiliary output, that is likely located on the back of the amplifier.

Once you have captured the location sound, there are any number of ways to get it back to the station, as covered earlier in this chapter, such as a Marti, cell phone, analog or digital phone hybrid, and wireless Internet connection. Because a lot of news is done on the fly, the simplest system often works the best. And sometimes, when push comes to shove, calling the station on a phone and placing the speaker of your recorder up to the phone is the quickest way to get the audio back to the station.

Suggested Activities

1. Select a site for a mock commercial radio remote. Visit the site and conduct a site survey. Decide upon the talent, transmission, and monitoring system. Create a checklist of the equipment that would be necessary to do the remote.
2. Select a sporting event for a mock radio sports remote. Visit the site and conduct a site survey. Decide upon the talent, transmission, and monitoring system. What unique or action sounds could you mic to make the broadcast more interesting? Create a checklist of the equipment that would be necessary to do the remote.
3. A city council is meeting to make a major announcement regarding an industrial park. The six council members will appear at the site and stand as a group to break ground with a gold shovel. If your station is covering this major event, how would you mic the event so that each council member's comments can be recorded? How many ways could you mic the event? Make a checklist of equipment for the method you choose.

Web Sites for More Information

For more information about:

- *breakout boxes,* visit Professional Sound Corporation at www.professionalsound.com
- *codecs for POTS and ISDN,* visit www.comrex.com
- *handheld satellite phones,* visit www.globalstarusa.com
- *portable satellite phone uplinks,* visit www.nera.no
- *radio remote pickup transmitters,* visit Marti Electronics at www.martielectronics.com
- *remote analog phone hybrids,* visit www.jkaudio.com

Pro Speak

You should be able to use these terms in your everyday conversations with other professionals.

A/D—The abbreviation for an analog-to-digital audio converter.

breakout box—A device designed to allow audio distribution at press conferences through multiple mic or line-level outputs.

codec—A digital audio device that codes analog audio into digital audio and decodes digital audio back into analog audio.

courtesy lines—Telephone lines that are available in the press area of a sports venue for visiting sportscasters to use without charge. Depending on the facility, the line may be a POTS or an ISDN line. Most have long-distance service disabled, other than toll-free exchanges such as 800, 888, etc.

D/A—The abbreviation for a digital-to-analog audio converter.

draw—Something to attract people to an event or a location: a gimmick or enticement.

duplex devices—Audio devices that allow bidirectional communications on a single line or radio-frequency transmission.

ENG—Abbreviation for electronic news gathering, or location spot-news coverage.

GPS—Abbreviation for Global Positioning System. A satellite-based navigation system made up of a network of satellites that enables pinpoint location identification.

GSM—An abbreviation for Global System for Mobile Communications.

ISDN—Abbreviation for Integrated Services Digital Network. A dial-up digital line capable of transmitting 128 kilobits of studio-quality audio data and 16 kilobits of telephone-switching data.

ISP—Abbreviation for Internet service provider.

LEO—Abbreviation for low earth orbit. A term used to describe satellites orbiting earth at between 300 and 500 miles high.

mic flag—A plastic nameplate, or cover, that goes on a microphone with the station's call letters or logo.

mult—Same as a breakout box, a device designed to allow audio distribution at press conferences through multiple mic or line-level outputs.

off-air monitor—An actual air signal taken from a radio for monitoring purposes.

phone hybrid—An electronic device used to connect broadcast equipment with a telephone line so that audio can be sent and received on the phone line.

pool audio feed—A single-point audio feed for the press, usually accomplished with a mult or breakout box.

vendor involvement—When the vendor of a product or service provides support to a local business in the form of product to give away or expert staff to help demonstrate the product. This kind of involvement with the local business can be quite varied from manufacturer to manufacturer.

CHAPTER 12

Interfacing with the Net

Background

Radio is the ultimate chameleon. From its very beginning, radio has been forced by competing media to change its colors on a regular basis to remain competitive. Radio has been through a number of challenges in its history, and each time it has emerged renewed and strengthened.

In the mid-to-late 1990s, dot-com radio stations were touted as the next wave that was going to decimate traditional radio, with their incredible variety of stations and worldwide reach. There were those who predicted that the dot-com stations would enjoy their biggest success once the Internet became wireless. Imagine that: Using wireless technology to deliver a radio station's programming . . . it's called radio, and it's been around more than eighty years.

The late-nineties' collapse of the dot-coms demonstrated that just because something can be done technically, that does not ensure a commercial success.

So why do production people need to understand the Internet and their station's involvement with it? Consolidation within the industry has come to require that each person in the station take a holistic approach, understanding how the different departments work together to form the whole. Radio employees are no longer isolated in their own tiny little worlds within the station. Now more than ever, it is important for you to consider the entire station and understand your role in its operation. And although you might not be involved in every aspect of the station's web operation, you should understand how it contributes to the overall success of the radio station. It would be easy to say that the dreaded dragon Internet has been slain and there is nothing to fear. Nevertheless, this author is reminded of something baseball pitching legend Satchel Paige (according to ballplayer Dizzy Dean, the greatest pitcher of all time) once said: "Don't look back. Something may be gaining on you." With respect to the Internet, radio must fully embrace the technology and move forward, using the Internet as a station resource to extend its positioning statement and branding concepts to impact listeners' lives.

The Challenge of Competing with Another Medium

The Internet is a dual-edged sword with respect to radio and other media. The present relationship between radio and the Internet is very similar to the love/hate relationship that once existed between cable television and local television stations. On the one hand, the Internet is a competitive threat to radio, with the ability to steal listeners and station advertising revenue. On the other hand, the Internet represents a tremendous opportunity to expand a radio station's reach, to provide a tangible presence for listener interaction, and to provide a steady source of **nontraditional revenue.**

Trends in media convergence and the Internet's ability to present traditional media in a nontraditional way make it abundantly clear that radio must embrace the Internet and learn to use its best qualities to enhance a radio station. There is an old saying, "Keep your friends close, your enemies even closer." Radio cannot afford *not* to be involved with the Internet.

Why Radio Needs the Internet

The first involvement with the Internet for most stations was webcasting their on-air signal on the net. Although it was cool to do so because every other station was doing it, the question that had to be answered was why? How did this activity benefit the radio station? After the passage of the Digital Millennium Copyright Act of 1998 **(DMCA),** most stations dropped their on-air signal from the Internet because they didn't want to pay the digital music copyright fees. Many stations discovered that the music was not really necessary and found better, and far more creative, uses for their web sites. Radio stations also discovered a new source of nontraditional revenue. Today, well over half of radio stations report that they depend on their web site as a source of nontraditional income.

How Radio Uses the Internet

One of the primary reasons advertisers use radio is that the medium allows them to target specific demographic and psychographic groups so that their advertising is more effective in reaching potential customers. Another key reason advertisers choose radio is that it allows them to target local areas; radio is a local medium. The Internet provides a station the opportunity for a global audience. Although the Internet may add a few listeners to the station, the reality is that these listeners have little monetary value to the station. An advertiser buys commercials on a station because the advertiser values the audience and the business the local audience can bring. Local advertisers can't sell the Internet listeners their products or services because most Internet listeners live too far away from the local market.

Typically, when advertisers think of the Internet, they think on a global scale, the ability to reach a worldwide audience. So how is it that radio, whose specialty is targeting local customers, relates to the Internet, whose specialty is offering a worldwide audience?

Linking Two Dissimilar Media

Even though most local advertisers won't be able to sell anything to faraway Internet listeners, global businesses will be happy to sell to local customers. A radio station can search out global businesses located within its market and show them how to generate increased revenues by targeting local customers with radio. For that matter, the station can pitch the unique demographic and economic qualities of its local market to any Internet-based business, even a faraway one, that might benefit from targeting the station's listeners. For example, an Internet-based travel agency in Orlando, Florida, could certainly sell warm, sunny vacations at the beach with wintertime radio advertising in New York City.

In addition, realizing that more than seventy percent of radio listeners have some type of access to a computer and the Internet, a radio station can make a good case to a local business to increase revenues by targeting radio listeners and directing them to its web site. For example, it makes perfect sense for a local car dealership to direct radio listeners to the dealership's web site to schedule their own service appointments on line. If an advertiser has an easy-to-remember web address, it should be used as a powerful call to action in a radio ad. There is not a better, more immediate, response to a radio ad than a listener logging on to the advertiser's web site and buying something within minutes of hearing the radio ad.

Although the Internet and radio are two distinctly different media, when combined they form an incredibly powerful marketing tool to solve a local or global business's problems and needs. The reality is that a radio station's local qualities and the Internet's global qualities are not at odds with one another after all. They strengthen one another.

Programming a Web Site

Although it may sound like the programming department's job to program the station web site, the fact is that a production person is likely going to be involved in some aspect of the project. Just as it is important for you to understand how the radio station is programmed and how production plays a vital role in the execution of the programming, it is important for you to understand the overall impact a web site has on a station and your role in its success.

A radio station must give listeners a reason to visit its web site other than "Visit our web site!" For a moment, forget broadcasting the station's on-air signal on the web site and concentrate on visual content. How can you make the site work without the music? Make it interactive. Remember, a listener is constantly asking "What's in it for me?" A station must offer something on its web site that listeners value, or something that solves a problem listeners have, to get them to visit the web site (see Fig. **12.1**). You need to think of programming for your station's web site as radio with graphics and pictures (or was that television?).

The creation of the station's web site is going to take more than a computer geek with a pocket protector pounding out **HTML.** It requires the work of several people from programming, promotion, and production. The web site must be artistically and graphically pleasing to the station's target demographic. The graphic design of a country station's web site is going to be a lot different from the design of one for a hard-rock station. Regardless of the style, the site has to be easy to read, it has to be functional, and it has to carry out the station's positioning statement and branding concepts.

Many stations have a second web site featuring the sales department. The sales web site can serve as a production showcase featuring demos of the station's best production work. The sales department's web site can offer materials created from the Radio Advertising Bureau's research on the benefits of radio advertising. The station can also offer sales and marketing information about the specific demographic and psychographic groups that compose the station's audience.

As a further service to clients, some stations offer a secure area of the sales web site to allow advertisers to check their account information and current advertising schedule, generate an online invoice, and pay for their ads with a credit card. They can even download and play back a copy of their current ad.

A really great station web site takes a lot of people working together to keep it up-to-date and fresh, all working under the watchful eyes of the webmaster.

Web Words: A New Vocabulary

To understand effectively what everyone in the station is talking about, it is necessary to learn a few industry terms that describe important aspects of the station's web site. Probably the two most often-used terms are *broadband* and *narrowband*. These terms refer to the type of web connection or access. To a consumer, broadband typically refers to a high-speed connection like a cable modem or digital subscriber line **(DSL)** phone line with a connection speed of 200 Kbps (kilobits per second) or higher. For a radio station, a broadband connection might be a T-1 class line at 1.544 Mbps (megabits per second). A T-1 line is often referred to as a "big pipe" in the industry and is necessary to serve a large number of listeners simultaneously. A narrowband connection typically refers to a consumer dial-

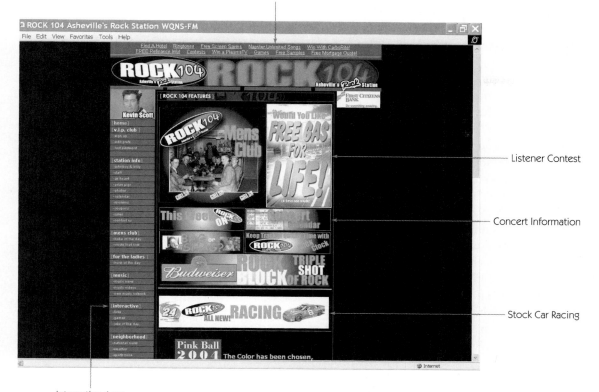

Services and Free Items

Listener Contest

Concert Information

Stock Car Racing

Interactive Area
(games, joke of the day, etc.)

Figure 12.1

Listener service features are a reason for listeners to visit a station's web site. Look carefully at the site above; it is filled with interactive links to involve the listeners in the station and its activities.

up modem that has a connection speed of less than 200 Kbps.

A term that is very important to the success of the station's web site is "banner ad." A banner ad is a creative graphic that displays an advertisement. The size and shape of these vary from company to company but typically measure about seven inches by three-quarters inch. However, some stations divide that in halves or thirds to generate more income. Closely related to the banner

ad is an "ad view." An ad view occurs when someone downloads the banner ad.

A term often misunderstood, with respect to a web site, is the term "hits." Although many people think that the number of hits on a site is an important number to share with advertisers, the fact is that a hit is nothing more than a request to the web site. If a web page has fourteen graphics and a user downloads the page, the site owner gets credit for fourteen hits. A hit does not indicate that anyone saw anything, and it is an unrealistic term to use when measuring the effectiveness of a web site. A more important term for stations, with respect to advertisers, is CAD, or confirmed advertisements delivered. An outside third party, using a site-tracking or auditing system, confirms CAD numbers. From the CAD numbers it is easy for a station and advertiser to calculate the CPM or cost per thousand (M is the Roman numeral for 1,000). This is the cost to reach 1,000 viewers of the web site.

Few advertisers purchase banner ads based on views or hits; most advertisers pay only for "click throughs." A click-through occurs when a viewer clicks on a banner ad and is taken to the advertiser's web site. The "click-through rate" is the percentage, among all the people who view the station's web page, of those who click-through to the advertiser's web site. Most banner advertising today is paid for on a per-click through basis; alternatively, the owner of the web page where the click-through originated receives a percentage of each product sold from the advertiser's web site.

There are several reasons for this pay-as-you-go compensation plan. First, just because someone goes to a web page does not mean that the person is going to see a particular banner ad. (For one thing, a viewer may be using ad-blocking software, in which case the ad is never seen.) Second, advertisers found that the overall return on their advertising investment on the Internet was otherwise too low to justify the cost. Notice that, with the thousands, even millions, of web pages to advertise on, there is little or no exclusivity of the medium (the number of radio station licenses, by contrast, is limited by the FCC, providing an intrinsic value in and of itself because of the exclusivity of the medium). And then, whereas the web is a global medium and can generate some impressive web page statistics, how many of the viewers can actually become paying customers?

Although there are a number of other web terms, the terms and concepts introduced here are a few of the most basic terms webmasters and salespeople use to describe some of the important aspects of the station's web site.

Web Site Content

With everyone in the station potentially contributing ideas to the web site, the webmaster has his or her hands full staying focused on the site's programming goals. Chief among the goals is maintaining the station's positioning statement and branding concepts. Below is a very limited list of the things a station could use its web site for; notice that webcasting the station's on-air signal is not even on the list (see Fig. **12.2**).

- client advertising and links to clients' web sites
- printable client coupons with links to clients' web sites
- restaurant and club listings with links to their web sites
- concert promotion and advertising with a link to the promoter's web site
- concert ticket advertising and links to ticket vendors
- station contests, contest rules, contest entry forms
- station clubs or fan groups associated with shows
- purchase-and-print tickets to station-sponsored events
- live studio web cams
- instant music requests directed to the jock in the studio via instant messenger
- photos of staff, station events
- interviews with station staff

Services and Free Items

VIP Club
Membership

Station
Information

Men's Club

Items for Women

Music Features

Interactive Area
(games, joke
of the day, etc.)

Listener Contest

Concert
Information

Stock Car Racing

Figure 12.2

The web site above is an example of a site that takes full advantage of just about
every aspect of potential listener involvement, from links to advertisers to joining a
station club.

- on-air staff schedules
- remote schedules or station event schedules
- music lists, even the hourly playlists
- advertising links to music companies or fan web sites
- station music charts
- music news
- music message boards for music discussion
- paid music videos for visitors to watch or download
- music or station surveys
- cross-promotion of other stations in your market group

- weather
- news headlines
- community public-service links
- video games to play (increases site visits and click-throughs)
- health, beauty, and pet links (everyone is interested in these three and they increase site visits and click-throughs)
- downloads for audio/video players

Interestingly, many items on the preceding list involve audio or production in some form. Every one of them is not only a reason to visit a site but also has commercial possibilities for generating nontraditional revenues. For example, a station can partner with retail web sites that sell things its listeners are interested in. The radio station receives a per-click-through fee or a percentage of each sale made from a click-through. The technology is incredible and allows a station to do just about anything it can dream up, including placing web cams at remotes.

Technical and Economic Considerations

Just as technology allows a station to be incredibly creative with its web site, it also limits what a station can do with a web site. One of the unique qualities of the Internet is that the creator of a web site cannot control the quality that the end user experiences. For example, a webmaster creates a site using a twenty-one-inch monitor and the latest software and computer. The webmaster has broadband Internet access to view the site with, and on his or her computer it looks incredible, audio and video clips included.

However, what the end user experiences is another matter altogether. The end user is likely using a dial-up modem to access the Internet, a seventeen-inch monitor, and a computer that is a couple of years old. The site looks good, but the pictures and video clips seemingly take forever to load. Is the end user seeing the same thing the webmaster sees? Not unless the webmaster takes into account "the average site visitor" when designing the site. Most people do not wait much longer than fifteen to twenty seconds for a web page to load. To make sure they are keeping the average visitor in mind, webmasters often keep an older computer in the office, with a smaller monitor and a dial-up modem, to test the site from time to time.

Economically, **streaming** on the Internet is quite different from broadcasting an on-air signal. Traditional radio broadcasting involves a signal that listeners are free to listen to at will. No matter how many listeners tune in, the broadcaster's operational costs remain the same. However, a station streaming audio on the web has to purchase enough bandwidth from an Internet service provider for a given number of listeners to hear the station. Every new listener adds to the station's costs. The concept of paying for each listener to access a station's signal is still a new concept to radio and one that many broadcasters find tough to justify. Some stations charge a small monthly subscription fee ($4.99) for their web streaming service to help defray the bandwidth and music copyright costs.

As a practical example, let's assume a station has a weekly on-air audience of 100,000 people. If the station had just five percent as many web listeners, they would be paying to stream audio to 5,000 people per week. As a broadcaster, which makes more sense, investing your money to reach 100,000 local listeners or investing your money in bandwidth for 5,000 who may or may not be local? After analyzing the costs involved, many broadcasters have found that in their particular situation, the costs for streaming far outweigh the benefits.

Audio Production for the Internet

Streaming Audio

Streaming audio on the Internet is similar to sending audio files on the Internet; however, it is a little more complicated. Sending an audio file is a one-time data transfer; streaming audio is a continuous real-time event. Trying to send a full-frequency, high-quality audio signal takes an incredible amount of bandwidth, both on the part of the sender and on the part of the receiver. Since it is already assumed that the consumer is an average site visitor, then something has to be done to make the audio fit on the web so that the consumer can listen to it on his or her dial-up or cable modem.

The solution to the problem of streaming good-quality audio involves using perceptual audio coding or data compression, sometimes referred to as lossy compression (this is similar to the process used in transferring mp3 audio files on the Internet. **Perceptual audio coding** is a method of compressing, encoding, and finally decoding audio that takes advantage of how humans perceive sound to achieve a significant reduction in the size of the data stream. Properly done, it entails little or no perceptible loss of audio quality. Basically, the audio processor discards everything the listener can't hear, such as the very low and high frequencies. Next, based on how your ears perceive sound, other unnecessary audio data is also eliminated from the stream.

Another factor besides human hearing that determines which audio frequencies stay and which are discarded is the connection speed. A computer server and licensed software are used to encode the audio; the listener's player is used to decode the audio. With a cable modem or DSL connection, the music can be encoded to near CD quality, but at low dial-up bandwidths, a lot of the audio data is tossed, and the result is a signal that sounds about like AM radio. Later in the chapter the various audio encoding products are discussed.

Regardless of the bandwidth, the quality of the audio sent to the codec for streaming is important. Typically, an audio production person wants to tweak and process audio to get every competitive sonic edge he or she can to attract listeners. Although this works well for a station's on-air signal, where the transmission and reception meet FCC guidelines, the web offers interesting challenges. The quality of the signal transmitted and received is dependent on a number of factors the production person cannot control, such as the quality of the Internet connection that the average site visitor is using.

Basically, good streaming audio comes down to sending the codec a quality signal to start with. Streaming audio needs to have an excellent signal-to-noise ratio, and the frequency response should be left flat, or unaltered. The codec's job is made easier through the use of high- and low-pass filters, eliminating the audio frequencies above and below what the web easily transmits. About the only audio processing necessary for a streaming signal is some light compression. The compressor should be adjusted for a mild compression ratio of 4:1 or 5:1, with approximately 3 dB of compression, just to level the peaks. Set the compressor's output to 0 dB.

Heavy compression, limiting, and equalization should be avoided, as the most commonly used streaming audio codecs do not work well with audio that has been heavily processed. Audio processing for streaming audio is truly a case where less is more.

Audio Clips

Preparing audio clips for the web is slightly different from streaming audio, in that the clips are small files that in some cases are downloaded and then played back, as opposed to being streamed. Just as with streaming audio, though, you need excellent audio quality to begin with. Assuming that you are preparing your clip on a DAW, start by normalizing the clip for the maximum audio level. Normalize the audio to only ninety-five percent, because some audio codecs have problems handling audio that has been normalized to one hundred percent.

Although normalizing audio raises the volume level of the clip's loudest passages, the quiet passages of the clip remain at a much lower level. Typically, quiet passages do not encode well, so it is a good practice to follow the normalization process with mild compression to raise the level of the quieter passages. Use the same compression settings mentioned earlier for streaming audio.

EQ can be added to an audio clip in an attempt to make it stand out. As discussed in an earlier chapter, it is always best to cut audio frequencies first to see if the desired effect can be achieved that way. In other words, clean away the sounds masking what it is you want to stand out. For example, to clean up a clip that features voice, cut everything below 100 Hz and roll off the frequencies above 7,500 kHz. Then, if the voice still needs help, add two or three dB of boost between 1 and 4 kHz.

Webcasting

Respecting the Music

Whether or not a station chooses to webcast an on-air signal is the station's decision; however, it is a decision that must be made in consultation with legal counsel. Technologically, it is easy to put an audio stream on the Internet. However, to do so within the applicable copyright laws requires some basic knowledge and legal assistance to insure that all of the music-license conditions are met prior to putting copyrighted works on the web.

Performance Rights

The two aspects of copyright that broadcasters are most concerned with are performance rights and sound-recording rights. The performance rights are the rights to perform publicly a music work. In the case of a radio station, it is the right to broadcast the music. Usually, the artist, composer, author, or publisher holds the performance rights to the music, depending on who created the work and contractually owns the rights. Because it is impossible for musical artists to keep track of all the broadcasters in the country using their work, artists sign contracts with performance-rights organizations to manage their works.

Radio stations pay fees to the three performance-rights organizations that represent songwriters and musicians. The fees each station pays are based upon station music-use reports and station financial statements. The performance-rights management organizations are the American Society of Composers, Authors, and Publishers (ASCAP), Broadcast Music, Incorporated (BMI), and the Society of European Stage Authors and Composers (SESAC). Based on the estimated airplay of each artist's work, the organizations divide the station fees among the various artists they represent.

Sound-Recording Rights

The sound-recording rights to a song are the rights associated with the physical recording itself—how the musical notes were recorded, edited, mastered, and released to the public, the creative work of the recording process. The company that recorded, produced, manufactured, and distributed the recording usually holds the sound-recording rights, although some artists retain the sound-recording rights to their work.

Radio stations do not pay sound-recording rights fees to broadcast music works on the air. Years ago, when such laws were originally proposed, the broadcasting industry prevailed before Congress and laws were passed in the broadcast industry's favor. This is not the case for streamed music on the Internet, however. The Digital Millennium Copyright Act of 1998 (DMCA) established, for the first time, that owners of the sound recording had the right to authorize digital public performances and to be paid for such performances.

The DMCA covers webcasting, cable, satellite digital audio services, and future forms of digital transmission yet to be determined. Traditional on-air radio broadcasts remain exempt from the DMCA.

The fee structure for sound-recording rights on the Internet is based upon detailed computerized records that are required, by law, to be maintained by the webcaster. Unlike with radio broadcast performance rights, the operator of a web site pays a per-song, per-listener fee. In addition to the performance/listener fee, the web site operator pays an annual license fee.

The initial response of many radio stations to the 1998 DMCA was to discontinue all webcasting, due to the extensive record-keeping requirements and per-performance fee structure. So although the music industry sought payment for sound-recording rights, the broadcasting industry responded by initially discontinuing streaming of its on-air signals until they could figure out a business plan to support the activity. Some radio stations simply webcast audio cuts from their morning shows and work for which they hold all rights, such as sportscasts or contest promotional announcements. However, even these audio clips have to be carefully screened for protected material.

Unless a broadcaster holds a sound-recording license, he or she must be extremely careful not to transmit anything other than an **"incidental performance"** of a protected sound recording. An incidental performance includes, but is not limited to, such things as brief musical transitions in and out of programs and commercial stop sets, and brief performances during news, sports, or talk programming. However, an incidental performance cannot include an entire sound record-

ing and in no case can it be longer than thirty seconds. What is, and is not, an incidental performance is defined by federal copyright statute.

A radio station can broadcast a musical or nonmusical work on the Internet without paying a sound-recording license fee, provided the owner has given the station permission to do so. For example, a music company might provide a station with an audio clip from an upcoming CD to tease listeners with. A music company might also pay the station to feature the music or music video on its web site. A radio station can also broadcast nonmusical events such as high school sports, city council meetings, and other events for which it has acquired the rights. For example, a university might retain the Internet rights to its sporting events and sell the games via the Internet to relatives of participating students and alumni.

The issue of copyright in our country goes back to our founding fathers and the constitution (yes, it is a constitutional right). Likewise, so does the history of copyright lawmaking and litigation brought by copyright holders, as is currently the situation with the many pending copyright suits resulting from new technologies. As a production person, you must abide by your company policies on webcasting and placing audio clips on the Internet. When it comes to questions and decisions regarding copyright, the station's legal counsel makes the final determinations for the station.

Audio Transmission Formats

When audio is transmitted using the AM or FM band, a radio-station engineer makes sure the station's signal complies with the technical rules and regulations of the FCC. This ensures a uniform signal that all AM and FM radios can receive. Likewise, manufacturers certify that the radios they build comply with certain FCC rules and regulations. The end result is that the audio quality the listener receives is fairly uniform.

When it comes to streaming audio on the Internet, though, there are no uniform guidelines for either the transmission of the audio or the receivers used by the consumer. Another factor is that the bandwidth the radio station uses to stream the signal is usually many times wider than that used by the consumer, who likely is on a dial-up line. Just as a webmaster has to consider the average site visitor in setting up a web page's graphic design, the station engineer has to consider the average listener when selecting a method to stream audio.

There are quite a few variables and costs, including the original audio source, the streaming server, streaming software, and available bandwidth, that affect the number of simultaneous listeners a station can serve. To try and cover each possible situation in detail is beyond the scope of this text. Three major companies are recognized as the providers of industry-standard streaming audio codecs.

QuickTime

QuickTime is a product of Apple Computer. The unique aspect of QuickTime is that the software is open-sourced. The computer codes used to create Apple's Real-Time Transport Protocol/Real-Time Streaming Protocol engine are available free of charge to any software developer for adoption and use. QuickTime supports a number of audio formats, including MP3 and MP4.

Although Apple created the product, there are several versions of the software for other platforms and operating systems, such as Linux and Windows. The open-sourced software is modified to fit other platforms by changing platform-specific computer-source files.

A QuickTime server can originate up to 4,000 audio streams per server. Of course, the best aspect of QuickTime is that the server software is free, as is the basic player for the listener. A "pro" version of the basic QuickTime player, that has additional features, is available for a nominal fee.

RealNetworks

RealNetworks pioneered streaming audio and video and offers a broad range of products to stream both. As with all of the major media-delivery companies, RealNetworks offers audio-encoding software in various price ranges (including free), based on capacity, to create and send audio products on the Internet. Depending on the number of audio streams desired, the audio-encoding software can cost several thousand dollars. Using RealNetworks products, a single server can handle up to 10,000 audio streams at once.

The basic player (RealPlayer) for the listener is offered as a free download and sometimes comes bundled with other software on new computers (see Fig. **12.3**). An upgrade to a RealNetworks player with additional features is available for a nominal fee.

Windows Media Player

Windows Media Player is the complement to the Windows operating system. Like the other products on the market, Windows Media Player offers a host of features to play back audio streams (see Fig. **12.4**). Like its competitors, the Windows Media Player offers very good performance for users on dial-up con-

Figure 12.3

RealNetworks pioneered streaming audio. The basic RealPlayer is offered as a free download and sometimes comes bundled with other software on new computers. RealNetworks streaming software is capable of streaming up to 10,000 simultaneous audio streams with one computer server.

nections. For those with broadband connections, Windows Media Player offers home-theater-quality 5.1 surround-sound audio and video. People using a dial-up connection can download the 5.1 surround audio files and then play them back.

Windows Media Player site developers pay a licensing fee based on the number of audio streams desired. Windows Media Players are bundled with original equipment software or can be downloaded separately free of charge.

Which Internet Codec Is Right for Your Station?

All three of the major codecs on the market are excellent products that do what they are de-signed to do. As a production person, you are not very likely to be asked to make the decision as to which codec your station should choose, but you should be aware of the factors that go into such a decision. Choosing one is not an easy task; the choice has to be based on your station's specific needs. Which codec your station decides on is going to be based on a number of factors. One of the primary factors is cost of the server, software, and any per-stream or per-listener software licensing fees. Other considerations include the audio-quality level your station desires, the number of streams that are needed, the bandwidth that is available for streaming, whether or not you are using web cams in the radio station, and how "universal" you want your streaming product to be.

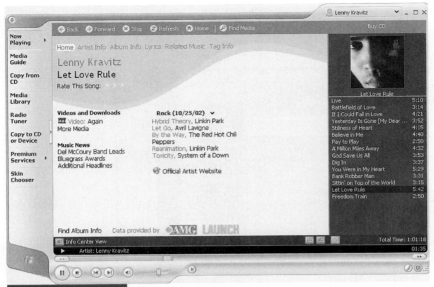

Figure 12.4

Windows Media Player offers a host of features to play back audio streams, offering very good performance for users on dial-up connections. For those with broadband connections, Windows Media Player offers home-theater-quality 5.1 surround-sound audio and video. Those using a dial-up connection can download the 5.1 surround audio files and then play them back.

The final decision is going to come down to which codec makes the best business sense for your station to adopt and which one the station's engineering staff is most comfortable working with.

Suggested Activities

1. Visit at least three major-market radio station web sites. Are any of the web sites streaming music? If not, do they say why? Make a list of the different categories of links that are on each site, such as those for news, weather, staff photos, and so on. Do you see any trends as to what these radio stations are featuring on their web sites?

2. Using three major-market radio station web sites, make a list of the commercial or income-producing links on the site. Do you see any trends as to the types of commercial links the stations are promoting, such as restaurants, music stores, and so forth?

3. Look at three major-market radio station web sites. Are the stations doing any web-based contests? If so, what kind or style? Can you enter the contest on the web, or do you have to listen to the station first?

4. Visit the web site of your favorite radio station. Has the radio station carried its on-air positioning statement and branding concept to the web?

Web Sites for More Information

For more information about:

- *copyright laws,* visit the United States Copyright Office at www.copyright.gov

- *music performance rights,* visit the American Society of Composers, Authors, and Publishers at www.ascap.com; Broadcast Music, Incorporated, at www.bmi.com; and The Society of European Stage Authors and Composers at www.sesac.com

- *Internet audio players or codecs,* visit Microsoft at www.microsoft.com; RealNetworks at www.realnetworks.com; and Apple Computers at www.apple.com

- *sound-recording copyrights and webcasting,* visit the Recording Industry Association of America at www.riaa.com

Pro Speak

You should be able to use these terms in your everyday conversations with other professionals.

DMCA—Abbreviation for the Digital Millennium Copyright Act of 1998.

DSL—Abbreviation for digital subscriber line. An Internet connection made over a regular, twisted-pair telephone line capable of carrying data and a telephone conversation at the same time. Popular for home and small business use.

HTML—Abbreviation for Hyper Text Mark-up Language, a computer language used in the creation of web sites that allows sites to be easily linked together.

incidental performance—A very brief performance of a portion of a musical work going into program or commercial stop sets. In no case the entire musical selection, regardless of length, and in no case longer than thirty seconds. Defined by federal copyright statutes.

nontraditional revenue—Revenue generated by a radio station from anything other than commercial-time sales. Examples include events a station sponsors, such as job fairs and car shows, or ad sales from the station's web site.

perceptual audio coding—A method of compressing, encoding, and decoding audio data files that takes advantage of the properties of the human perception of sound to achieve a size reduction of the data file with little or no perceptible loss of quality.

streaming—A term used to describe transmitting audio on the Internet. Usually used to describe a continuous, real-time-audio feed, such as an on-air signal.

CHAPTER 13

From Here to There: Radio and Audio Transmission in a Digital World

In this chapter, you are going to learn about the methods of producing and transmitting digital audio on the Internet. You will also learn about high-definition radio and the production challenges it presents, as well as digital satellite radio services and the basics behind **AM** and **FM** broadcasting. Before there was radio there was broadcasting, which is not even an electronic term. Broadcasting is a farming term for sowing seeds, or casting them over a broad area. The term was applied to early radio since the radio message was cast out to listeners over a broad area.

Internet Audio Transmission for Commercial and Production Transfer

The days of shipping a reel of tape, cassette, or CD are long gone, thanks to the Internet and data-compression techniques that allow the transfer of quality audio on the Internet. The key word in the last sentence is quality. What has made this possible is our ever-increasing need for speed—the desire not only for broadband data transmission on the Internet, but to "get it now," to push a deadline right until the last moment. Amazingly, the Internet gives us an essential tool to do just that.

For competitive reasons, advertising agencies often wait until the last moment to send a commercial to a station via the Internet, knowing the commercial is going to arrive at the station within moments. The commercial is digitally transferred to the station's main server and is ready to go on the air in minutes. Likewise, the Internet provides a station with a powerful tool to exchange commercials and production work with other stations in local, regional, or national groups.

What is so incredible about transferring audio on the Internet is that there are so many different, creative ways it can be done. In this chapter you are going to learn some of the more widely used methods to transfer audio, keeping in mind that it could all change next week with someone's new data-compression system or networking concept.

Internet Connection Speeds

The quantity of data, or audio, that a radio station can transmit and receive on the Internet is directly related to the bandwidth, or the connection speed. Whereas audio can be transmitted to the Internet via a dial-up phone line, it takes considerable time to transfer large audio files and is not practical for a radio station or production facility. The available options beyond dial-up are numerous, based on the station's location and the local services available. Ranked by speed, from slowest to fastest, some of the viable options include cable modems, DSL (digital subscriber lines), or a **T-1** leased line.

A cable modem typically is able to transmit and receive data at a rate of 1 million bits per second (1 megabit) and qualifies to be called broadband, or high speed. This transmit/receive rate is about twenty times faster than that of the standard dial-up Internet connection. Although monthly fees are relatively low, cable Internet access is a shared service. If your neighbors all have cable and log on at the same time you do, the connection speed slows down proportionally.

A DSL line uses a standard phone line to transmit both voice and data simultaneously via a special modem. A DSL line can transmit data at speeds of up to 1.5 megabits per second, depending on the distance to the nearest telephone company switching center. The maximum distance a subscriber can be located from a switch center is three miles. Unlike the cable modem, a DSL line is not a shared service. Subscribers pay for the service based on where they are located and the speed of service they select. Although DSL service fees vary from area to area, one thing remains constant: the faster the data speed, the higher the monthly fee.

The faster option is a T-1 leased line. A T-1 line is a dedicated line that transmits and receives data at a speed of 1.544 megabits per second. Typically, a market group of several radio stations shares a T-1 line, thanks to the line's huge capacity to transmit and receive data. However, it would not be unusual for a market group of stations to have more than one T-1 connection to the Internet, using one for a local area network, another for a wide area network, and a third for all of the on-air studios. A shared arrangement like this allows the group to put the business-oriented local and wide area networks (LAN and WAN) behind a secure firewall (either a physical electronic device or software that prevents hackers from breaking into the computer networks), while giving studio talent the freedom to surf for show-prep material and interact with listeners via instant messenger. Depending on location and availability, a T-1 connection typically costs several hundred dollars a month.

The very fastest practical leased line is a **T-3** that can transmit and receive data at the blistering speed of 44.736 megabits per second, but a T-3 line would only be used for a large facility requiring a huge amount of bandwidth, comparable to an Internet service provider.

Local Area Network (LAN)

A local area network is usually a radio station's first means of exchanging audio with other computers. A local area network is just what the name implies: The computers within a local station or station group are all linked together so that they can share information.

One of the major advantages of a computer-based DAW is networking with other workstations in the same facility through a local area network. For example, a radio station might have two production rooms and a newsroom, each with a DAW. All three computers can be networked together to share files and also networked to the station's main control room or station server. When a commercial or news story is produced, it is instantly accessible anywhere in the radio station. Simply dragging and dropping files into folders easily transfers them from machine to machine. Each computer in a LAN system typically has Internet access.

Wide Area Network (WAN)

A wide area network is the next step up from a LAN. Broadcast stations within a regional or national group use WANs so that stations can share files over larger geographic areas. Stations can share files with other stations for any number of reasons, from voice-tracking radio shows to delivering custom production or commercial dubs, to sharing news stories.

Internet File Transfer Protocol (FTP)

Before the World Wide Web, with its flashy graphics and point-and-click icons, there was the Internet. Technically speaking, the World Wide Web operates on the Internet. The Internet is a vast network of networks over which large data files are easily transferred using file transfer protocols, or FTP.

To send and receive files using FTP, all that is required is an Internet connection and two pieces of software, an FTP server and a client. The FTP server software is at one end of the

Figure 13.1

FTP (file transfer protocol) is a very powerful way to move large files from one location to another. In the example above, the files in your computer appear on the left, the files on the server appear on the right. Moving a file from one to another is as simple as clicking on one of the two directional arrows between the two windows.   *Courtesy Ipswitch WS_FTP Pro.*

connection and the client software is at the other. The FTP server turns your computer into a very simple server, without all the flashy pictures and graphics. The FTP server only delivers files.

To retrieve a file from a server, you need FTP client software that is the equivalent of a very simple web browser. Again, no flashy pictures or icons. When the FTP client is launched, it asks for the web address of the computer you want to connect to and your client log-in name and password. The client connects to the server and two side-by-side windows are displayed. One window lists the files on your computer, and the other lists the files on the FTP server that are available for you to download (see Fig. **13.1**). When you

have identified the file you want, double-click on the file and the transfer begins to your computer. You can also highlight the file and click the directional arrows between the two windows to start the transfer.

One of the reasons that FTP works so well is that it has a very powerful error-checking feature. Each data packet, or segment of data that is received, is compared to the original file on the server. If the data packet is identical to the original, the FTP client accepts it and then the next packet is transmitted. If there is an error, the client asks the server to resend the packet. The FTP software reports a successful file transfer only when every bit of the data has been successfully received. Due to the accurate error-checking ability of the FTP client and server software, "quality in" equals "quality out."

Quality is one of the big things that FTP has going for it. At broadband connection speeds, it is not necessary to use any type of data compression or encoding. Consequently, it is important to understand that any production you put up on your server for someone to retrieve had better be good, clean, quality audio.

Millions of data files are transferred every day using FTP on the Internet. Although FTP is not as fancy as a WAN, it certainly is just as functional. FTP gives smaller regional broadcast groups and individual program producers the ability to transfer audio files without the expense of leased WAN lines. Independent production studios use FTP to transfer audio files across the country from studio to studio or to advertising agencies and back.

The final aspect of FTP that makes it so interesting is that there are a number of free versions of the server and client software available, such as WS_FTP LE.

mp3 and mp2 File Transfer

There are two things that potentially stand in the way of transferring quality audio on the World Wide Web. The first is the amount of hard drive space required to store audio files on a computer. A typical one-minute, CD-quality, stereo-audio file occupies 10 megabytes of hard drive space. The second is the bandwidth needed to send such large files over the web. Most consumers using POTS (plain old telephone service) have an average dial-up connection speed of 30 kilobits per second. To send a four-minute, CD-quality song that way would take approximately four hours. One of two things has to happen: either the bandwidth has to be significantly increased or the amount of data has to be reduced.

In 1987, work began at the Fraunhofer Institute in Germany to develop data compression and perceptual audio coding to reduce the size of an audio file and still retain the perceived audio quality. The International Organization for Standardization foresaw the coming need for video and audio data compression and formed The Moving Pictures Experts Group (MPEG) to standardize these methods. Two popular data compression technologies were developed as a result of their research, MPEG Audio Layer-3 (or MP3 as it is popularly known), and MPEG-2. MPEG-2 is primarily a professional format used in the television and motion picture industry. Some broadcast software companies also use MPEG-2 as their preferred file-storage format.

An MP3 codec (encoder/decoder) compresses, or shrinks, a CD-quality audio file by a factor of 12, maintaining the original perceived CD-sound quality. This dramatic reduction in file size makes the transfer of quality audio files relatively easy for just about anyone. Thanks to the small file size, huge amounts of music or audio can be stored on hard drives or CDs. For example, using MP3 data compression, about 150 encoded songs can be stored on a CD.

A key to successfully using MP3 audio compression is the quality of the codec. There are many free MP3 codecs on the Internet and, although there are some good ones, many leave a lot to be desired when it comes to quality audio. Most professional MP3 codecs are based directly on the original Fraunhofer research and research done by Thomson Multimedia.

One of the features of most MP3 codecs is an adjustable bit rate. The bit rate determines the audio quality and the storage space necessary for the data. Typically, a 128-kilobit-per-second bit rate produces 15-kHz, CD-quality audio using a 12:1 compression ratio. An audio file for a one-minute, CD-quality commercial is approximately 10 megabytes and compresses to about an 850-kilobyte mp3 file. Although it results in a slightly larger file size, most producers use higher bit rates (of 192 or 256 kilobits per second) for more accurate reproduction of the original audio.

The mp3PRO codec was developed by Thomson Multimedia and is an improved version of MP3. An mp3PRO codec provides higher fidelity audio files that are half the size of an MP3. What formerly took a 128-kilobit-per-second bit rate to equal CD-quality audio takes only a 64-kilobit bit rate with mp3PRO. For example, using MP3 compression, about 150 encoded songs can be stored on a CD, whereas the mp3PRO codec is capable of doubling the capacity to 300 songs on a CD. An mp3PRO codec is included as a part of the Adobe Audition software that came with this text.

Web Hosting and E-Mailing Audio Files

Two of the most popular ways for professionals to transfer mp3 files easily on the Internet are posting the mp3 file to a web page and attaching the file to e-mail. Web sites work well for file retrieval. There are several ad-posting services that specialize in hosting commercial and program files for stations to download. Web distribution of a commercial provides a substantial cost savings over sending commercial dubs to individual stations. If necessary, the web page can be secured with a password to prevent unauthorized downloads.

An audio file can be attached to e-mail just like any other file. Such e-mail can be addressed to one person or to a number of people for mass distribution. The only drawback to e-mailing mp3 files is that sometimes the receiver's mailbox is full or their Internet service provider limits the file size of e-mail attachments. However, this problem can be avoided by simply asking the person to

whom you want to send a file whether they can receive it.

ISDN (Integrated Services Digital Network)

Stations and production facilities are often required to receive or deliver real-time digital audio to another studio or facility. It might be something as simple as a voice talent delivering a set of liners or sweepers or as complicated as producing an entire show from a remote location. The use of an ISDN line and audio codecs not only makes the job easy, but their use provides studio-quality audio to work with. ISDN lines are also popular for broadcasting sporting events.

An ISDN codec is capable of sending and receiving CD-quality audio with a frequency response of up to 20 kHz over a single ISDN telephone line. To link with another station or production facility, dial the phone number of the codec you want to connect to. When the codec receiving the call answers, the two codecs take a moment to exchange audio coding information and complete the link. Once the link is completed, the audio feed can begin. Audio can be sent both ways simultaneously on an ISDN line. After the audio has been sent, the caller simply hangs up. For a sporting event or other remote broadcast, the remote site talent sends audio to the studio and the studio can send cues and other information to the remote site.

The ISDN Transmission System

ISDN is a digital "switched" international telecommunications network that carries voice and data over existing telephone net-

Figure 13.2

A studio ISDN codec serves as the interface between the station's control boards and the remote audio sources. The station can send and receive full-frequency digital audio to and from other locations.

works for point-to-point audio delivery. The term "switched" indicates that an ISDN line is assigned a telephone number and that calls are routed just like with POTS.

ISDN lines are designed to carry large amounts of data. The typical installation in a radio station uses a unit that provides two channels of 64-kilobit-per-second data for audio and one channel, at 16 kilobits per second, for data. All three channels are delivered on one standard telephone pair, or wire.

ISDN is a full-duplex service and delivers digital audio in both directions simultaneously. This is accomplished by using one of the audio channels in a send mode and the other channel in the receive mode. For example, during a sports broadcast the announcers can carry on a conversation with the in-studio announcer over the ISDN line and both can be on the air at the same time. The data channel is used primarily to carry telephone network signaling data.

An ISDN line requires a codec at each end. The codec is plugged in just like a telephone and has a telephone dial pad on the front (see Fig. 13.2). The codec serves as the interface between the station's control boards and the remote audio sources. ISDN codecs use standardized algorithms for transferring digital-audio data. The more popular ones are G.722, G.711, and MPEG-Layer 2 and 3 audio coding.

Because ISDN uses a dial-up line, the rates for the service are quite reasonable (you only pay for what you use).

Benefits of ISDN

ISDN lines are widely available and are quite common at sports stadiums. ISDN offers two-way, studio-quality, audio transmission from point to point on an as-needed basis. It is particularly useful for transferring liners and sweepers from voice talent, voice-tracking radio shows, and transmitting live sporting events or remote broadcasts. ISDN is much less expensive than leasing satellite time for such events, and much more portable. Using standardized audio-coding algorithms, like G.722, the various brands of codecs can talk to one another to exchange audio.

Although Internet or e-mail delivery of single commercials or promos works quite well, ISDN is better suited for longer-form audio transmission. For example, you can establish an ISDN link with the station's voice talent and coach him or her through a liner session as you listen. It is like having the voice talent in the studio with you.

Even though the ISDN lines are relatively inexpensive, it should be noted that ISDN codecs are priced in the $3,000–$5,000-dollar range.

HD Radio: AM and FM In-Band-On-Channel (IBOC) Digital Transmission

The analog technology used in AM and FM broadcasting remained essentially unchanged for more than fifty years. With the rapid development of digital audio, however, it was only a matter of time before a digital transmission system was developed to deliver high-quality digital AM and FM broadcast signals. The system, called high definition or "HD Radio," was developed by iBiquity Digital Corporation and approved by the FCC for implementation in late 2002.

HD Radio is the marketing term for IBOC, which is short for "in-band-on-channel." An HD Radio signal uses an AM or FM radio station's existing FCC-assigned frequency (in band) and bandwidth (on channel). The system offers a number of advantages to broadcasters and consumers alike, the first of these being greatly improved audio quality. In addition to traditional stereo transmissions, HD Radio offers the option to transmit 5.1 surround sound.

A second major advantage of HD Radio digital transmission is backward and forward compatibility using present AM and FM radio station frequencies. A radio station converting to HD Radio continues to broadcast its present analog signal for as long as necessary. Consumers can continue to listen to their favorite stations until they choose to buy a digital radio. The analog/digital changeover is similar to when television made the transition from black-and-white to color.

HD Radio transmission opened the door, not only to high-quality audio, but to a whole new range of digital information and entertainment services that stations can offer. Sophisticated data-compression techniques further enhance this ability, allowing more data to be transmitted within the original bandwidth of an AM or FM station.

Such data services include text displays on the radio or on a display screen in a car's back seat, providing listeners more information about the song that is playing or allowing the station to pass along information services such as weather, traffic, sports, and news. Stations can offer these additional data services free or on a subscription basis. Other possibilities include listener-controlled, on-demand, main-channel audio services that permit listeners to store the radio signal and then fast-forward, rewind, pause, or play back the signal, using a built-in program guide transmitted by the station. Another possible HD Radio use is transmitting secondary audio services to the main channel. Needless to say, text advertising can also be sent to the radio's display, so that when listeners hear a phone number in an ad, they see it on the display.

The HD Radio Transmission System

AM and FM HD Radio transmission systems are very much alike. Both systems simultaneously transmit an analog and digital audio signal as well as data services. To create an HD Radio signal, a station's analog transmitter is equipped with a device to combine and piggyback the analog audio, digital audio, and data signal onto the radio station's frequency. In the simplest of terms, a "hybrid" analog/digital signal is created. At some point in the future, when most people have converted to digital radios, a station may choose to discontinue transmitting the analog signal. To go deeper into the complex technical aspects of the HD Radio signal transmission is beyond the scope of this text.

The average cost to upgrade a radio station to an HD Radio hybrid analog/digital signal is approximately somewhere between $75,000 and $300,000, provided the station has a recently manufactured transmitter. Older transmitters must be replaced, since they are not capable of transmitting the sophisticated analog/digital hybrid signal.

There is no mandatory implementation date for HD Radio; the changeover is occurring gradually as each station sees the benefits to be gained from the conversion to HD Radio. However, the technology used to transmit the signal is like a moving target. The technology used to transmit the signal today is likely going to change in the future as we develop better methods to transmit the digital data.

HD Radio System Benefits

There are a number of major benefits to be gained by stations converting to the HD Radio digital-transmission system; chief among them is audio quality. Traditional analog AM and FM audio quality is dependent on the bandwidth of the radio signal. Digital signals do not require as much bandwidth as do present analog signals, so it is easier to transmit a high-quality digital audio signal.

AM HD Radio provides FM-like audio quality, giving the once-nearly-forgotten band a new life. An additional benefit for AM, thanks to new sophisticated radios, is that the static and noise that were once common on the AM band are eliminated. Likewise, FM HD Radio signals provide improved, CD-like quality.

HD radios use digital processors and powerful algorithms to provide improved reception by electronically sorting through all the incoming signals. By intelligently selecting the most powerful signals, noise, static, and distortion can be eliminated under most conditions.

Competitive Benefits of HD Radio

There are at least five major competitive benefits to be gained when a station switches to HD Radio. Firstly, the station gains the technical improvements in the station's audio quality and the marketing strategy that labels the station as High Definition. Secondly, the ability to transmit data services offers opportunities to increase radio station income from new, nontraditional, revenue sources. Thirdly, intelligent receivers improve reception and eliminate the common problems of static, noise, and distortion; possibly improving and increasing audience ratings. Fourthly, HD Radio offers growth opportunities for broadcasters, retailers, automobile dealers, and aftermarket stereo shops to partner and sell new radio products using radio advertising. Fifthly, the improved digital audio quality allows land-based radio stations to compete more effectively for listeners against digital satellite radio companies whose big selling point is "digital quality."

Software-Defined Radios

Software-defined radios **(SDR)**, although related to HD Radio, are stand-alone products designed to receive either analog or digital radio signals.

In a traditional radio design, the received radio signal is routed through a number of different electrical circuits before you ever hear it. The design of the radio's internal components is extremely critical, since they are processing the high-frequency radio waves.

Software-defined radios, on the other hand, rather than being filled with a number of different circuits as traditional radios are, have as few as two microprocessor chips, each smaller than a quarter. Essentially, a software-defined radio is a small computer designed to decode radio signals with incredible accuracy. A software-defined radio receives a radio signal and immediately converts the signal into digital data at the input of the radio. The radio's software processes the data and extracts the usable radio signals, eliminating noise, static, and interference from other radio stations.

Because the radio is designed around software, it can be included in many computer-based devices that you would not normally think of as having a radio, such as your PDA (personal digital assistant) or cell phone.

HD Radio Production, a New Dimension

High-definition radio production presents a whole new set of challenges, particularly to AM radio. For the first time, an FM listener has CD-like quality and an AM listener has near-FM-like quality. With new HD radios and high-quality factory-auto-sound systems, the listener is able to hear with clarity what he or she have been missing up until now. For the first time, the listener can hear what you hear in the studio. Suddenly, it is more important than ever to be aware of audio quality.

The Challenges of HD Radio Production

For FM broadcasters, the leap to HD is not that severe if they have a modern digital facility. However, if ever there were a case to apply the old computer adage "garbage in equals garbage out," this is it. Heavy audio process-

ing such as compression, limiting, and sloppy equalization are not only going to be noticed, but annoying. Poor audio quality becomes a valid reason for a listener to tune out.

For AM radio, the change to HD is much more dramatic. In some cases, stations have to be completely rewired for digital stereo audio. Keep in mind that for over eighty years, AM radio was limited to broadcasting only those audio frequencies between 50 Hz and 7,500 kHz, or about half the human hearing range. For years, AM broadcasters didn't really worry too much about full-frequency audio quality. It wasn't necessary. Often, the mantra regarding AM audio quality was "don't worry, it's just AM." HD radio provides AM with a dramatic change in audio quality, an entirely new sound, and one that is going to make AM stations more competitive with FM.

HD radio is a moving target. As the technology continues to develop, stations will have to improve their audio quality to keep up with the demand from consumers with high-quality radios. Although most stations are going to be satisfied with a stereo HD startup, there are those stations that will make the leap to 5.1 HD surround sound as it develops.

Mixing Production in 5.1 Surround Sound

Radio has the DVD to thank for the popularity of 5.1 surround sound. In a consumer-driven digital-audio marketplace, there are numerous 5.1 home theater audio systems available for less than $350 that produce impressive results and generate consumer demand for the recorded product. With the first high-quality DVD-A players now in cars, the logical extension is 5.1 surround sound HD Radio.

Producing and mixing in 5.1 surround sound is different in several ways from mixing in stereo. The goal is to produce a more lifelike sound field or image—to create realism, a feeling of being there. Surround sound creates a more realistic acoustic image than stereo by increasing the number of channels and speakers on which those channels are played back. A 5.1 surround system has five channels of full-range audio, from 20 Hz to 20 kHz; the five channels are the left front, center front, right front, left rear, and right rear. The sixth channel, or the .1 channel, is the LFE (Low Frequency Effects or Enhancement) channel, which has a limited frequency response (20 Hz to 90 Hz or 120 Hz to 150 Hz, depending on the system).

In a 5.1 surround sound recording, the front left, center, and right speakers typically carry the bulk of the audio to create the width of the sound field. The two rear channels add depth to the sound field, using both the natural ambient sounds present when the recording was made and any electronic reverb or delays that have been added. In other words, imagine yourself seated in row ten, center, at a concert, and mix to create that feeling.

An alternative school of thought puts the listener in the very center of the musical performance, with the instruments and players situated around them; yet another puts the listener in the conductor's position. How you mix 5.1 surround sound has a lot to do with your perception of reality, or how you want people to perceive reality. Just as with stereo mixes, try to avoid the urge to put five different people in the five different possible locations of the surround-sound field. Although 5.1 surround sound is well established, there are no hard and fast rules of what should go where when it comes to sonic positioning in 5.1 surround sound.

Digital Satellite Radio Services

Digital satellite radio services are an alternative to **terrestrial-based** AM and FM radio stations. There are several major differences between satellite radio services and terrestrial-based radio stations, the primary one being that satellite services charge a monthly subscription fee. There are two major satellite radio service providers: XM Satellite Radio and Sirius Satellite Radio.

The Digital Satellite Radio Transmission System

The satellite transmission system starts with a typical on-air studio. Instead of feeding an AM or FM transmitter, though, the studio's digital signal feeds a satellite modulator. The modulator generates the ultra-high-frequency signal (gigahertz) that transmits the audio to a series of satellites in **geo-synchronous orbit** (the satellites remain in a stationary position with respect to the earth) 22,000 miles above the United States. The satellites retransmit the digital signals back down to earth in a broad **footprint,** or coverage area (see Fig. **13.3**).

To receive a typical satellite signal, a reflective dish is required to pick up and focus the weak signal. Digital satellite radio services use very high-power transmitters so that only a small antenna, which can easily be mounted on a car or in a portable radio, is required. Radios capable of receiving digital satellite radio services can also receive terrestrial AM and FM signals. Although we typically think of satellite-based radio as being in an auto, there are also portable satellite radios and units designed for the home.

Text in image:

SATELLiTE RADiO

Two Boeing 702 Satellites beam XM directly to listeners

ROLL

ROCK

Terrestrial Repeater

XM Headquarters
1500 Eckington Place NE,
Washington, DC 20002

Choose up to 100 channels of programming

AM/FM/XM radios and small antenna receive XM seamlessly from coast to coast

© 2001 XM Satellite Radio Inc. All rights reserved.

Figure 13.3

Digital satellite radio signals travel thousands of miles before reaching your car or home. Thanks to very high-power satellite transmitters, only a small antenna, which can easily be mounted on a car or in a portable radio, is required.

A question that often arises concerns what happens when a satellite-radio-equipped car goes under a bridge or into a tunnel: Can the car's antenna "see" the satellite (receive the signal)? This is actually not a problem, because satellite radios receive the digital signal and store several seconds of it in a storage or buffer area of the radio before playing it back. When a car passes under a bridge, the radio continues to play the signal stored in the buffer and then catches up to the satellite once the car emerges from under the bridge. This is done seamlessly, and the listener is not aware of what is happening. (In long tunnels or parking garages, loss of signal is possible, in which case the listener can switch to terrestrial AM/FM signals. However, in a tunnel or under a large mass of concrete and steel, such as a bridge, even terrestrial-based signals may not come in well.)

Competitive Benefits of Digital Satellite Radio

Both of the satellite radio providers feature a large number of music channels mixed with numerous channels of news, talk, and information programming. In addition to over 100 channels of basic service, providers are offering "premium" channels, such as the Playboy Radio Channel, for which there is an additional monthly charge.

When originally conceived, there was great debate about how fast satellite radio would outdate terrestrial-based AM and FM radio stations. The reality has turned out to be that they are two different broadcast services serving two different needs. Each service has a number of advantages and disadvantages. The primary disadvantage of satellite radio is that listeners must pay for something that traditionally, for over eighty years, has been free.

Satellite-based digital radio offers the distinct advantage of being able to broadcast to the entire continental United States. From the listeners' perspective, this allows them to enjoy the same channel as they travel, no matter where they go. For people who travel a lot, like truck drivers, this is a valuable service. For that same reason, however—just *because* the satellite radio services are national radio services—they are not capable of offering detailed local programming such as the local personalities, news, and sports that listeners often enjoy during morning and afternoon drive times. To overcome this disadvantage, satellite providers are now providing weather and traffic report channels in a limited number of major metropolitan areas.

The satellite services were the first to broadcast high-fidelity digital signals. This is a big selling point of satellite radio. However, with the advent of HD Radio digital-transmission systems, terrestrial AM and FM stations can remain competitive. Prices for satellite radios are comparable to prices for standard AM/FM stereo radios. In addition, car manufacturers include satellite-equipped radios in many models as a standard feature.

As to whether satellite or terrestrial radio is "better," the answer to that question ultimately lies with the consumer.

Analog Radio Transmission Methods

HD Radio is taking the industry in a new direction technically. And although the basics of radio transmission might not be interesting to everyone, here they are for those who want to know how a traditional analog radio signal gets from point A to point B. (Remember, it is the analog signal onto which the HD digital signal is piggybacked.) The following is a

Radio Frequency Bands

| AM Radio Band | Short Wave and Mobile Radio Services | VHF TV Channels 2–6 | FM Radio Band | VHF TV Channels 7–13 | Microwave Frequencies |

540–1600 kHz,
106 Possible Positions
on the Radio Dial

88.1–108.1 mHz,
100 Possible Positions
on the Radio Dial

Figure 13.4

The small chart above shows how the AM and FM radio bands relate to other frequencies in the radio frequency spectrum. A complete chart of all available radio frequencies is quite extensive and requires a large wall chart to display properly. Such charts are available for purchase from the FCC.

rather nontechnical discussion of the AM and FM transmission methods upon which HD Radio is based.

AM Transmission

Transmitting a radio signal involves attaching, or superimposing, an audio signal onto a much-higher-frequency electromagnetic wave, called a radio-frequency **carrier wave.** Although very few people realize it, the carrier wave is the frequency or dial position of a radio station. The process of superimposing audio onto the carrier wave is called **modulation.** There are two common forms of modulation or attaching an audio signal onto a radio wave: AM and FM.

AM radio was the first method of transmitting radiotelephony, or voice signals, and was developed over a hundred years ago. AM is the abbreviation for amplitude modulation. If you remember from chapter 2, the term *ampli-*

tude refers to the height of a sine wave. The term *modulation* means change. Modulating, or changing, the amplitude of a radio-frequency carrier wave creates an AM radio signal.

The "standard" AM radio band in the United States is between 535 kHz and 1605 kHz (see Fig. **13.4**). The FCC assigned 540 kHz as the first radio station in the band; the last station is at 1600 kHz. Stations are separated by 10 kHz intervals across the band. For example, the first station is at 540 kHz, the next is at 550 kHz, then 560 kHz, and so forth. The FCC coordinates and assigns all of the frequencies to avoid interference.

In addition to the "standard" AM broadcast band, the FCC has assigned the extreme upper and lower areas of the AM band for specific purposes. On the low end of the band, 530 kHz is assigned to AM travelers' information services. On the high end of the band, 1590 through 1700 kHz are assigned to a class of regional stations.

Audio Sine Wave

Sound from
Microphone

Carrier Wave
Created by the
Transmitter

Amplitude
Modulator

Amplitude **M**odulated Radio
Wave or AM Radio Signal

Figure 13.5

AM radio uses the image of the audio sine wave to modulate, or vary, the amplitude (height) of the AM carrier wave. When the AM radio signal arrives at the receiver, the radio's circuitry detects the carrier wave and demodulates the signal. The demodulation process separates the audio from the constantly changing carrier wave and sends the audio to the radio's amplifier and speaker.

An AM transmitter generates a high-power, radio-frequency carrier wave on the channel, or frequency, assigned by the FCC, such as 740 kHz. The carrier wave is so named because it is used to carry the audio to the radio receiver. A silent radio carrier is unmodulated, or unchanged, from its original state.

To broadcast audio on an AM station, the audio signal from the station's control board is sent to the modulator in the transmitter. The modulator uses the rapid changes of the audio signal's amplitude to modulate, or change, the amplitude of the high-power carrier wave. The modulator superimposes the audio onto the powerful carrier wave that is sent to the station's transmitting antenna. The amplitude of the carrier wave becomes identical to, and tracks with, the amplitude of the original audio signal (see Fig. **13.5**).

When the AM radio signal arrives at the receiver, the radio's circuitry detects the carrier wave and demodulates the signal. The demodulation process separates the audio from the carrier and sends the audio to the radio's amplifier and speaker.

AM radio broadcasts with a limited audio-frequency response because of the narrow bandwidth assigned to each station by the FCC. AM radio is limited to transmitting the audio frequencies between 50 Hz and 7,500 Hz, or about half of the human hearing range. Because of this limited audio-frequency response, AM does not have the bright, open sound of FM. Another drawback to the radio frequencies in the AM band is that they are subject to atmospheric noise and static from a number of sources, especially lightning.

Typically, an AM radio station broadcasts a single channel of audio (monaural). Although a number of methods of broadcasting AM stereo were developed in the early 1990s, broadcasters and receiver manufacturers never agreed upon an industry standard.

An AM radio station antenna is the radio tower itself, or a set of vertical cables mounted just off the face of the tower and running parallel to it. AM radio station towers are energized with high voltage and are dangerous. The tower is insulated at its base and where the guy wires connect to the tower. *NEVER* go inside the safety fence at the base of a tower when it is energized, unless the station engineer escorts you. Under some conditions, high levels of radio frequency power can be encountered near the tower and can be hazardous to your health. The technical term for radio-frequency energy is nonionizing radiation. In simplest terms, it's like walking into a microwave oven. Observe all safety precautions and warning signs (see Fig. **13.6**).

Figure 13.6

Although you cannot see or feel radio waves, under some conditions, high levels of radio-frequency power can be encountered near a radio tower. Such high levels of power can be hazardous to your health and you should obey all safety signs.

Classes of AM Stations

AM radio stations are classified by the FCC into four power and frequency classifications, labeled Class A through D, on *local, regional,* and *clear channels.* Such classes allow a maximum number of stations to serve the country without interfering with one another.

Local channels are assigned by the FCC to stations that are intended to serve their community of license and a limited area around it. Local channels are limited to a maximum power of 1,000 watts. Local stations may remain on at full power during the nighttime hours.

Regional channels are assigned by the FCC to stations that are intended to serve larger geographic areas. A regional channel operates with higher transmitter power at night, provided the station uses a directional antenna to aim the signal in a specific direction to prevent interference with other stations.

Clear channels (no relation to the company) are assigned to only a few, select radio stations that the FCC classes as "dominant." A typical clear-channel station has a maximum power of 50 kilowatts (50,000 watts) and, using an omnidirectional antenna, provides nighttime service to a 750-mile radius from the station. The maximum number of clear-channel stations assigned to a single frequency is two. In such cases, the two stations are located great distances from one another to prevent interference. Examples of clear channel-stations include WGN, Chicago; WCBS, New York; and KFI, Los Angeles.

Groundwave Propagation

An AM radio station signal can travel much farther than an FM signal because of the radio frequencies and antenna designs involved. An AM radio signal travels over the earth's surface primarily by conduction. The technical term for the signal's groundhugging ability is **groundwave propagation.** Daytime AM signal coverage is usually limited by the FCC to 100 miles for the most powerful stations.

Skywave Propagation

As the sun starts to go down, AM radio signals begin to travel great distances, thanks to a phenomenon called **skywave propagation.** This occurs as the long wavelengths of the AM signals interact with the radically shifting layers of the ionosphere several miles above the earth's surface. The phenomenon starts at sunset and continues through the night. AM signals often travel hundreds, or thousands, of miles as the signals travel up to the ionosphere and are reflected back down to earth. Because of this phenomenon, some stations have to reduce power, change the direction they transmit in, or go off the air to prevent interference with other stations.

FM Transmission

Edwin Armstrong developed FM radio in the early 1930s. Due to a series of patent fights with RCA (which Armstrong eventually won), the implementation of FM broadcasting was delayed at least twenty years.

The FM radio band in the United States includes the frequencies from 88 mHz to 108 mHz and is located between channels 6 and 7 in the television broadcast band (again, see Fig. **13.4**). The FCC assigned 88.1 mHz as the first radio station in the band; the last station is at 107.9 mHz. Stations are separated by 200 kHz intervals across the band. For example, the first station is at 88.1 mHz, the next is at 88.3 mHz, then 88.5 mHz, and so forth. There is room for 100 channels in the FM band. The FCC assigns the channels to radio stations based on location and power to prevent interference with other stations.

FM is the abbreviation for frequency modulation. Rather than modulate the amplitude of the radio carrier wave, as in AM broadcasting, FM modulates, or changes, the frequency of the carrier wave. An FM transmitter generates a high-power, radio-frequency carrier wave (the carrier-wave frequency is the channel assigned by the FCC, such as 88.1 mHz). When looked at on an oscilloscope, the unmodulated sine waves of the radio carrier appear identical in amplitude and frequency (see Fig. **13.7**).

To broadcast audio on an FM station, the audio signal from the station's control board is sent to the modulator or, as it is often referred to, the "FM exciter." The modulator uses the variations in the amplitude of the audio signal to modulate the frequency of the high-power carrier wave being sent to the station's transmitting antenna. As the audio's amplitude varies up and down, the modulator tracks it and changes the frequency of the carrier wave slightly above or below the station's carrier frequency. The maximum change permitted by the FCC in the carrier frequency is 75 kHz above or below the carrier.

FM Radio Transmission

Audio Sine Wave

Sound from
Microphone

FM Exciter
(modulator)

Carrier Wave
Created by the
Transmitter

Frequency Modulated Radio
Wave or FM Radio Signal

Figure 13.7

The FM exciter uses the image of the audio sine wave to modulate, or vary, the frequency of the FM carrier wave. When the FM radio signal arrives at the receiver, the radio's circuitry detects the carrier wave and demodulates the signal. The demodulation process separates the audio from the constantly changing carrier wave and sends the audio to the radio's amplifier and speakers.

When the FM radio signal arrives at the receiver, the radio's circuitry detects the carrier wave and demodulates the signal. The demodulation process separates the audio from the carrier and sends the audio to the radio's amplifier and speakers.

Unlike AM radio stations that are spaced closely together on the band, FM radio stations are spaced much farther apart (200 kHz). The wider separation allows FM signals to have a wider bandwidth and thus transmit a wider audio frequency range. FM radio can transmit audio frequencies from 50 Hz to 15,000 Hz, or very close to the average person's complete hearing range. To deliver the additional audio information to a radio receiver for stereo FM (transmitting two audio signals, left and right channel), a sub-carrier is attached to the main radio carrier wave.

Stereo FM broadcasts are not subject to the electrical interference and static experienced by AM broadcasts. FM multipath distortion is one problem that does plague FM broadcasts in mountainous regions or cities with tall buildings. Unlike the AM signal, the FM signal does not have a groundwave that follows the contours of the earth. Instead, an FM signal travels in a straight line until it hits something, like a tall building or the side of a mountain, and is reflected in another direction. Multipath distortion typically occurs in a car radio as the original signal and reflected signals arrive at the car radio at slightly different times. The radio has difficulty receiving

Figure 13.8

An FM antenna is mounted to the side of the tower with the tower serving only as a supporting structure. The two antenna elements pictured above are part of an antenna that can have several elements, depending on the power of the station.

the various signals and the result is an undesirable distortion of the audio's high frequencies. If the car is moving, multipath distortion can cause the radio signal to fade in and out rapidly.

An FM signal is transmitted from an antenna mounted at, or near, the top of a tower (see Fig. **13.8**). The tower is simply a supporting structure for the antenna. However, you should *NEVER* climb an FM tower while the antenna is energized. High levels of radio-frequency power (nonionizing radiation) can be encountered that are hazardous to your health. Due to the higher frequencies involved in FM, it can be even more dangerous than the nonionizing radiation given off by an AM tower. Tower climbing is dangerous. Observe all safety precautions and warning signs when near any FM tower.

Classes of FM Stations

In contrast to an AM signal, which follows the curvature of the earth, an FM signal simply travels in a straight line off into space. The earth's surface curves out of sight about every ninety miles, and so the line-of-sight FM signal path effectively limits the range of a full-power FM station to approximately sixty to ninety miles, depending on terrain.

An FM station operates at its FCC-assigned power twenty-four hours a day. The FCC has established eight different classes of FM stations, based on antenna height above average terrain **(HAAT)** and the effective radiated power **(ERP)** needed to cover a specific geographic or service area. The specific classification of a station is based on a set of complex calculations designed to deliver a specific power level of radio signal at a specific distance from the station's antenna. Because FM signals travel by line-of-sight, the higher the antenna, the further the signal will travel; and the combination of antenna height and power determines how far an FM signal will travel.

As an example, a Class A FM station operates with 6,000 watts of power and an antenna height of up to 100 meters (330 feet). At the other end of the spectrum, a Class C FM station operates with 100,000 watts of power and an antenna height of up to 600 meters (1,980 feet). (Sometimes geography works in a station's favor. For example, a radio station placed its FM transmitter on top of a 5,000-foot-tall mountain. Due to the extreme height, the station was required by the FCC to reduce its power to only 200 watts. Although 200 watts of power is not at all impressive, the height of the antenna more than compensated for the low power. Since there is nothing to block the view of the antenna for many miles, the line-of-sight coverage for the station is excellent.)

Suggested Activities

1. Plan an evening to experience AM sky-wave propagation. Wait until after the sun goes down and, using either a table-model AM radio with an antenna or your car radio, slowly tune the AM band and see how many stations you can identify. Hold a contest to see who can log a station from the longest distance.

2. Contact the director of engineering for a local radio station and arrange an engineering tour of both an AM and FM radio station. Find out how each is handling the changeover from an analog to digital transmission system in its physical plant.

3. Download from the Internet a free shareware copy of an FTP server and client program. After loading them on your computer and that of another, try exchanging an audio file with each other.

4. Using the MP3 codec that came with Cool Edit Pro, practice converting audio files to the MP3 format and playing them back again. With your personal web page or one that you have permission to use, practice posting an audio file on the web site and downloading it.

5. Create a one-minute audio file; then compress it, using an MP3 codec. Attach the compressed file to e-mail and send it to a friend. Keep in mind that the e-mail and attached file might be too large for some e-mail providers to handle. Try several until you can send one successfully.

Web Sites for More Information

For more information on:

- *File Transfer Protocol*, visit Ipswitch, Inc., at www.ipswitch.com or www.ftpplanet.com

- *HD Radio*, visit iBiquity at www.ibiquity.com

- *ISDN*, visit Telos Systems at www.telos-systems.com

- *mp3PRO*, visit Thomson Multimedia at www.mp3licensing.com

- *MPEG Audio Layer-2 and MPEG Audio Layer-3*, visit Fraunhofer IIS at http://www.iis.fraunhofer.de

- *satellite-based radio services*, visit XM Satellite Radio at www.xmradio.com or Sirius at www.sirius.com

- *skywave and groundwave propagation*, visit the Federal Communications Commission at www.fcc.gov

- *software-defined radios*, visit Blaupunkt Radio at www.blaupunktusa.com

Pro Speak

You should be able to use these terms in your everyday conversations with other professionals.

AM—The abbreviation for amplitude modulation. The AM radio band extends from 535 kHz to 1605 kHz.

bandwidth—With reference to a radio carrier wave, bandwidth is the space on the radio band occupied by the radio carrier-wave frequency and the audio that has been superimposed upon it. The superimposed audio signal widens the radio carrier by adding sidebands just above and below the assigned carrier frequency. The carrier wave and the upper and lower sidebands of the signal compose the bandwidth of a signal.

carrier wave—The high-frequency radio wave transmitted by a radio or television station that has been amplitude or frequency modulated.

ERP—An abbreviation for effective radiated power. When applied to an FM station, the term specifies in watts how much power the station can use to transmit its signal, as measured at the antenna.

FM—The abbreviation for frequency modulation. The FM radio band extends from 88 mHz to 108 mHz.

footprint—A satellite signal's geographic coverage area on earth.

geo-synchronous orbit—An orbit that places a satellite approximately 22,000 miles above the earth so that it rotates at the same speed as the earth, maintaining a fixed position in space.

groundwave propagation—The property of physics that allows amplitude-modulated radio carrier signals to follow the earth's surface through conduction.

HAAT—Abbreviation for height above average terrain. Applied to an FM radio station, the term specifies in meters the height of the station's transmitting antenna above the average terrain that surrounds it.

modulation—Change; in this case, the process of changing a silent carrier with either amplitude or frequency modulation.

SDR—Abbreviation for software-defined radio. A radio that converts the incoming radio signal into a digital data stream and then processes the data to extract the usable signals.

skywave propagation—A phenomenon that occurs as the long wavelengths of the AM signals interact with the radically shifting layers of the ionosphere several miles above the earth's surface at night, causing AM signals to travel great distances.

T-1—The technical designation for a direct-leased Internet connection that is capable of transferring 1.544 megabits of data per second.

T-3—The technical designation for a direct-leased Internet connection that is capable of transferring 44.736 megabits of data per second.

terrestrial-based—Fancy term for earth-based.

CHAPTER 14

Programming, Production, and Measuring Success

Radio is under attack. As we have discussed repeatedly in the previous chapters, it keeps surviving, but that doesn't mean it isn't still under attack. In case you hadn't noticed, the digital age is bringing an onslaught of electronic devices to the marketplace. Each new technology, and the convergence it brings, is a challenge to radio, an opportunity to steal away some of radio's audience. What do you call a handheld device that has a miniature keyboard, liquid-crystal display, handles your e-mail, text messaging, paging, stores the names and addresses of your hundred closest friends, stores and plays mp3 music files, lets you download and play video games, has an FM radio and a built-in camera, and lets you make phone calls? The cell phone being described is just one example of the incredible convergence of technology that is continuing to evolve.

Radio is under attack from every eighteen- to twenty-four-year-old who likely has more music stored on his or her computer than the average radio station has in its entire music library. Most portable MP3 players hold more music than a radio station can play in a day, and young people are turning to technology to give them the music rotation they want when they want it. Radio no longer has the stranglehold it once had on presenting new music or being the driving force behind music. What's worse is that this group of young people is soon going to move up into the eighteen- to forty-nine-year-old age group that advertisers spend big bucks to reach through radio.

Although we may be impressed with the technology, one thing remains clear: It is not digital technology we listen to; what we listen to are the people and the programming that *use* the technology to deliver their messages. To succeed with a new generation, radio is going to have to return to its roots of presenting entertaining personalities and delivering real-time interaction with listeners, something an MP3 player or web connection can't do. And although satellite-delivered radio signals are impressive, they are not local and cannot interact with local listeners.

That is where you come in. As a production person, you are not only going to be involved in production, but you are going to be a part of the team of people that has to develop the next generation of radio to appeal to young people. The kind of personality-based entertainment radio that is going to dominate the medium in the next few years requires lots of production. As a part of this transformation, you are going to get to help create, develop, and carry out your radio station's program format.

As a production person, you need to understand that programming a radio station is not based on someone's hunches, guesses, or feelings. Programming is based upon a mix of quantitative and qualitative research, including tools like **psychographic** or lifestyle research. Programming involves talented individuals who are capable of interpreting this data, developing a unique format, and selecting, motivating, and coaching on-air talent. It is not an easy job.

The success or failure of a radio station in a rated market is measured by its Arbitron audience ratings. Businesses, ad agencies, and competitors use the ratings as a benchmark to judge your station's success by. This is not necessarily so in smaller markets where the measure of success comes directly from the experience of the business community. If Bob's Hardware bought ads on your station and it sold all the widgets it was advertising, you have a great radio station.

It is important that a production person understand programming and ratings, as they work closely with the PD, promotions department, and sales on many projects. Producers get a lot of guidance and cues from these people because the creative product they are asked to create has to fit within the station's programming, positioning, and branding concepts.

Arbitron Audience Ratings

Two words that strike fear into even the bravest of radio souls are "the book." This is an element of the business that no one in the radio station can control, except by doing the best possible job. It is not necessary that a production person be able to explain all of the ratings data and do detailed audience-number breakouts. But, it is important that you understand the basic terms and what the ratings mean, because they will become a part of your daily working vocabulary in the industry.

The Arbitron Company conducts audience research several times a year (depending on market size). Typically, if the radio station is in one of the approximately 250 designated market areas, the station is rated four times a year, based on audience research conducted during a twelve-week-long survey period. In nearly 100 larger markets, Arbitron research is carried out on a continuous, year-round basis. At the end of each survey period, the ratings book is issued to the subscribing stations. In addition to the printed hard copy of the book, many stations subscribe to a computer service from Arbitron called Tapscan that, among other things, provides an electronic copy of the materials and detailed market analysis.

The actual survey is a very serious piece of research (see Fig. **14.1**). In many markets, the data it contains is a major factor in determining how well the radio station will be able to sell advertising. The data is not difficult to

comprehend if you understand the three basic types of audience estimates being reported: Average Quarter-Hour, Cume, and Time Spent Listening.

Average Quarter-Hour

The first audience estimate, Average Quarter-Hour, is itself comprised of three individual rankings: the Average Quarter-Hour (AQH) Persons, AQH Rating, and AQH Shares (again, see Fig. **14.1**). The Average Quarter-Hour Persons is the estimated number of people listening to a particular radio station for at least five minutes during any quarter-hour period in a specific daypart. The estimate is broken down into Arbitron's standardized demographic age groups and dayparts, including weekdays and weekends. Among the standard age groupings are persons 18–34, 18–49, 25–49, 25–54, and 35–64. The age groupings also are further broken down into men and women. The AQH Persons estimate helps advertisers determine how many potential people can hear their radio ad in any given fifteen-minute time period.

The Average Quarter-Hour Rating is the estimated number of radio station listeners expressed as a percent of the total population of the measured survey area in any quarter-hour period in a specific daypart (see Fig. **14.1**). Each percent is referred to as a rating point. To arrive at the Average Quarter-Hour Rating, Arbitron uses the following formula:

$$\frac{\text{Average Quarter-Hour Persons}}{\text{Survey Area Population}} \times 100$$
$$= \text{Average Quarter-Hour Rating}$$

This estimate is broken down into the standard demographic age groups and dayparts, including weekdays and weekends. The Average Quarter-Hour Rating tells advertisers the estimated percent of the total population in

Sections of the Arbitron Radio Market Report

The Listener Estimates

Target Listener Trends

Persons 12+

	Monday-Sunday 6AM-MID				Monday-Friday 6AM-10AM				Monday-Friday 10AM-3PM				Monday-Fri 3PM-7P		
	AQH (00)	Cume (00)	AQH Rtg	AQH Shr	AQH (00)	Cume (00)	AQH Rtg	AQH Shr	AQH (00)	Cume (00)	AQH Rtg	AQH Shr	AQH (00)	Cume (00)	
WAAA-FM															
SP '01	118	1731	1.9	9.9	167	1118	2.6	10.8	177	923	2.8	10.8	165	1172	
WI '01	123	1980	1.9	10.1	155	908	2.4	9.6	186	1064	2.9	10.9	152	1115	
FA '00	101	2120	1.6	9.0	110	1110	1.7	7.2	130	1207	2.0	8.8	130	1312	
SU '00	115	2238	1.8	9.3	144	1233	2.2	9.3	144	1202	2.2	8.4	148	1264	
4-Book	114	2017	1.8	9.6	144	1092	2.2	9.2	159	1099	2.5	9.7	149	1216	
SP '00	126	2259	2.0	10.5	172	1272	2.7	11.1	193	1207	3.0	11.7	153	1492	
WBBB-FM															
SP '01	118	1731	1.9	9.9	167	1118	2.6	10.8	177	923	2.8	10.8	165	1172	
WI '01	123	1980	1.9	10.1	155	908	2.4	9.6	186	1064	2.9	10.9	152	1115	
FA '00	101	2120	1.6	9.0	110	1110	1.7	7.2	130	1207	2.0	8.8	148	1312	
SU '00	115	2238	1.8	9.3	144	1233	2.2	9.3	144	1202	2.2	8.4	148	1264	
4-Book	114	2017	1.8	9.6	144	1092	2.2	9.2	159	1099	2.5	9.7	149	1216	
SP '00	126	2259	2.0	10.5	172	1272	2.7	11.1	193	1207	3.0	11.7	153	1492	
WCCC-FM															
SP '01	118	1731	1.9	9.9	167	908	2.6	10.8	177	923	2.8	10.8	165	1172	
WI '01	123	1980	1.9	10.1	155	908	2.4	9.6	186	1064	2.9	10.9	152	1115	
FA '00	101	2120	1.6	9.0	110	1110	1.7	7.2	130	1207	2.0	8.8	130	1312	
SU '00	115	2238	1.8	9.3	144	1233	2.2	9.3	144	1202	2.2	8.4	148	1264	
4-Book	114	2017	1.8	9.6	144	1092	2.2	9.2	159	1099	2.5	9.7	149	1216	
SP '00	126	2259	2.0	10.5	172	1272	2.7	11.1	193	1207	3.0	11.7	153	1492	
WDDD-FM															
SP '01	118	1731	1.9	9.9	167	1118	2.6	10.8	177	923	2.8	10.8	152	1115	
WI '01	123	1980	1.9	10.1	155	908	2.4	9.6	186	1064	2.9	10.9	152	1115	
FA '00	101	2120	1.6	9.0	110	1110	1.7	7.2	130	1207	2.0	8.8	130	1312	
SU '00	115	2238	1.8	9.3	144	1233	2.2	9.3	144	1202	2.2	8.4	148	1264	
4-Book	114	2017	1.8	9.6	144	1092	2.2	9.2	159	1099	2.5	9.7	149	1216	
SP '00	126	2259	2.0	10.5	172	1272	2.7	11.1	193	1207	3.0	11.7	153	1492	
WEEE-FM															
SP '01	118	1731	1.9	9.9	167	1118	2.6	10.8	177	923	2.8	10.8	152	1115	
WI '01	123	1980	1.9	10.1	155	908	2.4	9.6	186	1064	2.9	10.9	152	1115	
FA '00	101	2120	1.6	9.0	110	1110	1.7	7.2	130	1207	2.0	8.8	130	1312	
SU '00	115	2238	1.8	9.3	144	1233	2.2	9.3	144	1202	2.2	8.4	149	1216	
4-Book	114	2017	1.8	9.6	144	1092	2.2	9.2	159	1099	2.5	9.7	149	1216	
SP '00	126	2259	2.0	10.5	172	1272	2.7	11.1	193	1207	3.0	11.7	153	1492	
WFFF-FM															
SP '01	118	1731	1.9	9.9	167	1118	2.6	10.8	177	923	2.8	10.8	165	1172	
WI '01	123	1980	1.9	10.1	155	908	2.4	9.6	186	1064	2.9	10.9	152	1115	
FA '00	101	2120	1.6	9.0	110	1110	1.7	7.2	130	1207	2.0	8.8	130	1312	
SU '00	115	2238	1.8	9.3	144	1233	2.2	9.3	144	1202	2.2	8.4	148	1264	
4-Book	114	2017	1.8	9.6	144	1092	2.2	9.2	159	1099	2.5	9.7	149	1216	
SP '00	126	2259	2.0	10.5	172	1272	2.7	11.1	193	1207	3.0	11.7	153	1492	
WGGG-FM															
SP '01	118	1731	1.9	9.9	167	1118	2.6	10.8	177	923	2.8	10.8	165	1172	
WI '01	123	1980	1.9	12.1	155	908	2.4	9.6	186	1064	2.9	10.9	152	1115	
FA '00	101	2120	1.6	9.0	110	1110	1.7	7.2	130	1207	2.0	8.8	130	1312	
SU '00	115	2238	1.8	9.3	144	1233	2.2	9.3	144	1202	2.2	8.4	148	1264	
4-Book	114	2017	1.8	9.6	144	1092	2.2	9.2	159	1099	2.5	9.7	149	1216	
SP '00	126	2259	2.0	10.5	172	1272	2.7	11.1	193	1207	3.0	11.7	153	1492	
WHHH-FM															
SP '01	118	1731	1.9	9.9	167	1118	2.6	10.8	177	923	2.8	10.8	165	1172	2.4	10.3	59	657
WI '01	123	1980	1.9	10.1	155	908	2.4	9.6	186	1064	2.9	10.9	152	1115	2.4	10.3	52	657
FA '00	101	2120	1.6	9.0	110	1110	1.7	7.2	130	1207	2.0	8.8	130	1312	2.0	9.5	46	784
SU '00	115	2238	1.8	9.3	144	1233	2.2	9.3	144	1202	2.2	8.4	148	1264	2.3	10.2	51	873
4-Book	114	2017	1.8	9.6	144	1092	2.2	9.2	159	1099	2.5	9.7	149	1216	2.3	10.3	52	708
SP '00	126	2259	2.0	10.5	172	1272	2.7	11.1	193	1207	3.0	11.7	153	1492	2.4	10.2	54	891
TOTALS															
SP '01	118	1731	1.9	9.9	167	1118	2.6	10.8	177	923	2.8	10.8	165	1172	2.6	11.3	59	517	.9	8.3
WI '01	123	1980	1.9	10.1	167	908	2.6	9.6	186	1207	2.9	10.9	165	1115	2.4	10.3	52	657	.8	7.4
FA '00	101	2120	1.6	9.0	110	1110	1.7	7.2	130	1207	2.0	8.8	148	1312	2.0	9.5	46	784	.7	7.8
SU '00	115	2238	1.8	9.3	144	1233	2.2	9.3	144	1202	2.2	8.4	148	1264	2.3	10.2	51	873	.8	6.7
4-Book	114	2017	1.8	9.6	144	1092	2.2	9.2	159	1099	2.5	9.7	149	1216	2.3	10.3	52	708	.8	7.6
SP '00	126	2259	2.0	10.5	172	1272	2.7	11.1	193	1207	3.0	11.7	153	1492	2.4	10.2	54	891	.8	7.3

** Station(s) not reported this survey.

* Listener estimates adjusted for reported broadcast change.

• Station(s) changed call letters - see Page 13.

4-Book: Avg. of current and previous 3 surveys.
2-Book: Avg. of most recent 2 surveys.

SURVEY PERIOD

YOUR MARKET | 15

Target Listener Trends

Report Features, Standard Report

Demos: P12+; Persons, Men and Women 12-24, 18-34, 18-49, 25-49, 25-54, 35-64; and Teens 12-17

Estimates: AQH (00), Cume (00), AQH Rating, AQH Share trends and multibook average

Dayparts: M-S 6A-Mid, M-F 6A-10A, M-F 10A-3P, M-F 3P-7P, M-F 7P-Mid

Report Features, Condensed Report

Demos: P12+; Persons, Men and Women 18-34, 18-49, 25-54, 35-64

Estimates: AQH (00), Cume (00), AQH Rating, AQH Share trends and multibook average

Dayparts: M-S 6A-Mid, M-F 6A-10A, M-F 10A-3P, M-F 3P-7P, M-F 7P-Mid

ARBITRON

Figure 14.1

Although quite detailed in its presentation, the data contained in an Arbitron survey is easy to comprehend providing you understand the three basic types of audience estimates. In many markets, Arbitron ratings are a major factor in determining how well the radio station will be able to sell advertising.

the measured survey area that is listening to your radio station.

The Average Quarter-Hour Share is the estimated number of radio station listeners expressed as a percentage of the people who were listening to the radio in any quarter-hour period in a specific daypart (again, see Fig. **14.1**). The estimate is broken down into the standard demographic age groups and dayparts, including weekdays and weekends. The estimate tells advertisers what percent of the survey area radio audience is tuned into the radio station at any given time.

Cume

The second audience estimate, Cume, is comprised of two different rankings: the Cume Persons, short for cumulative persons, and Cume Ratings (again, see Fig. **14.1**). The Cume Persons are the total estimated number of *different* radio listeners who listened to the radio station for at least five minutes in any quarter-hour period in a specific daypart. No matter how long the listener stayed tuned to the station, the person is only counted *once*. This estimate is broken down into the standard demographic age groups and dayparts, including weekdays and weekends. (In addition, Arbitron provides the Exclusive Cume Persons ranking, which is the estimated number of different listeners in the area who listened to *only one* radio station in a given daypart.)

The Cume Person estimates tell advertisers the total number of different people that listen to the radio station in a given time period, or put a different way, the total number of different people they could reach with their ads. A Cume Rating is also calculated by Arbitron, as a percent of the total survey population.

Time Spent Listening

The last category of the Arbitron audience estimate is Time Spent Listening. This is the number of quarter-hours the *average* person spent listening to the radio station in a given daypart. Obviously, the radio station with the longest Time Spent Listening has a very loyal audience. This estimate tells advertisers what the chances are of the same listener hearing their ad more than once in a given time period.

In addition to the three basic audience estimates, the Arbitron data can be used to develop additional estimates and information valuable to the programming and sales departments. When it comes to the ratings, regardless of the company conducting the research, there has always been a lot of debate among broadcasters about specific survey methods and the number of valid survey participants needed to get accurate results. Although this topic can be endlessly debated from a scientific standpoint, the reality is that advertising agencies, public relations firms, media-buying services, and the radio station's competitors all depend on the Arbitron ratings and use them as a benchmark by which to judge a station's performance.

Music and Format Selection

One of the first programming tools a program director learns about is music. Prior to becoming a program director, a person may have had personal favorites with regard to artists and styles of music. When it comes to the business of radio, though, personal favorites get set to the side. The first thing a program director learns about music is that music is a commodity. As a commodity, music has a shelf life that is dependent on the wants and

With dozens of formats and thousands of Radio stations nationwide, there's a station that's just right for every consumer. In 2003, there are 10,754 commercial Radio stations on the air in the U.S. Below is a list of the most popular Radio formats and their station counts.

Radio Format Analysis

Rank	Format	# Stations
1	Country	2088
2	News/Talk	1224
3	Oldies	807
4	Adult Contemporary	692
5	Hispanic	628
6	Adult Standards	497
7	CHR (Top 40)	491
8	Sports	429
9	Classic Rock	425
10	Hot AC	399
11	Religion (Teaching, Variety)	347
12	Soft Adult Contemporary	336
13	Rock	273
14	Black Gospel	253
15T	Classic Hits	237
15T	Southern Gospel	237
17	R&B	207
18	Modern Rock	189
19	Contemporary Christian	167
20	Urban AC	128
21	Ethnic	102
22	Alternative Rock	99
23	Jazz	90
24	R&B Adult/Oldies	66
25	Gospel	64
26	Pre-Teen	60
27	Modern AC	51
28	Variety	36
29	Classical	32
30	Easy Listening	18
31	Other/Format Not Available	1

Source: M Street Corp.,® 2003

*An additional 149 stations were licensed under construction permits for future broadcast.

Radio

Figure 14.2

The Radio Advertising Bureau (RAB) has the world's largest library of radio industry research. Typically, the top format for radio stations is Country followed by News/Talk. *From the RAB Radio Marketing Guide and Fact Book.*

desires of the customer, or listener. The music's shelf life is based on what is in style and popular. The average song has a life of four to six weeks. Just like any other commodity, music is intended to be bought and sold by the people who produce it. That is how they make their living.

The second thing that a program director learns about music is that music is just one of the tools that a radio station uses to attract listeners. Just as the carpenter selects a specific type of saw to cut a specific type of wood, the program director selects a specific style of music to reach a specific **target audience.** If reaching that target audience requires a particular type or style of music, then that is the tool that gets selected, regardless of whether or not the PD personally likes the music (see Fig. **14.2**).

Sometimes the tool used to attract listeners is not music. There might be a strong demand in a market for a news- or sports-talk format.

Other alternative formats that a station might consider include foreign-language (most notably Spanish-language) programming, religious programming, or ethnic programming, if any of those potential target audiences is not being served. Remember, the PD is seeking to reach a specific target audience, and sometimes that requires some very creative approaches.

Program directors who know their craft can work with just about any format, because they understand the tools they have to work with. They understand that it is their job to research and to become familiar with the target audience and then determine how best to reach that audience and attract them as regular listeners.

Researching a Market

Before the competitive advantages of one format over another in a market can be considered, a PD needs to answer three seemingly simple questions about the market: What do I know about the market? What don't I know about the market? and What do I need or want to know about the market? Each question logically leads to the next.

In the process of answering these questions, a PD discovers that there are three elements in a radio market over which he or she does not have control: the station's coverage area, the area's population, and the number of competitors the station has. These three elements will impact every decision program directors make. Although they cannot control these elements, their best offense against them is an in-depth knowledge of the radio marketplace.

Footprint

The first element a PD has no control over is the radio station's coverage area, or footprint.

The FCC determined the geographic area that the station's signal could reach when the station license was granted, based on a number of technical factors. The station's engineering staff can provide the PD with detailed maps and drawings, showing where the station's signal is strongest and weakest (see Fig. **14.3**). By examining the geographic area with the station's engineer, the PD can better define the market and focus the station research only on the areas that can receive the station's signal.

The station engineers can also show the PD the competing radio stations' coverage areas, including signal strengths and weaknesses. These detailed engineering drawings are a matter of public record and can be obtained from the FCC engineering database for each radio station. This is truly a case where it pays to know your enemy.

Population

The second element that a PD has no control over is the population that lives within the radio station's coverage area. The PD has no control over who moves in and out of the area, or the unique economic, social, or demographic profile of the people who live in the coverage area.

Although PDs can't control the population, they certainly can identify who is in the population through demographic research. This knowledge can be used for a competitive advantage.

Competitors

The third element the PD cannot control is the number of radio stations in the market he or she is competing against. The FCC decides

Figure 14.3

A coverage map is a scientific chart of where the radio station's signal extends to and what quality of signal the listener can expect to receive. The map above shows a 100,000-watt FM radio station at 95.1 mHz. Persons within the coverage area (big circle) should expect to pick up the radio station on just about any kind of radio in any location.

what radio stations go where. Unlike any other type of business, the number of radio stations in a market is controlled and limited. In this respect, the competing businesses are limited in size and number. When conducting format research, most PDs carefully examine every radio station in the market. Depending on the size of the market, it is entirely possible that there is more than one radio station at-

tempting to be successful with the same format. The fact is, if a radio station is extremely successful, someone will launch an assault on the station's market position, hoping to steal some of the station's rating points.

As a PD examines the uncontrollable elements just listed, it is important to keep in mind the PD's three original questions: What do I know about the market? What don't I know about the market? and What do I need or want to know about the market? Market knowledge and competitive intelligence are some of the most serious aspects of programming a radio station.

In-Depth Format Analysis

After all of the data has been gathered and analyzed for a market, it is time to start narrowing the format possibilities. Format analysis begins by brainstorming and making a list of all the possible format options. Format analysis is based around a business model, just as with any other business looking for new customers.

One of the interesting things about radio programming is that what other businesses call customers, the radio industry calls listeners. In reality, though, listeners are customers of what the radio station has to offer. Do listeners and customers get treated differently? Although radio's customers are not going to spend any money with the radio station, they do spend something that is just as valuable—their time. If enough of these customers give the station their time, ratings go up, advertising rates increase, and advertising clients buy more time on the radio station, providing the cash the station needs to succeed in business.

Any business looks for two types of customers. The first is a customer who is not being served by any other business. The second is a group of customers that is not being served well. Following this basic plan, a program director first determines whether there is any group of people within the marketplace that is not being served. The PD is looking for a hole in the marketplace, an audience that the other radio stations have overlooked. The group of people the PD would like to find is one that fits into one of the standardized radio demographic groups, such as adults 25 to 54 or young adults 18 to 34. These are called target demographics or demos. By selecting a demo that fits an accepted industry standard, the target audience is much easier to market and sell to advertisers. The PD also examines the other radio stations in the market for weaknesses, to see whether there are any audiences that are being under-served by another station.

Selling the Target Demographic

With a target demo identified, the PD consults with the station's general manager and sales manager on the next step of the format-selection process, based upon a question: If the station can achieve market dominance or a strong ratings position with the target demo, are there advertisers willing to pay to reach the audience? In other words, what is the monetary value of the selected target demo? The radio station may be able to deliver a huge audience in a particular demographic segment of the population, but are they consumers? What businesses want to talk to the radio station's target demo? Does the target demo buy things, and what do those people buy (see Fig. **14.4**)? These are critical questions that must be answered.

For example, a radio station develops a format appealing to 12-to-17-year-olds and has the highest rating in this target demo in a major metropolitan city. This is fabulous—or is it? Are 12-to-17-year-olds good consumers? What kinds of products and services do they buy? Do 12-to-17-year-olds buy new cars, open bank accounts, use credit cards, consume beer, join health clubs, purchase furniture, take vacations, dine out at nice restaurants, or buy major appliances? All of these

Alternative

Purchasing Behavior
Alternative fans are 33 percent more likely than average to live in a household planning to purchase a new SUV and 31 percent more likely to buy a new compact car in the next 12 months. They spend a little more on groceries per week than the general population.

They are 52 percent more likely than the norm to use home computer banking and 56 percent more likely to use online investing.

Leisure Activities
Alternative listeners are far more likely than the general population to engage in exhilarating leisure activities such as extreme sports (144 percent more likely) and snow-skiing (81 percent more likely). Alternative fans are number one in movie attendance.

Nearly a quarter have eaten at a fast-food restaurant 10+ times in the past 30 days.

Alternative Strengths
This format's listeners are more likely to:

	% of Category Alternative Listeners Represent	% of Alternative Listeners	Index (100= National Average)
Live in a household planning to buy a new SUV in the next 12 months	14.0%	4.3%	133
Live in a household planning to buy a new compact car in the next 12 months	13.8%	1.5%	131
Live in a household that has used online investing in the past 12 months	16.3%	7.6%	156
Live in a household that uses online banking	15.9%	16.3%	152
Live in a household that has spent $200+ on groceries in the past 7 days	11.9%	9.2%	113
Have participated in in-line skating in the past 12 months	21.8%	9.4%	208
Have participated in extreme sports in the past 12 months	25.6%	3.0%	244
Have gone snow-skiing in the past 12 months	19.0%	9.0%	181
Have attended movies 3+ times in the past 3 months	15.6%	29.6%	149
Have eaten at fast-food restaurant 10 or more times in the past 30 days	13.6%	23.9%	130
Have children in household	12.2%	48.1%	116

Note: *Due to rounding, totals may differ.*
Source: *Format definitions are from Scarborough USA, Release 1, 2003.*

29 Radio Today 2004 Edition | © 2004 Arbitron Inc.

Figure 14.4

As a group, listeners of particular music formats exhibit specific trends as consumers. The report above carefully examines those who listen to Alternative rock music. One interesting fact about Alternative listeners is that nearly twenty-five percent have eaten at a fast-food restaurant ten or more times in the last thirty days. Fans of Alternative music are also the number one group in movie attendance. *Radio Today courtesy of Arbitron, Inc.*

business categories are major radio advertisers and are *not* looking for 12-to-17-year-old customers. Typically, this young demographic group tends to purchase consumables rather than durables. They spend their money on things like fast food, cosmetics, and clothing.

The revenue-producing potential of the target audience is the bottom line with respect to a format. With the chosen audience, will the sales department be able to generate the revenue required to meet the station's income projections and produce the needed return on investment? Is there another target demo that has more revenue potential?

There are no easy answers to the preceding critical questions. Most radio stations do formal market research to find the answers. Stations want to know everything they can about their geographic service area and their target demo. On the quantitative side, stations want to know the number of households, the average number of people living in those households, how long it takes those people to commute to work every morning, the average household income, and the average spendable income, to name just a few data categories. Qualitatively, the radio station wants to know what brands and models of cars these people drive, what kind of beer they like, how many times they eat out each week and what kinds of restaurants they eat in, how many trips they make to the grocery store each week, even whether they do their laundry at home or in a laundromat.

Many radio stations hire outside firms to do quantitative and qualitative research, feeling that because the firm is an outsider it may see and find things the station staff has overlooked or is just not familiar with. In larger markets, a station or regional group may have an in-house audience-research specialist.

Once the target demo that can produce the most revenue potential for the radio station is clearly identified, the PD takes the next step in the programming process: Find out what the target demo wants to listen to, and then give it to them!

At this point in the process, audience surveys and **focus groups** are conducted with people in the target demo who reside in the coverage area. In some respects, audience research helps to validate the market research the station has already conducted to identify the target demo. What the radio station wants to know from this research is what the target demo wants to listen to. Although it is easy to make a guess, sometimes local and regional factors come into play and what you thought might work turns out to be just the opposite. Another round of surveys is often conducted with businesspeople to make sure the target demo reflects the businesses' potential customers.

Strategy and Tactics

Once a program format is decided upon, the PD develops the strategy and tactics for the presentation of the format to the listener. Just as in the military, the strategy is the overall plan, and the tactics are the specific elements needed to carry out the plan. For example, market research shows that there is a large population of eighteen to thirty-four-year-old males in the station's coverage area that is not being targeted by any other media. The PD decides the best strategy for reaching this very desirable demographic is with Alternative rock music and promotion of the lifestyle that surrounds it.

The tactics employed to reach and hold this audience could include high rotation of the top twenty hits, fewer commercial stop sets, and announcers with in-your-face attitudes, edgy language, and lots of concert promotions, special events, and contests. The strategy and tactics developed by the PD determine how the radio station ultimately communicates with listeners.

The Program Director's Duties

Program directors focus on four goals during the format design. Firstly, the format presentation must be exciting enough to cause the target demographic to listen to the radio station in the first place. Secondly, the program flow of the format must maintain the listeners' interest to a point that causes them to listen longer. Thirdly, the air staff must be trained by the PD in how to communicate with the target listeners so that they return and listen again. And fourthly, and this is critical, the format must be designed in a way that listeners clearly know which station they are listening to, as well as being able to recall the station when participating in the audience ratings. In all of the decisions a PD must make about the format, the fulfillment of these four goals must be kept in mind.

Music Mix and Rotation

Program directors are responsible for determining a station's music mix and rotation. They develop schedules that regulate how the music format is going to flow each hour and how many of what kind of song are played. These detailed hourly schedules are called play clocks (see Fig. **14.5**). The PD creates as many play clocks as necessary to accomplish the programming goals. Play clocks often rotate or change from daypart to daypart. (The morning drive daypart is typically 6 a.m. to 10 a.m., midday is 10 a.m. to 2 p.m., afternoon drive runs from 2 p.m. to 6 p.m., evenings from 6 p.m. to 10 p.m., and overnights from 10 p.m. to 6 a.m. Music in the morning drive show is arranged and rotated differently than that in the midday or afternoon drive dayparts.)

Play clocks are arranged in a way that promotes the smoothest music flow and the longest time spent listening. PDs carefully figure out how often the music needs to rotate and how often a song is played. When the number-one hit in the station's format is played, how long is it until it can be played again? When a two-year-old song in the format is played, how soon does it come up again in the rotation? A day? Three days? PDs make

these determinations prior to the format ever going on the air, based on format research and what has worked well in similar markets.

Most PDs use a music-scheduling program for this tedious aspect of their job. The approved music list is loaded into a computer program, with each song having a number of identifying qualities assigned to it that the computer looks for when making a music list for a particular daypart (see Fig. **14.6**). A music software program makes the PD's job much more manageable and frees the PD up to spend time on other aspects of their job, such as working with talent.

Program Elements

In addition to programming the music, the PD selects all of the program elements that occur each hour. How many traffic reports will there be? Will there be news, weather, and sports? How do air personalities say the time and temperature? Every element is examined for every minute of every hour. Specific guidelines are established that guide air personalities in giving the time, promoting music and programming, giving the weather, and knowing whether or not they are to talk over music, among other things. PDs create and enforce programming rules associated with each element. PDs do not hesitate one second to tell the air staff when it has gone beyond the format limits or violates the station's programming guidelines.

Selecting a Promotional Voice

Another important aspect of the program director's job is to select the radio station's promotional voice for station imaging. This is the voice that you hear promoting the station with liners and sweepers like, "Seattle's home for

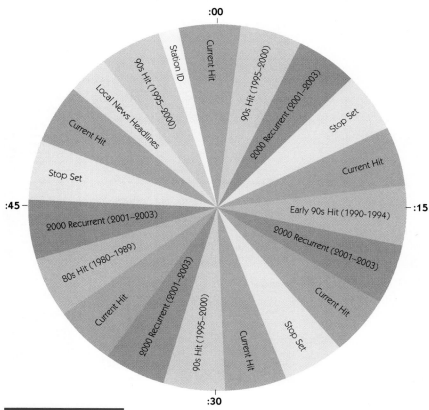

Sample Play Clock

Figure 14.5

A play clock is used by the program director to plan the music and program flow. Usually created with music scheduling software, play clocks may rotate or change from daypart to daypart and can be quite detailed.

classic rock hits, Y-100!" These can be "dry," with no music or sound effects, or fully produced, with music and a signature sound effect the station chooses to use as an identifier (see demo CD, cut 91).

As a general rule, the PD selects this distinctive voice from outside the market to create a personality and image for the radio station that is unique, standing out from all of the other radio stations. The PD has several options when purchasing imaging. Imaging may be purchased fully produced, with music sweeps and effects backing up the voice, or the PD may decide to let the production department produce everything and just order dry voice tracks.

The promotional voice is sacred. It is always the promotional voice, and it should

Figure 14.6

Music is critically important. Using music selection software, each song can have a number of identifying qualities assigned to it by the music or program director. The computer looks for these qualities when creating a music list for a particular daypart. *Courtesy RCS, Inc.*

never be used to voice commercials, since the PD does not want to tie the station imaging and slogans directly to commercials with the same voice.

If a station elects to use singing jingles, these are produced by an outside source, to the PD's specifications, so that they complement the music format of the station. Just as with every other element of each hour, the PD

sets the rules on how imaging and jingles are used in each daypart.

Formatics and Inventory Control

Just as in a regular business with products on shelves, the minutes of time the radio station has for sale are referred to as its inventory.

PDs are particularly sensitive to how the station's inventory intrudes into the format. Each particular format, based on the target demo, tolerates only so many commercials each hour. Once that point is reached, the audience reacts negatively, and the commercials become known as a tune-out factor. Ratings suffer and revenues drop. The PD, in conjunction with the general manager and sales manager, determines the maximum number of commercials that can be sold on the station each hour.

The PD also determines the best commercial placement within each hour, based on the desired flow of the format. Generally, commercials are grouped together into stop sets, or breaks. The PD determines the commercial load, or how many commercials are played in the stop set, and in most cases, the order in which the different styles of commercials are played. The PD also sets the rules as to how the commercials are placed with regard to music. For example, can a commercial be butted up directly to music? Likely not, since that means you would be tying the music directly to the commercials—a negative image most PDs would rather avoid.

PDs, along with the general and sales managers, also help develop the station's commercial-acceptance policy. What kinds of commercials are allowed on the air? What kinds of products are acceptable, and what kinds of products do not fit the format? Some products are banned outright and are not allowed on the air. For example, some stations do not accept ads for hard liquor, condoms, or feminine-hygiene products; whereas other stations may accept these commercials, depending on the format, time of day, and target demo. The PD, working in conjunction with sales, writes policy on how many commercials a sponsor can buy in one hour, in one daypart,

and in one day. PDs, working with sales, establish the rules for product separation, meaning how close together two commercials in the same product category, such as restaurants, can be placed. These are written policies that account executives are required to follow when selling commercial time or inventory.

PDs from time to time butt heads with the sales department. If the radio station is doing particularly well and is sold out in several dayparts, the sales department may be tempted to ask for, and in some cases demand, more inventory each hour. Sales claims they have clients waiting to buy the time, and they likely do. Usually, these battles are fought in the general manager's office between the sales manager and the program director, with the general manager being responsible for making the final decision. Typically, when a station is sold out in a daypart, with clients waiting to get on the air, the laws of supply and demand dictate that the price of the commercials goes up rather than making more inventory available and risking listener tune-out.

Comparison-Shopping a Format

Radio stations that have chosen to put their on-air signals on the Internet make a PD's job of comparison-shopping music formats much easier. PDs can check out web sites and listen to similar formats in other markets around the country for ideas. This is not necessarily a good thing, however. Taken to the extreme, a program director risks losing the originality and unique personality of the radio station if he or she tries to copycat a format from a radio station in another market. PDs who survey several radio stations playing the same format generally find that the format has a different sound from market to market. This is because each PD has, in theory, fine-tuned the format to fit his or her market.

Coordinating All of the Program Elements

Overall, the PD uses all of the elements discussed to assemble a living, breathing radio station. Just like a person, the radio station develops a personality and a distinctive style in everything it does that listeners identify with and relate to. This is called positioning the radio station so that listeners identify your radio station as *the* home, or *the* source, for their lifestyle and their kind of music.

The PD serves as the coach of a talented team of on-air professionals brought together to create the product that the sales department markets and sells to advertisers. Within the radio station's structure, the PD supervises the on-air personalities and the news, sports, and production departments. Typically, he or she works with the air talent and support staff in the station to make sure each person is focused and on goal.

PDs not only keep track of everything occurring in their radio stations, but it is also their job to find out and keep track of everything the competition is doing. PDs supervise and oversee competitive intelligence-gathering. It is quite common for different staff members of a radio station to be assigned a competitor to track and monitor.

Format Delivery

After resolving all the preceding issues described in this chapter, the program director must resolve one final issue with regard to the radio station's format presentation. His or her decision is usually made based on the projected profitability of the station format. The question is: should the presentation of the format be live, live-assist, automated, or syndicated?

Live Radio

A live format is based on air personalities in the studio working their shows, following the format, taking phone calls from listeners, and working creatively with news people, traffic reporters, and the weather person. There might even be a program producer doing a lot of these tasks for the talent during the show. There is a lot of studio activity and interaction between the various people appearing on the show (see Fig. **14.7**).

The advantage of a live format is that it allows talent to stretch its legs and be creative. Tremendous creativity occurs as the different people who make up a show play off one another and entertain the audience, adding a great deal of spontaneity to the show.

The downside of a live show is that all these people cost money. Another downside is that if the live personalities become popular and do well in the ratings, which should be a good thing for the station, they demand greater salaries, which is not a good thing for the station. As well, if the personalities do exceptionally well in the ratings, some other station may try to woo them away with even greater monetary compensation. Personalities can also become difficult to deal with as they become popular and realize they are worth more money. Sometimes it is very difficult to keep popular talent within the format guidelines, since they become teenagers reincarnated. They know all and see all and, to them,

Figure 14.7

A live format is based on air personalities in the studio working their show, following the format, taking phone calls from listeners, and working creatively with news people, traffic reporters, and the weather person. Often one person serves as a producer (center) to keep the show moving and handle technical details.

anyone in authority is an idiot, because they are the stars!

For all these reasons, live radio is more expensive to produce and thus requires a lot more station revenue to support.

Live-Assist Radio

A live-assist format is based on a live air personality in the studio, with computers and outsourced talent doing much of the additional work. Pre-selected music is on one computer, and commercials and imaging are on another; in some systems, everything is loaded into one computer (see Fig. **14.8**). The music and commercials have been loaded into the computers based on music logs generated by the music director and program logs created by the traffic director. Basically, all the announcer is doing is hitting a space bar on a computer keyboard to start each music segment or commercial stop set. News may come from a local TV news anchor over a digital audio link to the radio station. The air personality and the TV anchor banter back and forth just before or after the news and, as far as the listener is concerned, the two are sitting in the same studio. Weather may come from a

Figure 14.8

Even small-market radio stations have adopted live-assist formats. Thanks to the two computers in this control room, the announcer has more time to be creative. The announcer does not have to worry about a lot of minor details during his show because many of the tasks are automated.

service like Accu-Weather, and traffic reports are outsourced as well.

Advantages of a live-assist format include greatly reduced talent costs. The station is only dealing with one or maybe two people for the morning show. A live-assist show gives the PD considerable control over every element of the station sound, since the music and program elements are all programmed into a computer. Because many of the tasks are automated, the on-air talent has more time to be creative. Thanks to the computers, announcer errors due to "brain fade" are reduced, and the format can be executed very efficiently.

There are not a lot of downside issues with live-assist. In fact, a lot of live shows use elements of live-assist. If live-assist is done carefully, the audience never knows how the show is being produced. If there is a downside to live-assist, it is that creativity may suffer if the talent sees himself or herself as just button pushers. But then again, that is where the role of the PD as a talent coach comes in.

Automated Radio

An automated format involves live announcers pre-recording their stop sets into a computer that has been loaded with the program and music logs; this is sometimes referred to as voice-tracking a show, which was described

Figure 14.9

Computer automation and live-assist systems put radio station resources at the announcer's finger tips. On the tool bar across the top is the station clock and audio meters. In the upper left of the screen is the station log, or playlist. Below the playlist in the lower left is the station imaging (jingles). On the right of the screen are the six playback decks into which any audio cut from the left side of the screen can be placed for use on-air. Announcers can configure the screen to suit their particular needs or show format. *Courtesy ENCO Systems.*

in chapter 9. In smaller markets, the on-air staff is often made up of former announcers who have gone on to become sales account executives or to some other position in the station—fewer people doing more work, producing more profit.

The station retains all of the control over its music, play clocks, and format, just like a regular station. All of the music and program ele-

ments are stored in files on a computer hard drive. Included in the format are stop sets in which the announcer can talk, do weather and news, and announce the music. These announcer stop sets are assigned a file on the hard drive for the announcer to record into, just like everything else on the program log that has been loaded into the computer (see Fig. **14.9**).

The PD loads the music logs into the computer, and the traffic director loads the program logs into the computer. The computer merges the two together to produce a complete day, ready to air unattended. The on-air personality receives a printout of the log prior to the show to see where the stop sets are and what he or she needs to do or say during breaks. Using the production room, the personality records the stop sets into the assigned computer files. It takes about thirty minutes for a personality to record and load a four-hour show into the computer.

This allows someone such as an sales account executive to come into the station, record a show, and then be out on the street all day selling time for the radio station. It allows PDs to do their shows and then have the rest of the day free to work on station projects, rather than being tied to a control room for four hours every day.

The morning show is likely to be recorded during the afternoon of the previous day. The midday and afternoon drive shows are often recorded in the morning, and the evening and overnight are recorded before everyone goes home at 5 p.m.

Taken to a higher level, automation is being used on a regional and national basis. There is no reason the air personality has to be physically in your radio station to record his or her stop sets. A station equipped with a WAN, a digital telephone line, or a digital satellite down-link can use talent located anywhere on the planet. Likewise, with music-scheduling software, the program director does not have to be located in your station either.

The nation's largest chain of radio stations, Clear Channel Communications, uses this level of voice tracking and automation to bring major-market talent to smaller markets served by the company. For less than $10,000 a year, the small-market radio station gets a major-market talent without all of the costs, such as a salary or benefits, normally associated with hiring someone.

A local station staff member prepares information for the talent doing the voice tracking, such as pronunciation guides, local-event schedules, landmarks, scores from local sports teams, and the names of high schools and universities in the area. In some cases, the radio station sets up a web site with all of this information so that the voice-tracking talent can access it any time he or she is ready to cut their tracks.

Because of the incredibly large talent pool such national media companies have to draw from, the local station's voice tracking for the morning show may come from Chicago, middays from Orlando, and afternoon drive from Los Angeles. In fact, in addition to a live-air shift in the major market where he or she is based, voice-tracking talent can do as many as three or four voice-tracked shows a day for stations in the smaller markets. Despite what you might think, with a good production person looking after the system it is virtually impossible for local residents to tell where the talent is located, since the show has been localized.

Advantages of voice-tracked automation include reduced cost, reduced cost, and reduced cost. Automation greatly reduces talent and operating costs, with most members of the station's staff pulling double duty. PDs have much greater control over the format, and it is very difficult for the announcer to make a mistake on the air, since a computer is running the show.

Thanks to the efficiency and savings of automation, a smaller market station ends up with a top-notch program director and a better-sounding product than the local live show it might otherwise have produced. Automation frees up station and staff resources while retaining the local sound. Because computers are literally operating the radio station, it can run unattended, meaning that from 5 p.m. until 8 a.m. the station operates with the lights out and everyone home snug in bed. The same thing applies to weekends. If there is a problem, the computer calls or pages someone. Actually, the computer has a list of several people to call, in descending order of importance, and continues calling until someone answers and gives it a PIN number telling the computer to stop calling. Done well, it is very effective and very profitable, and local listeners will never have any idea where the talent is coming from.

A downside of automation is that it involves computers and attention to detail. Computers can fail; lightning and power surges can kill computers. However, when computers are properly protected and maintained, they operate for long periods (thousands of hours) of time without calling in sick or needing a day off to go see the dentist. And with the cost of computers so low, many stations operate what are called mirror computers. The mirror computer mimics everything the on-air computer does and is on standby, ready to go on-air should the main computer fail.

Syndicated Radio

A syndicated show or programming service is similar to automation. Using such a service, an entire radio station can be located in a closet, and a small one at that. The syndicated format provider delivers major-market-sounding talent and music. Syndicators spend a great deal of money on research and programming their format. The station receives the program service over a digital satellite link. The format has detailed play clocks, just like a regular radio station, with fixed-length local breaks each hour for insertion of com-

mercial stop sets, news, weather, traffic, or whatever the station wants to program in these local stop sets (see Fig. **14.10**).

The satellite link is tied to a computer in which all of the local program elements are stored. The station traffic director loads the station's daily program log into the computer. A local production person is in charge of making sure the elements of the format, such as commercials, news, and weathercasts, are loaded into the computer and are ready for playback. The format provider uses digital commands to tell the local computer when to take a commercial stop set or other local break.

What can really make a system like this come to life is how well the local station handles station identity. Each announcer from the syndicated program service provides a number of imaging liners that incorporates the local station's call letters and location or local station slogan. Each announcer's localized imaging liners are stored in separate files on the station computer. Just like the digital commands from the format provider that trigger the local stop sets, digital commands tell the local computer which announcer is on the air and what image liners to have ready to play when the announcer sends the command to play one. Suddenly, the national announcer is a local announcer because his or her imaging, using your call letters, locations, and so forth, is played at appropriate times during the show. National announcers can even introduce the local news and weather. By keeping these up to date, your announcers can talk about local events and things going on in the community. These imaging liners are freshened by the national announcer as needed.

Advantages of the syndicated program format are even greater reduced cost, reduced cost, and reduced cost. Because the syndicated

Scott Shannon's TRUE OLDIES CHANNEL

TRUE OLDIES

FLEX CLOCK 1
5:00 AM - 10:00 AM (CT)
Monday - Friday

COMMERCIAL TIME
Minimum: 2:00 Local/2:00 Net/4:00 Total
Maximum: 18:00 Local/2:00 Net/20:00 Total

RECOMMENDED SPOT PLACEMENT
A. 35:00 Mandatory Break (3:00 - Must Fill)
B. 48:00 Optional Break 5:00
    Includes ● ABC News 2:00
C. 17:00 Optional Break (5:00)
D. 8:00 Optional Break (5:00)

CLOSURE FUNCTIONS:
1. Local Call Letters (:03)**
2. Local Liner (:05)**
3. Local Liner 2 (:05)**
4. Local ID (:04)
5. Local Optional (5:00)
6. Local Mandatory (3:00)
7. Net Spot Recording Cue
13. Automated Time Sync at 59:58*

Time Sync @59:58*

13
4
5
:00
:55
:05
:10
Local Optional 5:00
5
:50
● ABC News
Local Optional 5:00
:15
:45
Local Mandatory 3:00
Net Spots 2:00
Local Optional 5:00
:40
:20
5
:35
:25
6
:30
7

ALL TIMES ARE APPROXIMATE
* EXACT TIME
Local Call Letters and **Local Liners** run variably within the hour.
● ABC News (2:00) at beginning of 5:00 Optional Break
© 2004 ABC Radio Networks
Effective Date: April 1, 2004

abc RADIO NETWORKS
america listens to abc

Figure 14.10

Syndicated formats have detailed play clocks, just like a regular radio station, with fixed-length local breaks each hour for insertion of commercial stop sets, news, weather, traffic, or whatever the station wants to program in these local stop sets. By creatively using the stop sets, a station can truly sound local.

format is thoroughly researched and uses major-market talent, it allows a station to have a solid, well-constructed format that has strong listener appeal. If the local radio station does a good job of localizing the syndicated format by keeping imaging liners up to date and adding news, weather, sports, and so on, it is very difficult for a listener to tell what is going on. The major advantage of a syndicated format is a major-market sound at a very low cost to the radio station. It is not unusual for such a station to show a consistent fifty to seventy percent return on investment.

Although appearing similar to automation, the syndicated format is less flexible and requires more advance planning and attention to detail on the part of the local station. Another disadvantage is that the station has no control over the music or the format elements; those are determined by the national syndicator.

The station depends on the syndicator for the station's personality. The station plans everything in advance so that the syndicated talent can cut localized materials and promotional announcements. Basically, such a station has to work "inside the box." However, people who are skilled at working with a syndicated format can stretch the limits of the box with creative solutions to the restrictions they have to work with.

With syndication as with automation, all of the comments we made earlier regarding the reliability and the failures involved in using computers still apply.

The Format-Delivery Decision

The PD, in consultation with the general manager and the general sales manager, makes the decision on which method to choose to execute the format. As previously stated, this is a business decision based on the costs associated with the format and the projected return on investment that is required to support the station.

In some cases, a station may choose more than one of the various styles of presentation. For example, in a large market, a station might choose a live personality in the critical morning drive rating period, with a producer, host, sidekick, news and sports person. Midday, the station may shift gears and switch to live-assist with a live air personality producing his or her own show. Afternoon drive, another critical rating daypart, is likely to be a live personality show. As the station transitions into the evening hours, when ratings typically drop due to competition from television, the station might switch back to a live-assist personality. For overnights, from midnight to 5 or 6 a.m., typically the smallest audience of the day, the station picks up a syndicated show so that the station operates unattended, thanks to the computers.

However, even in a large market, a station may decide to go with one of the nationally syndicated morning shows. Don't think for one moment that a show has to be local and live to do well in the ratings. Such shows have proven many program directors very wrong in the live-versus-syndicated programming war. Typically, a lot of news- or sports-talk programming is syndicated, and stations do very well with it.

A smaller-market radio station might choose a live morning show and then automate the rest of the day. Another small-market alternative would be to use a live morning show and then switch over to a syndicated format for the rest of the day.

By availing themselves of the technology that is available, PDs can maximize their budget resources, putting live talent in the dayparts where it is needed the most to earn rating points, and at the same time, controlling costs and helping to generate the most revenue for the radio station.

The Production Person's Role in Programming

Although it may not be obvious, there is one common denominator critical to the success of each format-delivery method: the production person. Each format-delivery method requires a production person for it to be successful.

On a live-formatted station, the production person is focused on producing commercials, station promotions, and imaging for the station as a whole. The production person works closely with the PD so that the personality, style, and attitude expressed by these elements mesh with the format.

A live show likely has a producer who is responsible for creating many of the bits and show elements that make the show a success. Producers often seek a production person's assistance on projects that may be beyond the producer's capabilities. A live-assist station likely asks more of production people, calling on them to produce special program elements for the live-assist personality, in addition to regular production duties. Although there are differences from the live format, they usually are not that great.

A local-automated radio station uses the services of a production person slightly differently. Although producing commercials, station promotions, and imaging, the production person's focus may shift to include responsibilities with regard to the automation system. The production person often is declared the "computer king or queen" and is responsible for making sure every element of the automation is loaded onto the hard drives properly. This includes making sure that logs are loaded properly, maintaining the system files, and

being the gatekeeper for everything that gets loaded into or out of the computer.

An automated station using regional- and national-level talent may require a production person to assume some of the duties of a program producer. Such duties might include supplying the distant talent with local information and timely details about the community to localize each show and verifying that the voice-tracking talent's stop sets are in the system. In this situation, the production person's role becomes critical, since the producer is responsible for the presentation of the show on the local station in addition to his or her regular duties as previously outlined.

A syndicated format is almost entirely dependent on a producer to coordinate between the national format and the local elements necessary to make a complete radio station. In this instance, the production person takes on the role of running the radio station 24/7. Production people produce everything that is loaded into the computer to interface with the satellite-delivered format, including news, weather, sports, and so forth. Very likely, the producer is also responsible for recording and producing all of the station imaging from the national announcers to localize the radio station. This requires advance planning on the production person's part to make sure that all of the elements are created and loaded into the computer.

As stated before, the method of format delivery is selected based on a business decision, just as the format selection was made. To say that one of these methods of format delivery is not as good as another would be a serious error. Each method of delivery has a place and a purpose in the industry. As an example, there are many family-owned, small-market radio stations that would have gone dark years ago had it not been for nationally syndicated formats delivered via satellite.

Interestingly, it was the smaller markets that embraced the new computer technologies first, as a means of economic survival. By helping to reduce operating costs, these services have made it possible for small-market stations to operate on a profitable basis, producing good earnings for their owners. At the same time, the small-market operators broadcast a much-better-sounding product than if they were using all local talent.

There are those who claim technology is eliminating jobs from the radio industry. It is not so much a question of eliminating jobs as it is changing job descriptions to make use of technology. The end result is a better quality product for the listener. What is ironic is that the value of production people sometimes increases as the market size decreases, because their role in the final on-air product becomes so critical. Production people and their computers become the radio station!

Suggested Activities

1. Visit the web sites listed for radio station automation systems (iMediaTouch and Enco Systems). Download a free trial copy of their software for running a radio station. Try it out on your computer and experiment with it. Come up with three different reasons a particular system would or would not work for a radio station.
2. Visit the web site for ABC 24-Hour Radio Formats and look at the various twenty-four-hour formats that are available. Do you see any you recognize that are on the air in your community?
3. Visit the web site for the Arbitron Company and look at all of the different kinds of listening data that is available that was not covered in this chapter. Also, examine the methods that Arbitron uses to collect

the audience rating data used to formulate the radio ratings.

Web Sites for More Information

For more information about:

- *audience ratings,* visit the Arbitron Company at www.arbitron.com
- *music-scheduling systems,* visit RCS Sound Software at www.rcsworks.com
- *radio station automation systems,* visit iMediaTouch at www.omt.net or Enco Systems at www.enco.com
- *syndicated radio formats,* visit ABC 24-Hour Radio Formats at www.abcradio.com

Pro Speak

You should be able to use these terms in your everyday conversations with other professionals.

focus groups—A qualitative market research tool in which a group of people with common demographics and similar attitudes are surveyed and questioned on a particular topic by a trained moderator.

psychographic—Determining how a person or group of people thinks about a particular product or service: what their image is of your product and how they see themselves relating to your product.

target audience—A group of people that a radio station has selected to try to reach with the station's programming. Typically, this audience can be identified both quantitatively and qualitatively.

CHAPTER 15

Getting Your First Job in Radio

Your parents have asked you a thousand times, maybe two thousand times: What's the job market like in radio? How much are you going to make when you graduate? Depending on whom you talk to, you may hear a story of doom and gloom for graduates entering radio. You'll likely be told how consolidation has certainly killed the radio job market. And yet, although consolidation has certainly changed the radio business, the demand for creative, *qualified* talent is as strong as ever. What has changed dramatically is that the job market for mediocre talent is quickly drying up, just as it is in other industries.

The professional experience of this author has included working as a program director, as major-market on-air talent, as a sales manager, and as a general manager. When he left the industry after more than twenty years to pursue teaching, he left a job as the affiliate relations director for one of the top three statewide radio networks in the country. This author's experience reflects that, with regard to job openings, radio stations always have a need for an aggressive, qualified, talented, creative individual who makes the effort to be the best in the market.

As to what your starting salary is going to be: there is no way to know. Because salaries vary depending the region of the country, the size of the market, and size of the station, the best way to find out about salaries in your particular area is to talk to a program director or a human resources person at one of your area radio stations. He or she can give you some figures based on your experience level and the market you are interested in. Also, don't hesitate to talk to your state broadcasters' association; those groups generally can give you a good idea of pay scales for the various areas of your state. The pur-pose of this chapter is to give you some *advice* on how to land your first job in radio. We use the term "advice" because, as you are going to learn, there are no hard-and-fast rules when you are dealing with creative people.

Getting your first job in radio is entirely up to you (unless your Uncle Bob owns the station). Radio stations don't show up on campus begging people to fill positions and offering lucrative starting salaries because there is a talent shortage. There is a great line from the movie *Barefoot in the Park*, "There are watchers in this world and there are doers. And the watchers sit around watching the doers do." No one is going to hand you a job. You are going to have to walk up and take it.

It would be easy to say that you could get all of the information in this chapter from your career services office on campus—you cannot. Although that office is prepared to help most students land a first job, it is not typically prepared for talent-based industries like radio, television, and acting. The information in this chapter is based on many years in the industry and a few other helpful hints.

Internship: Getting the Jump on the Competition

If you wait until the semester before you graduate to begin your job search, you're late. About a year late, to be exact. Early in your junior year in college, at the latest, you should begin taking the first steps necessary to land a full-time position in radio.

Figure 15.1

An internship can be a valuable experience and provide a student the opportunity to explore a career. Radio station staffs are glad to see someone express an interest in their field and are willing to help you learn the industry when you ask for their help. The two students above are getting hands-on experience under the direction of the production director (behind the desk).

The Planning Process

A job search starts with the planning of an internship at a radio station. Although some universities require an internship in the media to get a degree in communications, many do not. You need an internship, however, whether the university you attend requires one or not. If you have to, set one up as a special topic in an independent-study class with a professor (see Fig. **15.1**). (And to get the one question on the top of most potential interns' minds out of the way up front: most internship opportunities are unpaid.)

Start planning your internship at the beginning of your junior year so that you can sched-ule the internship, ideally, in the summer between your junior and senior years. Summer is a good time because, depending on where your internship is located, you can possibly lower your expenses by living with family, friends, or relatives. In some places, however, depending on the market and the hiring trends in your particular area, you may find that your second-to-last semester or last semester is a better time than the summer, because in many markets, stations offer positions to outstanding interns at the end of the internship. This is something to discuss with your professors. Regardless of the timing of your internship, plan for it well in advance.

Depending on the number of hours you devote to the internship each week, you might be able to hold a paid, part-time job as well. You should plan your internship to give you a total of at least 160 hours of professional workplace experience.

Selecting a Station

Station selection is important to a good internship. Firstly, the station should be a commercial station, unless you want to work in public radio. Secondly, the station should be in the largest market that is reachable from your home or the university (again, so you don't have to spend a fortune on living expenses). The larger the market, the better your resume reads. And thirdly, you should do some research and select the top-rated radio station in that market, even if you're not too thrilled with its music format.

In addition to how it reads on your resume, why should you select the top-rated station in the largest market you can? Through your internship, you have the opportunity actively to seek out someone in the industry to become your mentor, or learning partner. You're looking for someone to help guide you and to share his or her professional knowledge with you. Doesn't it make sense to work with the best and find out how the best do what it is they do? The professional you are seeking as a mentor, or learning partner, did not achieve his or her position by accident.

Another reason to select the best station in the market is so that you can network with top industry professionals. These experienced pros have contacts that could be valuable to you later during your job search. For example, if you have an excellent internship experience, your supervisor may be able to offer you a job when you graduate. If not,

that person may be able to call friends at other stations and help you find another opening. That's the kind of result you want. We'll talk more about networking later in the chapter.

Asking for an Internship

No one is going to hand you an internship. You have to ask for one. Most stations, especially near universities, have someone who coordinates student internships. Your first call to the station is for surveillance purposes: Your only task is to get the internship coordinator's name, title, and proper address.

If you're planning for a summer internship, make that first call to the station in early December, well before the holidays. Then immediately make the second call. You have a better chance of getting through to the internship coordinator right away because you are going to ask for that person confidently and by name. The internship coordinator is likely to tell you that you are calling early for a summer internship and that you should call back in January or February. That's fine, because no matter how the call goes, it gives you the opportunity to demonstrate how professional you are by sending a follow-up letter. Remember: Be aggressive, creative, and professional.

The follow-up letter should arrive within a day or two of your call. Thank the person for taking your call, briefly introduce yourself, and tell the person you *will* contact him or her in January, or whenever you are told (see Fig. **15.2**). The letter must be professional in every respect, from the grammar and spelling to the 24-pound, 25 percent cotton-fiber stationery and matching envelope. Under no circumstances may there be spelling or grammatical errors in that letter. Other than your phone call, the letter is the first tangible impression

Mike Roberts
Program Director
WRPC
26 Radio Lane
Charlotte, NC 28723

Dear Mr. Roberts,

Thank you for taking my call today and explaining WRPC's summer internship program. I was particularly impressed with the training program you offer interns over the summer. I have no problem with your 15-hours-per-week minimum as I must complete 160 hours at a radio station to receive course credit. I will be going online in the next few days and completing the WRPC internship application there, which I will then send to you by next week.

This spring I will complete both my radio production and my radio programming classes, as you suggested. In addition to Adobe Audition, I am also becoming skilled in Pro Tools. I would really like to spend some of my internship time in production, as well as in the promotion department.

Again, thank you for taking time with me and I will plan on calling you the second week in March to set up an appointment for an internship interview.

Best Regards,

Tasheera Miller

12407 East 46th Street
Charlotte, NC 28723
704.555.1212 Home 877.555.1212 Cell
tmiller101@peoplelink.net

Figure 15.2

Sample follow-up letter.

you are making on this person. How do you want to be remembered?

The letter should never be more than one page long. Under your signature and typed name, place your contact information, including address, e-mail address, and phone number. (A word about e-mail addresses is in order here. Some young people have jokey e-mail addresses. But you need a professional-looking e-mail address that includes your name, or a portion of your name, at whatever dot com or dot net. This makes it easier for the person to associate the e-mail address with your name and to remember you. Besides, "bubba-redneck@quickmail.net" just does not cut it professionally.)

With regard to the phone number you provide, make sure you have voicemail or an answering machine at that number and you have a professional-sounding outgoing message that includes your name. If a potential employer were to call you about an interview and heard a recorded message sung by you and your roommate about "drinking beer and having sex"—chances are that he or she would not leave a message!

The envelope for your letter should have the same professional appearance as the letter. With the information you obtained earlier, address the letter to the specific person you talked to. It should be addressed on a computer printer, making sure your return address matches the one on the letter inside. Last, but not least, put a stamp on the letter. *Never* use a postage meter to send a thank-you letter. It makes it look impersonal and like all the other junk mail the person receives. Letters with stamps draw people's attention.

After the letter arrives, demonstrate a little aggressiveness and make your follow-up call to the station three to five days earlier than you said you would. Continue to maintain contact with this person every three to four weeks, with a phone call and a follow-up letter each time.

At this point, you already have a much better chance of landing the internship you want, thanks to the professional nature with which you have approached the internship coordinator and your persistence in following up. Your actions demonstrate that the internship is important to you and that you value the opportunity he or she may extend to you. Ask and you get; don't and you won't.

How to Gain More from Your Internship

An internship is the opportunity to gain valid professional experience and can be extremely valuable. It is an opportunity to explore your desired career in a professional work environment. How much you gain, though, is up to you. Be upfront with the internship coordinator about what you want to learn and experience while doing your internship.

Your approach to a successful internship must be a professional one. For several weeks, you are going to get the opportunity to work in a radio station. There are a number of things you can do to make your experience much more rewarding, so make the most of your opportunity!

Before arriving at your first day of work, make a phone call to your supervisor. Ask that person when he or she would like you to report and also ask what the standard business attire, or dress code, is for the area you are working in. Follow the supervisor's lead. Regardless of how the other employees look, avoid excessive jewelry and forget the tongue piercing, extreme hairstyle, or heavy-duty perfume or cologne.

You are entering a professional radio work environment. Time is money, time is money, time is money! Set your watch and adjust your lifestyle to the station time standard. *Never* be one second late for anything. Better to be five minutes early and appear energetic and on time than to be a minute late and appear as if you don't care. Late is a four-letter word.

Make it your goal to remember the name of everyone you meet and, likewise, make sure everyone knows your name. Your internship is an excellent time to network with people in the industry and to pair up with someone similar to you to become your mentor, or learning

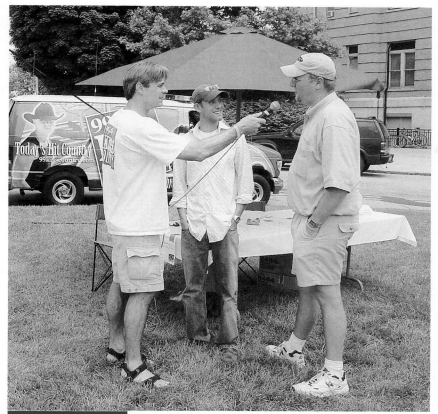

Figure 15.3

As an intern at a radio station (center), take advantage of every opportunity offered to you. Radio is a 24/7 business, and many opportunities may come outside the regular 8-to-5 business day. If someone extends an invitation to you to participate in a station event or promotion, like this event, after office hours or on a weekend, take it.

partner. The guidance of a mentor can pay big dividends later when you are seeking your first position.

Take advantage of every opportunity offered to you. Radio is a 24/7 business, and many opportunities may come outside the regular 8-to-5 business day. If someone extends an invitation to you to participate in a station event or promotion after office hours or on a weekend, take it (see Fig. **15.3**). Make

yourself available to do anything that is asked of you. No matter how simple the task may seem, do it better than anyone has ever done it before. Don't be afraid to try new things.

Above all else, ask lots of questions. That's why you are there, to learn. There is no such thing as a dumb question. You'll find most industry professionals are as interested in you as you are in learning how to do things in a professional manner. The most certain way to get an answer to any question you have is to ask the person for his or her opinion. For example, "What do you think is the best way to . . . ?" When asked for an opinion on the best way to do something, most pros are more than happy to share their knowledge.

When you ask a lot of questions, establish good communications with the industry professionals you're working with, and are unafraid to ask and answer questions, unexpected things can happen. During a morning sales meeting, a student intern at a major market radio station asked a question about a promotion that was in the planning stages. The sales manager turned the question around and asked her how *she* would handle the promotion if it were her project. She answered with an idea she had picked up in sales class. It was a fresh approach to the promotion that the sales manager had not heard of. Imagine her shock as the sales manager adopted her approach to the promotion on the spot! By the way, that question landed her a major-market sales position straight out of college. The key to her success was that she was alert, observed what was going on, and when *asked* for her opinion was ready with an intelligent answer.

Another student who did an internship with a top-rated large-market morning team really wanted to be a morning show producer and worked very hard at the craft for several weeks alongside the show's producer. With about a week left in his internship, one day he asked if there was any way the producer would consider allowing him to produce just one show. He was stunned when the show's producer stood up and said, "Take it, it's yours" and left the studio. For the last week of his internship the student produced the show under the guidance of the regular producer. The producer later told the student the reason he had allowed him to take the show: The pro-

ducer had decided that if the student had enough confidence in the skills he had learned to ask the question, he would give him a chance. Thanks to a good radio-oriented resume and an outstanding internship experience, the student started work at that station two days before he graduated.

While doing your internship, keep copies of any work you do or projects that you contribute to. (Be sure to get your supervisor's permission to make copies, as some materials may be copyrighted, or it may be a violation of station policy to copy and remove such materials from the station.) These materials are valuable for your audition disc to demonstrate professional experience. For radio, air checks and production you worked on are great.

Although you will probably be required to work a minimum number of hours to satisfy the requirements of an internship anyway, this author strongly suggests that you become as involved in the station as your supervisor allows. Network with everyone you meet and do your assigned job better than anyone who has ever done it.

Networking

At least eighty percent of the job opportunities in radio are discovered through networking. Fewer than ten percent of radio jobs ever show up in the classified section of a newspaper. Networking is all about making contacts. As you meet people, begin to build your network of contacts, communicating with them on a regular basis and adding more people to your network over time. Be selective about whom you add to your network. You should be able to get along well with each person and, quite frankly, each one should like you.

Figure 15.4

These days most of us (especially men) tend to neglect the art of handwriting notes, but a handwritten thank-you note always makes a good impression.

Organize your network by keeping a business card from each person you meet or by adding him or her to your personal digital assistant, because a good network has too many names and numbers for you to keep in your head. Include the person's name, addresses, phone numbers, e-mail address, and any bit of information you think is important about this person. You can also trade contacts and information with others in your network. If you truly desire to be a pro at networking, send each new person you meet a short thank-you note or letter. The fact that you took the time to send a note puts you one step above everyone else professionally (see Fig. **15.4**).

Networking is centered around the exchange of information and advice. When the time comes to find employment, *do not* pick up the phone and call everyone in your network asking for a job. The best way to approach someone in your network when you are looking for a position is to ask for some type of help, or advice. You can ask someone in your network for job-search advice, for the best places to find information and position listings, for career-planning advice, state-of-the-industry advice, or advice about a particular company. You need to be seen as seeking guidance from the people in your network, not asking them for a job.

By using this approach, you are positioning yourself as someone who is seeking to better herself or himself through knowledge. When you ask for someone's advice, you are telling that individual that you respect his or her opinions and thoughts. People are much more willing to help someone asking for advice; it makes them feel like their opinion is valued and respected. Which of the following approaches would work better for you?

> Dave, I met you at a station promotion and I am about to graduate from college. I've waited a little late to start my job search and I am desperately looking for a position so that I won't have to move back home with my parents. Dave, you got any jobs open right now?"

Or . . .

> Dave, Jim Green at Clear Channel in Orlando suggested I contact you. Jim was my internship supervisor and he mentioned that you work in radio production. I am just starting a career in production and I am looking for someone who can give me some good advice about the best way to get started. Could we get together sometime next week? I would sincerely appreciate any time you could give me.

When you meet, ask for advice on seeking that first position and how to get a career off to a good start. Often, people are happy to share contacts and leads with someone asking for help. If they don't know of anything, they may refer you to someone in their network of people who might have something. Just as before, send a thank-you note or letter after your meeting. You will get a call the next time they hear of a job opening.

The best example of successful networking is the following unsolicited e-mail this author received from a student.

> Ultimately, it was my internship with XXXX that sealed the deal for my new job. This is no joke, it took about a month to get hired. So pass along to graduating students that they will have to be patient and aggressive at the same time or they'll get discouraged very fast. I can't stress the importance of the internship. People always talk about that first position as "getting your foot in the door," well the internship is ultimately getting your foot in the door. You just can't beat the importance of all those contacts you meet with during your internship.

The student landed a job in a top-50 market. Networking is a powerful means of finding a job.

Resume

You might be tempted to skip over this section of the chapter, thinking that resumes are generic, one-size-fits-all things that the folks in your college career services office will do for you. But stop and consider this: It is estimated that ninety-eight percent of the resumes being handed to potential employers do not even begin to describe adequately or do justice to the candidate whose name and personal information appears on them. Writing a great radio resume is just like writing a great radio commercial. Forget the advertiser and focus on solving the customer's problems and needs, and the product (you) will sell. Likewise, focus your resume on showing how you can solve a particular employer's problems and needs, and you've likely got an interview.

With regard to your resume, there is only one rule set in concrete, steel-reinforced, and armor-plated. Under no circumstances can it include a single spelling or typographical error. The best resumes are well organized and often professionally prepared. After you have met the requirements of rule number one, then you can get creative and use some color, graphics, and creative packaging. The industry buzzword for a professionally designed and prepared resume is "career design." Career designers are people who specialize in preparing resumes and graphically marketing people.

Formatting Your Resume

When it comes time to write your resume, you need to select a format or style. Two of the most popular resume formats don't work particularly well for starting out in radio. The first kind is a chronological resume. As the name implies, this is a chronological listing of the jobs you have held, working backward from the present. Under each job you list your skills and achievements. Although very informative, a chronological-style resume is not very creative. The focus of the format is on personal growth and job-to-job continuity. Employers tend to look at these historically, to see whether you have had steady upward growth in your career development, but this is pretty hard to do if you are a student just starting out and don't have years of experience to list on your resume.

The second popular resume format that won't work so well for your purposes is a functional resume. This is one that begins with a couple of paragraphs centered on a broad description of your qualifications, abilities, certifications, skills, and how great you are. Your employment history is secondary in importance to the opening and provides few details about the positions you have held or what you may have accomplished at each job. The focus of a functional format is on what you have done, but not on where or how you did it. Although functional resumes appear very creative, employers tend to be cautious when someone presents this type of resume, particularly someone fresh out of college. The general thinking is that if you can't list your jobs in chronological order and what you accomplished at each, you might be trying to hide something like gaps in employment or frequent job changes.

An ideal resume for someone starting in radio combines these two formats. The resume opens with a section detailing your market value and why you are worth considering. This is the "Hey, look at me" section of your resume. You present your skills, qualifications, and accomplishments just as you would in the functional resume. The creative opening is then followed with a typical chronological listing of the positions you have held, working backward from the present. Under each job, list your skills and achievements, just as you would in a chronological resume (see Fig. **15.5**).

The benefit of the combination-style resume is that it allows you to sell your assets as a potential employee right up front, to get the employer's attention. You start by showing how you can solve his or her problems and needs. The detailed chronological section supports the opening. Likewise, the opening adds a creative touch to the rather dull chronological listing. It allows you to add some bulk to your resume that's not fluff or nonsense. The combination style appeals to employers because it demonstrates creativity, backed up with a job history the employer can track. In essence, it is the best of both worlds.

Targeting Your Resume

Unlike a generic resume intended for general applications, a radio resume needs to be focused and targeted at the specific station and market you are applying to. Instead of a one-style-fits-all resume, you need one that presents your talents, skills, abilities, and experience in a manner that matches the needs of a specific station. Targeting a station involves carefully looking at the requirements for the

Mark R. King

Current: P.O. Box 3XXX, Anytown, NC 28723, 828.293.XXXX
Permanent: 4118 Utopia Dr., Charlotte, NC 28226, 704.341.XXXX
E-mail: mrking1950@supermail.com

Objective
To excel in broadcast sales, using my team building skills and exemplary verbal, adaptive, listening, and organizational skills.

Summary of Qualifications
- Radio Advertising Bureau, Radio Marketing Professional, certification # R-618923
- Interpersonal skills that build relationships based on trust
- Optimistic outlook when faced with difficult sales situations
- As a broadcast student, I was underwriting sales coordinator for WWCU-FM at Western Carolina University during my junior and senior years.
- Skilled with industry software such as ACT!, Pro Tools, and Adobe Audition

Career Profile
Underwriting Sales Coordinator, WWCU-FM, Cullowhee, NC   **2003-04**
- Developed sales projections, conducted meetings, established goals and budgets
- Carried full account list, 19 active accounts
- Supervised two underwriting sales people
- Supervised underwriting continuity
- Consistently exceeded sales projections and met budgets

Sugar Hill Records, Durham, NC   **Summer 2002**
- Organized and developed sound scan markets for street teams

Intern, Welk Music Group: Vanguard and Sugar Hill Records Corporate Offices, Los Angeles, CA   **Summer 2001**
- Assisted promotions, sales, marketing, new media and publicity departments

Community Service and Volunteer Work
Habitat for Humanity, Charlotte, NC   **1997-1999**
- Helped construct 17 homes for low-income families

Fundraising events for community organizations
- A.W.A.K.E. Foundation for battered women and children

Education
Western Carolina University, Cullowhee, NC   **May, 2004**
- B.S. in Communications (GPA 3.87)
- Major: Electronic Media
- Minor: Marketing

Technology
- Microsoft Windows XP, Professional
- Microsoft Office, Professional
- ACT! sales management software
- Pro Tools and Adobe Audition digital audio software

Personal Interests
- Auto Racing
- Community Baseball League

Letters of reference provided upon request.

Figure 15.5

position. The requirements are, in essence, the program director's statement of the station's problems and needs. After you analyze the problems and needs, adjust the copy on your resume to match the position requirements item by item. Answer as many of the stated problems and needs as you can with your skills and abilities. Look at the example resume in Fig. **15.5**. Can you tell what kind of position this student is seeking?

The other aspect of targeting a radio station is how you go about presenting yourself and your accomplishments. Most people tend to just list their former positions and responsibilities. Big whoop, most employers don't care about your prior responsibilities; they want to know what did you accomplish, what did you achieve for your previous employer? Instead of listing the responsibilities of each position you have held, list your accomplishments. For example, look at the two following statements: Which looks, reads, and sounds better? Which candidate would interest you?

> I was responsible for the production department at WWCU at Western Carolina University and managed a staff of five students.

Or

> As production director at WWCU at Western Carolina University, I streamlined production work flow and increased efficiency, resulting in a 20-percent reduction in the time needed to get public service and underwriting announcements on the air. I was honored three times with local Addy awards for public service campaigns. As a result of the new procedures, outstanding quality, and fast turnaround time, my department operated more efficiently, resulting in a significant cost savings for our university station.

Analyze your previous jobs by what you accomplished. Learn some of the broadcast industry buzzwords and phrases such as:

inventory control

improved profitability

turnaround

implemented new procedures

identifying and resolving problems

increased return on investment

introduced new technologies

improved productivity

Keep in mind that responsibilities have never solved a problem or met an employer's needs—accomplishments have. Make sure everything on your resume accurately represents your accomplishments and answers the specific job qualities or skills requested in the ad. Look again at the student resume in Fig **15.5** and pick out the achievements and buzzwords.

Resume Contents

If you have not figured it out by now, resume writing is critical to your successful employment. There are a number of good books and publications on resume writing; use them for ideas. You should also take a look at the materials in your university career placement office for ideas. Keep in mind, though, that you are applying to a creativity-based business. What follows is a very basic listing of what should and should not appear in your resume for a radio station, or any other business, for that matter.

Information That Does Not Go on Your Resume

There are a number of personal information items that you do not put on your resume. Although your name may give the employer a clue as to your gender, do not list yourself as male or female. Never list your date of birth, social security number, age, height, weight, health, race, citizenship, ethnicity, religion, sexual preference, or whether you are single, with a domestic partner, married, divorced, have children, dependents other than children, or are a single parent. You should not state or imply any family plans you may or may not have regarding marriage, domestic partners, or starting a family. Statements of religious beliefs are also not appropriate on a professional resume.

If you have a question about what information an employer can require you to divulge, visit the web site of the Equal Employment Opportunity Commission.

The Header

At the top of your resume, a header contains all of your personal contact information. The header should have your name, address (both university and permanent if you are still in school), and appropriate phone numbers, including cell phone, pager, fax machine, and e-mail address. A word of caution: *Do not* use a current work phone number, fax number, or e-mail address. This is a red flag to a potential employer that you abuse company resources for personal gain.

There are two places to put the header at the top of the resume: in the center, or somewhere else. A centered header is considered the traditional style, and any other position is considered a creative style. Using recent books and publications, examine a number of creative resume samples and see if there is a style that looks professional and fits your personality. Radio people tend to be creative and like to see creative approaches to projects. Remember: Keep it professional and creative with neat, clean lines, not avant-garde.

Goals and Objectives

Below the header is the first opportunity to sell yourself, your first opportunity to land an interview. Imagine yourself as an employer for just a moment. As you begin to read a resume, what do you want to see? If you are like most employers, you are asking a couple of questions: "Why am I reading this? What does this person have that I am interested in? What can this person do to help solve my problems and make our company more profitable?"

You must have a specific goal, or objective, that clearly demonstrates to a station how you can solve its problems and needs or that you were told about through your network. Most resumes have incredibly vague and meaningless career goals or objective statements. For example, one that sounds like it came out of a can, is overused, and means nothing is "I am seeking a position with a market-leading radio station." Many employers will simply toss resumes with those words into the "no thanks" pile. Resumes that are even more likely to hit that pile contain the words "I am open to any position in your station you might wish to consider me for." If you don't know what you need, where you are going, and how you are going to get there, then no one is interested in you, period.

As someone entering the job market for the first time, your goals and objectives are going to be different from those of an experienced pro. You need to target personal attributes and qualifications that meet the stated needs of the prospective employer, then back them up with any related experience you might have. You need to let the reader see that you have potential.

Start by making a list of your skills, talents, and outstanding achievements in college. Analyze your internship for things you accomplished or excelled at. Select items from your list that address the stated qualifications of the position you are seeking. A good way to start off your resume is with a quote from your internship supervisor, or other industry professional, followed by your goals and objectives. Here is an example from a recently graduated student:

"It is hard to believe that Lashea is a college student. Her creativity, writing skills, and mastery of digital audio gear are outstanding and helped her fit right in at XXXX. In fact, the quality of her work was so good several of our sales department though he was one of our full-time production people."

Mike Roberts, Program Director,
XXXX, Knoxville, TN

Goals and Objectives

I am seeking a full-time production position with a demanding, creative, radio production department in the Pensacola, Florida, area. I want to be involved with a station that needs a team player with an excellent track record of productive work relationships and on-time production delivery.

Notice that rather than leaving the goals and objectives as a single sentence, this student took the opportunity to address a specific qualification or requirement that had been listed for the position she was seeking. Just as a commercial has to attract the listener's attention in its first few seconds, the person who reads your resume needs to see something in the first fifteen to twenty seconds to cause him or her to read further. A resume is a marketing tool for you, and your choice of words and the messages you deliver are critical. The reader needs to see something that lets him or her know that you have potential and deserve some attention. A resume has two basic pur-

poses. The first is to get the employer's attention and an interview. The second is to build your confidence and "pump you up" through your own personal inventory of skills and realizing what you really do have to offer an employer.

Sometimes, in doing a personal inventory, a student realizes he or she does not have a lot of professional experience to put on a resume. If you think this is a big negative, you are mistaken. For example, a student was interviewing in a top-30 market for a sales position. He was worried he would be asked about his lack of professional experience. He received the following good advice as to how to turn the objection into a benefit. If you are told that you have a great resume but that you lack professional experience, tell the interviewer: "You are correct and this is to WXXX's benefit because I don't bring years of bad work habits with me. You can help me develop my professional skills and work ethic in *exactly* the manner your company desires." The interviewer agreed, and the student was hired into a top 30 market. If someone asks you what you have to offer his or her station, be prepared to tell them.

Career Profile

The terms "Employment" and "Employment History" are very dull words. Your "Career Profile" sounds a little more exciting as a section following the introduction, the goals and objectives, and a summary of your outstanding qualifications. Although you design your goals and objectives to catch the employer's eye, your career profile is typically what draws the most attention from a prospective employer. This section of your resume begins with your current job and works backward, chronologically. Include your internship under your career profile, clearly listed as an internship. (Remember that any gaps in your career-profile time line, without an adequate explanation, are an automatic red flag to an employer.)

If you have gaps in your career time line, explain them in a simple, straightforward manner. For example, "attending college" is a perfectly acceptable explanation, as is "medical leave of absence" or "personal leave of absence." Although employers can ask you about things like your college experience, they may not legally ask you about medical or personal issues. Because of the variety of situations, how to handle a specific gap on your resume is something best discussed with a career placement counselor at your university.

For each employer you should list:

name of the corporation, station call letters, if applicable, and city

dates of employment rounded off to nearest month

title or position

specific things you accomplished for the employer

experience and skill sets required to carry out the position's duties

You should *not* list supervisor's names, company phone numbers, or reasons for leaving.

Be sure to put most of the emphasis on your skills and how you used them to accomplish things or on your achievements while holding the position. One of the jobs some people shy away from listing on their resume is waitress, waiter, or server. Waiting tables, however, is actually a good example of how you can find

skills and abilities in just about every field. A waitress or waiter has to deal with a number of different restaurant staff members. That is called "excellent employee relations" or "able to work with people from a diverse number of backgrounds." And also: you did not wait on tables; you waited on restaurant customers. Make one serious mistake, and customers never return. That is called "great customer relations skills" or "able to work with a variety of customers simultaneously." Employers know that being a server in a restaurant for any length of time demonstrates excellent people skills.

Your present employer receives the most attention in your resume; give progressively less space to each employer as you work backward. Normally, you need to go back only ten years and, in the case of college students, not even that far, since your employment history is probably not that lengthy.

As you write each employment description, use positive power words, or buzzwords, as they convey your professionalism and knowledge. Keep the focus on your accomplishments and how they contributed to the profitability of the business. For example, look at the following and decide which you think sounds better to a potential employer.

I helped install the new production computer software.

Or

I worked on the installation of new, enhanced, production computer software, which resulted in increased productivity and improved work flow in the production department.

Notice how the second statement is a positive statement that includes accomplishments and benefits.

Take a look through broadcast trade publications, web sites, and the professional want-ad section of a major Sunday newspaper. Look at the words employers use to describe the positions they are hiring for. Learn to speak their language!

Education

The education section of your resume can go either toward the end of the resume, if you have a significant work history, or near the beginning of the resume, if you are a recent graduate with a more limited work history. Where you place the education section is your choice.

The education section begins with your most recent degree, the year you earned it, and the institution where you earned the degree. If you graduated magna or summa cum laude, this should also be listed with your degree. If you had a GPA of 3.0 or above, list it along with your degree. It is not necessary to list your high school diploma.

In addition to your degree, you may also choose to list significant honors, awards, or scholarships you have received, along with any special licenses or certifications you have earned. In particular, list any college classes that have direct applicability to the job you are applying for. If you did a major research project that directly applies to the field or position you are applying for, you should list it as well. List your membership in any honorary professional, fraternal, and social organizations that relate to the position you are applying for.

Miscellaneous Sections

There are many things that distinguish you as an individual that you may wish to include toward the end of your resume, under various headings. If you served in the military and were honorably discharged, briefly mention this under a heading of Military Service. However, keep the listing simple, using only terms a civilian can understand. If your military service was directly related to the position you are applying for, it is appropriate for you to go into detail about your military career. For example, if you are applying for a position at a radio or television station and you served with Armed Forces Radio and Television, the details of your military service could be beneficial. Again, any details about your military career need to be written in plain English so that a civilian can easily understand what you did and where you did it; stay away from military abbreviations.

Do you speak a second language fluently? You might not think this is important, but in a global economy it is an increasingly valuable job skill. Not every radio station client speaks English well. In some markets, this skill is critical enough that it should be listed at the very beginning of your resume. For example, you are a valuable employee if you speak Spanish in any major metropolitan area, particularly in cities like Miami, Atlanta, or New York.

Certifications and membership in student and professional organizations should be listed on your resume if they relate to the position you are seeking. For example, a sales person who has earned the Radio Marketing Professional certification from the Radio Advertising Bureau should list this information on his or her resume. Engineering students should list any FCC licenses or Society of Broadcast Engineers certifications held. Certifications and memberships are listed as Professional Memberships or Professional Certifications.

Community service and volunteer work is an excellent indicator of character. Many employers like to see a history of community involvement. In particular, radio stations require that on-air staff become involved in community projects and maintain a high profile in the community. If you serve on any community boards or service group boards, this information should be included on your resume (again, see Fig. **15.5**). Community involvement is listed under a Community Service heading.

Most radio production people are capable of operating a number of different digital audio software programs and equipment. Tell your potential employer which such abilities you have, in a section of your resume entitled Technology or Technological Skills. List the hardware and software you are proficient with. List whether you are Mac, PC, or dual-platform proficient, and what major computer operating systems you are familiar with (again, see Fig. **15.5**). Employers want to see that your computer and software skills are current.

And finally, there are Personal Interests. These are listings that can spark conversation and show a potential employer you have a life outside work. These are particularly good to list if they relate to your work. As an example, this author collects vintage microphones and radios. He is also an advanced, open-water scuba diver and enjoys sports car racing. The microphones and radios show a historical interest in radio work. The scuba diving reflects taking calculated risks on a regular basis. The sports car racing reflects that he is competitive, a good quality to have in one of the most competitive industries in the world. You should devote only a simple one-line listing for each item to give your potential employer an idea of who you are outside work.

References

Normally, you state "References furnished upon request" at the end of your resume. References are not usually listed on the resume, but they certainly deserve some attention as they are a critical part of the hiring process for most employers.

The reason you do not put the names of references and their phone numbers on your resume is that most former employers will only confirm dates of employment during a telephone reference request. Yet your potential future employer will want more information than that, and this is when letters of reference are a good idea.

Most employers want to see and verify references. As a student starting out, you can enhance your professional status with the prospective employer by having five or six current reference letters ready for examination when requested. Rule number one with respect to references is to use only professional references, not family members or friends. References from people you worked with during your internship are very appropriate. As a recent grad, academic references from professors whose classes have direct applicability to the position you are applying for are also appropriate. Rule number two is that reference letters *must* be on company letterhead. There are no exceptions. Rule number three is that reference letters should not be more than one page long.

Prepare your reference letters as you are putting together your resume. Make a list of five or six individuals who will provide you a favorable reference, and contact them. Tell them what you are doing and ask if they would help you in your job search by providing a favorable reference letter. When asked, most people are pleased to help. If your resume is ready, send each individual a copy so he or she will have a good picture of what you are seeking to accomplish.

Typically, one of two things happens when a person agrees to give you a reference. The person either asks you to write the body of the letter (the best situation), or the person asks you what you want the letter to say. In either case, you need a letter that supports the critical elements of your resume and highlights your specific accomplishments. If the person is going to write the letter, it is appropriate to tell the person what the letter needs to say, or to coach the person on how you want the letter written.

When you receive a reference letter that has been written for you, promptly send a thank-you note to the person expressing your gratitude for his or her support of your job search. Along with your thank-you note, you should send the person a copy of your resume if you haven't already done so. Explain that it is for reference purposes should a prospective employer call him or her for more information. Keep in touch with your references and contact them after each interview so that you can keep them up to date on your job search. Let them share in some of your excitement of finding a new job.

Once you have your reference letters in hand, take them to a professional copier service and have color copies made. Create a title sheet with the header "PROFESSIONAL REFERENCE LETTERS." On the title sheet, list the references by name, the company each represents, their address, and phone number. Place the copies of the reference letters behind the title sheet and have them bound at a professional copier service or office supply store. When submitted with your resume, such a presentation gives you a great deal of credibility. In effect, you and five business leaders are applying for the position.

Keep three copies of your resume and references with you at all times when interviewing or networking. You need three so that you have two back-ups in case anyone else asks for a copy during an interview or while you are talking to someone. Remember, broadcasters typically need someone yesterday. They work in minutes and seconds and are accustomed to things happening fast. If someone you meet asks for a resume and references—hand it to them on the spot! If you are attending a job fair, carry a dozen resume/reference packages with you.

Audition CD

Now you have an application letter, a resume, your references, and you are ready to apply for your first job at a radio station. Right? Not quite. Remember, this is a talent-based industry, and potential employers want you to demonstrate your skills for them in the form of an audition. Almost all radio positions require an audition CD that showcases your best work.

Your audition CD should not be more than four (preferably 3.5) minutes of your very best work. If you are applying for a morning drive position, you can extend the time frame up to ten minutes, if you feel it is necessary. Something to keep in mind is that the person who listens to your CD has likely never met you. Your CD is both your introduction and who you are, to some degree. The prospective employer interviews the best-sounding audition CD.

Creativity is the key when it comes to the audition CD. Your CD needs to stand out from the pack and deliver the message that you have all the necessary skills to create exciting "theater-of-the-mind" product. At the very most, you are going to have fifteen to twenty seconds to catch the ear of the person reviewing the audition CDs. The first fifteen seconds need to be bright and expressive and need to reach out and grab the listener by the throat and scream "listen to me!" If it does not, your

CD becomes a flying object directed at the trash can or part of a glittering mobile of "nice tries" hanging in the PD's office.

Start the audition with your shortest, *best* work, and follow it with a series of fast-paced segments and cuts that move from one aspect to another of your production skills. The segments need to be in the twenty to thirty seconds long. Think of your CD as telling a story with an incredible beginning, good middle, and a great ending. Save your *second-best* work for the end of the CD because you need to leave the person impressed. It is important to have a high *wow* factor at the end of your CD because this is what motivates the program director to pick up the phone and call you.

For a production person, the content of your audition CD needs to include at least five commercial segments or complete commercials. You need to include as much multitrack demo material as possible. Show the extremes to which you can go: from a soft, caring, funeral-home commercial to a multitrack concert commercial. Include a couple of station promos, sweepers, and liners. Once your audition CD starts, there should be no spaces or gaps. It's a steady barrage of great production work with a super ending.

Listen to the first audition on the demo CD (see demo CD, cut 92). The audition was a class assignment and was produced entirely in a studio by a college junior who had never held a position in radio. His target: an edgy Alternative station. Although it may not be the style of music you prefer, listen carefully to the production. Creatively mix your segments so that the listener is teased and wants to hear more, rather than just lining up one commercial after another. Don't be afraid to develop a short imaging sound effect, such as the record noise and static at the beginning of the demo or the sound of a radio being tuned, to go between segments. This same create-it-in-a-stu-

dio style can be used for an announcer looking for that first position.

For an experienced announcer seeking an air shift, the content of the CD needs to be focused on your on-air personality (see demo CD, cut 93). The student on the demo had extensive on-air experience before re-entering college. If you are working, even on a part-time basis, you should be air-checking yourself every day. Make your air checks using a digital recorder. From these air checks, edit your best work together, keeping in mind that the focus is on you. Although you may talk over music or talk about upcoming artists and station events, edit out as much of the music as possible. For example, as soon as you finish talking over the intro to a song, cut to the next segment. The program director does not need to hear any music.

The physical presentation of your CD is just as important as what is on the CD. Use a quality CDR and, after you have burned it, listen to it in a CD player other than the one on your computer. The presentation of your CD needs to demonstrate to your prospective employer that you are a pro. Your CD must be clearly labeled. There are a number of software/label products that can create a professional label on your computer. The label should appear as neat, clean, and professional as possible. Remove the jacket and liner card that came in the CD case and replace them with ones you create with the CD label software.

Be sure your CD label and jacket liner have your name, address, phone number, and e-mail address clearly displayed (see Fig. **15.6**). Believe it or not, these sometimes end up in some pretty strange places in a radio station, and if they are not labeled, they are history. Often, they get passed around among the individuals making the hiring decision.

Remember, your audition CD is the first impression you make on a prospective employer. If your materials look sloppy, you are per-

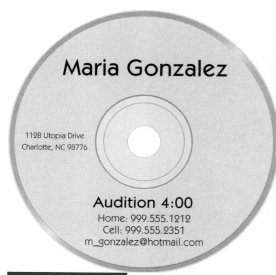

Maria Gonzalez

1128 Utopia Drive
Charlotte, NC 98776

Audition 4:00
Home: 999.555.1212
Cell: 999.555.2351
m_gonzalez@hotmail.com

Figure 15.6

Sometimes simple is best. The CD label above clearly displays the applicant's name, address, two phone numbers, and e-mail address. Keep in mind when you label your CD that it may become separated from your resume, and you never know where it will end up. It is important to have complete contact information on the disc.

ceived as sloppy. If they look poorly done, you are perceived as someone who cannot handle details and lacks professional standards. First impressions are lasting impressions.

Packaging Your Application

With your resume, professional references, and audition CD you are ready to write a cover letter and ship your package to a prospective employer. The cover letter and the package should be addressed to the individual doing the hiring. Never send a package to "Program Director" or "Station Manager." If you do not know the name of the program di-

rector, check the station's web site or call the station to get the person's exact name, title, and mailing address. If you are given a post office box number, ask for the station's Federal Express delivery address.

Rule number one of sending materials: Send them flat, never folded. Rule number two: *never* send your materials in a brown or manila envelope. Junk mail comes in brown or manila envelopes. The large padded envelope you select to send your materials in is critical. Distinguish your package so that it stands out from all the rest. At the very least, purchase some large, bright white envelopes to send your materials in. Sending your materials via U.S. Postal Priority Mail is an even better way to distinguish your package from the rest. Use the bright, colorful, free envelope the post office provides for this service (see Fig. **15.7**). Even if you are mailing your package to a station in the town where you live, send it via priority mail. Priority mail attracts attention and gets opened. It also subtly says to the employer that you value the application and the opportunity.

Even the label on your envelope says something about you. Purchase some computer address labels and prepare the address and return address labels on your computer.

If the potential employer is located out of town and you are really interested in the position, send your materials via Federal Express, next-morning delivery, and require a signature. This lets the employer know you are a professional and you are serious.

The Creative Approach to Package Delivery

You are formally warned: Read this section of the chapter at your own risk. What follows are several highly unusual ways to deliver a resume/audition CD package that have been used by creative people to land jobs in

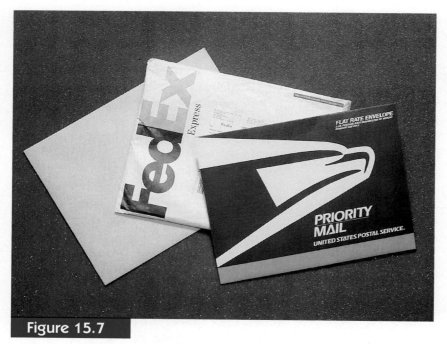

How you package your resume and materials is important. If you were a program director, which of the envelopes above would you open first?

various-sized markets. However, although some production or program directors will regard these types of packaging as highly creative, others will regard them as highly unprofessional and will ignore or toss your package. For the most part, the following delivery attempts were not first approaches but attempts to get attention when the normal methods didn't work.

It is recommended that you *not* use the exact approaches described here, but use them as inspiration for your own creative ideas. (It won't look so original and creative if someone else is doing exactly the same thing you are, now will it?)

An announcer who had worked his way through college delivering hot pizza in thirty minutes or less did what seemed natural to him. He took a clean, large pizza box and

placed his resume, references, and audition CD inside. He also included a handwritten note that said "I'm hot and I deliver!" He had a friend from his old employer deliver the "pizza" to the person accepting the applications.

Having been on an athletic scholarship and having lots of pairs of running shoes, a morning "sidekick" announcer took one of her old shoe boxes and put her application materials inside. She taped a large note on the outside of the box that read "Use the enclosed to help your morning team run off and leave the competition!" She used a local messenger service to deliver the box to the person accepting applications, with a signature required for delivery.

You have to love technology to appreciate what this production person did: He bought an inexpensive phone and programmed his home phone number into every memory button on the phone, including redial. He shipped the phone and his application materials overnight to the person accepting the applications. On the phone was a note that read "The incredibly creative production person who sent you this package is on the other end of the phone. Plug it in and hit redial!"

Possibly the mother of all attention-getters was a jock who shipped a live Maine lobster to a program director with a note that read, "Not afraid of hot water. In fact, I'll dive right in!"

These are just a few of the creative methods applicants have used to get someone's attention, and although approaches like these may certainly get your materials looked at, you still have to have the qualifications to get an interview and the proven abilities to get the job.

The Electronic Resume and Audition

Typically, a printed copy of your resume is sent along with your audition CD to a prospective employer. However, keep in mind that radio is sometimes a "got-to-have-it-yesterday" business. Although sending a package overnight is quick, there is a faster way, if requested, to get your resume to a program director. Send your resume and audition electronically.

Have your completed resume converted into an electronic file such as an Adobe .pdf file. A .pdf file is easily attached to an e-mail and delivered instantly. (Although a word processor file can also be attached to an e-mail message, it is not protected from alteration or accidental modification through error as the .pdf is.)

Convert your audition CD to a high-quality MP3 format, such as the mp3PRO format found in the Adobe Audition digital audio workstation software included with this text. You can also use a standard MP3 recorder set to a high bit rate, such as 256 kbps. Such files can easily be attached to an e-mail or placed on your web site for the employer to retrieve.

With electronic copies of your resume and audition you are ready to respond to ads that request you to send materials electronically. Checking the major broadcast companies' web-based job listings, it is quite common to see "electronically send your resume, MP3 air check, and any other relevant information to . . ."

Tracking an Application's Progress

Once your carefully prepared package has been sent and delivered to the appropriate person, what do you do? Wait. Then wait some more. Remember: Radio is different when it comes to getting a job. If you answered an ad in a broadcast trade publication, very likely the ad said "NO calls." There is a reason for this. It is not unusual for a trade-publication ad to generate more than a hundred responses for a program director to consider. Some of the applicants are qualified; the vast majority, however, are not.

Program directors are human beings. In today's marketplace, program directors often handle the programming for more than one station. Their time is very valuable. Do you really think they have the time to take over a hundred phone calls from potential applicants, many of whom are not qualified to begin with? Resist the urge to call if the ad says "NO calls." You'll only be annoying the person you want to impress, and besides, the chances are very high that you won't get through anyway because the program director has told the receptionist (gatekeeper) to block all calls regarding the position.

If, on the other hand, the ad did not say "no calls," then go for it. It may not be easy to get through to a busy person. No matter how frustrated you are that the person has not returned a call or you have not gotten to talk to that person, *never* challenge the receptionist/gatekeeper. In fact, make some small talk and tell the person you understand he or she has one of the toughest jobs in the station. Thank the person for any help he or she can give you. If the person takes a liking to you, you may get through. However, if the person feels you do not appreciate his or her position, your calls will never get through. Treat people the way you would like to be treated.

Is there any other way to get to the program director? Try a simple e-mail. And if or when you do get through to the program director with a phone call or an e-mail, keep it short and simple. Tell the program director you know he or she is swamped but that you just wanted to confirm that the package you sent had arrived and thank him or her for consideration. *Do not* try to advance the call or e-mail past this point. All you want to do is confirm that your package arrived and say thank you. If *the director* wants to advance the conversation, answer any questions politely, but don't get pushy.

What you have to understand about radio is that program directors *do* call the people they are interested in, without hesitation. They are constantly searching for the best talent to fill the positions they have. During the career of this author, I once delivered a resume and audition to a major-market news/talk station on Wednesday morning, was called Wednesday afternoon, interviewed Thursday morning, and reported for work on Friday. The process does not always happen that fast, but radio stations *do* move when it's time to move.

Suggested Activities

1. Go on-line or round up some industry trade publications like *Radio and Records* or *Broadcasting and Cable*. Look at the ads and the positions listed, paying particular attention to the language used in the ads. Look for words and phrases you can incorporate into your cover letter and resume.

2. Visit your state broadcasters' association web site. Many have employment clearing houses or "job banks" that list available positions around the state. Search for something that appeals to you. Review your resume to see what changes you would need to make to fine-tune it to apply for the particular job.

3. Go to the library and find the *Broadcasting and Cable Yearbook* or a copy of the latest *Standard Rate and Data*. Both of these reference books provide current listings for all of the radio and television stations in the Unites States. Learn how to read the listings so that you can find out valuable information about a station, including names of personnel, phone numbers, and addresses.

4. Visit the web site of the National Association of Broadcasters at www.nab.org and click on the "Career Center." The career center has job listings for radio and television stations all over the country. You also can post your resume and visit links to other broadcasting job banks. This is an incredible resource. Explore the site and become familiar with all of the services offered for the job-seeker.

Web Sites for More Information

For more information about

- *broadcasting job bank and career development,* visit the National Association of Broadcasters at www.nab.org

- *employment opportunities with each of the major station chains,* visit each of the individual corporate web sites

- *personal information required or not on a job application or resume,* visit the EEOC at www.eeoc.gov

Appendix

Each cut on the demonstration CD has a narrative explaining what you will hear and what key element you should listen for.

CHAPTER 1

Cut 1   A sample commercial with the music and copy mismatched.

Cut 2   A sample commercial with the music properly matched to the copy.

CHAPTER 2

Cut 3   Audio frequency sweep from 100 Hz through 20 kHz, with the major frequencies announced.

Cut 4   Audio frequency sweep from 50 Hz to 5 kHz at a fixed sound level, to demonstrate perceived sound level changes.

Cut 5   A fixed frequency audio signal with the sound level varied to demonstrate a perceived frequency change.

Cut 6   Shuttle launch recorded at the Kennedy Space Center press site to demonstrate how it takes nearly 15 seconds for the sound to arrive from the launch pad, which is 3.1 miles away.

Cut 7   Demonstration of music recorded 180 degrees out of phase.

CHAPTER 3

Cut 8   Vocal demonstration of the proximity effect using an AKG 414 microphone.

Cut 9   Demonstration of a ribbon microphone's open natural sound.

Cut 10   Demonstration of the proximity effect with a ribbon microphone at various distances up to 3 feet.

Cut 11   Vocal recording with an AKG 414 at 3 feet, 2 feet, 1 foot, and 6 inches from the face of the microphone.

Cut 12   Omnidirectional microphone pattern demonstration with an AKG 414 microphone.

Cut 13   Bidirectional microphone pattern demonstration with an AKG 414 microphone.

Cut 14   Cardioid microphone pattern demonstration with an AKG 414 demonstrating 0-degree vs. 180-degree sensitivity.

Cut 15   Hyper-cardioid microphone pattern demonstration.

Cut 16   A demonstration of polar frequency response by rotating an AKG 414 while in the super-cardioid pattern and speaking into it.

Cut 17   Demonstration of an AKG 414 microphone, without a shock mount, and the building noise and rumble it picks up.

Cut 18   Recording of birds and mountain stream in the Joyce Kilmer Forest.

Cut 19 Recording of whitewater rafters on the Nantahala River.

Cut 20 A recording of a direct and an ambient microphone demonstrating the various mixes that can be created from the two tracks.

Cut 21 Popping "P" demonstration.

Cut 22 Demonstration of a Shure SM 81 with and without a pop filter.

Cut 23 Demonstration of a Sennheiser 421 II with a person speaking directly into the front of the mic, popping "P's," and the same person speaking into the same microphone, turned 90 degrees to the side.

Cut 24 Demonstration of a Sennheiser 421 II outside, without a windscreen, on a windy day, and the same microphone with a windscreen, under the same conditions.

Cut 25 Demonstration of a person speaking directly into a lavalier microphone placed at the lips.

Cut 26 Demonstration of a shotgun microphone's audio pickup compared to an omnidirectional microphone at the same distance from the sound source.

CHAPTER 4

Cut 27 A demonstration of equalization by placing one sound above or below another and "carving" an equalization "hole" to demonstrate height in a mix.

Cut 28 A demonstration of panning to help provide width in a mix.

Cut 29 A demonstration of reverb to help provide depth in a mix.

CHAPTER 6

Cut 30 An example of an announcer's voice with and without a voice processor.

Cut 31 An example of an announcer's voice with and without compression over music to demonstrate how compression raises the voice above the music.

Cut 32 A whisper that is compressed and becomes a loud whisper.

Cut 33 An example of an announcer's voice comparing a 4:1 compression ratio to a 15:1 compression ratio.

Cut 34 An example of an announcer's voice demonstrating a compressor pumping.

Cut 35 An example of an announcer's voice with limiting applied.

Cut 36 An example of an announcer's voice with expansion applied.

Cut 37 An example of an announcer's voice using a noise gate.

Cut 38 A demonstration of a high-pass filter cutting or removing building rumble.

Cut 39 A demonstration of a low-pass filter cutting or removing the high end from a vocal.

Cut 40 A demonstration of a notch filter removing pops and clicks.

Cut 41 A demonstration of a de-esser on an announcer's voice.

Cut 42 An equalization demonstration to show the effects of boosting and cutting frequencies.

Cut 43 An example of an announcer's voice with 40 milliseconds of slap delay.

Cut 44 An example of an announcer's voice with 40 milliseconds of slap delay and feedback.

Cut 45 An example of an announcer's voice with less than 35 milliseconds of slap delay.

Cut 46   An example of an announcer's voice with reverb, demonstrating three different-sized rooms or spaces.

Cut 47   A recording of a piano without reverb, compared to piano with small reverb and short delay to make it sound bigger than life.

Cut 48   A recording of a music bed and how to move it behind or in front of a vocal, using reverb.

Cut 49   A demonstration of a 20- to 35-millisecond chorus effect on a piano recording.

Cut 50   A demonstration of the phase-shift effect.

Cut 51   A demonstration of a 10- to 20-millisecond flanging effect.

Cut 52   A demonstration of the re-amping effect.

Cut 53   A demonstration of normalizing a vocal.

Cut 54   A demonstration of adjusting the input on a PreSonus voice processor.

Cut 55   A demonstration of adjusting the compressor controls on a PreSonus voice processor.

Cut 56   A demonstration of adjusting the expander on a PreSonus voice processor.

Cut 57   A demonstration of adjusting the de-esser on a PreSonus voice processor.

Cut 58   A demonstration of adjusting the shelving filters on a PreSonus voice processor.

Cut 59   A demonstration of adjusting the peak limiter on a PreSonus voice processor.

Cut 60   A demonstration of the Eventide Harmonizer and its effect on voice.

CHAPTER 7

Cut 61   An example of a commercial in which the advertiser talks only about his business and uses industry jargon. (Amy's Cookie Factory)

Cut 62   An example of a commercial in which the advertiser stresses customer benefits. (Amy's Cookie Factory)

Cut 63   An example of a commercial that uses "we" and "us" versus one that uses the business's name instead. (Amy's Cookie Factory)

Cut 64   An example of how confusing telephone numbers can be in a commercial and a better way to present them.

Cut 65   An example of a good wrap at the end of a commercial.

CHAPTER 8

Cut 66   A demonstration showing how too many sound effects ruin a commercial.

Cut 67   Two different reads of a commercial to demonstrate the differences in presentation of the same material.

Cut 68   An original, unedited, location recording of the historic Baldwin steam engine number 722 owned by the Great Smoky Mountains Railroad, Dillsboro, NC, for sound effects editing purposes.

Cut 69   An "OK" read of a commercial with the announcer doing several pickups so that the production person can edit to the read he or she likes.

Cut 70   A 60-second music cut created with music loops from the music CD that is included with the text.

Cut 71   A comparison of an unprocessed voice track and the same voice track with mild compression and reverb, demonstrating how the processed voice blends with the commercial.

Cut 72 A 60-second agency commercial with space for a 10-second tag at the end for local copy.

Cut 73 A 60-second agency commercial with a donut in the middle for local copy.

Cut 74 A news story that has been unethically enhanced using sound effects and audio processing.

Cut 75 A person saying the numbers one through ten in random order, with breath sounds between each; this is an editing exercise.

CHAPTER 10

Cut 76 Radio station sweeper demonstration.
Cut 77 A national award-winning promo.
Cut 78 Morning show promo.
Cut 79 Promotional voice demonstrations.
Cut 80 Promotional voice doing sample liners.
Cut 81 Promotional voice doing sample sweepers.
Cut 82 Highly produced sweeper sample.
Cut 83 Transition sweeper from music to news.
Cut 84 Sample sweeper with station ID buried inside.
Cut 85 Demo of jingles from TM Century.

CHAPTER 11

Cut 86 Thirty seconds of a remote broadcast on a POTS line.
Cut 87 Thirty seconds of a remote broadcast on a POTS codec.
Cut 88 Thirty seconds of a remote broadcast on an ISDN codec.

Cut 89 Thirty seconds of a remote broadcast on a Marti VHF remote pickup transmitter.

Cut 90 Thirty seconds of a remote broadcast on a satellite phone.

CHAPTER 14

Cut 91 An audition of imaging including liners and sweepers from Jeff Laurence.

CHAPTER 15

Cut 92 Actual student production audition CD.
Cut 93 Actual air talent's audition CD.

Digital Radio Production Music CD

Chapter 5

Cut 1	Carolina Blues—full mixed version	1:35
Cut 2	Carolina Blues—piano track	1:35
Cut 3	Carolina Blues—bass track	1:35
Cut 4	Carolina Blues—drum track	1:35
Cut 5	Carolina Blues—rhythm guitar track	1:35
Cut 6	Carolina Blues—lead guitar track	1:35
Cut 7	Rock 1	1:30
Cut 8	Rock 2	1:00
Cut 9	Swing	1:00
Cut 10	Funky	0:59
Cut 11	Funky Too	1:00
Cut 12	Smooth	1:00
Cut 13	Sweet	0:59
Cut 14	Pretty (waltz)	1:00
Cut 15	A Bit of Bach	2:00
Cut 16	Mozart	1:00

Cut 17	Far East Loop	1:00		Cut 29	Drum 5, Fill Only-A	0:03
Cut 18	Reggae Loop	1:00		Cut 30	Drum 6, Fill Only-B	0:02
Cut 19	Garage Loop	1:00		Cut 31	Drum 7, Ending Only	0:09
Cut 20	Dirty Loop	1:00		Cut 32	Drum 8, Pattern with Crash	0:10
Cut 21	News and Public Affairs Bed (full version)	1:00		Cut 33	Drum 9, Pattern with Ride	0:13
Cut 22	News and Public Affairs Bed (short)	0:30		Cut 34	Drum 10, Pattern with 8ths	0:10
Cut 23	News and Public Affairs Bed Bumper 1	0:15		Cut 35	Drum 11, Pattern with 8ths + Open Hat	0:10
Cut 24	News and Public Affairs Bed Bumper 2	0:05		Cut 36	Drum 12, Pattern with 8ths + Crash	0:10
Cut 25	Drum 1, Basic Pattern	0:10		Cut 37	Drum 13, Pattern with Ride	0:13
Cut 26	Drum 2, Pattern with Fill-A	0:14		Cut 38	Drum 14, Pattern with 16ths	0:10
Cut 27	Drum 3, Pattern with Fill-B	0:10		Cut 39	Drum 15, Pattern with 16ths + Crash	0:10
Cut 28	Drum 4, Pattern with Fill-C	0:10		Cut 40	Drum 16, End Hit Only	0:05

Glossary

A/D: Analog-to-digital audio converter. (chapter 11)

acoustical phase: A difference in time between two or more sine waves, measured in degrees. (chapter 2)

active crossover: A powered speaker crossover network with adjustable crossover frequencies. (chapter 4)

ADAT: Alesis digital audiotape is a digital audio-recording system that uses S-VHS videotapes to record up to eight channels of digital audio. (chapter 5)

AM: Amplitude modulation. The AM radio band extends from 535 kHz to 1605 kHz. (chapter 13)

amplitude: Amplitude represents the strength, or loudness, of a sound or audio signal without regard for its frequency. The height of the sine wave can be measured either in decibels, for sound, or voltage, for audio signals. (chapter 2)

Arbitron: The primary radio audience measurement service. Arbitron ratings are often referred to as "the book," since the ratings are published in book form each quarter. (chapter 10)

ASCAP: American Society of Composers, Authors, and Publishers. A membership-based performing rights organization that protects the copyrights of members' works by licensing and distributing royalties for the performances of their copyrighted works. (chapter 1)

attack time: The fixed or adjustable length of time it takes for an audio processor to sense the presence of audio and react to the audio, measured in milliseconds. (chapter 6)

audio: Latin, "to hear"; sound that has been converted into electrical energy. (chapter 3)

balanced microphone cable: A microphone cable or line in which there is a positive wire, a negative wire, and a shield, or earth ground, surrounding the positive and negative wires. (chapter 3)

band-pass filter: An audio filter that has a high and low cutoff frequency, allowing only the frequencies in between to pass unaffected. (chapter 6)

bandwidth: With reference to a radio carrier wave, bandwidth is the space on the radio band occupied by the radio carrier-wave frequency and the audio that has been superimposed upon it. The superimposed audio signal widens the radio carrier by adding sidebands just above and below the assigned carrier frequency. The carrier wave and the upper and lower sidebands of the signal compose the bandwidth of a signal. (chapter 13)

barometric air pressure: A measure of the weight of the atmosphere, or air, pressing down on earth. It averages approximately 29.92 inches of mercury at mean sea level, which is the equivalent of 14.7 pounds per square inch. Barometric pressure varies with altitude, getting lighter as the altitude increases. (chapter 2)

bass boost: Another term for proximity effect. (chapter 3)

bidirectional: A microphone pattern that has maximum sensitivity at 0 and 180 degrees and maximum rejection at 90 and 270 degrees. (chapter 3)

BMI: Broadcast Music, Incorporated. A membership-based performing rights organization that protects the copyrights of members' works by licensing and distributing royalties for the performances of their copyrighted works. (chapter 1)

BNC: An unbalanced coaxial cable connector with a bayonet-type locking system invented by Paul Neill and Carl Concelman, thus the name Bayonet Neill-Concelman. Typically found on video and digital audio cables. The center conductor of the cable is connected to a pin, and the shield is connected to a barrel surrounding the pin. A rotating ring outside the barrel locks the cable to any female connector. (chapter 5)

branding: A marketing plan that seeks to provide a clear differentiation from the other stations in the marketplace, based on the station's overall identity and attitude as defined by the listener. (chapter 10)

breakout box: A device designed to allow audio distribution at press conferences through multiple mic or line-level outputs. (chapter 11)

bright: A sound rich in high frequencies. (chapter 6)

bus: A common point in an audio device into which several inputs feed and are joined together. (chapter 4)

butt plug: A wireless transmitter designed for plugging into the base of a microphone. (chapter 3)

call-out research: Research conducted by a radio station or a research firm to ask listeners questions about how they perceive the station's music format; often used to keep a station's music format on track from week to week. (chapter 1)

cardioid: A heart-shaped microphone pattern with maximum sensitivity at 0 degrees and maximum rejection at 180 degrees. (chapter 3)

carrier wave: The high-frequency radio wave transmitted by a radio station that has been amplitude or frequency modulated. (chapter 13)

centerline: An imaginary line extending straight out from the face of a microphone, or 0-degree axis. (chapter 3)

codec: Encoder/decoder; used to describe digital communication devices that encode data into a digital format before transmission and decode the data after the transmission. (chapters 11, 13)

coincident pair: Stereo microphone placement in which the two microphones are placed one above the other on a horizontal plane facing the sound source. With the heads serving as the rotation point, one is aimed at the right side of the sound source, the other at the left side. (chapter 3)

combo mode: When the on-air radio talent serves as the show's engineer as well, running the control board and other elements of the show in addition to announcing. (chapter 4)

commercial inventory: The number of commercials that a radio station has to offer for sale. Commercial inventory can be broken down into weekly, daily, and hourly inventory. (chapter 1)

commercial inventory load: How many commercials are actually scheduled to run in a given time period such as an hour, half hour, or quarter hour. (chapter 1)

compression: An audio processing technique in which the highest audio peaks are automatically turned down, reducing the dynamic range of the audio signal in a direct ratio to the audio input level; a form of automatic volume control. (chapter 5)

compression ratio: The fixed or adjustable ratio of the input to the output of an audio compressor. (chapter 6)

condenser microphone: A microphone that uses an electrostatic field to convert sound into audio and requires a polarizing voltage and preamplifier. (chapter 3)

constructive interference: When two sine waves are just slightly out of phase with one another but are still together in their cycles of compression and rarefaction. Constructive interference tends to increase the amplitude, reinforcing the sound waves. (chapter 2)

continuity coordinator: The individual who is responsible for writing all of the commercial and promotional copy that goes on the air. (chapter 8)

core audience: The primary target demographic of a radio station. (chapter 10)

courtesy lines: Telephone lines that are available in the press area of a sports venue for visiting sportscasters to use without charge. Depending on the facility, the line may be a POTS or an ISDN line. Most have long-distance service disabled, other than toll-free exchanges such as 800, 888, etc. (chapter 11)

crispy: A sound with extended high-frequency response, like the sizzle of crisp bacon frying. (chapter 6)

critical distance: The distance from the sound source at which the ratio of direct-to-reverberant sound is equal, or 1; abbreviated Dc. (chapter 3)

D/A: The abbreviation for a digital-to-analog audio converter. (chapter 11)

dark: A sound that is the direct opposite of bright; dull with a weak high-frequency response. (chapter 6)

DAW: Digital audio workstation is the term generally applied to a computer-based digital recording system that incorporates the ability to record, store, manipulate, transport, and deliver digital audio products. (chapter 5)

daypart: A broadcast industry term that classifies a specific time period of radio listening. (chapter 10)

dead studio: A studio or a location that has no natural reverberation or echo. (chapter 6)

dead-studio sound: A studio is said to be a "dead studio" when there is little or no natural reverberation—the less reverberation, the more dead the studio. (chapter 8)

decibels: A unit of measurement developed by Alexander Graham Bell to measure the loss of signal over one mile of telephone line. Because the bel is such a large unit, most measurements are made in tenths (deci) of a bel, thus the decibel. A decibel can be expressed as a volume of acoustic sound-pressure level or, for audio signals, as a voltage reading. (chapter 2)

de-esser: A specialty compressor that has a variable frequency range used to reduce sibilant *ess* sounds in speech between 6 kHz and 8 kHz. (chapter 6)

demographics: Demographic information consists of statistical data about a particular group of people. For example, the radio station targets 18-to-34-year-old single males living in Jackson County who have an annual income of over $15,000. (chapter 1)

destructive interference: When two sine waves are out of phase with one another and their cycles of compression and rarefaction are occurring at different times. Destructive interference tends to decrease the amplitude and weaken the sound waves. (chapter 2)

digital condenser microphone: A condenser microphone with a built-in preamplifier that includes an analog-to-digital converter and digital output only. (chapter 3)

diversity receiver: A wireless microphone receiver using two tuners and two antennas to eliminate noise and dropouts. (chapter 3)

DMCA: Digital Millennium Copyright Act of 1998. (chapter 12)

donut: A type of agency-supplied commercial that has a hole in the middle of the ad for the insertion of local copy. (chapter 8)

draw: Something to attract people to an event or a location: a gimmick or enticement. (chapter 11)

driver: An individual speaker within a speaker cabinet; each driver consists of a moving-coil transducer that converts analog electrical energy into acoustic energy. (chapter 4)

dry signal: An original, unprocessed audio signal being sent from an audio console to an outboard audio processor, such as a reverb or delay unit. (chapter 4)

DSL: Digital subscriber line. An Internet connection made over a regular, twisted-pair telephone line capable of carrying data and a telephone conversation at the same time. Popular for home and small business use. (chapters 12 and 13)

DSP: Digital signal processor is a device for the manipulation and modification of audio signals, such as reverb, delay, or dynamics processing. (chapter 5)

DTRS: Digital tape recording system that uses Hi8 videotape as the recording medium, with the capability to record eight channels of digital audio. (chapter 5)

dubs: Slang for the word duplicate, a term used for a copy or copies of an original. (chapter 7)

duplex devices: Audio devices that allow bidirectional communications on a single line or radio-frequency transmission. (chapter 11)

DVD: The digital versatile disc is an optical storage medium that offers a number of both audio and video storage formats. Depending on the format, a DVD can store data on both sides of the disc, two layers deep. (chapter 5)

DVD-A: A digital versatile disc that contains only audio. (chapter 5)

dynamic microphone: A moving-coil microphone. (chapter 3)

dynamic range: The difference betwen the softest and loudest part of a sound, measured in decibels (dB). A dynamic range of 95 dB, for example, indicates that the loudest sound is 95 dB louder than the softest sound. (chapter 2)

electret-condenser microphone: A condenser microphone that, although it does not require a polarizing voltage, does require a battery to run the preamplifier. (chapter 3)

ENG: Electronic news gathering, or location spot-news coverage. (chapter 11)

ERP: Effective radiated power. When applied to an FM station, the term specifies in watts how much power the station can use to transmit its signal, as measured at the antenna. (chapter 13)

external marketing: Any medium or marketing tool outside the radio station such as billboards, newspaper ads, and television commercials used to promote the radio station. (chapter 1)

fatter: A sound with a good, solid, low-frequency response with emphasis in the 100 Hz to 300 Hz range. (chapter 6)

feedback: A condition that occurs when a microphone is left open near a monitor speaker, creating a loud howling or whistling sound. The microphone picks up the amplified sound from the speaker and sends it back through the system, re-generating the signal over and over. (chapter 4)

FM: Frequency modulation. The FM radio band extends from 88 mHz to 108 mHz. (chapter 13)

focus groups: A qualitative market research tool in which a group of people with common demographics and similar attitudes are surveyed and questioned on a particular topic by a trained moderator. (chapter 14)

footprint: A satellite signal's geographic coverage area on earth. (chapter 13)

frequency: The number of complete cycles that occur in one second of time; expressed as cycles per second. (chapter 2)

frequency: The number of times a radio ad airs during a given period of time. (chapter 7)

frequency-response curve: A plotted chart that shows how a microphone responds to various frequencies, called flat if the microphone treats all frequencies equally. (chapter 3)

FTP: File transfer protocol, a system for exchanging computer files with another computer, using the Internet as opposed to the World Wide Web. (chapter 5)

gaffer's tape: Available in colors, gaffer's tape has the strength of duct tape without the sticky mess afterwards. (chapter 3)

gain staging: Matching a microphone's maximum output voltage to the preamplifier's maximum input voltage to prevent overload. (chapter 3)

gating: An audio processing technique that acts just as its name implies, as a gate. When audio is above a preset level, the gate allows it to pass. When the audio level drops below the preset level

the gate closes, blocking the background noise. (chapter 5)

geo-synchronous orbit: An orbit that places a satellite approximately 22,000 miles above the earth so that it rotates at the same speed as the earth, maintaining a fixed position in space. (chapter 13)

gooseneck: A piece of flexible metal conduit used to support a microphone. (chapter 3)

GPS: Global Positioning System. A satellite-based navigation system made up of a network of satellites that enables pinpoint location identification. (chapter 11)

groundwave propagation: The property of physics that allows amplitude-modulated radio carrier signals to follow the earth's surface through conduction. (chapter 13)

GSM: Global System for Mobile Communications. (chapter 11)

HAAT: Height above average terrain. Applied to an FM radio station, the term specifies in meters the height of the station's transmitting antenna above the average terrain that surrounds it. (chapter 13)

hard clipping: An audio condition in which the audio is driven beyond distortion to the point that the edges of the sine waves start breaking up. (chapter 3)

harmonic: A harmonic is a sound created by multiplying the fundamental frequency or first harmonic. The second harmonic is two times the fundamental; the third harmonic is three times the fundamental, etc. (chapter 2)

headroom: The additional capacity of an audio device to handle level increases above average working levels to protect from transients, overload, and distortion. (chapter 4)

high-pass filter: A filter that blocks audio frequencies below a specific frequency, allowing those frequencies above the specified frequency to pass. (chapter 4)

hollow: A sound that has a mid-frequency dip similar to when you cup your hands around your mouth and talk. (chapter 6)

HTML: Hyper Text Mark-up Language, a computer language used in the creation of web sites that allows sites to be linked together easily. (chapter 12)

hyper-cardioid: An elongated, heart-shaped cardioid pattern used primarily in shotgun microphones to allow the microphones to be moved farther from the sound source without increasing the apparent room reverberation. (chapter 3)

IFB: Interruptible foldback. A method for sending a monitor signal to the talent while also being able to talk to him or her through an earpiece or headphone; a sophisticated intercom system. (chapter 11)

image transfer: When an audio track from a television commercial is used as a stand-alone radio commercial, causing the radio listener to visualize the images of the matching television commercial. (chapter 7)

imaging: Radio station imaging consists of the short live and recorded elements that are used between segments of a station's programming that tie everything together, creating a station's signature sound. As an example, "Kansas City's home for good-time rock-and-roll oldies, Super Cool 107-9." (chapter 1)

incidental performance: A very brief performance of a portion of a musical work going into program or commercial breaks. In no case the entire musical selection, regardless of length, and in no case longer than 30 seconds. Defined by federal copyright statutes. (chapter 12)

infrasonic: Sounds or audio signals that fall below the average person's hearing range, typically 20 Hz and lower. (chapter 2)

internal marketing: Any marketing tool or promotion tool used on a radio station to attract more listeners, such as contests, T-shirts, bumper stickers, etc. (chapter 1)

interruptible foldback (IFB): A type of intercom or communications system that allows the control board operator or producer to talk to the talent. (chapter 4)

ISDN: Integrated Services Digital Network. A dial-up digital line capable of transmitting 128 kilobits of studio-quality audio data and 16 kilobits of telephone switching data. (chapter 11)

ISP: Internet Service Provider. (chapter 11)

Krispy Kreme donut: A Southern delicacy, wonderfully light donuts slathered in mouth-watering sugar frosting, often used to entice the crew to show up in the morning; a sugar-delivery device. (chapter 3)

LAN: A local area network is a computer interconnection system for sharing data between or among computers within a company or media facility at one location. (chapter 5)

lav: Lavalier, which comes from the French word lavaliere or "pendant," a microphone worn on the body. Pronounced like "lava" from a volcano, just dropping the last a. (chapter 3)

LEO: Low earth orbit. A term used to describe satellites orbiting earth at between 300 and 500 miles high. (chapter 11)

limiting: An audio processing technique that automatically controls audio levels that approach a preset maximum audio level. When the preset level is reached, the audio is turned down so that it does not exceed the preset level. (chapter 5)

listener fatigue: A condition brought on by misadjusted audio processing, causing the listener to become consciously, or subconsciously, tired of listening to a musical selection or radio station. (chapter 6)

loudness distortion: Distortion that is caused by overpowering an electronic device, such as a speaker, thereby exceeding its capabilities and producing a very harsh and distorted sound. (chapter 4)

low-pass filter: A filter that blocks audio frequencies above a specific frequency, allowing those frequencies below the specified frequency to pass. (chapter 4)

maximum sound-pressure level: The maximum dB-SPL that a microphone can reproduce before going into distortion and then failure. (chapter 3)

MD: Minidisc is a registered trademark of Sony and refers to a disc enclosed in a small cartridge. The 2 1/2-inch-diameter disc records and plays back near-CD-quality audio using a combination magnetic/optical system. (chapter 2)

metro area: A metropolitan city's area as defined by the U.S. Government's Office of Management and Budget, also generally accepted by the major rating services as a designated geographical area. (chapter 10)

mic: Pronounced "Mike"; industry abbreviation for microphone ("mics" is used for more than one mic). (chapter 3)

mic flag: A plastic nameplate, or cover, that goes on a microphone with the station's call letters or logo. (chapter 11)

micron: An outdated term still in common usage that has since been replaced with the term micrometer. A micron, or micrometer, is one millionth of a meter, or about 1/25,000th of an inch. (chapter 3)

middle/side microphone: A stereo microphone incorporating a cardioid element facing forward and a bidirectional element facing out the sides of the microphone. The combination of the middle element and the separate halves of the bidirectional element create the left and right channels. (chapter 3)

modulation: Change; in this case, the process of changing a silent carrier with either amplitude or frequency modulation. (chapter 13)

MP3: Motion Picture Experts Group Layer 3 audio compression compresses, or shrinks, CD-quality audio files by a factor of twelve or more, maintaining the original, perceived CD-quality sound so that audio files can be transferred via the World Wide Web. (chapter 1)

muddy: muffled-sounding audio, not clear, with too much reverb at the lower frequencies. (chapter 6)

mult: Same as a breakout box, a device designed to allow audio distribution at press conferences through multiple mic or line-level outputs. (chapter 11)

national rep: A national representative is a person or company that represents a radio station to large, national advertising agencies handling regional or national products. (chapter 1)

near-coincident pair: Stereo microphone placement in which the two microphones are placed one above the other on a horizontal plane, facing the sound source. With the midpoint of the mic bodies serving as the rotation point, one is aimed at the right side of the sound source, the other at the left side. (chapter 3)

near-field monitors: Smaller monitor speakers placed very near the mixing position, often at the front of the console. (chapter 4)

needle-drop basis: An old radio term used to describe paying for production music on a per-cut-used basis. (chapter 8)

noise: Electrical noise, which appears as hiss in an audio signal, measured in negative dB. The higher the negative figure, the better. (chapter 3)

nontraditional revenue: Revenue generated by a radio station from anything other than commercial-time sales. Examples include events a station sponsors, such as job fairs and car shows, or banner ad sales from the station's web site. (chapter 12)

notch filter: An audio filter designed to eliminate a very narrow bandwidth of sound, creating a notch in the frequency. Generally used to eliminate unwanted sounds. (chapter 6)

off-air monitor: An actual air signal taken from a radio set for monitoring purposes. (chapter 11)

off axis: Outside of the centerline of a microphone's directional pattern, usually measured in degrees. (chapter 3)

off-axis coloration: The change in the frequency response and sensitivity of a microphone as it is turned away from a sound source and aimed in a different direction. (chapter 3)

omnidirectional: A microphone pattern that allows the microphone to pick up sound from all directions equally. (chapter 3)

overload: The point at which a microphone's output will overpower the preamplifier it is plugged into. (chapter 3)

overtone: A sound or audio signal that occurs in between the harmonics or multiples of a fundamental frequency. (chapter 2)

pan control: Panoramic control, a sonic positioning control that allows the input to a mixer channel to be assigned to the left channel or the right channel, or to remain in the center channel for a mono signal. (chapter 4)

parabolic reflector: A microphone that uses a large parabolic dish to focus sound onto the microphone; used to pick up distant sounds, and commonly seen on sports sidelines. (chapter 3)

passive crossover: A crossover network comprised of electronic components whose values are fixed, with the audio requiring no electrical power to pass through the network. (chapter 4)

pattern: The term used to describe the directional characteristics of a microphone. (chapter 3)

perceptual audio coding: A method of compressing, encoding, and decoding audio data files that takes advantage of the properties of the human perception of sound to achieve a size reduction of the data file with little or no perceptible loss of quality. (chapter 12)

phantom power: Power supplied to a condenser microphone from a source such as a control board, portable mixing board, or other outside source through the microphone cable. (chapter 3)

phone hybrid: An electronic device used to connect broadcast equipment with a telephone line so that audio can be sent and received on the phone line. (chapter 11)

polar frequency response: The frequency-response curve of a microphone measured at various points in the microphone pattern. (chapter 3)

pool audio feed: A single-point audio feed for the press, usually accomplished with a mult or breakout box. (chapter 11)

pop filter: An acoustic foam filter within a microphone, used to prevent popping plosive sounds from reaching the microphone element. (chapter 3)

popper stopper: A fine mesh screen placed a few inches off the face of a microphone to prevent popping plosive sounds from reaching the microphone element. (chapter 3)

positioning statement: A unique selling proposition, or slogan, used by a station to separate itself from the competition. (chapter 10)

pot: Potentiometer; technical term for a volume control. (chapter 4)

POTS: A telephone company term for Plain Old Telephone Service, or a dial-up, hard-line telephone connection. (chapter 6)

preamplifier: A voltage multiplier used to boost the weak signal of a microphone to a usable audio level. (chapter 3)

prosumer: Prosumer equipment is equipment that offers many professional features but is not built to rigid professional standards. It is generally priced in between consumer and professional-level equipment. (chapter 3)

proximity effect: The closer you move to a directional microphone, the more bass it appears to have. (chapter 3)

psychographic: Determining how people or groups of people thinks about a particular product or service: what their image is of your product and how they see themselves relating to your product. (chapter 14)

qualitative research: Research centered on a person or group's lifestyle choices. For example, the radio station targets 18-to-34-year-old single males living in Jackson County who rent an apartment, make monthly car payments on a 2004, or newer, vehicle, eat out three times a week, drink domestic beer, and go to the movies twice a month. (chapter 1)

quantitative research: Research centered on numerical or statistical data; most commonly audience ratings research to determine the number of listeners a radio station has. (chapter 1)

quantization: The process of assigning a binary number to each of the samples or voltage readings taken during the analog-to-digital audio conversion. (chapter 2)

release time: The fixed, or adjustable, length of time it takes for an audio processor, such as a compressor or limiter, to return a signal to its normal level after processing, measured in milliseconds. (chapter 6)

RF: Radio frequency. (chapter 13)

ribbon: A member of the dynamic class of microphones; the ribbon uses a thin ribbon of metal as the sound pickup element. (chapter 3)

rubber ducky: A flexible radio antenna made from silicone-based rubber products that can be bent and flexed without damage to the antenna coil contained within. (chapter 3)

SACD: A joint product of Sony and Philips that uses a two-layer, CD-sized disc to reproduce both 5.1 surround sound and standard stereo using Direct Stream Digital encoding, which is a one-bit system with a sampling rate of 2,822,400 samples per second. (chapter 2)

SDR: Software-defined radio. A radio that converts the incoming radio signal into a digital data stream and then processes the data to extract the usable signals. (chapter 13)

self-powered speakers: Speakers that have amplifiers built into them so that an audio feed from a mixer or control board can be fed directly into the speaker. (chapter 4)

sensitivity: An electrical measurement in either dBV or millivolts that tells what the audio output of the microphone will be at a given sound-pressure input level. (chapter 3)

SESAC: Society of European Stage Authors and Composers. A membership-based performing rights organization that protects the copyrights of members' works by licensing and distributing royalties for their performance. (chapter 1)

SFX: Sound effects. (chapter 8)

shock mount: A device designed to hold a microphone and isolate it from vibrations that might enter the microphone body and cause undesirable sounds. (chapter 3)

shotgun microphone: A microphone designed with a long tube in front of the microphone element to focus the sound and increase the microphone's direct-to-reverberant sound ratio. (chapter 3)

skywave propagation: A phenomenon that occurs as the long wavelengths of the AM signals interact with the radically shifting layers of the ionosphere several miles above the earth's surface at night, causing AM signals to travel great distances. (chapter 13)

slate: The radio equivalent of the beginning of a scene in a television or film shoot, when someone holds a slate, or "clapboard," in front of a camera with the production name, scene number, take number, roll number, director, producer and date, to identify the material later. In radio, this is done audibly, with a slate mic, so that a production person can identify the audio cuts. (chapter 4)

sound: Acoustic energy traveling through a medium such as air or water. (chapter 3)

sound design: The overall sound quality of a radio station that sets it apart from others. (chapter 10)

spaced pair: Stereo microphone placement in which two microphones are spaced a distance apart following the three-to-one rule: three feet of separation for each one foot of distance from the sound source. (chapter 3)

SPDIF: Sony/Philips Digital InterFace is a standard digital-audio-file-transfer format using 75-ohm coaxial cable. (chapter 5)

spectrum use fees: Fees charged by the FCC to broadcasters for the use of the public airwaves. (chapter 1)

spit screen: A fine mesh screen placed a few inches off the face of a microphone to prevent popping plosive sounds and spit from reaching the microphone element; same as a popper stopper. (chapter 3)

spot: Slang term for a radio or television commercial. *Don't use this word.* Although advertising salespeople call them spots, clients typically think in terms of ads or commercials. (chapter 7)

stop set: A break in a station's music programming, composed of a jock talking, commercials, and promotional announcements. (chapter 7)

streaming: A term used to describe transmitting audio on the Internet. Usually used to describe a continuous, real-time-audio feed, such as an on-air signal. (chapter 12)

subwoofer: A speaker designed to handle those sounds from 16 Hz to about 100 Hz. (chapter 2)

Super Audio Compact Disc (SACD): A joint product of Sony and Philips that uses a two-layer, CD-sized disc to reproduce both 5.1 surround sound and standard stereo using Direct Stream Digital encoding, which is a one-bit system with a sampling rate of 2,822,400 samples per second. (chapter 5)

super-cardioid: A heart-shaped microphone pattern with maximum sensitivity at 0 degrees and maximum rejection at 180 degrees. Super-cardioid microphones are even less sensitive to the sides than a cardioid microphone. (chapter 3)

sweet spot: The physical location in a concert hall or studio where there is the least phase cancellation of live sound and where the direct-to-ambient sound ratio is in proper proportion. (chapter 6)

T-1: The technical designation for a direct-leased Internet connection that is capable of transferring 1.544 megabits of data per second. (chapter 13)

T-3: The technical designation for a direct-leased Internet connection that is capable of transferring 44.736 megabits of data per second. (chapter 13)

T/S connector: A one-quarter-inch-diameter connector with the tip as positive and the sleeve as negative and shield or earth ground. (chapter 3)

tag: A 10- to 15-second space at the end of an agency ad over which the local station puts copy. (chapter 8)

target audience: A group of people that a radio station has selected to try to reach with the station's programming. Typically, this audience can be identified both quantitatively and qualitatively. (chapter 14)

terrestrial based: Fancy term for earth based. (chapter 13)

threshold: When used in relation to an audio processor, an adjustment that sets the audio level at which the device will become active and begin processing. (chapter 6)

time spent listening: An audience ratings measurement indicating the number of quarter-hour time segments the average person spends listening to a radio station in a given time period, such as a week. (chapter 10)

tinny: A sound that has an almost telephone-like quality to it. A very narrow-band sound that sounds as if it were coming through a tin can or over a telephone. (chapter 6)

TOS LINK: The name given a system of fiber-optic cables and connectors developed by Toshiba and used for the transmission of SPDIF digital audio. (chapter 5)

transient: A sound that has a very fast attack, or rise in volume, and is slow to trail off. Examples include a snare drum and consonants in human speech. (chapter 3)

transient response: How a microphone reacts to transients, or sounds, with a fast attack that trail off slowly. (chapter 3)

TRS connector: A one-quarter-inch-diameter balanced connector with the tip as positive, the ring as negative, and the sleeve as shield or earth ground. (chapter 3)

tune out: Any psychoacoustic element of a radio station's signal that is annoying to the listener. Often referred to as a tune-out factor. (chapter 6)

UHF: Ultra High Frequency, a band of frequencies assigned to television channels 14 through 83; 14 through 69 are also assigned to wireless frequencies. (chapter 3)

ultrasonic: Sounds or audio signals occurring above the average person's hearing range, typically above 20,000 Hz. (chapter 2)

unbalanced cable: A microphone cable or line that only has one positive conductor, with the shield acting as both the negative and the shield. (chapter 3)

unidirectional: A generic term for a directional microphone, meaning one direction. (chapter 3)

unity gain: A gain of one; the position on a fader at which the ideal operating level of 0 VU (volume units) occurs. A device with unity gain does not raise or lower the volume, or gain, of a signal. (chapter 4)

variable-pattern microphone: A microphone that has more than one pattern. Pattern selection can be changed with a switch on the microphone. (chapter 3)

vendor involvement: When the vendor of a product or service provides support to a local business in the form of product to give away or expert staff to help demonstrate the product. This kind of involvement with the local business can be quite varied from manufacturer to manufacturer. (chapter 11)

VHF: Very High Frequency, a band of frequencies assigned to television channels 2 through 13 and to wireless microphones. (chapter 3)

wall wart: A self-contained power supply, for running portable equipment, that plugs directly into the wall and down-converts 110 volts AC to a DC voltage. (chapter 4)

WAN: A wide area network is a computer interconnection system for sharing data among computers within a company or media facility at multiple geographic locations. (chapter 5)

wet signal: A processed audio signal that is returning to a control board after audio processing such as reverb or delay. (chapter 4)

windscreen: An acoustic foam cover for the head of a microphone, used to block wind outdoors. (chapter 3)

XLR connector: A balanced microphone connector, sometimes referred to as a Cannon Connector, after the man and the company that invented it. A connector in which there are pins or sockets for the positive, negative, and shield or earth ground. (chapter 3)

X-Y stereo configuration: Stereo microphone placement in which the two microphones are placed one above the other in a horizontal plane and aimed in either a coincident or near-coincident manner. (chapter 3)

Annotated Bibliography

Books and General Works

Alten, Stanley. *Audio in Media, 5th ed.* Belmont, CA: Wadsworth Publishing Company, 1999. An extensive introduction to sound theory and its application to the various media including radio, television, film, and the recording industry.

Arbitron Radio Description of Methodology. New York: Arbitron, Inc., 2002. Web document.

Arbitron, Inc. *Arbitron Radio Market Report Reference Guide. Understanding and Using Radio Audience Estimates (Purple Book).* Available from http://www.arbitron.com

Bendinger, Bruce. *The Copy Workshop Workbook, 3rd ed.* Chicago, IL: The Copy Workshop, 2002. Basic to advanced copywriting skills and advertising campaign design. Emphasizes the role creativity plays along with writing skills in developing successful advertising campaigns.

Betrus, Michael and Jay A. Block. *101 Best Resumes.* New York: McGraw-Hill Companies, Inc., 1997. Resume design and presentation methods for the creative professional.

Cohen, Barry H. *Ten Ways to Screw Up an Ad Campaign.* Bloomington, IN: 1st Books Library, 2001. A creative approach to creating successful radio advertising campaign design.

Franz, David. *Producing in the Home Studio with Pro Tools.* Boston: Berklee Press, 2001. A guide to the use of Pro Tools in a home or semi-professional studio setting with emphasis on recording style and technique.

Keith, Michael C. *The Radio Station, 5th ed.* Woburn, MA: Focal Press, 2000. General operation of a radio station with selected materials related to radio production.

McCoy, Quincy. *No Static.* San Francisco: Miller Freeman Books, 1999. A historic perspective on radio programming with an analysis of the "formula" type programming that has dominated radio. McCoy provides several solutions to traditional programming problems that face the radio industry.

McLeish, Robert. *Radio Production, 4th ed.* Woburn, MA: Focal Press, 1999. A radio production text based on worldwide practices in radio.

Media Bureau, Federal Communications Commission. *The Public and Broadcasting.* Washington, DC: U.S. Government Printing Office, 1999. A guide for the general public to explain a radio station's legal and community service obligations.

Owsinski, Bobby. *The Mixing Engineer's Handbook.* Vallejo, CA: Intertec Publishing Corporation, 1999. Mixing basics combined with interviews from noted mixing and mastering engineers in the recording industry.

Radio Advertising Bureau. *Certified Radio Marketing Consultant.* Irving, TX: 2003. Advanced training for the professional radio salesperson seeking to obtain the Certified Radio Marketing Consultant certification.

Radio Advertising Bureau. *Radio Marketing Professional.* Irving, TX: 2003. A comprehensive training program for the beginning radio salesperson seeking to obtain the Radio Marketing Professional certification.

Reese, David E., and Lynne S. Gross. *Radio Production Worktext.* Woburn, MA: Focal Press, 2002. Basic audio production worktext with student exercises and audio CD.

West, Bill, and Jim Conlan. *Radio Advertising 101.5.* Houston, TX: Alpha Publishing Group, 1999. The basics of how radio advertising works and how to create radio advertising that gets attention and delivers customers.

Whitaker, Jerry C. *Master Handbook of Audio Production.* New York: McGraw-Hill, 2003. A purely technical treatment of audio with regard to good engineering practices.

White, Glen. *The Audio Dictionary,* CD-Rom Version 1.0. Seattle, WA: University of Washington

Press, 1999. A dictionary of audio terms and detailed explanations of concepts in audio, acoustics, and electronics.

Wood, Julia T. *Communication in Our Lives.* Belmont, CA: Wadsworth Publishing, 1997. A communications text that explores, among other things, the role that group communication plays in the creative process.

Periodicals

Broadcast Engineering, Radio. Technically oriented for radio professionals who design, operate, service, or maintain radio facilities. Monthly.

EQ. Recording projects, equipment reviews, and articles on studio recording technique. Targeted at the audio professional. Monthly.

Journal of Radio Studies. A journal of the Broadcast Education Association dedicated exclusively to the publication of scholarly radio research. Bi-annual.

Keyboard. Interviews with recording industry professionals about music and creative recording styles. Equipment reviews, recording techniques, education, and industry software are featured. Monthly.

Mix. A professional publication featuring education, industry trends, and equipment evaluations for the professional. Covers studio recording, audio for video, and audio for motion pictures. Monthly.

PC World. Based in computer technology for home and business and featuring articles on how to use and integrate computer-based technologies. Monthly.

ProSound News. Equipment reviews and technical articles on recording studios, music recording, and live venue presentations. Monthly.

Surround Professional. A professional publication dedicated to mixing and developing multi-channel surround sound projects for the recording industry, television, and motion picture productions. Monthly.

Technical Papers

Audio Engineering Society. (1991). *AES Recommended Practice for Digital Audio Engineering--Serial Multichannel Audio Digital Interface*

(MADI) AES10-1991 (r-1997). Retrieved October 9, 2002, from the World Wide Web: http://www.aes.org/standards/b_pub/aes10-1991.pdf

Audio Engineering Society. (1992–1998). *AES Standard for Professional Audio Equipment–Application of Connectors, Part 1, XLR-type Polarity and Gender.* Retrieved June 10, 2002, from the World Wide Web: http://www.ftp.aessc.org/standard/b_pub/aes14-1992.pdf

Audio Engineering Society. (1998). *AES Recommended Practice for Professional Digital Audio–Preferred Sampling Frequencies for Applications Employing Pulse-Code Modulation AES5-1998.* Retrieved October 9, 2002, from the World Wide Web: http://www.aes.org/standards/b_pub/aes5-1998.pdf

Audio Engineering Society. (2000). *AES Recommended Practice for Digital Audio Engineering–Serial Transmission Format For Two-Channel Linearly Represented Digital Audio Data AES 3-1992 (r1997).* Retrieved October 9, 2002, from the World Wide Web: http://www.aes.org/standards/b_pub/aes3-1992.pdf

Audio Engineering Society. (2001). *AES Information Document for Digital Audio Engineering–Transmission of AES3 Formatted Data by Unbalanced Cable AES-3id-2001.* Retrieved October 9, 2002, from the World Wide Web: http://www.aes.org/standards/b_pub/aes-3id-2001.pdf

Cohen, E., Shane, E., Tavares, F. (June 2002). *Journal of Radio Studies Forum.* Journal of Radio Studies, Vol. 9 #1, 1–7.

Fraunhofer ISS. (2001). *Basics about MPEG Perceptual Audio Coding.* Retrieved February 4, 2003, from the World Wide Web: http://www.iis.fraunhofer.de/amm/techinf/basics.html

Fraunhofer ISS. (2001). *MPEG Audio Layer-3.* Retrieved January 29, 2003, from the World Wide Web: http://www.iis.fraunhofer.de/amm/techinf/layer3/index.html

IEEE. (April 2002). *IEEE Approves Amendment to IEEE 1394 Standard for High-Speed Serial Busses Allowing Gigabit Signaling.* Retrieved June 3, 2003, from the World Wide Web: http://standards.ieee.org/announcements/1394bapp.html

National Institute for Occupational Safety and Health. (2002). *How to "Look" at Noise.* Retrieved March 7, 2002, from the World Wide Web: http://www.cdc.gov/niosh/noise/noisectd.html

Adobe Audition License

LICENSE AGREEMENT FOR ADOBE® AUDITION™ LOOPOLOGY CONTENT

IMPORTANT-READ CAREFULLY:

NOTICE TO USER : PLEASE READ THIS CONTRACT CAREFULLY. BY USING ALL OR ANY PORTION OF THE ADOBE AUDITION LOOPOLOGY CONTENT ("AUDIO CONTENT") YOU ACCEPT ALL THE TERMS AND CONDITIONS OF THIS AGREEMENT, INCLUDING, IN PARTICULAR THE LIMITATIONS ON: USE CONTAINED IN SECTION 2; TRANSFERABILITY IN SECTION 4; WARRANTY IN SECTION 6; AND LIABILITY IN SECTION 7. YOU AGREE THAT THIS AGREEMENT IS ENFORCEABLE LIKE ANY WRITTEN NEGOTIATED AGREEMENT SIGNED BY YOU. IF YOU DO NOT AGREE, DO NOT USE THIS AUDIO CONTENT. IF YOU ACQUIRED THE AUDIO CONTENT ON TANGIBLE MEDIA (e.g., CD) WITHOUT AN OPPORTUNITY TO REVIEW THIS LICENSE AND YOU DO NOT ACCEPT THIS AGREEMENT, YOU MAY OBTAIN A REFUND OF ANY AMOUNT YOU ORIGINALLY PAID IF YOU: (A) DO NOT USE THE AUDIO CONTENT AND (B) RETURN IT, WITH PROOF OF PAYMENT, TO THE LOCATION FROM WHICH IT WAS OBTAINED WITHIN THIRTY (30) DAYS OF THE PURCHASE DATE.

Adobe and its suppliers own all intellectual property in the Audio Content. Adobe permits you to Use the Audio Content only in accordance with the terms of this Agreement.

1. DEFINITIONS

"Adobe" means Adobe Systems Incorporated, a Delaware corporation, 345 Park Avenue, San Jose, California 95110, if subsection 8(a) of this Agreement applies; otherwise it means Adobe Systems Software Ireland Limited, Unit 3100, Lake Drive, City West Campus, Saggart D24, Republic of Ireland, a company organized under the laws of Ireland and an affiliate and licensee of Adobe Systems Incorporated.

"Audio Content" means any and all audio files either provided on tangible media alone, as part of an Adobe authorized product bundle or publication, or with an Adobe software product in a folder marked "Adobe Loopology Content" or similar legend; or downloadable or streamed from http://www.adobe.com, including, but not limited to, loops, beds, sound effects, and vocals.

"Use" or "Using" means to access, install, download, copy or otherwise benefit from using the functionality of the Audio Content.

2. GRANT OF LICENSE.

The Audio Content is the property of Adobe or its suppliers and is protected by United States Copyright Law and International treaty provisions. As long as you comply with all of the terms of this Audio Content License Agreement (this "Agreement") Adobe grants to you a non-exclusive license to use the Audio Content. Your rights and obligations with respect to the use of this Audio Content are as follows:

2.1 Audio Content. You may install and use one copy of the Audio Content on a single computer. The primary user of the computer on which the Audio Content is installed may make a second copy for his or her exclusive use on a home or portable computer.

2.2 Storage/Network Use. You may also store or install a copy of the Audio Content on a storage device, such as a network server, used only to install or run the Audio Content on your other computers over an internal network.

2.3 Mixing. You may mix the Audio Content to create derivative works based partially or completely on the Audio Content to create your own original compositions. However, neither the Audio Content nor any portion thereof may be resold or redistributed as loops, except as may be permitted under US copyright law.

2.4 Use of derivative works. You may play, sell, broadcast, or otherwise distribute derivative works based partially or completely on the Audio Content provided that your customers are restricted from obtaining direct access to the individual components licensed to you as part of the Audio Content. (This means, for purposes example only, that you may mix loops together to create your own songs and then sell or otherwise use those mixes commercially, but you may not redistribute either individual or series of music loops themselves, or otherwise give your customers or others direct access to the loops themselves.)

2.5 Distribution of MP3 or mp3PRO content. Supply of the Audio Content does not convey a license or imply any right to distribute MP3-encoded or mp3PRO-encoded data in revenue-generating broadcast systems (terrestrial, satellite, cable and/or other distribution channels), streaming applications (via Internet, intranets and/or other networks), other content distribution systems (pay-audio or audio-on-demand applications and the like) or on physical media (compact discs, digital versatile discs, semiconductor chips, hard drives, memory cards, and the like). An independent license for such use is required. For details, please visit http://mp3licensing.com.

2.6 Restrictions on Use. You may not: use, copy, modify, or transfer copies of the Audio Content except as provided for in this License; remove any proprietary notices or labels from the Audio Content; redistribute, sell, duplicate, or rent the Audio Content except as a non-separable part of a derivative work as noted herein;

or rent, lease, sublicense or assign the Audio Content or any copy thereof to another person or legal entity. Other than as part of your own original compositions, you may not modify, adopt translate, reverse engineer, decompile, disassemble, or create derivative works based on the Audio Content.

2.7 Termination. Without prejudice to any other rights, this License will terminate if you fail to comply with the terms and conditions of this License. In addition, Adobe may terminate this license by notifying you that your continued use of the Audio Content is prohibited. In the event this License is terminated for any reason, you must immediately stop using the Audio Content and destroy all copies of the Audio Content and all of its component parts.

3. INTELLECTUAL PROPERTY OWNERSHIP, COPYRIGHT PROTECTION. The Audio Content and any authorized copies that you make are the intellectual property of and are owned by Adobe Systems Incorporated and its suppliers. The structure, organization and code of the Audio Content are the valuable trade secrets and confidential information of Adobe Systems Incorporated and its suppliers. The Audio Content is protected by law, including without limitation the copyright laws of the United States and other countries, and by international treaty provisions. Except as expressly stated herein, this Agreement does not grant you any intellectual property rights in the Software and all rights not expressly granted are reserved by Adobe and its suppliers.

4. RESTRICTIONS.
4.1 Notices. You shall not copy the Software except as set forth in Section 2. Any copy of the Software that you make must contain the same copyright and other proprietary notices that appear on or in the Software.
4.2 Transfer. You may not rent, lease, sublicense, assign or transfer your rights in the Software, or authorize all or any portion of the Software to be copied onto another user's computer except as may be expressly permitted herein. You may, however, transfer all your rights to Use the Software to another person or legal entity provided that: (a) you also transfer (i) this Agreement, and (ii) the Software and all other software or hardware bundled or pre-installed with the Software, including all copies, Updates and prior versions, to such person or entity; (b) you retain no copies, including backups and copies stored on a computer; and (c) the receiving party accepts the terms and conditions of this Agreement and any other terms and conditions upon which you legally purchased a license to the Software. Notwithstanding the foregoing, you may not transfer education, pre-release, or not for resale copies of the Software.

5. NO WARRANTY. The Audio Content is being delivered to you "AS IS" and Adobe makes no warranty as to its use or performance. ADOBE AND ITS SUPPLIERS DO NOT AND CANNOT WARRANT THE PERFORMANCE OR RESULTS YOU MAY OBTAIN BY USING THE AUDIO CONTENT. EXCEPT FOR ANY WARRANTY, CONDITION, REPRESENTATION OR TERM TO THE EXTENT TO WHICH THE SAME CANNOT OR MAY NOT BE EXCLUDED OR LIMITED BY LAW APPLICABLE TO YOU IN YOUR JURISDICTION, ADOBE AND ITS SUPPLIERS MAKE NO WARRANTIES, CONDITIONS, REPRESENTATIONS, OR TERMS (EXPRESS OR IMPLIED WHETHER BY STATUTE, COMMON LAW, CUSTOM, USAGE OR OTHERWISE) AS TO ANY MATTER INCLUDING WITHOUT LIMITATION NONINFRINGEMENT

OF THIRD PARTY RIGHTS, MERCHANTABILITY, INTEGRATION, SATISFACTORY QUALITY, OR FITNESS FOR ANY PARTICULAR PURPOSE. The provisions of Section 5 and Section 6 shall survive the termination of this Agreement, howsoever caused, but this shall not imply or create any continued right to Use the Audio Content after termination of this Agreement.

6. LIMITATION OF LIABILITY. IN NO EVENT WILL ADOBE OR ITS SUPPLIERS BE LIABLE TO YOU FOR ANY DAMAGES, CLAIMS OR COSTS WHATSOEVER OR ANY CONSEQUENTIAL, INDIRECT, INCIDENTAL DAMAGES, OR ANY LOST PROFITS OR LOST SAVINGS, EVEN IF AN ADOBE REPRESENTATIVE HAS BEEN ADVISED OF THE POSSIBILITY OF SUCH LOSS, DAMAGES, CLAIMS OR COSTS OR FOR ANY CLAIM BY ANY THIRD PARTY. THE FOREGOING LIMITATIONS AND EXCLUSIONS APPLY TO THE EXTENT PERMITTED BY APPLICABLE LAW IN YOUR JURISDICTION. ADOBE'S AGGREGATE LIABILITY AND THAT OF ITS SUPPLIERS UNDER OR IN CONNECTION WITH THIS AGREEMENT SHALL BE LIMITED TO THE AMOUNT PAID FOR THE AUDIO CONTENT, IF ANY. Nothing contained in this Agreement limits Adobe's liability to you in the event of death or personal injury resulting from Adobe's negligence or for the tort of deceit (fraud). Adobe is acting on behalf of its suppliers for the purpose of disclaiming, excluding and/or limiting obligations, warranties and liability as provided in this Agreement, but in no other respects and for no other purpose. For further information, please see the jurisdiction specific information at the end of this Agreement, if any, or contact Adobe's Customer Support Department.

7. EXPORT RULES. You agree that the Audio Content will not be shipped, transferred or exported into any country or used in any manner prohibited by the United States Export Administration Act or any other export laws, restrictions or regulations (collectively the "Export Laws"). In addition, if the Audio Content is identified as export controlled items under the Export Laws, you represent and warrant that you are not a citizen, or otherwise located within, an embargoed nation (including without limitation Iran, Iraq, Syria, Sudan, Libya, Cuba, North Korea, and Serbia) and that you are not otherwise prohibited under the Export Laws from receiving the Audio Content. All rights to Use the Audio Content are granted on condition that such rights are forfeited if you fail to comply with the terms of this Agreement.

8. GOVERNING LAW. This Agreement will be governed by and construed in accordance with the substantive laws in force in: (a) the State of California, if a license to the Audio Content is obtained when you are in the United States, Canada, or Mexico; or (b) Japan, if a license to the Audio Content is obtained when you are in Japan, China, Korea, or other Southeast Asian country where all official languages are written in either an ideographic script (e.g., hanzi, kanji, or hanja), and/or other script based upon or similar in structure to an ideographic script, such as hangul or kana; or (c) Ireland, if a license to the Audio Content is obtained when you are in any other jurisdiction not described above. The respective courts of Santa Clara County, California when California law applies, Tokyo District Court in Japan, when Japanese law applies, and the competent courts of Ireland, when the law of Ireland applies, shall each have non-exclusive jurisdiction over all disputes relating to this Agreement. This Agreement will not be governed by the conflict of law rules of any jurisdiction or the United Na-

tions Convention on Contracts for the International Sale of Goods, the application of which is expressly excluded.

9. GENERAL PROVISIONS. If any part of this Agreement is found void and unenforceable, it will not affect the validity of the balance of the Agreement, which shall remain valid and enforceable according to its terms. This Agreement shall not prejudice the statutory rights of any party dealing as a consumer. For example, for consumers in New Zealand who obtain the Audio Content for personal, domestic or household use (not business purposes), this license is subject to the Consumer Guarantees Act. This Agreement may only be modified by a writing signed by an authorized officer of Adobe. Updates may be licensed to you by Adobe with additional or different terms. The English version of this Agreement shall be the version used when interpreting or construing this Agreement. This is the entire agreement between Adobe and you relating to the Audio Content and it supersedes any prior representations, discussions, undertakings, communications or advertising relating to the Audio Content.

10. NOTICE TO U.S. GOVERNMENT END USERS. The Audio Content and Documentation are "Commercial Item(s)," as that term is defined at 48 C.F.R. §2.101, consisting of "Commercial Computer Audio Content" and "Commercial Computer Audio Content Documentation," as such terms are used in 48 C.F.R. §12.212 or 48 C.F.R. §227.7202, as applicable. Consistent with 48 C.F.R. §12.212 or 48 C.F.R. §§227.7202-1 through 227.7202-4, as applicable, the Commercial Computer Audio Content and Commercial Computer Audio Content Documentation are being licensed to U.S. Government end users (a) only as Commercial Items and (b) with only those rights as are granted to all other end users pursuant to the terms and conditions herein. Unpublished-rights reserved under the copyright laws of the United States. Adobe Systems Incorporated, 345 Park Avenue, San Jose, CA 95110-2704, USA.

U.S. Government Licensing of Adobe Technology. You agree that when licensing Adobe Audio Content for acquisition by the U.S. Government, or any contractor therefore, you will license consistent with the policies set forth in 48 C.F.R. §12.212 (for civilian agencies) and 48 C.F.R. §§227-7202-1 and 227-7202-4 (for the Department of Defense). For U.S. Government End Users, Adobe agrees to comply with all applicable equal opportunity laws including, if appropriate, the provisions of Executive Order 11246, as amended, Section 402 of the Vietnam Era Veterans Readjustment Assistance Act of 1974 (38 USC 4212), and Section 503 of the Rehabilitation Act of 1973, as amended, and the regulations at 41 CFR Parts 60-1 through 60-60, 60-250, and 60-741. The affirmative action clause and regulations contained in the preceding sentence shall be incorporated by reference in this Agreement.

11. COMPLIANCE WITH LICENSES. If you are a business or organization, you agree that upon request from Adobe or Adobe's authorized representative, you will within thirty (30) days fully document and certify that use of any and all Audio Content at the time of the request is in conformity with your valid licenses from Adobe.

12. SPECIFIC EXCEPTIONS.
12.1 Limited Warranty for Users Residing in Germany or Austria. If you obtained the Audio Content in Germany or Austria, and you usually reside in such country, then Section 5 does not apply,

instead, Adobe warrants that the Audio Content provides the functionalities set forth in the Documentation (the "agreed upon functionalities") for the limited warranty period following receipt of the Audio Content when used on the recommended hardware configuration. As used in this Section, "limited warranty period" means one (1) year if you are a business user and two (2) years if you are not a business user. Non-substantial variation from the agreed upon functionalities shall not be considered and does not establish any warranty rights. THIS LIMITED WARRANTY DOES NOT APPLY TO AUDIO CONTENT PROVIDED TO YOU FREE OF CHARGE, FOR EXAMPLE, UPDATES, PRE-RELEASE, TRY-OUT, PRODUCT SAMPLER, NOT FOR RESALE (NFR) COPIES OF AUDIO CONTENT, OR AUDIO CONTENT THAT HAS BEEN ALTERED BY YOU, TO THE EXTENT SUCH ALTERATIONS CAUSED A DEFECT. To make a warranty claim, during the limited warranty period you must return, at our expense, the Audio Content and proof of purchase to the location where you obtained it. If the functionalities of the Audio Content vary substantially from the agreed upon functionalities, Adobe is entitled — by way of re-performance and at its own discretion — to repair or replace the Audio Content. If this fails, you are entitled to a reduction of the purchase price (reduction) or to cancel the purchase agreement (rescission). For further warranty information, please contact Adobe's Customer Support Department

12.2 Limitation of Liability for Users Residing in Germany and Austria.

12.2.1 If you obtained the Audio Content in Germany or Austria, and you usually reside in such country, then Section 7 does not apply, Instead, subject to the provisions in Section 12.2.2, Adobe's statutory liability for damages shall be limited as follows: (i) Adobe shall be liable only up to the amount of damages as typically foreseeable at the time of entering into the purchase agreement in respect of damages caused by a slightly negligent breach of a material contractual obligation and (ii) Adobe shall not be liable for damages caused by a slightly negligent breach of a non-material contractual obligation.

12.2.2 The aforesaid limitation of liability shall not apply to any mandatory statutory liability, in particular, to liability under the German Product Liability Act, liability for assuming a specific guarantee or liability for culpably caused personal injuries.

12.2.3 You are required to take all reasonable measures to avoid and reduce damages, in particular to make back-up copies of the Audio Content and your computer data subject to the provisions of this Agreement.

If you have any questions regarding this Agreement or if you wish to request any information from Adobe please use the address and contact information included with this product to contact the Adobe office serving your jurisdiction.

This License Agreement applies to all downloads and uses at any time unless and until a revised License Agreement is posted on Adobe.com. Thereafter, all new downloads and uses will be governed by the terms of the revised License Agreement. Adobe.com

Audition Loop EULA 012804_04:15

Index

format selection and, 365
job description for, 8–10
general sales manager (GSM), 9f, 10, 11, 13, 14, 15, 18
commercial production and, 19
job description for, 10
geo-synchronous orbit, **341**
gooseneck, **89**
GPS (Global Positioning System), 293–295, **303**
groundwave propagation, **337, 341**
group/market manager, 9
GSM (Global System for Mobile Communications), **303**

HAAT, **341**
hard clipping, **125,** 129
Hard drives, types of
for digital audio storage, 166–168, *167*
harmonics, **26, 43**
HD. *See* high-definition radio
headroom, **125**
hearing
frequencies and, 31
loss of, 29
loudness and, 29
hearing/audible spectrum, 25–28, 29
Hertz, Heinrich, 25, **43**
hertz/cycles per second, 25–28
high-definition radio (HD), 322
advantages of, 328
AM radio and, 330
benefits of, 329
cost of, 329
IBOC (in-band-on-channel), 328
producing/mixing for, 330–331
surround sound and, 328, 330–331
transmission systems, 328–329
high-pass filter, **125, 198**
hollowness, **198**
hot-swap hard drive, 156–157, *159*
House Ear Institute, 36
Howard Stern Show, 365

HTML, **308**

IFB (interruptible fold back), **99, 125,** 288
imaging, **12, 15, 21**
incidental performance, 315, **319**
income, projected quarterly, 19
Infinity Broadcasting, 2
infrasonic, **43**
Integrated Services Digital Network. *See* ISDN
interference, constructive/destructive, **34**
internal marketing, **21**
Internet, 6
advertising and, 307–308, 310, 322
audio clips, 313–314
audio quality and, 322
audio transmission via, 322
bandwidth, 322, **322,** 325
broadband/narrowband access, 308
codecs, 317–318
connection speeds, 322–323
data compression, 325
demographics/reach and, 307
File Transfer Protocol (FTP), 323–325, 324f
FTP v. WAN, 325
incidental performance and, 315
key industry terms, 308–309
music licensing and, 314
nontraditional revenue and, **306,** 311–312
performance/recording rights and, 314–315
radio's need of, 306–307
radio's use of, 307
streaming audio, **312**–313
technical/economic issues, 312
web site programming/content, 308–312, *309, 311*
webcasting via, **306**–307, 314–318
website use list, 310–311
World Wide Web and, 323

Internet audio
bit rates, 325–326
emailing files, 326
hard-drive capacity and, 325
Internet audio formats
perceptual audio coding, **313**
QuickTime, 316
RealNetworks, 316, *317*
streaming, **312**–313
Windows Media Player, 316–317, *318*
Internet service provider. *See* ISP
internships, 370–376
applying for, 372–374, 373f
interruptible fold back. *See* IFB
inventory control, 356–357
ISDN (Integrated Services Digital Network), 290, **303**
audio delivery via, 326–327
benefits/cost of, 327
codec, 327, *327*
codecs/signals, 290–291, *291, 294, 295*
ordering from telephone company, 298
transmission system, 326–327
ISP (Internet service provider), **303**

jingles, 275–276, 356
jobs, in radio, 370. *See also* résumé design
application packaging/tracking, 389–391, *390, 391–392*
applying for, 377–378
auditioning for, 387–391
career designers for, 378–379
internships, 370–376, *371, 375*
networking and, 376–378, 377f
planning for, 371–372
reference letters and, 386–387
résumé writing, 378–387
vocabulary and, 381

Krispy Kreme donuts, **89**

LCDs (liquid crystal displays), 110
LED (light-emitting diode) displays, 110

Pro Tools software *(continued)*
  mix window, 145, 151*f*, 152*f*,
    153*f*, 154*f*
  mixing with, 153
  plug-ins for, 144
  producing with, 145–153
  record controls, 148
  recording with, 146–149
  Selector function, 151, 152,
    157f
  transport window, 146
  Trimmer function, 151, 156*f*
  work areas of, 144–145
production
  long-form programming, 238
  mixing/processing/monitor-
    ing, 231–233
  recording, 224–226
production consoles
  auxiliary sends/returns on,
    108
  channel assignment/routing
    on, 106
  cost of, 102, 103, 104*f*
  EQ (frequency equalization)
    and, 102, 107
  filtering and, 107
  filters on, 107
  in-line layout of, 103, 104*f*
  input gain staging on, 105–106
  layout diagram of, 104*f*
  level controls/faders on, 106
  metering on, 108–110
  outboard gear and, 108
  pan (panoramic) controls, 102,
    107
production department, 16
  as station hub, 5, 5*f*
production director
  commercials and, 19
  job description for, 14–15
  market research and, 349
production order, commercial, 19
production person
  as artist, 7–8
  client relations and, 20, 200,
    203
  commercial production and,
    19–20
  creative services of, 5

digital signal processing by,
    195
  job description for, 15
  profitability and, 4
  role in programming, 366–367
  role/skills of, 4, 6–8
  sales staff and, 203
  workload of, 216
production pre-planning
  copyright issues in, 220
  music and, 218–221
  music libraries, 220
  scheduling studio time, 224
  script/timing, 217
  sound effects (SFX), **218**
  talent selection, 222–223
  track layout form, 219*f*
  track layout/studio prep,
    217–218
production staff, 14–15, *16*, 20
  as critical listeners, 252, *252*
program director (PD), 9*f*, 11–12,
    13, 16, 17, 20
  job description for, 11–12
  market research and, 349–353
  role/duties of, 353–358, 360,
    362, 365–366
  skills required of, 2
program elements, 354
  coordination of, 358
program log, 11*f*
program promotion, 269–271
"the programming side of the
    house," 11–18, 20
promotional announcements, 5,
    13, 15
promotional voice, 354–355,
    354–356
promotions department, 5, 5*f*, 14
promotions director, 20
  job description for, 13
prosumer equipment, **51**, **90–91**
proximity effect, **47, 91**
psychographic research, **344, 367**
public affairs programming, 5, 5*f*,
    15, 238
public service announcements
    (PSAs), 216
public service/community
    affairs director, 20

job description for, 13–14

qualitative research, **21**
quantitative research, **21**
quantization, **38, 43**

Radio Advertising Bureau, 20
  format analysis, 348*f*
radio station
  as a business, 2–4
  as organization, 8–18
radio station personnel
  interdependence of, 5, 5*f*, 18
  job descriptions for, 8–18
radio transmission basics
  AM (amplitude modulation),
    334–337, 335*f*
  band assignments, FCC, 334
  carrier wave, **334**
  FM (frequency modulation),
    337–339, 338*f*, *339*
  frequency bands, 334*f*
  modulation, 334, **334**
ratings, audience, 12, 15, 357
RealPlayer, 316
recorders, portable digital, 41*f*
recording
  on digital audio workstations
    (DAW), 132–134
  dimension/space in, 130–131
  music, 225
  sound effects, 225–226
  talent, 224–225
recording, digital, 128–129. *See
    also* digital audio work-
    station (DAW)
regional manager, 9
release time, **198**
remote broadcast transmission
    systems, 291–295
  A/D and D/A converters,
    37–40, 53, 132, **287, 302,
    303**
  cell phones, 289–*290*
  codec/duplex devices,
    287–288, 288*f*
  courtesy lines, **287**
  GSM (Global System for
    Mobile Communications),
    290